Communication Communication
DISCUS II
Communication
Communication
Script
CURSIVA RUSINOL
D0900190
Communicati
Communi
MISTRAL
Communication Communication Communication
COMMERCIAL SCRIPT
EXCELSIOR SCRIPT SEMIBOLD
KAUFMANN BOLD
MMUNICATION
Communication
STANDARD EXTENDED
Communication
STANDARD LIGHT EXTENDED
Communic
STANDARD BOLD C
GOTHIC CONDENSED
Communication
STANDARD EXTRALIGHT EXTENDED
Communication
STANDARD EXTRA BOLD COND
Sans Serif-Gothic
Communication
LYDIAN BOLD CONDENSED
Communication
LYDIAN BOLD
MICROGRAMMA EXTENDED
OMMUNICATI
COMMUNICA
RUSTIC
DANDY (H) 36
STREAMLINE
Ornamented
RAFFIA IN
COMMUNICATION
ARBORET
COMMU
GEORGIAN INITIALS
GOTHIC OUTLINE
GILL FLORIATED INITIALS
COM
PROFIL

The Student Journalist

Other books by Edmund C. Arnold

FUNCTIONAL NEWSPAPER DESIGN,
Harper & Bros., 1956

PROFITABLE NEWSPAPER ADVERTISING,
Harper & Bros., 1960

FEATURE PHOTOS THAT SELL,
Morgan & Morgan, 1960

INK ON PAPER: A HANDBOOK OF THE GRAPHIC ARTS,
Harper & Row, 1963

Other books by Hillier Krieghbaum

AMERICAN NEWSPAPER REPORTING OF SCIENCE NEWS,
Kansas State College, 1941

FACTS IN PERSPECTIVE: THE EDITORIAL PAGE AND NEWS INTERPRETATION,
Prentice-Hall, Inc., 1956

WHEN DOCTORS MEET REPORTERS,
New York University Press, 1957

SCIENCE, THE NEWS, AND THE PUBLIC,
New York University Press, 1958

The Student Journalist

A HANDBOOK FOR STAFF AND ADVISOR

BY

EDMUND C. ARNOLD

Chairman, Graphic Arts Department, School of Journalism, Syracuse University

AND

HILLIER KRIEGHBAUM

Chairman, Department of Journalism, Washington Square College of Arts and Science, New York University

1963 · NEW YORK UNIVERSITY PRESS

LIBRARY OF CONGRESS CATALOG CARD NUMBER: 63-11300
MANUFACTURED IN THE UNITED STATES OF AMERICA

To Kathleen Anne and Kay-K,
our teen-agers who looked over our shoulders
as we wrote this book for them and their peers.

Preface

"Nobody reads prefaces."

This is a common plaint of author and publisher. But you—thank you!—are disproving the saying. This is not unexpected; for you are a special kind of person.

The very fact that you have picked up this book indicates your unusual status. For the journalist—student or professional—is a person who constantly seeks out and explores many things that the average person passes by unseeing.

This preface, too, is unusual in that it will tell you how to do something you think you already know: how to read this book.

You'll see from the table of contents that this volume is divided into five books, on newspapers, magazines, and yearbooks. Please don't restrict your reading to only that section which most concerns you. Read the whole book, then concentrate on those things most specifically directed to your journalistic job. There are many cross references; so many basic principles apply to all publications that they shouldn't be repeated in all sections. You will constantly be referred to other chapters as you study the ones of your own primary interest. Look up the references promptly; they'll make your reading more productive. Use the index, too, for the same purpose.

You'll notice that technical terms used for the first time are set in Italics. These are words and phrases the journalistic world has adopted to make it easier to communicate within the profession. You'll find they will facilitate conversation with your colleagues, the printer, and the professional journalist.

These are by no means the only technical terms you'll meet in your inky career. There's a whole glossary at the end of this book; use it often.

You will also notice that certain sentences begin with a star like this ★. These are the most important axioms in journalism. They've been emphasized to stress their importance and also to make them easier to find if you want to quote an argument-clincher.

Above all, we hope you will find as much between the lines of this book as you'll find in type. That is the excitement, pleasure, pride, and satisfaction that your authors have found in journalism.

These same feelings have prompted the generous cooperation of many people and companies who have contributed materials used in this book. We are particularly grateful to: William J. Keller, Inc. of Buffalo; Foote & Davies, Atlanta; Mergenthaler Linotype Company; United Press International; Dr. Joseph M. Murphy and the Columbia Scholastic Press Association, of which he is executive secretary; Quill and Scroll Society and its executive secretary, Professor Lester G. Benz; Paul S. Swensson, executive director of The Newspaper Fund Inc.; Mrs. Sylvia B. Kline of North Central High School, Indianapolis; "College English" for permission to reprint an adaption of the article "Letter from a Triple-Threat Grammarian" by George W. Feinstein, which appeared in the April 1960 issue; Houghton Mifflin Company for quotation from Archibald MacLeish's *Ars Poetica;* The Macmillan Company for quotation from "Freedom of Information" by Herbert Brucker; Haber Typographers Inc., who furnished the specimens for the end papers; the Department of Journalism, Washington Square College of Arts and Science, New York University; School of Journalism, Syracuse University; the staffs of student publications reproduced in this book, and all the countless journalists and teachers who taught us the principles we hope to pass on to you.

Finally this book is also a warm welcome to you, the newest initiate into our profession, from two old newspapermen,

Edmund C. Arnold
Hillier Krieghbaum

Table of Contents

BOOK V THE PEOPLE IN JOURNALISM

The Student Journalist

BOOK ONE

School and Community Journalism

1. *The Nature of Journalism*

Mass media in school and society

Journalism is the most popular extracurricular activity in most high schools. While the total number of students involved in all athletics is considerably larger, no single sport attracts as many participants as student publications.

The average IQ of journalism students is almost always several notches above the school average.

Students who direct publications are included among the outstanding leaders; they rate as "big wheels."

Alumni keep closer contact with their journalism organizations and colleagues for a longer period of time than with those of any other activity.

Even those adults with vocations far removed from journalism look back on their service on high school publications as a highly interesting and rewarding experience in their scholastic careers.

There are many factors that contribute to the appeal of journalism.

Despite the debunking to which professional journalists subject their profession, it is still a glamorous field. The newsman or newswoman, whether dean of the White House correspondents, a foreign correspondent covering a faraway war, or a staffer on a school paper, has the respect—and envy—of most of his associates. He has entrée to places banned to the average citizen; he rubs elbows with the great, regardless of whether they are the star quarterback of his school or the premier of a great nation.

More than that, journalism fills a basic need for humans. We all want to know what's happening, and we enjoy being able to tell news to our friends. For those who want to perform a public service, journalism provides countless ready opportunities.

Every one of us is engaged in journalism much of the time. Think back to what you did during the past 24 hours. Most of your conversations—and there were many of them—were devoted to discussing happenings of the day, weren't they? That's journalism of a sort.

Personal transmittal of news is the most limited form of journalism. It's most specialized, too. With your best friend, you exchange news about the basketball team and classroom activities. With your parents, you discuss events around home, in the family, or among acquaintances. At a Stamp Club meeting, the news you give and receive is that of the world of philately.

Many topics interest your schoolmates, your family, and your fellow stamp collectors. To transmit this mass of information to many, many people by word of mouth is impractical, if not impossible, today. The old town crier did just such an assignment, but then the world was small and news of general interest was sparse.

To disseminate the mass of general information to a mass audience, we have—appropriately enough—the *mass media*. Included are newspapers, magazines, radio, television, newsreels, books, trade journals, house magazines, newsletters, public address systems, bulletin boards; and the list could go on and on.

As average Americans, we spend from three to six hours getting news from the mass media in addition to all the time we spend exchanging stories in conversations. That's the biggest chunk of time we devote to any spare-time activity. We work, at school or on the job, for eight hours, and then we sleep about the same amount. This involvement with the mass media is one of those "revolutions" that have taken place in the 20th century, and some social scientists are giving it detailed study.

As a student journalist, you are embarking upon one of the most important jobs in modern society: that of communicator. Thus you ought to understand at least the basic concepts of *communications theory* as well as the practical applications that will fill most of the pages of this book.

The Basics of Communication

Probably one of the first demonstrations of communication was when some primitive caveman grunted appropriately to his mate and she deciphered that he had killed a tiger during the hunt. This was a long way from modern mass communications, when a broadcaster in Europe can transmit his news message by voice and picture via an outer-space satellite to an American television audience, or a foreign correspondent can telephone halfway around the world to his editor in New York or in San Francisco and dictate a news story.

Despite all the technological progress, the basic principle remains the same. This is how communications researchers have diagramed it:

For a publication, in either a high school or a community, this diagram would become:

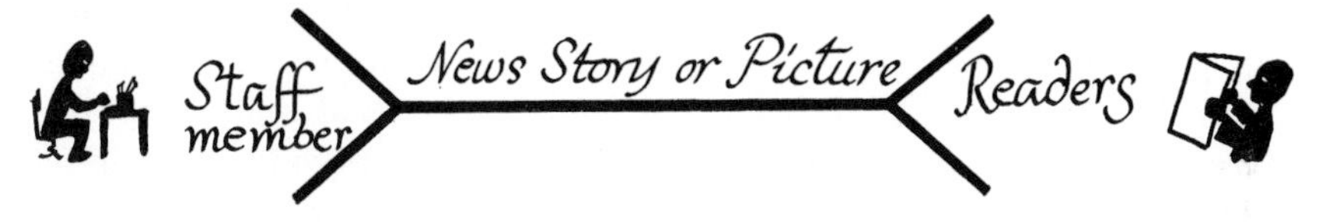

Ideal communication depends on the combined contributions of all three components. An inefficient or careless "sender" or staff writer may introduce what students of information theory call interference or *noise*. A tired or distracted "receiver" or reader may misunderstand the facts, despite their being accurate, and thus get the wrong impressions.

Some types of "message" are more compelling than others. For instance, a photograph may present some facts more graphically and therefore better than several hundred words of description. One writer may do a more dramatic story and thus be more effective than another.

Due to developments during recent decades, mankind now has not only the printed word but also television, radio, and motion pictures to help present the news of the world. But, while radio and television news programs have been gathering increasing attention, time, and praise, the average American still depends on the printed medium—his newspapers and magazines—for the bulk of his factual information about contemporary events. This is especially true of that part of reporting known as *reporting-in-depth: interpretation, explanation,* and *background.*

Because of this popular attitude toward the printed word, and even more because print is the medium that carries news of the high school world to its special audience of students, teachers, and parents, this book will concentrate on newspapers, literary magazines, yearbooks, and Mimeographed publications.

★ Each publication has a specialized job to do for a unique audience.

This is true whether the publication is a metropolitan daily with a national circulation, such as "The New York Times"; a small weekly in Devils Lake, N. D.; a monthly union periodical for printers; a quarterly literary magazine in a New York City high school; a yearbook at a small Pacific Coast college—or your own school publication. This uniqueness explains, in part, the deluge of words for Americans today.

★ The successful staff knows both its job and its audience.

Each successful publication is a happy marriage: of its main functions, as its staff conceives them, and the desires of its audience—its readers and subscribers.

Some publications gather news about important and interesting happenings around the world during the past 24 hours. They are properly known as NEWSpapers and appeal to the mass audience of a large community.

Others gather news of a special segment—a limited geographical area of a small town and its surrounding countryside, or the also restricted area of a profession, such as doctors or accountants; of a business speciality, such as supermarket managers or chemical manufacturers; or of a trade, such as carpenters or tailors. Each caters to its specialized group.

Still other periodicals provide literature and opinions for especially discriminating readers.

Some additional ones are mementos of memorable experiences, such as souvenirs of last summer's vacation trip to Yellowstone National Park and the Pacific Coast. These belong to the tourists who were there.

To meet all these demands, a gush of words recites the news of the world and every segment of it. These statistics for the major mass media will give you some idea of the magnitude of this flood:

Some 1,750 daily newspapers distribute more than 60 million copies.

Some 9,000 weekly papers have a total circulation approaching 25 million copies.

Some 8,000 general and specialized magazines print an average of 265 million copies for each issue.

Some 9,000 company publications or house magazines distribute 300 million copies to employees, stockholders, distributors, and buyers.

Some 165 million radio sets in homes, automobiles, and business establishments may be tuned to approximately 4,000 commercial stations.

Some 60 million television sets may be set for approximately 700 commercial or educational stations.

With this deluge, is it any wonder that a typical American sometimes feels as if he were drowning in words?

The Functions of a Publication

Although each publication's staff may see its job as somewhat different from all the others, some generalizations are possible.

The functions of a periodical are:

1. To inform the readers.
2. To influence them.

3. To amuse them.
4. To serve the readers and the community.

The *information function* might be served through an account of last Saturday's baseball game or a picture of the valedictorian receiving a $500 scholarship award. It might include an explanation of why the local school board was considering double sessions, plus a summary of arguments given for and against the proposal by parents and student leaders. (In addition, advertisements also carry information, some of which may intrigue potential buyers more than many news stories.)

The *opinion function* is traditionally achieved through the editorial columns. An illustration might be an appeal for greater attendance at football games or advice on how to study more effectively for final examinations. Arguments in editorials should always rest on factual accuracy and sound logic. The effort to influence readers also may occur in "Letters to the Editor" and in many columns that express individual viewpoints and not the opinions of the publication.

The *entertainment function* carries into journalistic practice the familiar saying, "All work and no play makes Jack a dull boy." A publication consisting only of straightaway facts and editorial appeals may be dull, so staffs like to lighten their news menus with humor, human interest, and other items that may amuse. For instance, an item might report the slip-of-the-tongue answer that brought laughs in English class.

The *service function* would include information on co-ed fashion trends, a schedule of school dances, or advertisements that would bring buyer and seller together in mutual benefit.

Staff members, especially those in high schools, may view their assignments from still another viewpoint: that of the format and the audience reaction to their publication.

The newspaper or news magazine, whether it is printed or Mimeographed, puts its chief emphasis on reciting what has happened since the last issue. What games were won, what honors given, what changes made in the faculty, what class officers elected, what guest speakers heard—these are the bare bones of each issue. Most students read these enthusiastically, but, except for the staff members, few will preserve all issues for years to come.

The literary magazine strives to provide recognition for good creative work, such as short stories, essays, poems, and playlets. Most students are interested to see each issue, but the copies that are preserved are the ones in which a student finds his own work.

The yearbook traditionally has been accepted as THE memento that is treasured for years. It becomes the unofficial record that practically every student keeps to recall his school days, the souvenir brought out by alumni when they get together to reminisce.

In the late 1940's, a group of educators and other distinguished nonjournalists participated in an evaluation of the press's performance and outlined ideals it might achieve. This group, under the chairmanship of Dr. Robert M. Hutchins, then chancellor of the University of Chicago and later to be associated with the Fund for the Republic, was known as the Commission on Freedom of the Press. What was said in its formal report, "A Free and Responsible Press" (University of Chicago Press, 1947), should interest those who are starting into news work. The title's twin emphasis on freedom and responsibility supplies a meaningful focus for any journalist's thoughts about his professional career and his duties. This is true of the staff members on a high school periodical just as much as the learned editorial board of a scholarly journal. Included in this small book was the following valid outline of ideals for a successful press in a democracy:

> Today our society needs, first, a truthful, comprehensive, and intelligent account of the day's events in a context which gives them meaning; second, a forum for the exchange of comment and criticism; third, a means of projecting the opinions and attitudes of the groups in the society to one another; fourth, a method of presenting and clarifying the goals and values of the society; and, fifth, a way of reaching every member of the society by the currents of information, thought, and feeling which the press supplies.

What Is News?

Since news ranks so prominently in any discussion of journalism and publications, let's take some time now to define what we are talking about. It isn't as easy as it might, at first glance, seem. Even professional journalists aren't quite sure themselves. And then some of the traditional definitions have been found deficient for this contemporary world of outer space, science, and a shrinking globe.

In the post-Civil War period nearly a century ago, a New York City newspaper editor phrased a definition that has passed into journalistic folklore:

"When a dog bites a man that is not news, but when a man bites a dog that is news."

When teachers started journalism classes in colleges more than 50 years ago, Professor Willard G. Bleyer of the University of Wisconsin evolved this definition:

"News is anything timely that interests a number of persons, and the best news is that which has the greatest interest for the greatest number."

These definitions of news neglected the increasing requirement for a publication's readers to be informed about the significant and the important, regardless of how interesting such happenings might be. In the second half of the 20th century, readers want, and will need, not only the interesting, the unusual, and the startling but also an accurate and balanced account of what is taking place.

For our purposes, then, we submit this definition:

News is the reporting of anything timely which has importance, use, or interest to a considerable number of persons in the publication's audience.

For a high school paper, this might include telling of changes in the state requirements for graduation (important), a schedule of classes for the spring semester (useful), and humorous incidents that took place backstage during rehearsals for the junior-senior play (interesting).

For a metropolitan daily, it might mean reporting Congressional action on tax revision (important), the times and stations of noteworthy radio and television programs (useful), and a short story on how firemen rescued a stranded cat from a treetop near City Hall (interesting).

For a trade publication, it might involve stories on recently established government regulations (important), descriptions of new products becoming available for the fall season (useful), and a personality sketch of a new president of a big company or union (interesting).

In the process of getting to the public, all news and feature stories are tested for six "angles" or handles to the news. If the story fails any of the six, it stands a chance of getting only passing attention or of being eliminated entirely.

These *angles* include:

1. *Today angle.* Is this recent news or a rehash of ancient history?

Newspapers and news magazines are geared to what has happened since the previous issue. Even background and interpretation of the news imply that there is a today angle which needs to have further explanation or elaboration. Almost no newsman considers it his job to educate the public, but to include an educational backdrop for a contemporary happening is considered within the boundary of the today angle.

By its very spelling, news implies those things that are NEW. (As a matter of history, the very earliest publications wrote about "newes," not news as we spell it.)

2. *Local angle.* Will this news interest our special audience?

A fire in their own community will interest most of the residents there, but unless there is something rather unusual it will have little interest for readers half a continent away. On the other hand, because the United States is a world power and what happens abroad may involve our citizens, many happenings halfway around the world may have local echoes. To document this, just think of the crossing of the South Korean boundary in 1950: a foreign news event, yes, but with plenty of local overtones in every United States community before the shooting stopped.

In this connection, reporters sometimes complain that their stories suffered because they lacked "N. I. H." When asked, they will translate, "Not Invented Here," and explain the facts of life regarding the importance of a local angle.

For the specialized publication, the equivalent of this local angle involves not geography but professional, business, trade, or union boundaries. A baker in New England, for example, would be interested in what a Chicago baking concern did to settle a union strike—even if it were nearly a thousand miles away.

3. *Prominence angle.* Does it concern interesting or important people or places?

Readers around the world are interested in almost anything that happens to the President of the United States. If he has a cold, news items are printed on front pages not only of United States papers but in all parts of the globe. Favorite actresses or well-known authors receive the same treatment.

Widely known locations, such as Broadway, Telegraph Hill, Red Square, the Arc de Triomphe, and the White House, receive special attention when events happen there.

4. *Consequence or importance angle.* Does this news have significant impact?

Some happenings—private and public—influence our lives until we die and we are never the same again. These are the things that involve us deeply. After the first successful orbiting of the earth by a man, the world was changed, and the news of this global flight got smash attention in every country. Revisions in the tax laws, technical though they may be, interest millions because these changes may raise or lower their payments to Uncle Sam.

5. *Human interest angle.* Does this news show an interesting, unusual human sidelight?

People, according to a saying, are interested in people. True, indeed. Even when they are not presidents, queens, famous authors, or actresses, previously little-known persons may do things that are worth reporting to a wide audience. A display of great heroism, an unusual or freak accident, a humorous twist—all these may have the essence of news. If the human interest angle concerns a prominent person, then the double bonus may send the news item onto front pages.

6. *Paper's policy* and *good taste.* Is this the sort of news we really want to print?

A specialized publication, obviously, is not interested in happenings outside of its particular field. The butchers' union paper has little interest in sales of cigarettes in California but this item might be of considerable appeal for chain store managers in the butcher's home town.

Some events conflict with the moral standards of the publication's audience. Even "The New York Times," a highly regarded publication, concedes this point in its slogan of "All the News That's Fit to Print." Most papers have their own "Fit-to-Print" test.

This brings us to an unresolved philosophical argument which has swept newspaper and magazine offices for generations: What news should a publication print?

Should it give the public what it wants to read or give the public what the staff thinks it needs to know?

This becomes a tug of war between the ideal of an influential social force in a democratic society and the brutal reality that a publication must at least break even financially over the long run if it is to survive. Until fairly recently a considerable number of publishers and editors seemed to favor giving readers what they wanted—or what they thought the public wanted. However, more and more newsmen seem to be swinging to the second philosophy. Greater education and increasing sophistication of the general public plus shifting interests in the modern scene are reinforcing the idea of giving readers what they need to know to function as participating members in a democracy, where the people make the fundamental decisions. Today this also seems to be what more individuals seem to want, instead of juicy tidbits of sensationalism on unrelieved news diets.

For most publications, the decision may not have to be either-or, but rather a choice of which way the staff consistently leans. No publication gives its readers only the vicarious thrill or the jazzy sensation. Certainly no paper or magazine of important circulation spreads out only legalistic and technical facts that might aid in making an informed decision on some civic problem. The successful publication today blends the important and the significant with the interesting and the exciting. This is done best when the important is told interestingly and the exciting is related to significance.

According to a story told by one of his associates, the late Adolph Ochs, who built "The New York Times" into a world famous newspaper, was kidded by an acquaintance during the 1920's about the extensive coverage the paper then was giving to a sensational murder trial. "The Times" had printed more column inches on the case than any other daily.

"How can you justify such sensationalism?" the man asked Mr. Ochs.

The publisher drew himself up and replied, "In 'The Times,' sir, it is not sensationalism; it is sociology."

And so it may be a generation later.

★ The emphasis determines news impact and its influence.

Students may (and rightly should) talk and think about a philosophy of journalism, including freedom of the press. These are important concepts for them to wrestle with.

But on most high school publications, with funds raised through school board appropriations of taxpayers' dollars or, possibly, through levies on all members of a student body, the practical phrase for the staff is more likely to be "freedom of a subsidized press." Their professional colleagues have the right and privilege to do as they please and then "to pay the piper" when things go wrong—in unpaid debts, irate partisans, legal obligations, and so forth. Students, however, have slightly different responsibilities, since their efforts represent a school and a student body, whether or not they will it, like it, or desire it. Their school and their fellow students are involved, and almost always staff members keep this focused in their minds. When they don't, they may be reprimanded or, in extreme cases, removed from their jobs.

Enlightened teachers, principals, superintendents, and school board members do not react to every pinprick of adverse comment as if it were major surgery. For example, criticisms of delays in cafeteria lines do not equate with accusations of embezzling funds. Unfortunately a few immature administrators seem to be incapable of distinguishing any differences of degree in criticism. The best advice for them is: Grow up. (But students generally should not provide that comment—if they hope to be graduated on schedule.) Honest and sincere criticism and advice should be welcomed by responsible school officials. And, generally, it is. This applies to comments on students as well as on administrators.

★ A publication's staff members should insure that their comments, especially in editorials and columns, meet the requirements of "honest and sincere criticism" and do not reflect bias, prejudice, and personal feuding.

If they follow this guideline and contribute to the school's well-being and improvement through news stories, features, editorials, and advertisements, then they should be well started along a career which will give them, as one experienced practitioner said, "a press pass to history in the making, a front-row seat at the passing show of life."

2. *On the Record*

The functions of school journalism

"Junior's going to be a journalist."

Such was a refrain in a song from a musical satire of a generation ago, and it expresses the attitude of tens of thousands of high school students as they sign up each year for beginners' jobs on school newspapers, magazines, and yearbooks. "Putting out the paper" has become one of the well established outside activities in an overwhelming majority of United States high schools.

School publications are no Johnny-come-lately among student activities. The United States government is younger than the first student issue of which we have a record—a neatly hand-written document, dated June, 1777, and put out by students of the William Penn Charter School in Philadelphia (Fig. 1). Please remember that this was only eleven months after the Continental Congress had adopted the Declaration of Independence in the same city, and a decade before the American Constitution was drafted. During the rest of 1777 and into most of 1778, approximately 60 copies of "The Students' Gazette" were written out by the pupils while the Revolutionary War was going on around them. If you are imaginative, you can visualize these students gathering information as troops marched past and writing it down meticulously with their quill pens.

The first printed school paper that we know today is "The Literary Journal," issued by the Latin School, Boston, Mass., under date of May 9, 1829. However, this obviously was not the initiator, for an article in the first issue of "The Literary Journal" explains that it was being started because similar publications had successfully been

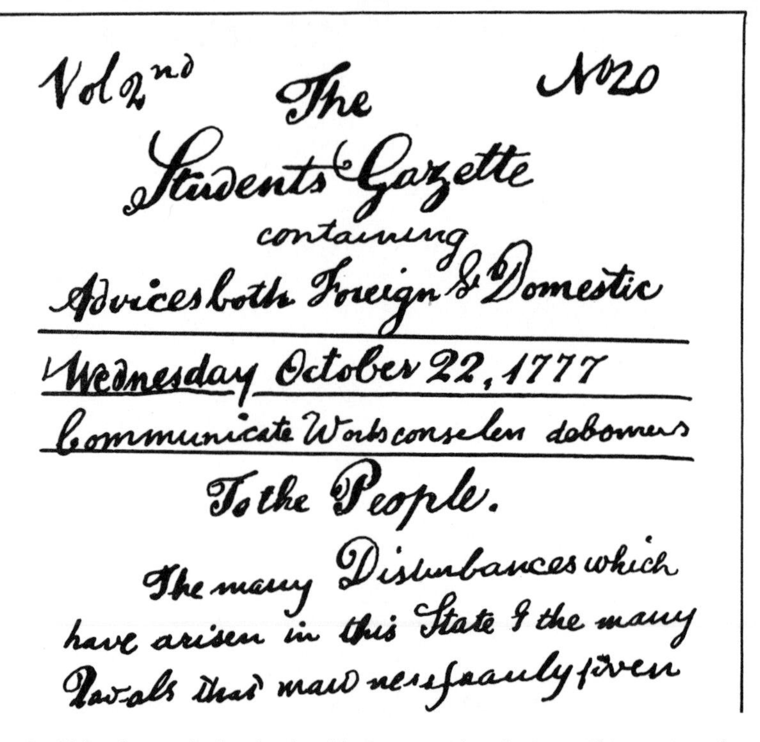

Vol 2nd The No 20
Students Gazette
containing
Advices both Foreign & Domestic

Wednesday October 22, 1777

To the People.

The many Disturbances which
have arisen in this State & the many

Fig. 1. Oldest known high school publication was handwritten. This portion of front page shows that first issue was produced during year Declaration of Independence was signed. (Courtesy Columbia Scholastic Press Assn.)

launched by others.

From these activities of long ago, a fantastically large harvest has grown. According to Dr. Joseph M. Murphy, director of the Columbia Scholastic Press Association, the best estimate on the number of high school periodicals today would be as follows:

Newspapers—16,000
Yearbooks—12,000
Magazines—1,500 to 2,000

In addition to these approximately 30,000 publications being distributed annually in American junior and senior public high schools plus private and parochial schools, Dr. Murphy reported that there may be some 9,000 other publications appearing in elementary and high schools every year. Some of these would be the departmental publications printed for students in the larger metropolitan schools.

An estimated cost of all these periodicals would amount to between $60 and $65 million. The cost of the yearbooks alone would approximate $45 million. No matter how an observer looks at school publications, he must be impressed by the gigantic operation that they have become in interest, student participation, and money.

The Rewards of High School Journalism

Did you ever hear the expression, "Well, it takes all kinds to make up a world"?

That's the way it is when students apply for positions on high school newspapers, magazines, and yearbooks. The motivations vary.

Some students try out for a school publication staff job because they dream of a day three or three-and-a-half years later when they may overhear some cute co-ed say to a friend, "Oh, that's Joe, the editor of the 'Clay High News.'" It may be the ego-whip of ambition. There's nothing wrong with that; individuals have attained some of the highest positions in the world because of just that drive. Just remember that the path to fame is not covered exclusively with roses without thorns. There is work and then more work—but it should be great fun, too.

Other students will attend the introductory recruiting meeting because they want to do "something." They may not have the right physique for football or track so they try the school paper, magazine, or yearbook. High school journalism will have rich rewards for them, too.

Still others may attempt to join the staff because they want to learn journalism or business. Possibly their fathers, favorite uncles, famous columnists they admire, or respected sports writers have inspired a desire to find out more about "the writing game" or how business operates. Working on a student publication certainly is one good way to find out.

For the student newsman or newswoman, it helps to develop that "nose for news" which so intrigues the curious nonjournalist, an ability to spot the unusual, the interesting, and the important and then to dig out the facts even if the persons interviewed are reluctant to give them. It stimulates a sense of accuracy, the unrelenting quest to get things right. It introduces students to a knowledge of journalistic techniques—organizing facts into logical news format, the rigid requirements of careful editing, and the exacting expertise of headline writing. Candidates for the business staff prepare themselves as relentlessly in their special fields.

Such high school jobs will yield vocational background that will provide considerable assets if the student desires to work on a college publication later or as a summertime replacement on his community paper.

Parents may urge their children to seek a publication staff job for still another reason: They may be thinking on to college and postgraduate careers.

In scanning college application forms, some admissions officers review outside activities as well as academic records. A major responsibility on a high school newspaper, magazine, or yearbook qualifies for extra marks here. While this motivation certainly tends toward the opportunistic, it won't prevent student staff members from benefiting and enjoying themselves just as much as any others who try out—if they'll just relax and work hard for the fun of it.

Possibly one of the greatest rewards of association with a school periodical has little to do with the initial reasons of the successful job applicant. This is the reward of a more mature personality, to become an individual who has developed with increasing responsibilities and who has assumed major obligations in his or her world. Almost as a by-product, but actually regarded by parents and teachers as more important than learning journalistic or business techniques and practices, is a capacity to think more clearly and an ability to express oneself more lucidly. This grows with astonishing rapidity for most senior staff members.

Like other outside activities, high school journalism stimulates regular working habits. (Students have to be methodical to maintain above-average grades to be eligible, and also to perform their publication assignments.) It develops initiative. (Successful newsmen strive for novel facts and novel techniques, and successful space or subscription salesmen have to try new methods, too.) It increases leadership qualities. (Any editor-in-chief or business manager has to direct a staff efficiently if the publication is to thrive.)

The high school student who heads the editorial or business staff of a highly regarded publication merits and generally wins the recognition of his classmates. He is acclaimed by his fellows as a high school V. I. P. He also has received many material and honorary rewards, including regional and even national awards if his efforts are sufficiently outstanding.

Working on publications is both rewarding and fun.

High School Press Associations

Most high school publications today belong to various press associations—state, regional, or national. Membership provides a wealth of useful information on how to put out a better publication as well as a regular evaluation of how judges think your efforts compare with those of other schools in the same general grouping. A truly outstanding newspaper, magazine, or yearbook may win fame when it ranks high in competition. Usually two senior representatives (plus a few others if the school's budget permits) will get a trip to the press association's annual convention and will listen to famous speakers.

All of these high school press associations seek to advance the cause of education generally, but they concentrate on competitions and evaluations of member publications to improve specific qualities of high school journalism. Consistently the good papers will win top honors and special recognition, but a specific win or loss by your own publication in any one year may not truly evaluate what that particular staff did. Placing low year after year does mean that something—possibly something drastic—should be done. Realistic staff members always will consider the judges' comments and, along with the faculty advisor, try to decide as objectively as possible what should be done.

High schools differ greatly and publications seek to achieve somewhat varied goals. Placed in the same category because of comparable school enrollment and printing process, two publications will be judged by a single set of standards although actually the staffs face vastly different problems. This is not to blame the judges, however, because no breakdown of categories could possibly take care of all the various differences. And despite all efforts, contest judges somehow turn out to be human beings with somewhat different ways of reacting.

One high school publication staff still tells with wide grins how some years ago their predecessors submitted one entry in a high school press association competition and then managed to sneak a second copy into the judging. One was rated in the "A" category while the other got "D."

★ Edit your publication for your readers, not for contest judges.

Oldest of the national high school press associations is the *National Scholastic Press Association (NSPA)*, founded in 1921 by Professor E. Marion Johnson at the University of Wisconsin. It started under the name of the Central Inter-Scholastic Press Association. When Professor Johnson shifted to the University of Minnesota in 1926, the headquarters moved along with him. When all of the then 48 states were represented by 1928, the name was changed to NSPA and Professor Fred Kildow, who had participated as a student when the group was set up, became the director. He was to hold the job for more than a third of a century as a Minnesota faculty member.

Membership is by publication rather than by school. Dues are approximately $10 a year depending on special services included. All member publications may subscribe to the official NSPA magazine, "The Scholastic Editor," at a special yearly rate.

NSPA services include a critical analysis of newspapers on a semiannual basis in 40 different groupings and of yearbooks on an annual basis. If newspapers wish continuous critiques, issue by issue, a special higher fee is charged. Evaluation booklets used in judging publications are mailed back to the submitting high schools. Certificates of "All-American" honors are given to the top twelve percent for newspapers and the top five percent for yearbooks in each of 40 groupings set up to insure fair consideration. Certificates also are awarded for publications in first, second, and third class ratings. Honors-winning newspapers and yearbooks may be borrowed from NSPA headquarters for a small fee plus shipping costs. Several workshops and conferences are held each year to help train new staff members.

The address is National Scholastic Press Association, Room 10, Journalism Building, University of Minnesota, Minneapolis 14, Minn.

The *Columbia Scholastic Press Association* (CSPA) was organized late in 1924 at Columbia University by Joseph M. Murphy. The first newspaper and magazine contest was held the following year and a yearbook competition was added in 1935.

CSPA membership is also by publication at low rates. Membership exceeds 3,000 publications. Faculty advisors may enroll in an Advisers Association for an additional $1.50, and that group includes more than 2,000 members. "The School Press Review," CSPA official publication, is printed monthly from October to May and is sent to each member publication without additional charge. Specialized aids for publication staff members also are distributed along with a style book and charts of proofreading symbols.

A two-day short course in yearbook production is conducted by CSPA during October and attracts more than 1,200 students and teachers. The CSPA annual convention, which takes place in March and is addressed by famous professional newsmen, may have as many as 5,000 participants.

In the evaluation competitions, divisions are established on the several school levels to insure fair grouping for each of the separate categories for newspapers, magazines, yearbooks, and duplicated publications. Differentiation also is provided between public and private schools; elementary schools, junior high schools, senior highs, colleges and universities; and by size of the school's population.

Ratings are given to publications based on scores achieved out of a possible 1,000 points. First Place goes to scores above 850, Second Place, 750 to 849, and so forth. Up to ten percent of First Place winners may be picked for *Medalist* awards because of "intangible qualities that become evident to the judges and which could be characterized as the personality of the entry."

Outstanding newspapers in each of the following competitions are given special *All-Columbian Honors:* headlines, news stories, editorials, sports, general features, and creative literary work. Magazines receive All-Columbian Honors for typography, general layout, stories and essays, verse, features, creative literary work, and art illustrations. Additional special awards are presented to individuals and publications for distinguished achievement in several fields.

Advisors who are adjudged to have directed outstanding work may be awarded *Gold Keys.*

The address is the Columbia Scholastic Press Association, Box 11, Low Memorial Library, Columbia University, New York 27, N. Y. Dr. Murphy is still director.

Roman Catholic parochial school publications may join the *Catholic*

School Press Association (CSPA). Some confusion may arise from two high school press groups having the same initials but a smart editor will be able to distinguish. In 1931 Professor Jeremiah L. O'Sullivan, then dean of the Marquette University College of Journalism, founded CSPA to stimulate and unify student journalism in Roman Catholic high schools.

Nominal CSPA dues cover a rating service, writing competitions, and a subscription to "Catholic School Editor," a quarterly magazine. Publications that score 800 or more points out of a possible 1,000 in evaluations are rated as *All-Catholic.* Newspapers, magazines, and yearbooks which, in the estimation of the judges, show outstanding work in any one department of the publication are rated *Newspapers (Magazines, Yearbooks) of Distinction.*

A national CSPA conference is held every two years for student editors and faculty advisors; on alternate years, various regional sessions are scheduled.

The address is Catholic School Press Association, 552 North Thirteenth Street, Milwaukee 3, Wis.

State and regional high school press groups hold much the same type of competitions and conferences as the national associations. In some metropolitan areas, professional journalistic organizations stage training sessions and competitions for student staff members. In New York City, for instance, the Overseas Press Club, Sigma Delta Chi, and Theta Sigma Phi—all three societies of professional journalists—combine to present an indoctrination program for high school staff members and to recognize outstanding student performance in various fields of writing.

Regional and state workshops and conferences for high school journalists also are being offered increasingly by colleges and universities giving journalism courses to their own students. Some of these institutions are holding sessions for one or two days during the school year, while others offer work during the summer months that may last as long as several weeks. These are designed for newly designated editors and business managers who want to prepare extensively for their new jobs.

Students who have the major responsibilities for next year's publications in a progressive high school should investigate the possibilities for such additional training. If their time schedules permit, they should participate and learn as much as they can.

Thanks to grants from The Newspaper Fund, Inc., which is financed by "The Wall Street Journal," faculty advisors during recent years have been attending summer short courses. In some of these, student editors and teachers have combined for a few joint lectures and discussion-workshop sessions. While The Newspaper Fund, Inc., has been seeking to stimulate interest and enthusiasm for journalism among high school teachers, publication staff members also have benefited from attending these joint sessions or later when the advisors got back to their high school jobs.

Certainly not to be omitted in any discussion of rewards is the international honorary society for high school journalists: *Quill and Scroll Society*. Organized in 1926 by George Gallup, a former college journalism teacher who later won world fame for his public opinion polls, Quill and Scroll Society seeks to encourage and reward achievements in creative writing, editing, and business management as well as to acquaint school officials, parents, and the general public with the values of high school journalism.

To be eligible for membership in this international honorary society, a student editorial or business staff member has to be in the upper third of his class, must have done superior work in some phase of journalism, and must be recommended by his advisor and approved by the society's executive secretary. Members receive the quarterly magazine "Quill and Scroll" and they may have their manuscripts criticized.

The address is Quill and Scroll Society, State University of Iowa, Iowa City, Iowa.

The "Worlds" of the Journalists

In most ways, a high school publication—its operations, its appeals to the audience, and its staff organization—may be compared with great similarity to a community paper or magazine. The relationship may be described as "the same but different." That means the guiding concepts and generalizations are rather close but the details can vary widely.

Newspapers—student and professional—assemble the news of recent happenings in their special "worlds." Both present these reports in overabundance, like a Swedish smorgasbord, for their special audiences to pick and choose.

For the community paper, the "world" with which it is concerned is that of the local area, the state, the nation, the globe, and now outer space, too. For a high school newspaper or news magazine, the "world" embraces the high school itself and all that happens in it, those places off campus where students congregate or to which they travel (such as on a visit to the out-of-town state capitol by social studies classes or to the local library by an English class), and other events anywhere that have direct impact on students and their lives. These last might involve new regulations from the state board of education, current books of special interest to teen-agers, television programs that relate to assignments in an American history class or a literature course, or special lectures at the community youth center.

The contemporary students' "world" does not stop at the edge of the school lawn or the boundaries of the athletics fields. High school students today do not live in a social cocoon—even if their grandparents may have. Too many student newspaper staffs forget that their readers are affected by events beyond the classroom walls.

However, a school paper is not a substitute for the local one that you and your parents read. It should not try to be one, either.

★ Don't build an "iron curtain" for news coverage. On the other hand, don't tackle the whole world as your news beat.

Some school papers convert the last issue of each term or each year into a general review of all that has happened around the school. This is approaching, in effect, the yearbook aspect and provides a memento for students who would not preserve every issue during the four years they were in classes.

Some schools model their news medium after the immensely popular news magazines. Consistency of style is a trademark of a professional news magazine and this is extremely difficult for high school staff members to attain. When a staff wants to publish a news magazine, its members must make efforts comparable to the work, study, and preparation which paved the way for their professional models. Because of the nearly impossible goal, high school efforts here usually fall short of success. Other schools attempt to blend typical newspaper content with a magazine format. This goal is more attainable but such an effort presents typographical complications. These will be discussed in Chapter 16.

The high school literary magazine, at its best, strives to come close to its counterparts for adults—the so-called *quality* and *opinion magazines.* Frequently under the aegis of the English department, such a magazine rewards classwork and special assignments of superior quality. Materials may include short stories, essays, poems, reviews, informational or background articles, and even short plays.

★ The successful literary magazine is a happy blending of fiction and nonfiction.

Students have experienced most of the spectrum of human emotions and a wide range of human experiences. They have something important to contribute, but they should not unduly strive to imitate the writing styles of their elders and, even more important, the ideas that older folks might better discuss. To publish what one student may think of the "sad state" of the international disarmament situation and his recommendations on what the world powers should do represents (1) the efforts of a near-genius, (2) a fantastic exhibition of egotism, or (3) extraordinarily poor editorial judgment. But when a student writer discusses a teen-age problem in either short story or article form, the chances are that the effort will interest not only students but adult readers, too.

★ With rare exceptions, the best material for literary magazines reflects student activities, thinking, and philosophy. It is not a parody of various journalistic patterns found in adult publications.

Unlike other high school publications, the yearbook has a wider span of time to cover; the previous issue in the series came out some 12 months earlier. There always is a highlighting emphasis on the seniors. Juniors' pictures are included and so are those of sophomores and freshmen, if possible; but the graduating class is the featured one.

The longer time span makes it possible to organize information with a totality that is missing in monthly and even quarterly publications. The season's evaluation and standings of the debating team may be told at once, not in installments as required for newspapers. The finality of a deadline does not bisect the football or basketball season. On the other hand, since one usually pays a penalty for every advantage, most yearbook editors have to struggle, for example, with a commencement story that has aged almost a year. They handle this by concentrating more on pictorial appeal than on text—or issue an *insert,* or *supplement.*

Another major problem for yearbook editors is to find some way to get pictures of students other than graduating seniors. A common reply to a yearbook salesman is, "I don't want to buy one; it won't have my picture in it." So staff members rack their minds to think up ideas to get more and more underclassmen's photographs. Some of the old standby methods are to include *group shots* of all members of clubs, societies, and class organizations, and of various competitions. If the school enrollment doesn't run into the thousands, special sections with individual pictures, smaller than those of seniors, may be scheduled. But all of these engravings and printing add to the costs.

★ When you include an individual's picture in a yearbook (and let him know about it), you have the most persuasive of arguments when it comes to selling him a copy.

The student newspaper, news magazine, literary magazine, and yearbook all present part of a school's story but each does it in a different way. Each appeals to different parts of the audience—the student body, in this case—and for differing reasons.

This is also true for the mass media that cater to the students and their elders. So again we see that, compared to high school publications, professional periodicals are the same but different.

3. *Organizing the Staff*

Team work is more than a phrase

Any publication's staff resembles a supreme command staff during a major war.

Whether professionals on a metropolitan daily or students on a high school quarterly magazine, staff members have especially assigned duties just as officers and men do in an army. The military man in charge is a commanding general. The journalistically comparable job would be that of *publisher* or *general manager,* on a community paper, and *editor-in-chief,* on a high school publication. Lesser commanders in the field of battle may be likened to the various subordinate editors. Then the army has its foot soldiers—the privates, corporals, and sergeants who do the muscle work, so to speak; publications have *reporters, copyreaders,* and *proofreaders.*

A typical community paper includes four major divisions: news department, editorial writing staff, business side, and mechanical department. Each has a separate and different function to perform.

The *news department* is concerned with gathering, editing or processing, and displaying the news and feature stories. The general in this field is known as either the *managing editor—M. E.*—or the *news editor.* Under him come the *city editor, telegraph* or *wire editor, sports editor, society* or *women's page editor, picture editor,* and *makeup editor.* Each of these supervises a staff which has special assignments that are fairly obvious from the titles. For instance, the sports editor assigns reporters to cover baseball games, boxing matches, golf tournaments, and other sporting events. His staff also compiles league standings and other statistics. Copyreading experts on sports usually edit all this copy, and either the sports editor or the chief of the sports copy desk decides how all this news is to be displayed in the columns assigned to sports in that issue of the publication. The telegraph or wire editor handles, with the aid of copyreaders, the news from outside the local area such as the state capitol, Washington, Europe, and Southeast Asia. This news comes over *press association Teletype* wires of the *Associated Press, United Press International,* or some other specialized wire service. Added to this may be dispatches from the publication's own foreign correspondents.

Practically all newspapers and magazines voice their opinions on what is happening in the world. This is done in their editorials. Some things they condemn; some they praise. At other times they want readers to take action, such as to vote for a certain political candidate, contribute to the Community Chest campaign, or simply think through a complicated international situation. The people who write these editorials are the *editorial writers* and their chief is called simply the *editor* or *editor of the editorial page.* Other individuals who speak for themselves and not in the name of the publication, as do the editorial writers, but who still voice opinions and subjective evaluations on the news are *columnists.*

Since newspapers and magazines don't grow on trees, some folk have to look after getting the money to pay salaries and bills. They work under the *business manager* and are concerned primarily with *circulation* and *advertising*. They also handle the books for records, receipts, payments, and so forth. They think up ideas that will *promote* the publication and keep its name before the public.

Then there are the people who actually get the ink on paper to produce the publication. They are in the *mechanical department* and the general in charge here is the *mechanical superintendent.* Found on his staff are the *typesetters* or *compositors, makeup men* who assemble the type for printing, proofreaders, *stereotypers, engravers,* and *pressmen.*

The High School Periodical's Staff

Basically, the staff organization on a high school publication is much the same as that of a community paper. However, since most schools do not do their own production, many of the processes of the mechanical department on a community paper are handled by a commercial concern. This does not apply for Mimeographed papers, which will be discussed in detail in Chapter 17.

While the student editor-in-chief usually must be the most important single person on a high school publication, he depends on regular channels of organization as does his counterpart on a community paper. For the business side, the chief student generally is the business manager, and he may be more important than the senior

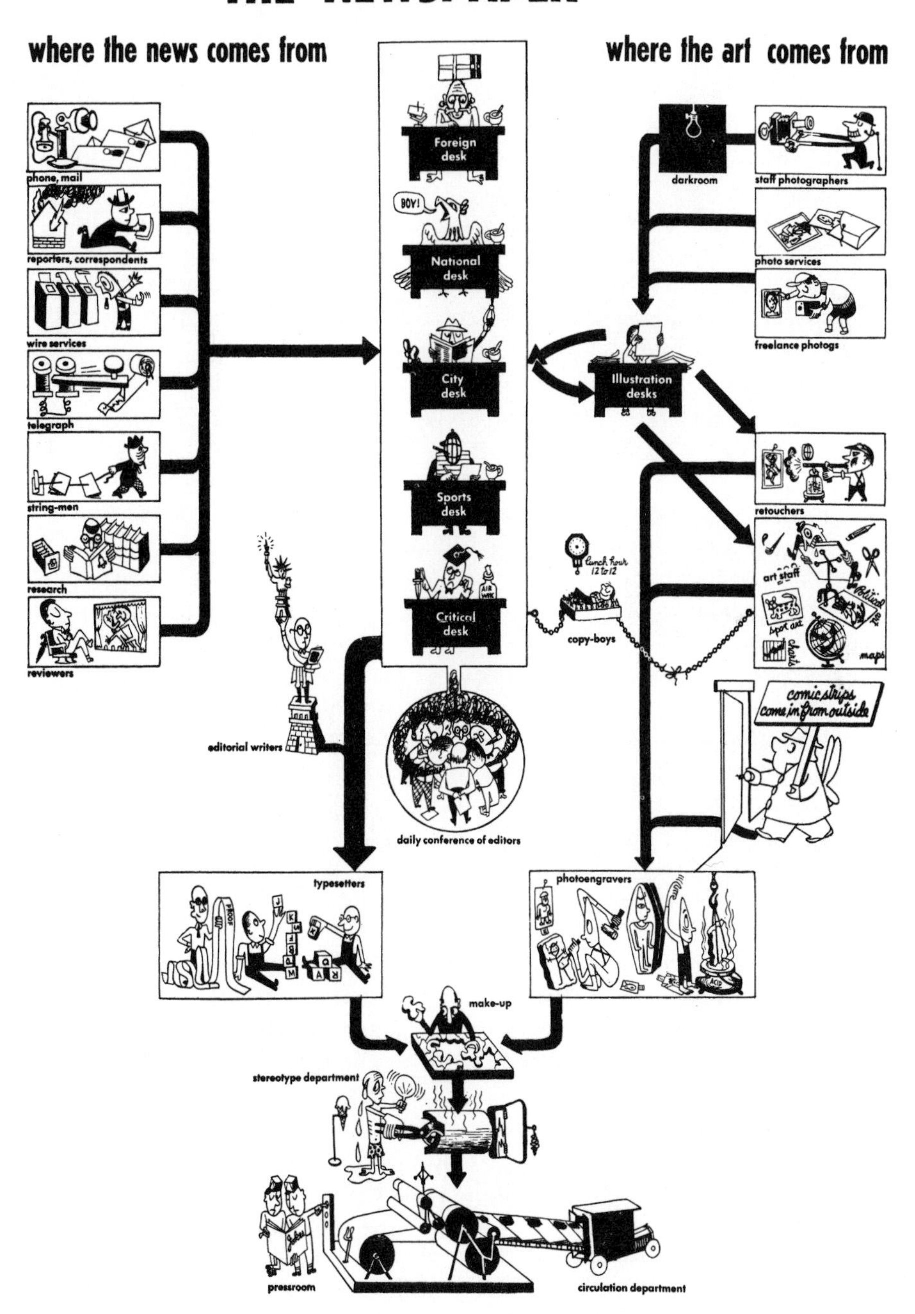

Fig. 2. Flow of news on large daily newspaper. (Adapted from a drawing by M. Bernstein, "PM.")

editor in a few cases. Some four-page school newspapers have solved the organization problem by naming four editors—one for front-page news, one for editorials and comments, one for features, one for sports.

On larger periodicals, the individual student who heads the staff that gathers, processes, and arranges the play of news and features is the news editor. On many papers, he gives reporters their *assignments* or instructions on what news and what *beats* to cover.

On a larger periodical's editorial side, as the news editor's bailiwick is known, there may be the following staff positions for subordinate editors:

Sports editor, who arranges for coverage of sports events that involve the school's teams. Attention should not be concentrated unduly on what varsity teams did; there are many other contests that rate coverage. Included should be co-ed intramural games as well as the boys' competitions.

Feature and department editor, who plans and supervises the coverage of special background, human interest, interview, or historical stories and who makes sure that departmental columns are on hand in good time. The beginner stands a better chance of doing passable work in writing features than in the possibly more exacting effort to achieve great literature through creative writing. Furthermore, teachers have found that the expertly done feature article possesses many of the qualities of great literature. Those who question this statement are referred to "A Treasury of Great Reporting," edited by Louis L. Snyder and Richard B. Morris (Essandess Paperback, Simon and Schuster, 1962) for examples of what the editors call "literature under pressure" from the 16th century to our own times.

Literary or *creative writing editor,* who obtains and edits the creative writing, such as short stories, essays, and verse, that may be printed in the periodical. On the traditional literary magazine, the literary editor would be a key staff member; in recent years, however, many high schools have turned to devoting only a section in the school newspaper to literary articles.

Picture editor, who is responsible for photographs and, even more important, for seeing that photographers are at the right place at the right time to shoot pictures for the paper. (It is difficult, sometimes impossible, to re-create a situation for the special benefit of a person with a camera.)

Editor of the editorial page, who arranges for the editorials and other opinion and comment columns that appear on this page. Often the editor-in-chief will want to handle the editorials himself, but a subordinate editor should be named to see that all the features on the editorial page are taken care of.

Exchange editor, who handles the mailing out of each issue to high schools with which your publication has "exchange" subscriptions and who also checks to insure that you receive copies in return. An up-

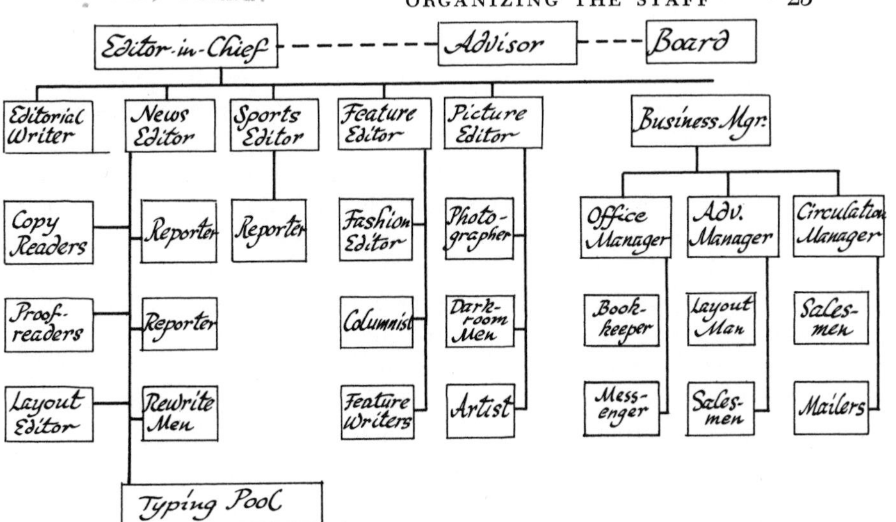

Fig. 3. Typical organizations of high school newspaper staffs. In lower chart, staff is organized by functions. Line editors are in judgment positions; service personnel aid all departments.

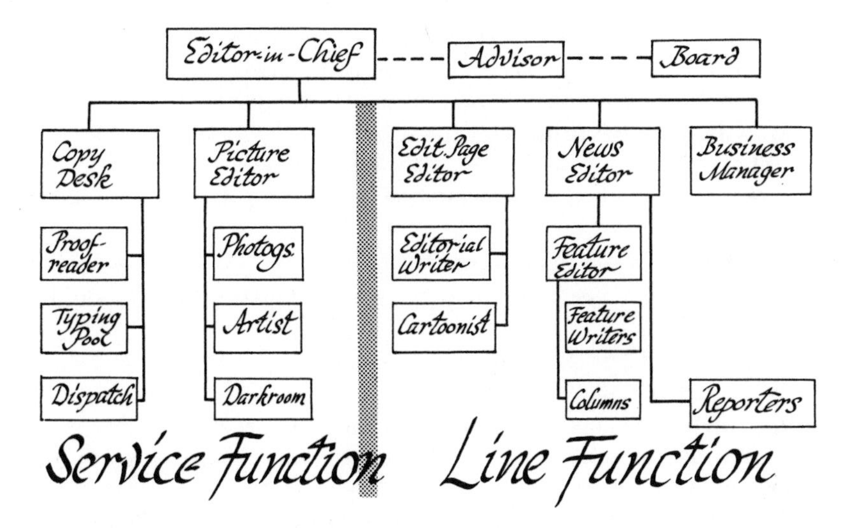

and-coming exchange editor scans incoming papers and magazines for possible story and feature ideas that might be passed on to the appropriate editor for adoption by your publication.

For the business manager, associates might include:

Advertising manager, who sells advertisements, collects fees, and supplies printed copies of the paper, or *tearsheets,* to the advertisers. In some schools, advertising is curtailed or prohibited; on such staffs, obviously, there is no advertising manager.

Circulation manager, who sells subscriptions and arranges distribution of copies to students in classrooms, teachers, school administrators (including members of the local school board), alumni, P. T. A.

officials, parents, and other friends of the school.

Office manager, the individual or group that keeps the records of money received and spent and other information needed for an efficient business operation.

Just as wars may be won or lost by poor commanding generals or by soldiers who fail to fight a good battle, so a poor editor-in-chief or business manager who does not provide sound instructions, or untrained, careless junior staff members who just don't carry out their assignments, may produce a sloppy publication in which no one can take pride and which will not win honors, awards, and recognition, even among the students who read it.

Now let's look at how students in these key positions might swing into action to produce a high school newspaper.

★ The editor-in-chief has the ultimate responsibility for getting the paper to press.

But, all along the way, this student should work with the senior subordinate editors and with the faculty advisor. Usually this cooperation would start with individual conferences or with a *senior editors* meeting to discuss the plans for the next issue. ("Senior editor," as used here, refers to a top staff member and does not designate the class year.) All sorts of decisions have to be made.

What will be the more important news stories?

How much advertising will there be?

What are some good feature story possibilities?

Are there any good human interest happenings that may be written up?

What about some interviews?

What pictures are available and what additional ones should be taken?

What should our editorials say this time?

What sports will be covered?

Are there any good ideas from exchange papers?

What may be done about tardy departmental contributors to make them more prompt?

When should the copyreaders be asked to report to edit copy and to write headlines?

What about a schedule for proofreading?

If deadlines have not already been arranged by the faculty advisor, printer, and editor, this early session should decide just what they will be for this issue.

Once these decisions are made, they funnel down to the reporters, copyreaders, photographers, and proofreaders. The process may be much the same as in the military "chain of command"—general to major, to lieutenant, to sergeant, to private. On a high school paper, a couple of these steps may be omitted. In other cases, the editor-in-chief may call a general staff meeting and tell every member at once.

Since good reporting is basic for a good publication, we should look at this type of work more carefully.

There are two kinds of reporters: *beat reporters* and *general assignment reporters*. Both are important and necessary; each has a different kind of job.

A beat reporter is assigned to dig up the news from an individual, an office, or a department. It is up to him to get all the news, regardless of whether his editor knows about it or not.

A beat reporter, for example, might be assigned to cover the principal's office. His job would be to talk to the principal's secretary and ask for news. Of course, the reporter would want to talk to the principal himself, but don't forget that news may come from many sources. Some of the best sources are assistants and associates—if they tell the facts correctly. The beat reporter might obtain information about next semester's new courses as approved by the school superintendent and just forwarded to the principal. He might find out about a visit to the school of a professor from a nearby university who wanted some of the students to participate in an experiment to test a new way to teach physics. He might learn of an alumnus who had been recently elected to Phi Beta Kappa and who had written about it to the principal or a teacher.

A general assignment reporter handles news about a special event or situation, such as a speech, club meeting, trip to a neighboring television station by a social studies class, or some other specific happening that the editor wants covered.

Such a general assignment reporter might be told to cover next Wednesday's assembly at which the student governing organization is going to reveal plans for the senior-junior prom. Another general assignment reporter might be assigned to interview the foreign exchange student from France who arrived just a few days ago and who is making friends in her classes.

When reporters, both those on beats and those on special assignments, have gathered their facts, they write these into journalistic articles. Some may be straight-away reports of events while others may be features on interviews or unusual happenings around the school. (See Chapters 5 and 6 for news and feature article writing.)

Reporters turn in their stories to the news editor or the feature and department editor, as appropriate. These editors look over the copy to see that it is, generally, in proper order, that the reporters have carried out their instructions, and that the stories are written in satisfactory style.

Then the copy is turned over to the copyreaders. These copy editors check the stories for errors of all sorts—factual, spelling, grammar, and interpretation. They make the capitalization, abbreviations, punctuation, and general style conform with that adopted for the publication. They make sure that the news item is the proper length, not too long and not too short. Then the copyreaders construct a headline, following the editors' instructions for proper size. (For further details on editing and headline writing, see Chapters 7 and 8.)

While the news department is providing copy for stories and pictures, the business staff has (if permitted by school regulations) solicited advertisements from local merchants, gathered the copy, and marked it with appropriate instructions to the printer.

Taking time off from his other duties, the editor-in-chief either writes the editorials or assigns that job to a special assistant who is expert in forceful expressions of opinion. Editorial policy is decided by the senior editors on most papers.

★ An editorial writer should always keep in mind that he is speaking for the entire publication, not just for himself.

Now the edited news copy, editorials, and advertisements are ready to go to the printer. But before that takes place, the responsible editor notes the heading or slug on all stories, their anticipated length, and the types of headlines given. The advertising staff does much the same for all its advertising copy. This information later is used in making up the pages from the *dummy* as discussed in Chapter 11.

Back from the printer come *galley proofs*, and then the proofreaders take over to insure that the version of the story set into type corresponds exactly with the marked-up or edited copy. When *page proofs* are approved or corrected, as appropriate, then the type is ready to be placed on the press and the journalists' brainchild finally is about to be born.

After the copies are printed, the business staff takes over the distribution to subscribers and, where advertisements are allowed, to advertisers who also want to see how their material looks in final printed form.

Regardless of whether it puts out a newspaper, magazine, or yearbook, a publication staff should have a place to meet and work. The problem of finding space should not be a recurring responsibility for an editor-in-chief and business manager; they will have enough problems without that one. If space for typewriters, supplies, and files is not handed down from year to year, which is by far the better policy, then the senior staff members and faculty advisor should try to solve this situation immediately after the students are chosen for their positions.

★ Every publication staff should have its own home, a regular place to work.

Once having obtained the space, key staff members should insure that it is kept as neat and tidy as possible. Some professional newspaper and magazine offices have floors littered with waste paper, but they should not become the ideals which school staffs vigorously try to imitate.

If at all possible, the staff should have a regular time to meet—

probably once a week after regular school hours at the beginning and much oftener when an issue's deadline is approaching. If your school is on two sessions each day, this may present a perplexing situation when it comes to holding meetings of the full staff. At the worst, it may be necessary to hold two split sessions, one for the early students and another for those who attend classes later. In any case, several senior staff members should attend both meetings so that there is a continuity in what takes place at both. Few football teams have to practice for a big game in split shifts, and the same arguments should be made with the school administration when it comes to getting approval for concessions on a publication's staff meetings. In some schools, seniors may be exempt from required studyhall attendance on rare occasions or emergencies. In such cases, they have to arrange their study programs so that they do homework at odd times and that their grades do not slip sufficiently to make them ineligible to continue to work on extracurricular activities.

The business manager, after discussion with the student editor-in-chief, should insure that adequate supplies are available. These should include typewriters, desks, copy paper, copy pencils, typewriter ribbons, paste pots, scissors, rulers for the copy desk, pencil sharpeners, and all the essential forms for the business office, such as receipts for subscriptions and advertising as well as for accounting of expenditures. Larger and more expensive items such as desks and typewriters usually are provided by the school administration or student governing organization and are handed down from one graduating staff to the next. Late in the spring or early in the summer, this equipment should be checked; if, for instance, typewriters need to be repaired or cleaned, this should be done before classes begin in the fall. Thus everything will be in good shape physically for the initial fall gathering of the staff.

The business manager may want to follow the example of some professional publications and have affixed to each piece of permanent equipment its price and date of purchase. It may surprise staff members to see how much more respect is shown a typewriter, for example, if a small, neat sign says:

Cost—$157.50
April 25, 1963

★ Stress responsibility of staff members for all equipment that they may use.

Another matter which has to be worked out in advance by the top editors, business office representatives, and the faculty advisor concerns the *free list* or exchange subscriptions. Every publication has complimentary and exchange copies, but, since each costs at least a few cents to print, lists should be thoughtfully and carefully compiled.

Complimentary copies usually are sent to members of the school board, superintendent, local newspapers, libraries (both school and community), some city officials, and regular advertisers. Some schools give free copies to the principal and department chairmen.

Exchanges between high school publications are valuable tools for student staffs. It sharpens the thinking of staff members to see what colleagues are doing under similar circumstances. Most exchanges will be with nearby schools. Their problems are similar; they may operate under the same school system. Information about their athletic teams will be of use to your sports staff. But distant exchanges are also valuable. It will be interesting, for instance, to find out differences between a school in Maine and one in California. Most exchanges should be with schools of about the same size and in the same kind and size of community or, at least, with common interests.

★ Studying exchanges produces many ideas for news coverage, features, and pictures.

While exchanges are useful tools for an alert staff, they are that only if they are read and inspected. All too often exchanges aren't even unwrapped and collect dust until a periodic housecleaning. To prevent this, the staff should decide at the start of each school year which papers the members would like to exchange with. Staffs of such papers should be asked if they want to exchange for one year. The list, when agreed upon, should be sent to the circulation department to prepare mailing lists.

★ There should always be at least one paper that is better than yours; it's good for the staff's soul to be reminded periodically that there is still room for improvement.

Prize-winning papers are often bombarded with exchange requests from all over the country. Often this becomes too great a burden. If a staff declines to exchange, don't sulk. If the paper is worth studying, it probably is worthwhile to buy a year's subscription.

The Nuts and Bolts of Staff Organization

An efficient editor wants to make sure that his staff is organized to gather news as a vacuum cleaner sweeps up dirt and lint.

Here is an efficient setup of high school beats:

1. Administration: principal's office, dean of students, vocational guidance, and possibly the office of the superintendent of schools.

2. Athletics: director of athletics, all coaches, and other assistants in the athletics department. The individual in charge of coverage might be the sports editor.

3. Academic department chairmen: all the supervisors for all the subjects taught. If yours is an exceptionally large high school, this beat would be so large that it would have to be split up among several reporters in order to give adequate coverage.

4. Advisors of all honorary societies.

5. Officers and advisors of all other clubs. Again, in a large school this beat would have to be divided.

6. Officers and advisors of all classes. Because junior and senior classes usually have more activities, persons assigned to these two might provide more news. But don't forget the freshmen and sophomores.

7. Activities such as drama, band, glee club, orchestra, debating, and publications. Never forget that your own school periodical should be reported just as any other activity is.

8. Nearby metropolitan daily. A student should be assigned to check and clip this newspaper for tips on happenings that would interest student readers. If this assignment is done properly, the individual responsible could have greater responsibility for a successful school paper than almost any other on the staff except the editor-in-chief and business manager. His assignment is to fill the *assignment book* and *future book* with ideas that will bloom later as fully developed news stories and feature articles.

Some beats, especially busy ones such as a principal's office, should be checked every other day for a weekly student paper and at least weekly, regardless of how infrequently the publication is issued. These repeated checkings will (1) allow more time for gathering background and writing up information, (2) prevent an administrator from forgetting or overlooking an event of interest because it happened so far in the past, and (3) avoid a traffic jam in news copy that could occur if every staff member made only one check on his beat a couple of days before the final deadline.

Other beats having little news need not be checked more than several times between issues. This will give time for writing if the news breaks early and will prevent scoops if it develops just before deadline.

★ A beat should be covered at least twice for each issue.

Most of the individuals you will be checking for information and interviewing for facts or comments are busy folk. There are many demands on their time. The courteous and efficient way is to set up an appointment to visit them—unless there is an emergency.

★ When possible, make an appointment with a news source.

Professional journalists have gotten smash stories from such unlikely sources as telephone operators and elevator men. A secretary to an important school administrator may, if you have her confidence, tip you off to something that will yield a front page story after you have checked it with her boss. Never print such tips without checking, because sometimes there is confusion on just what is taking place.

★ Good tips on news sometimes come from people who are not in high positions.

If a student hears about an event which would make an interesting, important, or useful story, it is his responsibility to let the editor-in-chief know. This is especially true if the happening is not on his regularly assigned beat. If a story seems to overlap several beats, the reporter should tell his editor and let him decide who will write it.

For instance, suppose a student assigned to the principal's office learns about a new athletics program. He should not assume that the sports editor or athletics department beat man already knows about it; just maybe he doesn't know. The editor will decide whether the administration or sports reporter will gather more material for a full-length story. Possibly both beat reporters will get all the information they can and then pool their news. The result thus may be more inclusive and more informational than if one had gathered the facts from his single beat and written them up.

Some happenings occur that are not included in the general division of beats. Here a staff reporter is sent out on an assignment to cover a specific event, such as a United Nations Day assembly or an inspection of the student cadet corps by a visiting U. S. Army officer.

To stoke the files with information on which to send out general assignment reporters, an editor maintains a future book, in which are scheduled all the forthcoming events that he knows about. He or his assistant will clip each issue of the student publication and file all items telling about coming events under the date on which they will take place. For example, if a Christmas party of the English Club is going to be held on December 18, that item will be clipped from the paper and filed under December 18. Then, early in December, the editor will assign a reporter to handle the club's party when it is held.

The business of giving out assignments may be done at a specific time to as many staff members as can attend then. More frequently, however, a list of assignments (sometimes including beat coverage, too, just to make sure all reporters are functioning as assumed) is posted on a bulletin board in the publication's office. Staff members should check regularly and frequently, daily if theirs is a weekly paper.

If the student reporter is free to carry out his assignment, he puts his initials after his name alongside the instructions.

If for some reason he can't carry out the assigned job, then he is responsible for notifying the editor or faculty advisor that he can't carry out the schedule. If a reporter becomes sick after agreeing to the assignment, he or his mother should notify the editor—or, in the editor's absence, tell the faculty advisor.

★ A reporter is on duty at all times.

Few gaps in performance can cause as much trouble for an editor and a publication as failure to carry out an assignment. Professional journalists have been honored for their devotion in getting the news to their publications. Let students perform as any other newsmen would.

A plaque honoring a reporter on the late "New York World" illustrates the respect which such faithful service may generate. Conspicuously displayed in the city room, this memento told how a newsman had sent his story on a big train wreck to his paper before he allowed his own serious injuries to be treated. Few high school students will be asked to make such a sacrifice, but it is a goal to keep constantly in mind.

★ Even when he is sick, a good reporter follows through; he notifies the proper person of his inability to cover the story.

★ Deadlines are sacred.

The High School Paper Within the Community Paper

Some high schools around the country have established their own publications by joining forces with the local community papers, either dailies or weeklies. At a specific time (say, on Tuesdays every other week or the third Thursday of every month of the school year), either a full page or a special section of the home town paper is devoted to school news prepared by the student staff.

In some communities, these pages are simply a sub-division of the regular paper with the same headline schedule and stylebook as the rest of the issue. In others, the students prepare an insert supplement with typography and makeup all their own.

Financing these papers-within-papers may be handled by a variety of methods. Some high school staffs use subscription fees to pay a specific amount, somewhat comparable to the full page advertisement rate. Others sell advertising for their page or section and thus utilize the practice of their professional colleagues to pay their own way. In a few communities, affluent publications have turned over space for student writing efforts as a public service. While this last method would seem to be a happy situation for reporters and editors, it deprives those interested in gathering experiences for careers on the business side of journalism.

Since the idea of a school page or section within the regular publication involves two groups, it is especially important that detailed mechanics of cooperation should be worked out well before the first issue's copy is submitted. The faculty advisor and senior editors should sit down with the community paper's responsible executives and arrange a schedule for submitting copy, returning proofs, presenting page dummies, and delivering copies—if any are to be sent to the high school for distribution there. Financial arrangements also should be developed carefully and realistically.

Editorial practices vary, but regardless of whether there is a special headline schedule and a different type of makeup, the rigid importance of keeping deadlines remains unbroken. A job printer may permit a wee bit of leeway but a daily or weekly has to appear when it is scheduled—even if the school copy has to be left out.

★ Make special efforts to meet deadlines if you are working with a local community paper.

If student staff members are using the general appearance of the community paper, then they should study the publication thoughtfully so that they will be able to present news stories, features, pictures, headlines, and makeup that are as close as possible to professional performance. In some ways this close association with the efforts of newsmen and newswomen who have spent years at their careers presents a stimulating challenge for highest possible achievements. Students, parents, teachers, and neighbors will—consciously or not—be comparing what you have done.

When the high school staff is given relatively free range of the composing room for choice of type faces, then the senior editors should study the typographical resources available and proceed with caution in efforts to experiment. Typography is full of booby traps for the amateurs and the staff should pay attention to the information and suggestions given in Chapters 9 and 11.

Practically all community papers will permit students to have their own nameplate (possibly only a variation of the paper's own name) and their own masthead. What is said later about picking a paper's name and about listing students on the masthead applies to the paper within a local paper.

The special student page or section has two advantages for staff members:

(1) Since their efforts go to all the community paper's subscribers, the public relations potentialities frequently are greater than for those school papers distributed only to students, faculty, and other special interest groups.

(2) Students come in closer contact with working newsmen and newswomen and thus may think they are in closer touch with "real" journalism.

Even in communities where each high school has its own publications, local papers carry material written by students about school affairs in regular news items, weekly columns, or special sections. One Boston daily has inaugurated a teen-age section written, edited, and illustrated by high school students of that area. Each of more than a dozen Greater Boston high schools was allotted half a page and students picked the subjects to be covered and how they were going to do it.

Qualities of Ideal Staff Members

If there could be a staff of saints who did nothing but the right thing for a high school publication, what characteristics would these staff members have in common?

This hypothetical question is helpful to contemplate. Graduates and teachers do not always agree on priorities of the characteristics, but we believe that most of the following points would be listed by any experienced group.

★ Each staff member should be well trained for his job and, preferably, should have risen through the ranks.

No substitute is available for good, old-fashioned, plain competence. If the staff member is to edit copy, he should know the copyreading symbols and he should have had enough practice to be able to do his assignment in reasonable time. If the staff member is going to cover a feature interview, he will gather his background facts before starting out, will arrange for a convenient time and place and then be there promptly, will ask probing questions that will uncover highlights of the personality and factual information, and then will write this up in language that will sing for the reader.

The best way to learn is to study what to do and to DO IT. You learn by doing. But you must always keep your eyes and mind open. There are things that you cannot learn from books, even textbooks. These you pick up yourself by doing.

★ The ideal senior editor or business manager must have executive ability.

This means the capacity to distribute work fairly evenly so that the news editor's staff is not overworked while the feature and department editor's staff is sitting around doing nothing. It also means that the business manager will know when to send his solicitors out to ask for advertisements and how to assign his staff to keep records of subscribers so that they will receive their publications promptly. Senior staff members must remember that they cannot do all the jobs themselves. They just can't sit in every editorial chair at the same time. Delegating duties and responsibilities is the most difficult thing a leader must learn.

Senior staff members, along with the teacher advisor, have a further duty to train their successors. Since most student publications shift their executives every year, a training program must be undertaken.

The editor-in-chief of a New York City girls' parochial school publication summed much of this up in the following comments about her year's work:

> This year has been memorable but a particular thing makes it even more so. I have discovered that one person cannot produce the entire paper alone, cannot (much as she might like to) write all the stories, headlines, and captions. This requires teamwork. Rather the main obligation of an editor-in-chief can be summed up in the word "responsibility," responsibility of seeing that deadlines are met and that assignments are fulfilled. This year I have not only tried to assume this responsibility, but I have also attempted to teach my successor this lesson.

★ Despite crises and disasters, ideal staff members remain cooperative and willing.

When things start going wrong, as they always will sometimes, is when it is most important to have willing hands and cool heads. This does not mean that staff members should cultivate a phony Pollyanna approach, but it does mean that when tempers are short because of mounting tensions at deadlines, all the staff will realize that a certain curtness is not to be taken as a major break in friendship. A solution is not to go away from the office and sulk but to offer your services to help relieve the burdens. If the staff confronts a major emergency, it is that much greater an opportunity to perform services "above and beyond the call of duty."

★ Successful staff members are persevering; they have a quality of "stick-to-itiveness."

If a person to be interviewed is rushed and doesn't have time to see a staff reporter until an inconvenient time for the reporter, he will see the individual at the inconvenient time. If hours are ticking away, the copyreader will stay on the job. The same will be true for the proofreaders. And so with all staff members who take their jobs seriously.

★ The staff members will be scholastically superior, and they will not become involved with many, if any, other outside activities.

Working on a high school publication can be exciting and fun but, even under favorable circumstances, it takes considerable time. If any important staff member is near the danger line scholastically, then any extra work demanded for the paper may plunge him into trouble. He may have to drop off the staff. Then there will be a frantic search for a replacement. Much the same situation occurs when an outstanding scholar becomes involved in too many outside activities, including a school publication. Many schools regulate how much extra work may be undertaken; others would be wise to do the same—at least for publications.

★ Ideal staff members present a neat appearance when they represent their publication and practice tidy work habits when they are in the office.

Every time a staff member goes after a story or an advertisement he represents not only himself but his publication and his school. Some of the people you meet may be making up their minds about what kind of paper and what type of school you serve. Dress neatly, be prompt and polite. You might well act with the good manners you would display on your first Saturday night dance with an especially attractive date.

To a large degree, the efficient operation of any periodical or yearbook depends on the good work habits of all its staff. A few messy souls can clutter up an office for all the workers.

In a talk to school journalists, Paul Swensson of The Newspaper Fund, Inc., summed up many of the ideal qualities when he identified the five parts of what he called "the face of a newsman" and then issued this invitation:

If you think you have a nose for news, if you have an eye for detail and distance, if your ears can hear the things unsaid, if you have a voice that carries, and if you have a chin for courage, come and join us.

Dedicate your talents to the voice of democracy, the world of the printed word, the world of free people and free press.

Journalism wants and needs your kind.

Selecting a Publication's Leaders

Selecting senior editors and business managers and then organizing the staff for the coming year resembles, in many ways, the working out of a jigsaw puzzle in which one has to get the right piece into the proper place. As with the puzzle-solver, the staff organizer may follow various methods, not one of which is guaranteed to be perfect under all circumstances.

Some students and a few advisors like to have the staff for next year chosen by a democratic balloting of this year's staff. This certainly conforms to the American ideal of democracy in action. But does it always work? NO!

In many instances, the balloting becomes a popularity contest to see which individual has the most friends. With rare exceptions, this stores up trouble for the following year's staff and advisor. The most popular student on the staff may not know enough about putting out the paper or magazine or yearbook. Or he may be a poor organizer. Those qualities which win votes rarely duplicate those needed by a successful editor.

This democratic election may bring another hazard. In some schools, unfortunately, there are cliques or groups of students, and these may gang up to support a candidate who may not be the best one. When this happens, awarding of lesser staff jobs too frequently is a reward for the support that elected the winner. In addition to being a poor way to run a publication, this method is almost sure to drive out most of the opposing group, including some who might have been exceptionally able staff members.

At the other extreme, there is the authoritarian technique whereby the advisor and other teachers select the student they think is best qualified. This eliminates the logrolling of school politics, but, with all due respect to teachers, it may not reflect the most accurate evaluation of how a student will get along with other staff members. There are some things that students don't always tell teachers. These may be important facts that could make a difference between a good or poor publication because of respect for the new editor and willingness to accept him as boss.

As frequently happens in life, a possible solution lies in compromise.

One way that has worked in many high schools is to have the senior editors of this year's staff plus the publications and class advisors pick the editor-in-chief and business manager for next year. This method combines the students' assessments with the teachers' evaluations. Thus it becomes more than a popularity contest and more than awarding the job to the hardest worker. After two or three years' work with the up-coming staff members, seniors should have an accurate idea of their capabilities and personality traits. With years on the staff and a year in a senior position on the publication, editors and business manager have a stake in seeing that paper, magazine, or yearbook continues in successful fashion. Teachers should bring a more mature assessment and should be able to obtain scholastic records and other teachers' personality ratings, if need be, in confidence. The teachers' role is to guard against any slips in case the seniors fall short in this exacting decision.

Never, though, should such a student-faculty selection board instinctively split along those lines. After all, both groups have the same interest: the welfare of the school and the continued excellence of the publication. Should irresponsible people fail to recognize this common interest and make the publications board a battlefield of campus politics, student representation should be curtailed or terminated. But any student who is mature and responsible enough to produce a good periodical hardly needs such admonition.

Many schools have found it helpful to have applicants for key staff positions file a formal application, stating their experience on the publication, other work in allied areas, scholastic record, list of other activities, and names of several students who might be checked as references. Such applications might well include a statement of purpose in which the applicant outlines his plans for the publication and lists the subeditors he would like to appoint. This procedure is especially good if the senior editors and business manager serve on the publication selection board.

★ Qualifications should be established and made well known. Applications should be solicited from all eligible students.

The selection board should interview each applicant—but remember that at a tense time like this an able student may not be as glib and articulate as one who has far fewer solid recommendations.

Some schools require that the editor-in-chief relinquish all other extracurricular activities. This idea is worth consideration, because many a student would be torn if he had to do this voluntarily. A board edict spares him the painful decision.

Actually there is no reason why a junior can't handle the top job. The selection board ought to use the same yardstick that a football coach does: Send in the best person without regard to his class affiliation.

★ Selection of the new staff for next year should be done and should be announced while senior editors are still around school.

This means that choices have to be made during the spring. This has two advantages:

1. In most cases, new senior staff members put out the last issue of the spring term under the watchful eyes of retiring editors and business manager. On a yearbook, the designated editors receive briefing conferences instead of actually holding their new jobs. In either case, the experienced predecessors can caution against possible boobytraps.

2. New editors and business manager have the summer to prepare for their new jobs. To aid newly appointed editors and business managers of high school publications, quite a few colleges and universities offer summer short courses. Spring appointments make it possible for some members on the new staff to take advantage of these.

The editor-in-chief has been given the highest honor a student can receive. With it come many duties and responsibilities. He is charged with every duty from identifying pictures to reading proof. He must use a carrot most of the time but not hesitate to swing the stick if a subordinate fails in his responsibilities. An editor must be utterly impartial; he can't save choice assignments for his best friends. He can't overplay one organization or activity because of his personal interest.

One of the first things that will confront new senior editors and business manager when they return in the fall is the job of interesting beginners in trying out for the publication staff. Announcements to the student body may be made at an all-school assembly, over a public address system, through bulletin board posters, or by Mimeographed material sent to each home room. Some of these will require permission from the school administration, but this should be forthcoming if a proper request is made. Recruiting is just as big a problem for the professional publication, too. This assignment may be a dramatic demonstration of the editor's career potential in journalism.

When a meeting for candidates is held, the editor-in-chief and business manager should outline opportunities for and advantages of working on the publication. Since the speakers will want to know the background and previous journalistic experiences of candidates, a simple application blank should be passed out, requesting these facts plus name, home room, home address and telephone number, other activities for which the candidate is trying out, and so forth.

A screening test should not be too exacting, but it should eliminate students who are only "status seekers" and are trying out for far too many outside activities. Those who successfully pass should then be launched into a training program. This includes a series of talks with some exercises that give staff applicants the barest essentials about the publication and journalistic techniques. The editor talks about the general policy of the publication and the business manager tells of his operations. Then the group splits into those interested in writing and editing and those wanting to join the business staff. At a second session, the editor discusses the organization of factual news information and of feature articles. Simple exercises in arranging news ideas are handed out. The business manager provides comparable facts and exercises concerning subscriptions, distribution, advertising, and office staff positions. At a third meeting, candidates are actually given minor assignments to complete for the publication. Homework in learning copyreading and proofreading symbols or subscription and advertising rates should be assigned. Finally those candidates who did well at these sessions, in their homework, and on their minor jobs should be considered for formal appointment. Shortly then their names will appear on the *masthead* and they are full staff members at the foot of the ladder which eventually may lead to the highest positions on the publication.

Many schools today have a journalism class as part of an accelerated English program or as a special honors class. This is a special boon for any editor-in-chief and business manager who wants new staff members who have some idea of "the score." Thus part of the training job may be done in the classroom instead of being handled by the editors themselves.

But no matter where a staff member begins, he may be taking his first step into a career that will make him the envy of his colleagues.

4. *The Language of Printing*

Technical terms of the craft

"The foreign languages I speak," said an editor once, "are French, Spanish, and printer's."

He exaggerated; but maybe not too much. For the printer has a jargon that has been accumulating for the past five hundred years. It is possible to carry on a perfectly understandable conversation with a printer in plain English. But often it is easier to speak to him in "printer."

You don't have to make a federal project of this. Yet, in mastering the jargon, you'll learn many of the basic principles of typography and layout as well as production. So you will be able to speak intelligently and concisely about a basic tool of journalism by noting the terms the graphic arts craftsman uses. Such terms are *Italicized* in this book and explained as they enter the discussion. Others are listed only in the glossary.

Typography is a long-range plan for the use of typographic elements; *layout* is the application of such principles to a specific situation. In the words of the soldier, typography is strategy; layout is tactics.

Both seek to make it easy, convenient, and rewarding for the reader not only to read, but to comprehend, printed communications. To do this, a difficult physical task must be made as easy as possible and a forbidding psychological task made more inviting.

Basic principles of typography and layout are applicable to all printed communications, including high school newspapers, magazines, and yearbooks.

We'll talk first about *letterpress,* not only because it's the oldest form of printing and most newspapers are produced by this method, but because an understanding of this classic method will make other methods easier to understand.

If you've ever used a rubber stamp—and who hasn't?—you've printed by letterpress. The method is also called *relief printing.* Type, pictures, and other elements are made with a raised printing surface which is inked and pressed onto the paper to *imprint* the image there.

Type for letterpress is usually *hot metal,* called that because it is produced from molten metal which is cast in a *mold,* or *matrix.* In the case of *foundry type,* this casting is done at a factory. The type resembles that used by children who place rubber letters into a wooden holder to form words. But printer's type is made of an alloy of lead, tin and antimony; it can't be squeezed.

Foundry type is used most frequently in large sizes, for headlines and advertising.

Most of the smaller type in a newspaper is set on a *Linotype.* This is a fascinating machine, invented in 1886 by Ottmar Mergenthaler. This name is a jawbreaker but must be remembered. For Mergenthaler, by mechanizing typesetting, which had been done entirely by hand up to that time, made it possible for us to have newspapers, magazines, and books at prices so low anyone can afford them. His name is as famous as that of Johann Gutenberg, the man who invented movable metal type. Up to the time of Johann's invention, about 1450, printing had been done from wooden blocks carved laboriously into all the letters on a page.

The Linotype is like a giraffe; it must be seen to be believed. And even then belief may come hard. When the operator touches a key on the *keyboard* of a Linotype, a matrix, or *mat,* is released from a container, the *magazine,* above and in front of him. This is a mold of the letter he needs. When enough matrices have been released to form a complete line, hot liquid metal is forced into them. The result is a single line of metallic type, a *slug.* After the line has been cast, the matrices are returned to their proper places in the magazine, ready to be formed into another line as the operator needs them.

The *Ludlow* is another *linecaster.* Like the Linotype, it produces a complete line of type as a single piece of metal. Ludlow matrices are assembled, cast, and redistributed by hand, and so it takes considerably longer to set type by this method than by the Linotype. Ludlow type is usually reserved for headlines and ads, where only a few words must be set.

When the type has been *composed,* no matter what the method, it is stored in a shallow, three-sided tray called a *galley.* While it is still in this container, it is used to print on a long, narrow piece of paper, the *galley proof.* This is read, not only by the printer's proofreader, but by the newspaper staff, to detect and correct any mistakes—

typographical errors or *typos*—which the compositor (typesetter) may have made.

While the type is being set, the *photoengraver* is making metal *plates* to print pictures. These are *photoengravings,* also called *engravings* or *cuts.* Often they're called *zincs,* for the metal most commonly used; but engravings are also made of copper and magnesium alloys.

Photographs and paintings are reproduced by *halftones.* The printer has only black ink and white paper to work with, while the photo has many tones of gray. To get the effect of gray in the newspaper, the engraver uses an optical illusion. He breaks down the original photo—by photographing it through a *screen*—into a mass of tiny dots. Where the dots are large and close together, the eye sees them as black or dark gray. Where dots are small and far apart, the eye sees them as a mass of light gray. By varying the size and proximity of the dots, the engraver creates the illusion of many kinds of gray. This halftone dot pattern is visible in a newspaper picture; on the slicker paper of magazines the dots are so fine they can be seen only with the aid of a magnifying glass.

The fineness of the dots, or the screen, is labeled by the number of lines of dots in a linear inch. For newspapers, *55-, 65-* or *85-line screens* are most common. For magazines, 120 is the most frequent.

Pen-and-ink-drawings, such as comic-strip cartoons, are printed from *zinc etchings,* or *line cuts.* These contain only lines or masses of black and white. Sometimes the effect of gray is created by using the *Ben Day* process or a *shading sheet.* Both of these methods add a regular pattern of dots or lines to ordinary line drawings. The dots of such *mechanical shading* can be distinguished from those of a halftone because Ben Day dots are always equal in size and distance from their neighbors while those of a halftone vary.

The best known shading sheets are called *Zip-A-Tone,* although there are many other trade names. These patterns are printed on sheets of transparent plastic with a waxy back. The artist cuts out the shape he needs, lays it on his drawing, and presses it down smoothly. It sticks without any other adhesive. Ben Day patterns are put on by the engraver.

In just a moment we shall be using the printer's measurements, for he has not only a language, but a measuring system all his own.

The basic unit is the *point,* approximately $\frac{1}{72}$ of an inch. (A point is .01384 inches. So 72 points make only .99648 inches. This bothers the purists but few journalists think that the difference of .00352 inches is worth quibbling about.) For our purposes, then:

★ 72 points = 1 inch.

★ 12 points = 1 *pica*

The pica is the most commonly used measurement. Only when he is working with advertising does the printer use inches. Then the unit is the *column inch,* an area 1 column wide and 1 inch deep. (Note that this measurement varies as the column width varies among newspapers.)

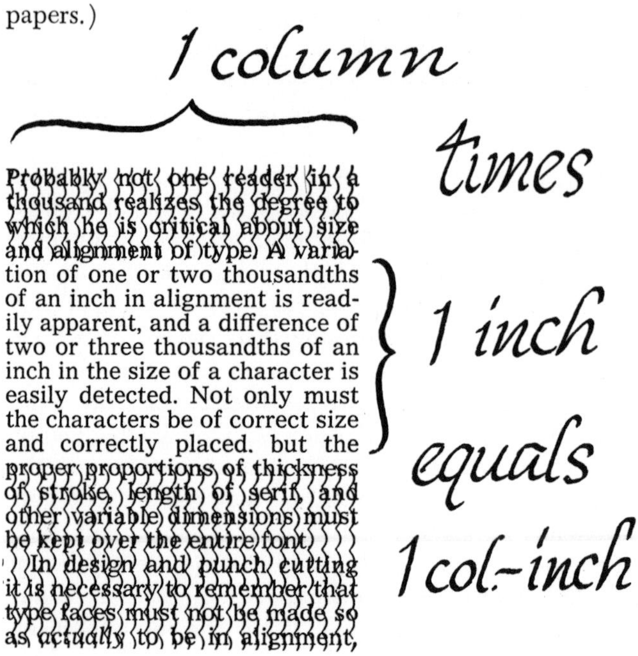

1 column

times

Probably not one reader in a thousand realizes the degree to which he is critical about size and alignment of type. A variation of one or two thousandths of an inch in alignment is readily apparent, and a difference of two or three thousandths of an inch in the size of a character is easily detected. Not only must the characters be of correct size and correctly placed. but the proper proportions of thickness of stroke, length of serif, and other variable dimensions must be kept over the entire font.
In design and punch cutting it is necessary to remember that type faces must not be made so as actually to be in alignment,

1 inch

equals

1 col.-inch

Fig. 4. One column inch, unit for measuring editorial and advertising content in newspaper.

After all the typographic elements have been prepared, they are taken from a wide shelf, the *bank,* where they have been stored, to the *stone,* a smooth table where the makeup man works. In the old days this was actually a slab of marble. Today it's usually a steel table, though it still goes by the venerable geological name.

Each page—or in the case of a small newspaper, a pair of pages—is made up inside a *chase,* a frame of steel. Where white space is to show on the printed page, the makeup man puts in low, nonprinting pieces of wood or metal. These strips, 2 points thick, are used to put more space between lines of type. Made of metal, they are called *leads* (phonetically, *ledds*). The phonetic spelling "ledd" will be used in this book to avoid confusion between these and *leads* (of news stories), pronounced *leeds.*

Thicker 6-point metal strips are called *slugs.* (These are not to be confused with Linotype slugs, a whole line of type.) Wider strips, usually a pica wide, are *reglets,* made of wood or metal. Larger material is *furniture.*

When all the printing elements are in the chase, each column must be made the same length as every other one. This is done by *justifying* them, inserting proper spacing so the column is completely filled. Justification of lines of type, making each line the same length, is done by increasing or decreasing the spacing between words so the type aligns exactly at both right and left margin. This is done automatically on the Linotype.

The unit composed of the justified page or pages—called a *form*—is *locked up* by means of metal wedges—*quoins*—which compress the form tightly into its metal frame.

Now comes the actual printing process.

Student newspapers are almost always printed on a *cylinder* or a *platen* press.

The cylinder press is best described by its common name, *flatbed*. The form lies on a flat surface, the *bed*. Rubber rollers move across the form to ink it. A sheet of paper is wrapped around a large cylinder. As the cylinder revolves, the bed moves under it so that the entire form is pressed upon the paper to print the page.

Cylinder presses vary in size, from a simple one used to print proofs up to one that will print four full newspaper pages in one *impression*.

Other names for the platen press are *clamshell* or *clapper*. The form is held vertically and inked by rollers that move down from the top. The platen is a flat surface that moves on a hinge at the bottom. The pressman places a sheet of blank paper on the platen. Like a clamshell closing—or applauding hands—the platen moves up to the type and presses the paper against the form. As the clamshell opens, the pressman removes the printed sheet with one hand and feeds a blank sheet onto the platen with the other. Clappers handle only small sheets: two pages of a 3-column newspaper, for instance.

A third kind of letterpress, the *rotary*, is used for printing daily newspapers. Its capacity is far too large for high school newspapers with their short *runs*, the number of copies printed. But we ought to take a quick look at what our big journalistic brothers use in their pressroom. Rotary presses print from curved plates. Paper is fed from a continuous roll and passes between the curved printing cylinder and a blank *impression cylinder*. After each page has been printed, front and back, the complete newspaper is folded and cut, all on the press by automatic operation.

When a paper has been printed on a flatbed or clapper, sheets are placed in proper order—*gathered*—and *folded*, either by hand or by machines which may be independent or attached to the press.

Two other printing processes are *offset* and *gravure*. Offset is discussed in later chapters; gravure is not used for student publications.

Colorful and broad as the printer's vocabulary may be, it is at least equalled by that of the typographer.

For writing—or printing—English, we use the Roman, or Latin, alphabet. This book will use the term *Latin* for a good reason you'll soon perceive.

The alphabet consists of *capitals* (*caps*) and *minuscules*, little letters. The latter are commonly called *lowercase* because in earlier days

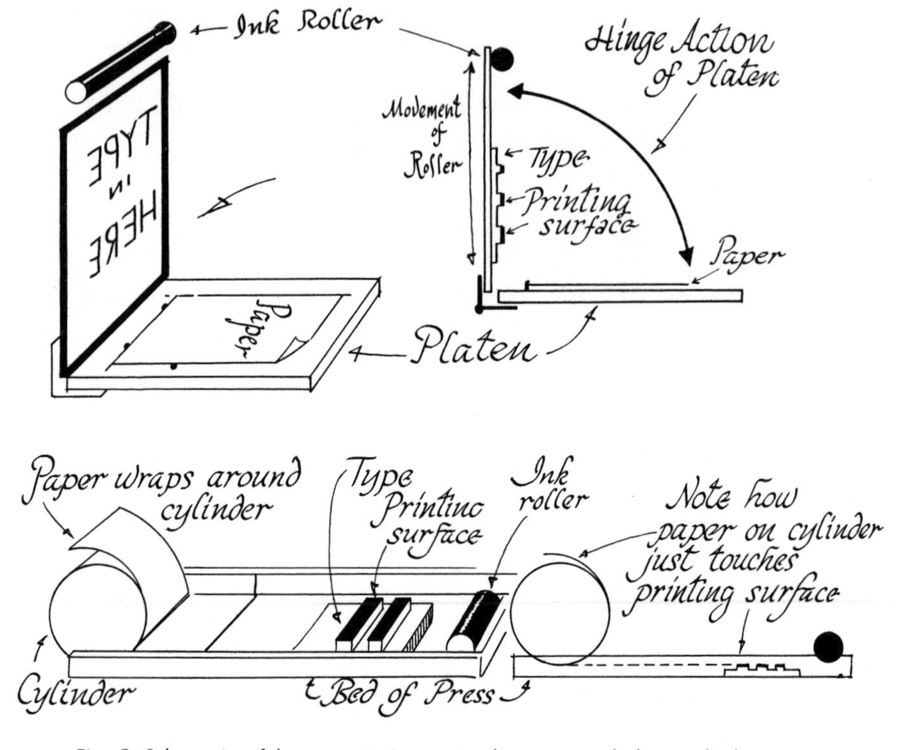

Fig. 5. Schematic of letterpress. At top is platen press; below, cylinder press.

type was stored in wooden boxes, one above the other, and the small letters were in the bottom case.

Letters are made up of *main strokes* and *hairlines,* the thinner strokes. When curves create a circle or a major portion of one, these are called *bowls.* Areas completely or partially enclosed by a bowl are called *voids* or *counters.*

There are three kinds of lowercase letters. *Primary letters* are those such as m, o and w. A line drawn across the bottom of these letters is the *baseline;* that along their top is the *meanline.* The distance between these lines is the *x-height.*

Letters such as b and d are called *ascenders* and their "necks" are given the same name. *Descenders* are both complete letters such as p and q and their downward projections. Punctuation marks are *points.* (Don't confuse them with "measurement points.")

There are almost as many styles of type, each called a *typeface,* as of human faces. At first, all type looks alike. But a second glance will show many differences, some marked, some subtle.

Like humans, types are first divided into *races.* The six major type races are Roman, Black Letter, Square Serif, Sans Serif, Script, and Ornamented.

On the next few pages are some cartoon mnemonics, a tongue-

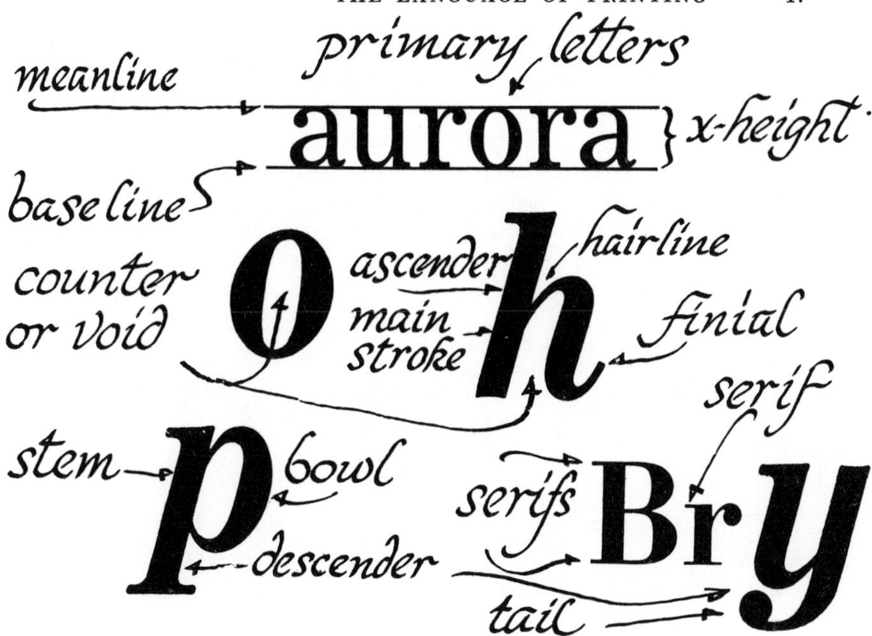

Fig. 6. Nomenclature of type.

twister that means "memory aid." This may not be the ultimate in scientific presentation but it is a helpful way to teach students to recognize type races.

Roman is the most familiar—and the oldest—form of our Latin alphabet. (And now you see why we prefer Latin as the name for our alphabet.) This type race developed in Rome and its most beautiful examples are still the inscriptions on the facades and pillars of that famous city. Characteristics of Roman are the thinning and swelling of curved strokes and the *serifs,* the tiny finishing lines at the end of main strokes.

This sketch of a Roman senator will help you remember the distinguishing features of the oldest of type races:

Note how the curved line swells and thins. The laurel wreath and the sandals made famous by Caesar's legions remind us of the serifs at the top and bottom.

Part of the Roman race are the *Italics,* named for the country of their origin. Like the Romans, the *Itlx* have strokes of varying thickness. Sometimes they have serifs; often they have curved finishing strokes, *finials*. Most striking characteristic is the slant to the right. This resembles handwriting, from which Italics originated.

What could be better to remind us of this tilt to the starboard than this sketch of another renowned Italianate creation, the Tower of Pisa:

When ancient scribes in what is now Germany tried to make Roman letters, they found that their recalcitrant quill pens wouldn't go around a corner without spattering ink all over the page. They solved this problem by reducing curves to a series of straight lines and creating *Text* or *Black Letter*. Its common, but incorrect, name is *Old English*. This race gets its name because it was used, in its infancy, to write the text of documents, usually those of the Church. So we can remind ourselves of its characteristics by this drawing which shows the sharp peaks of the "roofs" of this type:

Square Serif letters are usually monotonal, all strokes of equal weight. In some varieties, such as the popular P. T. Barnum, the serifs are heavier than the main strokes. We remember Square Serifs by a pun:

(This Wild West character couldn't be anything else than a "square sheriff," could he?)

Sans Serif is French for "without serifs." These letters are also monotonal and are entirely without serifs. An even worse pun helps us remember this race:

(Oh, yes! This is "a footprint on the Sans of time.")

In the same race as the Sans are the *Gothics*. These, too, are minus serifs. Originally they were *block letters* like those children cut out in kindergarten. Early Gothics were so ugly that when it came to naming them, someone suggested the most ugly thing he could think of. It was a barbarous Goth! See how his name reminds us of Gothic letters.

It must be remembered that Gothic refers to these warlike marauders, not to the graceful towers of Gothic churches. (In Europe, they avoid this confusion by calling this unpretty face *Grotesk.*)

Scripts—and their cousins, the *Cursives,* in the same race--duplicate handwriting. The only difference between them is that Script letters are tied together, like this happy couple:

Cursive letters are separated, but it should be pointed out that often this separation is tiny. Cursive comes from the Latin "cursus," running, and we remember it with the aid of this little cur-sive:

Ornamented letters are also called *Novelties.* There are as many ways to ornament a letter as to decorate a Christmas tree. If the ornamentation is within the letter, it's a *shaded* letter. If the decoration is outside the letter, it's a *shadowed* letter.

If you are shaded, your body is darkened. If you cast a shadow, it's thrown away from your body. This distinction may help you remember the words as they apply to letters:

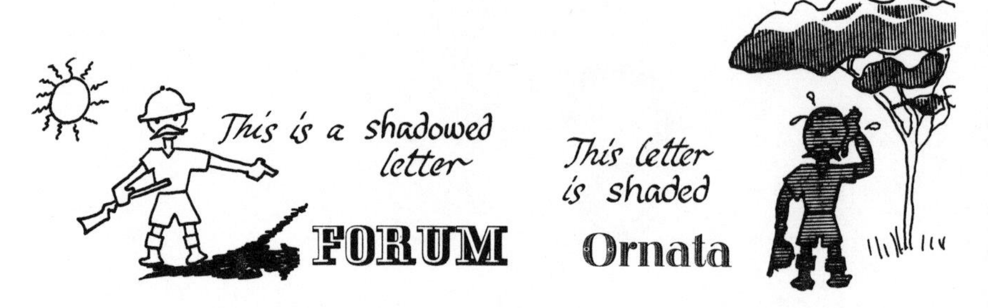

The simplest shading is a thin white line. If it runs down the middle of the letter, it's an *inline*. If it runs nearer one side of a stroke, it's a *shading line*. If only the silhouette of a letter is drawn, we have an *outline* letter.

Printers are often so proud of the words in their language that they use them on more than one occasion. That's what happened to Italic. Originally it was the slanted form of Roman. Today Italic is used to refer to all letters that slant to the right. While no one will be thrown into jail for using Italic in this way, it is better to refer to slanting versions of races other than Roman as *Oblique* letters.

Romans and Italics are divided into *Old Style* and *Modern* versions. Old Style is identified by a minimum difference between thick and thin strokes, by serifs that are bracketed and by the fact that round letters look as if they lean to the left with their thickest stroke at 2 and 8 o'clock and the thinnest at 11 and 5.

Notice how Old Style and Modern differ in this sketch:

Modern Romans have a marked difference between thicks and thins. Serifs are thin and straight, without brackets. Letters stand erect with the thinnest stroke at the very top and bottom and the widest at the outside of the curves.

It must be remembered that Old Style and Modern do not refer

Printing has perform *Old Style*

ROMAN Printing has perform *Modern*

Printing has performe *Italic*

TEXT Printing has perfor

SANS Printing has performed *Sans Serif*

Printing has performed a rol *Gothic*

SQUARE SERIF **Printing has p**

SCRIPT *Printing has performed* *Cursive*

Printing has perfo? *Script*

ORNA- PRINTING HAS *Shaded*

MENTED PRINTING HAS *Shadowed*

Fig. 7. Races of type.

to the date when the typeface was designed. The most famous Modern was designed at the time of the American Revolution; Hermann Zapf, a famed German designer, is cutting beautiful Old Styles today.

Those Romans and Italics which combine characteristics of Old Style and Modern are *Transitionals.*

Numbers, too, are Old Style or Modern. Modern numbers align top and bottom. Old Style 3, 4, 5, 7, and 9 drop below the baseline.

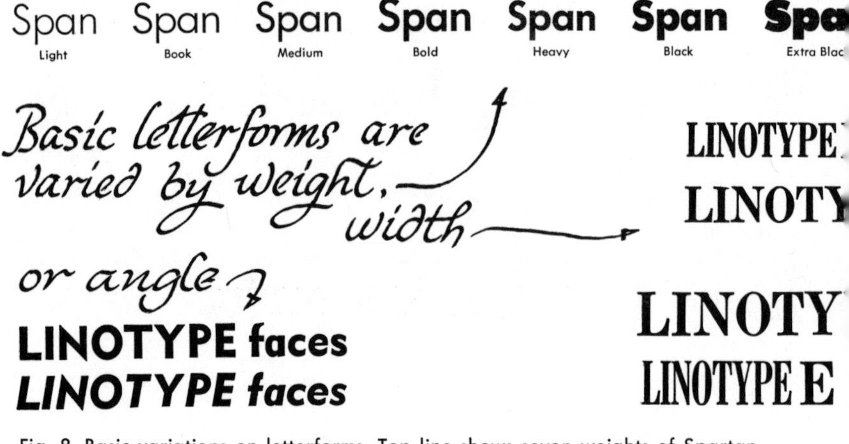

Fig. 8. Basic variations on letterforms. Top line shows seven weights of Spartan. Lower left shows change of angle to make Oblique letter. At right, each pair of lines is of same height with variation in width.

Type races, like human races, are divided into *families,* each with its own trade name. This may be the name of the designer, Bodoni, Goudy, or Craw; a national name such as Scotch, Caledonia, or Columbian; or names that are just names: Falcon, Fairfield, or Century.

Families are made up of *series.* They use the family name plus one or more adjectives that describe a basic variation in the form of the letter.

The normal letter is called *fullface* or *lightface.* Increasing the weight of the stroke makes it *boldface*—or even *extra bold.*

When the letter is squeezed but remains at the same height, it is a *Condensed;* when it's stretched out it's an *Extended.* The third variation, in angle, creates Italic or Oblique.

So a series name might be Caledonia Bold Italic or Cheltenham Extra Bold Condensed.

A series consists of all the sizes in a particular letter style. Each of these sizes is a *font.* So the name for a font is a size plus a series name: 6-point Spartan Bold, for instance. A font contains all the letters—caps and lowercase—punctuation, other characters, such as $, %, ¢, and &, and spacing material.

Type sizes are designated in points. In the old days, sizes were indicated by such resounding names as nonpareil, brevier and Columbian. Today only 5½-point type still is referred to by name, *agate.*

Six- through 12-point are commonly called *body sizes;* larger ones are *display sizes.* From agate through 12-point, type progresses through these sizes: *5½*, *6*, *7*, 7½, *8*, 8½, *9*, *10*, *11*, 11½, *12*. (Italicized ones are *regular sizes.*) In display, regular sizes are 14, 18, 24, 30, 36, 48, 60, 72. Type larger than that is usually made of wood instead of metal. A few series also have 21-, 27-, and 28-point sizes.

But it is the use, rather than the size, of type that gives it its common label. In a full-page ad, for instance, a block of copy might be set in 14- or 18-point type, which would, in this instance, be classified as body type. Or, in smaller newspapers, a 10-point might be used for headlines and thus become display type in this instance.

All newspaper body faces are Romans. They have the highest *readability,* the characteristic which makes it easy and pleasant to read large masses of type, columns of a newspaper or pages of a book.

Romans are often used for headlines, with Bodoni, Century, and Cheltenham the most popular, although the latter two are fast becoming too dated for modern use. Caledonia, a Transitional, is growing in popularity for headlines.

The Sans and Gothics have low readibility but the Sans have high *legibility,* the characteristic that makes a few words almost pop off a page and into the reader's mind. So the Sans are favorites for headlines, with Spartan and Tempo the most frequently used. Franklin Gothic is often used for *banners,* the heavy heads that go clear across the top of a page. Either of these serifless faces are also used for classified ads (and in telephone directories) where, although there is an extremely large mass of type, the reader actually will read only a few items.

Text is rarely used in newspapers except for nameplates and an occasional label head on deaths or on Christmas or Easter stories. Scripts, Cursives, and Ornamented letters are used only in advertising or on special column heads.

Square Serifs make good headlines but, oddly enough, have never been very popular with professional papers. The Squares are called *Egyptians* in Europe and their family names in America are all in that flavor: Memphis, Cairo, and Karnak, for example. Any of these faces will make a good headline schedule for the student paper.

The newspaper editor must use typography within specifications of the *format,* within available resources in body and headline type and facilities to reproduce photographs. In this area the high school editor has problems identical to those of the professional editor. Indeed, those typographic areas which are common to school and professional newspapers are far greater than those which differ.

BOOK TWO

The School Newspaper

5. *Reporting the News*

The reporter—leg man of the paper

To be a successful reporter on your school paper, you have to serve as the eyes and ears of the readers.

This means that you are the indispensable person on the staff, because without news there would be no publication. You have to go out to find the facts, to dig out information no matter how reluctant a news source may be to answer questions or how difficult it is to locate somebody who knows the real details. In addition, you have to write up the news, no matter how complicated, so that readers will be interested in what you say.

★ Only when readers get the message do you really serve as their eyes and ears.

Requirements of these two assignments—gathering the news and writing it—differ widely. In fact, they vary so much that on many dailies these duties may be given to different individuals. A reporter who is expert at unearthing facts, called a *leg man,* goes out to the scene of an event to collect details and to gather necessary notes. Then he telephones his information to a *rewrite man* who assembles it into a news story. On some newspapers, both get their share of credit by having the two names in a joint *by-line* at the top of the story. This split operation probably never will happen on your high school newspaper, but the metropolitan dailies' practice pointedly demonstrates a possible division of labors.

In this chapter, you will learn about these dual aspects of a reporter's job.

No matter how many reporters an editor has, he never has enough of them to be on hand for every newsworthy happening. He might have sufficient staff to cover planned events, such as club meetings, press conferences, conventions, and sporting events, but the unplanned happenings, such as fires, accidents, bank robberies, teen-age rumbles, and the like, also merit coverage. Seldom would a newsman be lucky enough to happen by when the unexpected occurred. Told by his editor to get the news, a reporter has to depend on secondhand sources.

If it is an assignment to cover a fire, the reporter might be there when the flames swept high and then a wall collapsed with a mighty roar. But he would talk to eyewitnesses who saw the first flames crackle out of second story windows. He would interview the experts who are on the scene, seek information of a special sort that might not be readily available elsewhere. For instance, he could ask the chief fire department officer about the probable cause and the number of firemen and kinds of equipment on hand. Of the building owner, he would inquire about his insurance and his estimate of the damages. He would seek anyone who had any information about the fire.

At a baseball game, a reporter notes the play-by-play account. But he also goes to the dressing rooms and talks to the players, and he interviews the umpires and quotes them on the reasons for a decision that brought boos from the home fans.

If a local celebrity is talking at your school assembly, you should follow this pattern of the professional newsmen: You note the chief points of the speaker's presentation. Jot down notes of key quotations so that you have an accurate record of his actual words. You may talk to the man himself or to the principal to find out further details. (Don't bother the speaker, however, for information available from other sources, either printed references such as "Who's Who in America" or faculty members who may know him. A competent reporter would have found this information long before the speaker ever reached the school.) During the interview, either before or after his talk, you gather new facts that may be added to your main account or handled as a *sidebar* or *with story* that is printed alongside the main report.

Gathering News

How would a good reporter gather information about an explosion and small fire in your chemistry laboratory if he had to handle the story for your paper?

First, find some student who was in the lab when the accident happened. You probably would interview the teacher, too. Since they were all at the scene, they might be expected to relate just what happened. However, individuals see, hear, smell, and feel things in different ways. Ask a trial lawyer and he will recite a story of the unreliability of witnesses.

So what do you do when you have to depend on a secondhand version of the event?

Most experienced reporters get a number of eyewitnesses and try to reconstruct the incident in their minds. Obviously not perfect, the method is generally better than depending on a single untrained observer.

In the case of the high school laboratory explosion and fire, you question the student who shouted the first warning as follows:

"Just where did you see the flame start?"

"How big was it?"

"What color was it?"

"What equipment was knocked over?"

"What was the student at that desk doing?"

"Where was the teacher?"

"What did he do?"

Then you interview the student at whose desk the explosion occurred. It turns out that his back was turned momentarily when the flame started so he hasn't the details of what first happened, but he tells you about the equipment that the previous student could not see.

You talk to the teacher. It turns out he was not looking at the desk where the accident started. But he does tell you about the damage and gives a tentative estimate of the cost of replacing equipment.

So from three eyewitnesses of various phases of the explosion and fire, you have enough information to start reconstruction of what happened at the first flash, the effects of the blast, and an estimate of the damage done. Possibly you might have gathered more details if you had been in the laboratory at the time of the explosion and fire. But then you, too, might not have been looking at the desk when the first flame shot out and you would have trouble making an accurate estimate of the damage if you had never bought laboratory supplies.

Professional reporters usually prepare in advance for interviewing or asking questions of a news source to elicit facts for publication. It would not be a bad idea for high school student journalists to follow that example. Three points in this preparation include:

1. Finding out about the individual you will interview.
2. Finding out about the topic you hope to have him discuss.
3. Drafting a few sample questions that you hope he will answer.

You may get information on individuals and topics from reference books, clippings, knowledgeable individuals—or have them in your own head as in the case of covering the laboratory fire and explosion. Remember, the more you know in background, the better impression you will make and the better will be the story you obtain.

If you are adequately briefed, you will not make the classic error of a young (and obviously inferior) cub reporter who went up to a visiting governor and asked, "By the way, sir, just what line of work are you in?" (The question was unanswered.)

Predetermined questions will give you a roadmap for the interview. They may prove especially handy in case you get stage fright when you enter the "presence." As a caution, however, don't let your previous thinking stand in the way of an even better story if the unexpected happens.

One of the authors, working for United Press, was interviewing the late Dr. Arthur H. Compton, Nobel laureate, to obtain a rather conventional feature on his philosophy about science and religion. Questions thought out in advance all had been answered. Almost to make conversation toward the end of the luncheon interview, the reporter inquired about the scientist's special field of cosmic ray research. Unexpectedly for the reporter, Dr. Compton disclosed a spectacular project with a high-altitude balloon he was preparing to launch within a few weeks. It made an exclusive story that was printed from coast to coast—but it was developed without any advance preparation in the way of scheduled questions.

Covering speeches or conventions, which are primarily a whole series of speeches, is a fairly frequent news assignment for student and professional reporters. Covering high school assemblies is one easy way to prepare yourself for what will be a common—and just maybe your first—assignment as a professional. Ascertain background about the speaker and his topic, as outlined above, and you will have some inkling of what his talk may include. As he starts to talk, take notes, sketching in his main points and jotting down any pithy remarks so that you may write them out in full as *direct quotes* or quotations as spoken. You will have—in your mind and reinforced by your notes—a bobtailed tape recording of what the man said. From this, you can construct a news story.

Other frequent assignments may involve people who are being honored, elected to clubs, chosen as officers, starred in sports. You may be asked to gather facts about these folk. You interview them. You talk to their friends—and their enemies. You go to their teachers. You may find facts in high school records, either official papers which the principal permits you to see or previous school newspapers, yearbooks, and the like.

No matter what the event he is covering, a reporter has his tools of the trade, just as a photographer has his camera and a doctor has his stethoscope. Pencil and paper are such tools for the newsman whether he goes out to gather facts on a bank robbery, interview a celebrity, or collect information on a beauty contest.

★ Be sure you have paper and pencil before you go out on a story.

Professional reporters frequently use white or yellow copy paper, folded into thirds along the long direction like a three-partition folding screen. They write on one outside third, then on the middle section, and next on the final third. They are careful to number each third so that there is no confusion as to the order of the thirds on a single sheet of paper.

A high school reporter, however, may wish to use a notebook. This is satisfactory because the student thus may preserve his notes for ready reference for a longer time.

After a lengthy interview, a professional may have pages of notes. To help him organize his ideas into a news story that presents the most important facts first, he goes back over the entire batch of penciled notes, marking the more important as some newspapers rate motion pictures—with stars. Those topics of key importance rate three or four stars (*** or ****) while those of secondary interest get only one or two (* or **). Those items of least importance are unstarred. Reporters thus narrow facts for a lead (*leed*) paragraph to a couple of competitors or to a single outstanding bit of news.

Newsmen and newswomen on press associations or daily newspapers have to write up their information promptly. Those working on monthly or quarterly publications are under no such deadline pressure. However, the professional will transcribe his notes before he forgets what they mean. Unless he has taken them in shorthand, some of the most important information may be in his head and not in his notes. If he waits several days or several weeks, he may forget what was in his head immediately after the interview. A school reporter must write up his notes promptly, even if he has taken them in a notebook, because his recall, too, may fade away.

★ The careful, competent reporter writes up his notes promptly.

If a writer is assembling material from a wide variety of sources or individuals, he transcribes his notes so that he has a full report on each interview shortly after it is finished. When he comes to write his final article, he goes over the batch of typewritten pages, including those bits of information he carried in his head from the interview and wrote down when he transcribed the notes.

Many beginners ask, "Should I learn shorthand?" There is no single, simple answer to this query. If an individual could become as familiar with shorthand as he is with English, it would be a tremendous help. However, if he has to concentrate on shorthand symbols instead of essentials of the news he is gathering, it is a liability. To bridge this difficulty, many reporters have worked out their own system of shorthand. When one of the authors was reporting in Washington, he used such symbols—taken from the Morse code—as "cgs" for Congress, "Whu" for White House, and so forth. Some headline words, such as "JFK" or "pres" for President Kennedy, are used frequently. Any system that you can use effectively and efficiently is okay.

Newsmen and newswomen follow different procedures for covering different types of news. Some are primarily eyewitness accounts and the reporter tells what he sees. Others depend on background that has to be gathered from many experts, and here the writer tells what he has heard.

If a student is assigned to write up a football, baseketball, or baseball game, he may sit in the designated press box or he may want to join a throng of home team rooters. If he is dealing with statistics, he probably should sit in the press box and check them with the official scorekeeper. If he is doing a color story, he will want to participate with his schoolmates in the crowd. This distinction separates most straight news from feature or color stories.

A track meet may be covered by close inspection (and thus coverage) of a few events or individual stars or it may be a roundup of the entire meet. The reporter should decide this before the event starts, being prepared always to shift mental gears if the news develops in a way other than expected.

A staff member assigned to write about the school play may sit in the audience or he may get permission to go back stage and tell what only members of the cast and production staff saw. Both are legitimate coverage; the one would be a review or criticism, the other would be a color story.

★ The type of story determines where a reporter goes to get it.

A telephone may be a tremendous assistance to a reporter making a fast check for last-minute information, but no conscientious beat man thinks that a telephone call is sufficient check to see if there is some news for him at various offices.

★ A beat reporter covers his run in person, except in the most exceptional emergency.

On the other hand, a student reporter who is performing in a professional manner will ask people he interviews or from whom he regularly gathers information for their telephone numbers. If there is some point he forgot or something that needs to be clarified, he can make a single telephone call to complete the assignment.

★ To be prepared for an emergency, a reporter will obtain telephone numbers from key people on his beat and others he may interview.

One journalism professor of earlier days told a story on himself that illustrates this point. He was assigned to cover a fire in the suburb of a large metropolis as one of his first jobs as a green cub reporter. A historic church was ablaze. After a long trip by street car and then a hike along a muddy road, he gathered what he thought were all the necessary facts. When he got back to his city room, he told his editor about the fire and how the steeple, largest in the area, had crashed to the ground in flames.

"How tall was the steeple?" the city editor asked.

The reporter was ashamed because he had to reply, "I don't know."

The editor's curt reply was, "Find out."

And the cub reporter had to go out to the suburb again to get the missing information, because this was before telephones were in general use and he had not bothered to ask for any phone numbers.

Although a reporter goes out on an assignment with scant physical supplies of a couple of sharpened pencils and a sheaf of scratch paper, a good one carries with him intangibles that are of the greatest importance.

He has an inquiring mind. He will not accept without weighing and, if need be, challenging the statements of others. He will try to obtain details that others failed to note. He needs good powers of observation to gather the colorful details. He is a responsible citizen.

Meyer Berger, late Pulitzer Prize winner whose color stories are included in many anthologies of great journalism, frequently spent hours reenacting the events of his assigned story. Once he climbed through a jail window to find additional colorful details for a news item on a prisoner's escape; he wanted to know what the man saw as he crawled into the open.

A reporter's intangibles are important to the public. Unless people in a democracy are adequately informed and enlightened, they do not have the basis for making wise decisions. One newspaper editor explained this when he said, "The reporter is as essential to the healthy working of our democratic society as the politician."

So it is with high school newspapers, too. A responsible staff presents the news around which it is possible to build better school spirit and provides the editorial leadership to clarify student goals and values.

But for high school and professional papers, the process begins with a reporter gathering facts, accurately, fully, and in such manner that they may be presented interestingly when written and published.

Putting Facts on Paper

The newsman's job, when he starts to write his *copy*, the typewritten draft of his story, is to so organize his information that it will attract and, if possible, hold the readers' attention until they are fully and accurately informed. Quite obviously, there are different ways of doing this.

The classic organization of news is to put the most important facts in the first paragraph, the next most important in the second, and so on, with the least significant at the end. This arrangement is the *inverted pyramid*. Among its natural advantages are these:

1. The reader gets the guts of the news at first glance. Thus his curiosity is satisfied early. If he is not especially interested in further details, he need not read to the end of the article for fear of missing the most important point.

2. In the composing room, the type for a story may more easily be *cut* or compressed in length—to fit available space—by throwing away

type from the last paragraphs, which contain the least essential facts.

Each of these assets has a liability and so some news stories follow a *chronological* sequence, starting at a low pitch and building up to a climax toward the end. Here vital information is held back to whet (not to satisfy, as in the inverted pyramid arrangement) the readers' curiosity. If the story has to be cut, sections have to be edited and compressed and then reset into type.

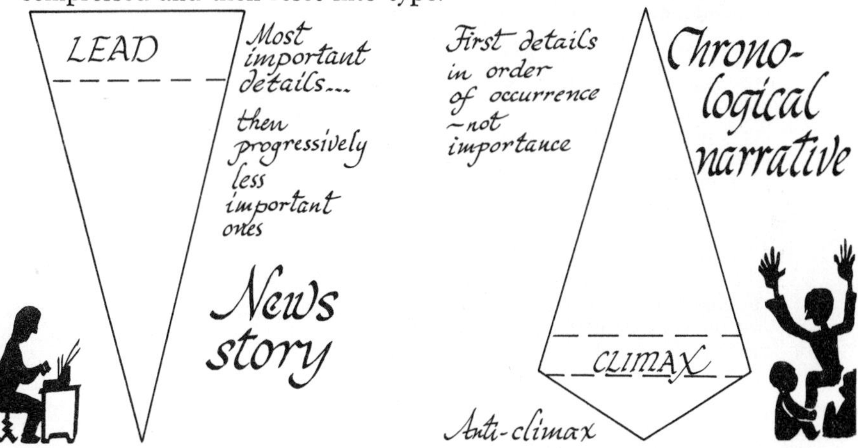

Fig. 9. Diagram shows differences in arrangement of material in news story and chronological narrative.

Other arrangements have their advocates—plus needs and advantages. Some stories start out with a wisecrack that attracts attention and the reader has to go on to find out the resolution. Frequently this is used for short items, often humorous, which are known as *shorts* or *brights*. Journalists may try other presentations of facts. If the effort attracts attention and holds it without readers' thinking it is too contrived, the writer has succeeded.

It is best to learn the conventions first and, having mastered these, experiment if you wish. A cub reporter has to practice the basics of newswriting just as a candidate for the varsity football squad does block and tackle repeatedly during early training.

Let's look at an example of an inverted pyramid organization in a news story that won national honors from the Columbia Scholastic Press Association and the Newspaper Information Service of the American Newspaper Publishers Association. Selected as best news story, the following text was written by Larry Maccubbin of "The Spectator," Granby High School, Norfolk, Va.:

Text	*Comments*
Norfolk's largest civil defense exercise in history, involving over 2,000 persons, was centered at Granby High School, December 7.	Summary lead paragraph

The simulated enemy attack "injured" or "killed" over 900 Granby boys and brought into action an area-wide cooperative effort between civil defense officials, hospitals, doctors, and local government officials.

Held on the nineteenth anniversary of the attack on Pearl Harbor, the mammoth exercise was designed to prevent any such surprise attack as occurred there from catching the country unaware. Mr. M. H. Hawley, Assistant State Coordinator of Civil Defense, echoed the statements of other civil defense officials in remarking that "the exercise has been extremely effective."

Pearl Harbor tie-in and official praise

Granby's gymnasium was turned into a central disaster area where public health nurses, civil defense authorities and about 25 volunteer workers tagged and "injured" all 900 Granby participants.

Number of participants and workers

"Casualties" ranged from broken bones to severe cuts and burns. Several persons were classified as "psychotics" and hundreds "suffered" from shock.

Types of "casualties"

Moulages, or artificial wounds, donated by the Norfolk Civil Defense headquarters, were made of clay, axle grease, cold cream, lipstick, and petroleum jelly.

Colorful details on artificial "wounds"

Coordinators of the drill left nothing to the imagination. Animal bones, obtained from area slaughterhouses, were taped to arms and legs to simulate broken bones. Blood, which was used more than any other substance, was made from glycerine, water, and vegetable coloring.

More colorful details

At 1:03 p.m. the first "take cover" warning sounded. Then, at 1:18 p.m., Navy Chief Boatswain's Mate S. C. Butler of the explosive ordinance disposal team, performed top honors by igniting two smoke bombs on Granby's athletic field. These bombs signaled the beginning of the evacuation of all 900 "casualties" to area hospitals.

Description of start of exercise

The "morgue," located in the Masonic Temple, across the street from Granby, accepted 50 "dead" boys representing an estimated 500 fatally injured students. A 200-bed emergency ward, brought by truck from Richmond, was set up at Nor-

Activities outside of school

folk Catholic High School. Hospitals in Norfolk, Portsmouth, and Suffolk handled an average of 100 "casualties" each.

Over 100 ambulances, vans, pickup trucks, and buses were used in the exercise to transport the boys to their assigned hospitals. Those boys who were not injured in the "attack" served as litter bearers.

Transportation of "victims"

A touch of realism was added when Phil Duncan, Granby, tripped while carrying a stretcher and sprained his ankle. This was the only injury caused by the "disaster" and was promptly taken care of.

Real accident

"Fatally injured" boys taken to the "morgue" were accompanied by an Honor Guard of 16 policemen from Portsmouth and Norfolk County. They were fingerprinted, tagged, identified if possible, measured, and prepared for a mass burial. Next of kin were notified and members of the clergy were standing by to administer last rites. Representatives from area funeral homes were also on hand and made the observation that the estimated 500 dead could be buried in about one week.

Details about the "morgue"

Representatives from Battle Creek, Michigan, recently the site of a similar "disaster," were present as were newsmen from local radio and television stations, newspapers, national wire services, and *Life* magazine. They expressed satisfaction with the drill and Mr. Douglas Moore, State Coordinator of Civil Defense, commented, "This is one of the best exercises in the state. The students were well prepared and we appreciate their earnest cooperation."

Visitors present and their comments

Look back over this story and you will see that each paragraph adds more details and that the readers could stop after any one of them and have a reasonably complete report of what happened. This is typical of inverted pyramid newswriting. If the author had followed the chronological sequence he would have started with the first "take cover" warning, but in such a story the reader would have had to go toward the end to find out many of the details included in the first summary paragraph.

The first paragraph or lead (*leed*) of an inverted pyramid story summarizes the essential facts of the news. This type of initial paragraph, as you might expect, is called a *summary lead.* It answers a series of questions that are always in readers' minds: Who? What? When? Where? Why? How? In the journalistic jargon, these are the *5 W's and H.*

Any one of the answers to these six questions could provide the key point to start the lead paragraph. Here are illustrations of how the same facts can be organized to feature the answer to any one of the 5 W's and H:

WHO?

Dr. John McQuire, Jefferson High School principal, announced at the weekly assembly Wednesday that students would have to attend school on the Thursday before Easter, previously listed as a holiday, because of time lost last month when the "big snow" caused cancellation of classes.

WHAT?

Classes will meet on the Thursday before Easter, previously listed as a holiday, so that students may make up time lost last month when school was closed because of the "big snow," Dr. John McQuire, Jefferson High School principal, said at Wednesday's weekly assembly.

WHEN?

Wednesday Dr. John McQuire, Jefferson High School principal, told students at the weekly assembly that they would have to attend classes on the Thursday before Easter . . .

WHERE?

At the weekly assembly, Dr. John McQuire, Jefferson High School principal, told students that they would have to attend classes on the Thursday before Easter . . .

WHY?

To make up time lost because Jefferson High School was closed last month because of the "big snow," students will have to attend classes on the Thursday before Easter . . .

HOW?

By attending classes on the Thursday before Easter, previously listed as a holiday, students will make up time lost when Jefferson High School was closed last month . . .

Leads which feature answers to the questions of "When?" and "Where?" need to have a special appropriateness to be effective; time and place usually do not merit such attention. "Who?" and "What?" are standard and conventional. People like to read about other people.

They are interested in things as people do them, or in what things do to people. You can seldom be far off base with either of these, but sometimes other ideas are even better.

To try to answer all 5 W's and H in a single paragraph tends to overburden the lead. Therefore, in recent years, more and more professional writers have included that information of paramount interest and left the remaining answers for the following paragraphs. This keeps the first paragraph to attractive length: not more than 35 to 40 words and generally shorter than that.

★ Don't clutter your lead paragraph with verbiage.

When a news writer uses the chronological arrangement of facts, he is turning his back deliberately on the inverted pyramid and summary lead paragraph. He is using the techniques of the fiction writer who starts at the beginning and goes on to the climax. This presupposes that readers will take time to go through to the end of the story; otherwise the whole point is missed. Hurried people may not do this, so you have to balance out the advantages of having a large majority of your potential readers get the news message from a summary lead against the curiosity and amusement of readers who will go all the way through to the end of the chronological presentation. A persuasive and skillful writer can so interest his readers that most of them will complete the story. But if every story were written this way who knows what might happen? The meat and potatoes diet of summary leads has to bulk large for any paper.

★ Don't overdo experimenting in news style.

Types of News Stories

Chances are that the news in high school newspapers will fall into certain major categories, similar to those of any community's daily. A school newspaper or news magazine eventually might print every type of news story, conceivably including crime news.

For both high school and community papers, *meetings* and *speeches* are the backbone of news coverage. For your school publication, you will cover the speakers and announcements at all-school assemblies and talks before departmental clubs; in your home town daily, you find news about the Rotary and Lions clubs written by staff members, as well as reports on sessions of the state legislature and Congress written by state capital and Washington correspondents. Your classmates may be just as interested in reading about the local YMCA physical director's talk on water safety at assembly as your home town adults are in reading about what your state's senator said in Washington about foreign aid to Latin America.

A conventional formula for covering a speech may be shown as follows, one side indicating topics in your notes and the other showing how the material is arranged in the news story:

Notes

1. Glad to be at high school.
2. Recalls when daughter attended the school.
3. Water safety important as summer is approaching.
4. A funny thing that happened to me while teaching swimming safety.
5. Key safety rule.
6. Ten rules in swimming with safety.
7. Summary conclusion on safety.
8. Hopes to see students in swimming classes.

News Story

1. Key safety rule.
2. Water safety important as summer is approaching. (Direct quote)
3. Ten rules in swimming with safety.

—o—

(Omit 1, 2, 4, 7, 8 from story.)

Since readers like to know exactly what a man said in his talk, you would sprinkle your article with direct quotes from the careful notes you made of interesting, pithy, and important sentences. Some quotations point up a viewpoint so well that they are incorporated into the common usage. For instance, Sir Winston Churchill first used "iron curtain" in a speech that was widely quoted, and thus it got into our famous phrases.

Reporters have to be extremely careful in using direct quotations; speakers—and readers—have justified complaint if you are not accurate. If you paraphrase what a man or woman said, you should not use quotation marks. To do so would make you a literary cheat, and no good reporter wants to be known as that.

★ Exercise the greatest care to insure accurate quotations.

When you are covering several speakers and assembly announcements as well, you pick out the most important item and treat it in the lead paragraph. In the third or fourth paragraph, however, you may want to follow a common practice of the professional newsman and include the other important items that happened. Then you conclude the report on the topic you used in your lead; if there is sufficient space, you then expand on the news mentioned in the third or fourth paragraph. In this way, you have constructed an inverted pyramid of descending news values. But you have insured that some mention is made of the secondary events.

If the announcements at the assembly were of greatest interest, you would start the story with them and then mention the guest speaker after several paragraphs. If you had enough space, you would include a full report of his address toward the end of the item. Some reporters prefer to write two stories, one on the announcements and another on the talk. These two stories might have a covering headline that spread over both leads, a *canopy* head, or run side by side, or even be quite widely separated.

Club meetings, PTA sessions, and other gatherings would be covered the same way as an assembly in the high school auditorium. Since the impact probably would be less, the stories would be shorter, but that would be the only essential difference.

A high school beat reporter assigned to cover the principal's office has much the same problems and responsibilities as a daily's city hall reporter covering the mayor. Both gather news about appointments, new regulations, and visitors, but when they write up the facts both are covering news of an administration. And both these assignments would not be too different, in basics, from that of the state capital reporter or Washington correspondent assigned to cover the governor or the President of the United States.

There are *personals* about students who are doing rather unusual things just as personals in your home town paper are short items telling what adults are doing. A prize-winning stamp collection would rate a story in a school paper just as one owned by the student's father would be reported in the home town daily. If the captain of the basketball team is in an automobile accident and goes to a hospital over night, it is news to your readers just as when the mayor gets sick during a political campaign and that is reported in the community paper.

In writing personals, it is best to use a summary lead with needed details in the following paragraphs. Seldom will such news be handled in chronological fashion unless the events are heavily loaded with *human interest* or personal and emotional material that lends itself to special treatment.

Both high school and community newspapers have considerable space devoted to *sports*. A sports writer gathers his facts and writes them up following the same basic techniques as other reporters. Rightly or wrongly, sports writers are permitted more freedom to experiment in their writing style than most other local reporters. Beginners in sports, abusing this unusual freedom in writing, pick up clichés of the sports fan and use them, misuse them, and overuse them until some high school publications—and a few weeklies and dailies—exhibit the worst writing of the entire paper in the trite language of the sports pages. To report some happening in an original manner is good but to be the 1,000th borrower of a hackneyed expression is an awful thing.

Interviews are another regular news category, whether a reporter is gathering facts about a news event, colorful details on an unusual personality, or opinions from an expert. Earlier in this chapter we told how to gather facts during an interview. One's success in writing an interview is limited only by insufficient familiarity with techniques, lack of imagination, or laziness. Variety is the keynote here. That is one reason why some of the greatest reporters have been experts in handling interviews; they would ferret out the essential facts and then paint them so alluringly that the readers were drawn through to the end of the write-up. Search out the human interest stories and *news features*, as contrasted to the *straight news* stories, in your favorite newspaper and you will find many examples of interviews worthy of your study and analysis.

Any dramatic or exciting news event does not need to be synthetically heightened by overwriting. In fact, such a performance ruins the built-in emotion for many readers.

An oft-repeated story in journalistic lore makes this point well. One experienced staff correspondent was sent out of town to cover a major disaster. He thought he would "shoot the works" in his dramatic lead. But before the telegraph operator could finish the lead sentence which began, "God sits on the hills and looks down sadly tonight on . . . ," the hard-boiled editor at the other end of the wire cut in with the request:

"Interview God!"

★ When you are writing a dramatic story, don't try to gild the lily.

The Nuts and Bolts of Newswriting

When you start to write your news story, there is a near-standard formula that you should follow. Here it is:

1. In the upper left-hand corner of each page of copy, put the *slugline* or identification of the story and the page number. On the second line, put your name and home room or phone number. Thus the top of a page might look like this:

Homecoming game—page 1 Smith (Room 12 B)	*or*	Honors assembly—2 Jones (OW 8-2298)

2. Begin the body of the story almost halfway down on the first page, so that the copy desk may make notations and possibly write a headline in the open space.

3. Leave about an inch of space at the top of subsequent pages.

4. Never write on both sides of a page.

5. Never single-space your copy. Some editors request their staff writers to double-space news copy; others ask for triple-space.

6. Type the word "more" at the bottom of each page except the last one. On the last page indicate the story's end with an appropriate symbol, such as your initials, "30," "###," or "—oo—."

7. Unless you have special permisson, always typewrite.

8. Adds and inserts should be marked appropriately and bear the slugline assigned to the story. Inserts should plainly indicate on what page and after what paragraph the material is to be placed.

An *add* or *addition* is further information that a reporter wants to attach to material that he has already submitted. For instance, further facts may be obtained from another news source for a story breaking just before deadline, and these must be included. However, if the new material is of primary importance, the facts may be written as an *insert* which will be put between paragraphs, either in the typewritten copy or in proof.

A really effective writer is able to transfer the ideas in his mind to his reader's with a minimum loss in meaning. This is the goal whether it is an author working on a novel which he hopes will reach the best seller list or a newsman telling for a Pacific Coast daily what happened at yesterday's session of the United Nations General Assembly.

But the more experienced reporters on United States publications have developed their own rules for effective writing after years of experience and thinking. These rules have almost become second nature to them. If you asked them how they do it, they would agree on a set of axioms that would look something like this:

1. Take time to organize your ideas before you start to write.
2. Use short, familiar words.
3. Translate technical jargon but maintain accuracy.
4. Use active verbs, not passive.
5. Strive for short sentences but don't make them all uniform.
6. Write short, terse paragraphs—but include a few longer ones, too.
7. Use anecdotes and stories; they humanize facts.
8. Dramatize figures and statistics.
9. Prune out extra words, verbiage.
10. Avoid editorializing—except in editorials or opinion statements.

★ A reporter has no editorial policy. He just tells what happened as he saw or heard it.

A reporter should write the full story that he has gathered. If the editor-in-chief and faculty advisor want to eliminate certain parts of news copy because of editorial policy, that is their decision. But it should never be done frivolously. In some cases, a reporter may be told in advance of guidelines for handling some event and, obviously, he should follow the instructions.

What should be a publication's policy about by-lines?

A by-line should be just what its name implies: a credit to an author for a reporting job. And if the senior staff editors are going to be fair, they will reward work only when it is well done. Some stories require research or news-gathering efforts almost superhuman. Other stories can sing happily and make readers laugh out loud; some make them cry because the events are so graphically written that emotions go right along with the words and phrases. Such superior efforts should be rewarded; one way is with a by-line.

A terrific photograph also may capture the emotion of an event or portray a situation so effectively that the photographer deserves his credit line or by-line, too. In that case, a by-line may be set in boldface type and put under the *cutline*. Even greater recognition and attention may be obtained for really outstanding performance by using the photographer's by-line under the *catchline* or heading. This latter is really exceptional and ordinarily should not be used more than a couple of times a year.

★ Publication of material with by-lines should always be based on policy, never on friendships.

Humorous columns, most opinion comments, and some stories such as those on plays, musical events, and debates, depend rather heavily on subjective evaluations. Many periodicals give by-lines to writers of these opinion-loaded articles. This is done because they do not, like the editorials, always reflects the policy of the publication itself.

★ A policy on awarding by-lines should be written out for all the staff to be aware of.

The decision on how to evaluate really superior work may be difficult for an editor and he may want to turn to the faculty advisor for confirmation of his initial reaction. Such a consultation will tend to eliminate playing favorites.

If several students collaborated on the assignment, such as a roundup from several news sources, full credit should be given to all those who helped. In that case, several names will appear in the by-line. This is done on a number of professional publications, even to the extent of a credit to an individual and then an "as-told-to" credit for the person who wrote it.

6. *Features and Opinions*

The newspaper interprets the news

> Nothing can be more misleading than the unrelated fact, just because it is a fact and hence impressive. Background, motives, surrounding circumstances, related events and issues all need to be understood and appraised as well as the immediate event.

So wrote Erwin Canham, distinguished editor of "The Christian Science Monitor," who frequently represents his journalistic colleagues and the United States government at various international conferences. The Boston editor was not advocating a rampage of bias and subjectivity in the papers; he simply was pleading for an adequate backdrop for current events.

The same problems that confront Mr. Canham and his fellow editors and publishers also have to be faced by students on high school papers. Both resolve their difficulties by using the same solutions: feature articles, columns, and editorials.

The previous chapter told how reporters must learn to keep their personal feelings, prejudices, and bias out of straight news stories. This chapter will discuss how a publication tries to help its readers understand events and make up their minds, how a paper, figuratively, throws its weight around—or at least tries to do so.

Feature Articles

"Do a feature on it!"

An editor may give this instruction to a reporter and a seasoned staff member will understand what to do. He will know that the factual basis for his writing will be much the same as that of a straight news reporter but that there is a difference in goals. In addition to informing readers, he will also try to present the flavor of a happening; he will tell its background, its significance, or its importance. Or he may portray the personality, the human interest aspects, of a key person involved. Or he may recite some humorous incident that took place.

A feature may range from a bright just long enough to provide a chuckle to many columns of explanation about some new and involved proposal. In other words, a feature might be three paragraphs on an amusing incident in history class or it might fill several columns and concern a whole new program for rescheduling all high school classes. A feature is not news reporting but is related to the news.

Interpretative features grow out of the news itself. A personality sketch, for instance, that is eagerly read this month might have fallen flat two months back because the individual wasn't in the news limelight yet. And it might attract almost as little interest a year later. Like a blacksmith, the feature writer has to strike while the iron is hot. This is why such material also is known as news features.

Features come in a wide assortment but the chief categories include:

1. Interpretative or news features. These explain, provide background, or tell how to do something.

2. Human interest. These may be shorts and brights or full-length biographical articles on an interesting or important person. Because "The New Yorker" magazine regularly prints such a *personality sketch* under the title of "*Profile*," that word also is used as a name for this group.

3. Vacation and travel. While this is primarily a category for community publications rather than high school papers, a few good features always are lying around on what students and teachers did during their summers or Christmas vacations. An enterprising staff will pry these out.

4. Anniversary or historical. When your school celebrates its 25th or 75th anniversary, students will be interested in what happened before. Many newspapers put out whole issues filled with many features when such an anniversary occurs. Students may be interested every year in the history of their school but, unless it happens to be an anniversary year, their curiosity will be largely unsatisfied. Community papers follow this same pattern, although some print "10 Years Ago" or "50 Years Back" columns on editorial pages.

5. Seasonal or holidays. Much the same as the previous group, these are geared to such occasions as Thanksgiving, Christmas, Easter, Commencement, and the like. Regular holidays provide almost daily opportunities for possible feature treatment. If you are interested in a detailed list of ideas for possible features, consult "Feature Photos That Sell" by Edmund C. Arnold (Morgan and Morgan, 1960) for an

idea worthy of treatment for every day in the year.

As a starter, however, here is a list of a few ideas, each worth a possible feature story, that take place month by month through the school year:

SEPTEMBER
New books in the library.
New faculty members.
Summer activities of students.
New elective courses.

OCTOBER
United Nations Assembly background.
Plans for scholarship examinations.

NOVEMBER
Thanksgiving.
Annual Book Week.
Senior jewelry orders due.
National Merit Scholarship examination semifinalists announced.

DECEMBER
Christmas holidays.
PTA Bazaar.
Students' vacation plans.

JANUARY
New electives to be offered.
Student organizations' plans for new term.
Faculty vacation trips.
Departmental plans and evaluations of achievements.

FEBRUARY
Entering freshman class.
Faculty changes.

MARCH
Class "celebrities" chosen.
St. Patrick's Day.

APRIL
April Fools' Day.
Inductions into national honorary societies.

MAY
Election of student government officers for next year.
Senior Proms, past versus present.
Seniors measured for caps and gowns.
Spring fashion show.

JUNE
Scholarships to graduates.
Graduations, past versus present.
Review of the year's activities.

Ideas for features may arise outside the school world just as well as from students, teachers, and school administrators.

In gathering features from the surrounding community, a staff member should insure that they are school-related, thus insuring that they will be considerably different from those in the local paper. For instance, students would be interested in employment opportunities in shops and stores around the school; this story might be gathered at the beginning of the school year on part-time employment or late in the spring for full-time summer jobs. Visiting speakers, concerts, and plays that visit your community but never come near the high school building may excite readers who want to build the well-rounded background of a "whole man."

Television currently is scheduling many programs of school interest.

Some early in the morning are geared for college credit and might attract superior high school students; others in the evening have broader appeal. An excellent production of Shakespeare on television may make one of his plays much more meaningful for an English class. Discussions of contemporary social problems or reports on national or world news might well stimulate students in social studies. In some communities, teachers assign programs that involve course subject matter for students to watch. If this is the case in your school, a feature might be written either about the classroom activities or about the television program itself.

Interviews, as such, may be handled either as straight news or as features. It depends on what goal a writer (and his editor) seek to achieve.

★ Feature writing demands ingenuity and special skills in both gathering facts and writing them.

Because of a looseness in use of the word "features" and because frequently they are printed on the feature page (often page 3 of a four-page publication), short stories, satires, poetry, short dramatic sketches, and other materials of this sort are chosen by the staff member who is known as feature editor. When selecting such material, he has problems much the same as the staff of the literary magazine, which will be discussed in Chapter 15.

Columns and Columnists

Although the newspaper's main functions are to transmit and interpret the news, an editor may need a column which serves as a repository for those light, fleeting, but interesting anecdotes that do not warrant handling as stories. Such a column gets high readership but this fact imposes increased responsibilities.

A chitchat column is not a traditional gossip column, which has no place in a school newspaper. The fact that John and Jane had a spat last week isn't news by any stretch of imagination—despite what Broadway and Hollywood columnists write about adults. Such a column may record genuinely humorous incidents in classrooms, bus, or locker rooms, boners from examinations and project papers, human interest happenings, and other observations. Here are some leads on possible ideas:

Has Billy Black found a Tanganyika stamp to complete a page in his album?

Has Sophia Stone received a recent letter from a pen pal in Tokyo?

Has Mike Malone been promoted in his after-school job?

Did Principal Jones meet an old Navy buddy at the educators' convention?

Has Miss Ward in home economics a favorite recipe for hot cross buns, chili con carne, or wiener schnitzel?

★ A chitchat column can help you attain a worthwhile goal: to get every student's name into print at least once a year.

When one of the authors was high school editor, he kept a list of every one of the 1,000 or so students. Each name was checked off when it appeared in the paper. Those names that remained unchecked were deliberately tracked down and a legitimate item about each soon appeared in print.

Class officers, athletes, and "Students Most Likely to Succeed" make the first or second issue because they are in activities. But what about Janet Davis? Her mother is an invalid and Jan must hurry home after classes to take care of small sisters and brothers and to cook dinner. She is an admirable member of the student body, no matter how inconspicuous, and deserves recognition in print. There's at least a column item in Jan but it will take ingenuity and work to dig it out. But the reward will be commensurate. It will come, not only from readership, but from the quiet pleasure of Jan and her family—and from the realization that you have done a constructive job of mining legitimate news from an unobvious source.

Because a chitchat column is so popular, the writer and his editor should keep these precepts in mind:

★ 1. Never write a column just to fill space.

It is better to write only half your allocated words with interesting material than to pad out to the full length with trash. You may even miss an issue entirely.

★ 2. Avoid embarrassing anyone.

In case of doubt, always delete an item of potential hurt.

★ 3. Don't grind a personal ax.

A student newspaper is not an arena for private combat but a channel for public communication. Feuds, either real or contrived, are not subject matter for a columnist. In one horrendous violation of this rule, a co-ed columnist used her space in an attempt to break up a friendship because she had long cast dreamy eyes on the male.

★ 4. Never write innuendo.

To say, "What blond football player is trying to date a sophomore cheer leader?" is pure garbage.

★ 5. Don't indulge in private jokes.

The paper belongs to the school, not to you or the columnist. You should edit your publication for every reader; it should not be necessary for him to have been on Ski Weekend to know what a columnist is talking about.

★ 6. Avoid even a suggestion of off-color references.

Double meanings should not be written with the hope that only a few people, possibly only the staff, will understand and get a private chuckle. Good taste governs this column, too.

Some school publications print a column comprised of students' contributions. They may be light verse, puns, parodies, satire, and short features. The rules listed above also apply here.

Like their parents, students spread their attention over a diversified range of out-of-school interests. A school publication thus may want to print information on such varied topics as popular records, co-ed fashions, teen-age fads, books, motion pictures, plays, radio, and television programs.

Much of this writing is straight news reporting on trends and announcements of forthcoming releases. The rest is biographical background on the stars and either *criticism* or *reviewing*. Since differences between these two terms have been blunted through recent misuse, it may be well to define them.

In a true criticism, a writer is giving his personal evaluation. His writing is subjective and the wise reader wants the opinions only of an authority. Here is opinion expressed because the critic is worthy of attention. On the other hand, a reviewer maintains objectivity and tells what happened but does not evaluate whether the performance was good or bad.

For instance, a review might report what the play was, the names of the players, what roles they had, how many acts there were, what the plot involved, and so forth. But, in the purist's sense of the word, a review would not tell whether the writer thought the players were ready to go on the Broadway stage next season or whether they should never consider the theater for a career. However, a reviewer might well tell the audience reactions to the performance.

A critic writes his own personal evaluations because his background and training are sufficient to make his opinions worthy of value and respect.

★ Write reviews rather than experiment with criticism—unless you have a background far beyond your peers.

By using reviews, students will avoid the pitfalls of writing either the caustic, sarcastic comments that critics sometimes shower on incompetent and sloppy professional performers or the Pollyanna praise of a sycophant who believes his schoolmates are near perfection.

Because the student market represents millions of dollars in potential purchasing power, high school publications are an appealing target for special press releases and, in larger cities, press conferences exclusively for their editors.

When a publisher sends a release on a new book that mentions your school or quotes a faculty member, it certainly rates mentioning; a general book on the problems of American high school education, however, should be (1) localized by getting comments of faculty and student leaders, (2) used as a basis for editorial comment, or (3) thrown into a wastepaper basket.

If an actress talked only about her new play at a press conference for student editors, the whole idea might well be dropped; if she told about her own high school training and offered advice to potential actors and actresses, then a report on the interview might interest readers.

New records are a bit stickier because a new song by a favorite still may not catch on; a news story mention may be all that it is worth. An editor, not a public relations man, should make the decision.

★ Some public relations efforts provide good stories; some press agentry represents exploitation of student editors—if they are suckers enough to print anything.

Editorials

When an editor gets an urge to "do something," he usually writes an editorial. This is true of editors whether they are on metropolitan dailies, monthly magazines, or high school publications. The editorial page is the one place where a paper tries to tell its readers what to do, what to think. A powerful weapon, it should be used with care and courage.

Purposes of an editorial may be classified as follows:

1. To influence readers. These *argumentative editorials* help to point thinking in a certain direction: an appeal to vote in the student election, a plea for greater school spirit, a rebuttal to a false opinion that is going around.

2. To add background information and explanation. These are *explanatory* or *informative editorials* that seek to fill gaps in knowledge: an explanation of why an extra class period is being required or background on football rivalry with Central High.

3. To amuse. These *change-of-pace editorials* include the humorous, those dealing with mood and color—the essay type—and *editorial paragraphs,* which may be puns, parodies, or wisecrack epigrams.

Editorial writing at its acme may change the future. In many ways, it is the climax of journalistic performance. It is a privilege to be awarded this assignment. As a consequence, editorial writers need greater thought, more care, and more forceful style than others on the paper. Their logic must be impeccable; their motives above reproach; their style powerful and persuasive. More than almost any other members of the staff, editorial writers must exhibit courage, possess an ability to find and to serve the truth as they see it.

★ Editorial writers must be sincere, displaying neither faulty logic nor phony style.

Professor Walter Steigleman of State University of Iowa analyzed 714 editorials submitted in the 1961 writers' contest of Quill and Scroll. Approximately one third of these editorials discussed students' personal problems, such as conduct in and out of class, slovenly dress, cheating, making the most of educational opportunity, and safer driving habits. Not quite a quarter concerned national and international problems, but these topics were treated in such contexts as the demands of

United States world leadership for informed students, federal aid to education, and students' adjustments to the "cold war" world. Approximately one in five treated extracurricular activities; more than half of these lamented "waning school spirit." One in eight dealt with student-administrative problems, such as more library facilities, defacing school property, and overemphasis on science courses. One tenth

Page 2 PROVISO PAGEANT Thursday, November 16, 1961

Thankful Thanksgiving

Before sitting down to enjoy that Thanksgiving turkey this year, let's think of the meaning behind the word "Thanksgiving." It should be a time of peaceful contemplation and true thanksgiving to God, and not merely a day on which to contract indigestion.

The tense and dangerous times in which we live force us to face the fact that world-wide warfare and destruction are not only possible but impending dangers.

We live in a land of plenty: Americans possess more food, clothes, and luxeries than any other people in the world. More than that, we have gifts which others envy more than material possions: we own religious, education al, and political freedom.

Yet, can easily lose these gifts which we have inherited from our founding fathers. If we begin to take these gifts for granted, we will become lax in our attitude towards protecting them.

This year, remember what we possess and give *thanks* on Thanksgiving.

Our Tie With the World

Adding machines could never count the number of words people say each day. We express our feelings towards the day and greet friends with words. "We use today's newspapers to start tomorrow's fire. A few of the words spoken or written are worth keeping." Their value is in the beauty of their use.

Books are our tie with the world. They fill in the gap between the beginning of time and the present. Literature has provided the means to aid the progress of language. Great teachers and books are weapons of warfare. Historians believe President Wilson's speech, in which he presented his Fourteen Points, played an important role in the surrender of Germany during World War 1.

The uses of books are endless.

They remain close, reliable friends.

Letters to the Editor

Sophomores Demand Action

After reading the column about the Social room, I have come to the conclusion that something must be done. Do students realize that if the administration decides to formally abolish the Social room, they will never be able to have this privilege again?

Movies may be shown, classes may be held in there, and, in short, students will be deprived of this privilege. Action is needed, one way or the other.

Verna Baughman, '64

Dear Editor:

I saw the column in the "Pageant" last week; and I, too, think that either more students should use the Social room; or it should be used for some other worthwhile activity.

Maybe it should be converted into a classroom. If students don't think enough of using it, what good is it? I think possibly the Social room could be used during study periods by honor roll students, somewhat as a student lounge.

Student lounges haven't been put into effect in Proviso as yet, and plans have not been very effective. Could our Social room be made into a student lounge?

Nancy Pruter, '64

Trooper Praises Audience

The success of "Mrs. McThing," our all-school play, surpassed our highest expectations. We, the members of the cast and crews, put untold effort into the production.

Miss Little, our director, helped us greatly. We were not sure, however, what effect the play would have on the student body. This was our greatest worry.

I am pleased to say that the conduct of our students deserves praise.

On behalf of the cast, I would like to thank each and everyone of the students who came to see the play.

Mary Ann Giannone, '62

by Dan Novotnak

Question: This is a time of year when we should be especially conscious of our blessings. What are you thankful for?

Alan Goldberg, '65: I am thankful for my new set of drums, but mainly I'm thankful for having the opportunity to get a good education.

Rita Brown, '65: Freedom of religion is what I prize most of all. There are many countries which don't have it.

Jerry Bieker, '64: I am thankful I am alive and able to go to school and take advantage of the opportunities this country gives us all to help us be a success.

Judy Samples, '64: I am thankful for having a wonderful school to go to, for all my friends, and for a good home.

Bob Hendrick, '63: I am thankful to be living in the best country in the world, and I'm thankful for my parents who give me such a good home.

Doris Bower, '62: I'm thankful to be alive, to be part of a happy family, to live in a nice neighborhood, and to go to a good school.

John Gibson, '62: I'm thankful that we are able to enjoy this almost presence of peace on earth, and in my opinion we are getting closer to it all the time.

by Sweetie Pie

HI GIRLS!

Today's the day of the college tea. I'm so excited.

All the upper-class girls look so nice in their pretty dresses and heels.

There's so much going on. Do you realize that Christmas is fast approaching, and we'll soon be going to Cook County hospital to give all the little children the toys we receive from the Girls' League Doll project?

The board members decided to put me in charge of posters from now on, so I'll need lots of help. If you'd like to help me, come to my first meeting on Oct. 29, in Room 249.

Here's some food for thought. I was just looking at the old League scrap books. I found the name of my older sister, the mascot before me. Her name was Lottie Leaguer.

Does anyone know when I, Sweetie Pie, came to Proviso? Maybe, you could ask your mothers, older sisters, or anyone who went to Proviso more than 10 years ago. If you find out, would you please drop the information off in Homeroom 206 before or after school on any day.

Yours in friendship,
SWEETIE PIE

PAGEANT SOAPBOX

by Hank Wessel

THANKSGIVING DAY is next Thursday. This provides us all with an opportunity to think seriously of our many blessings. This day serves as a reminder to not forget that we possess much more than other people.

When we are eating turkey, others will be eating dried bread—or nothing at all. When we are sitting in our warm homes, others will be in the cold.

This is certainly a dreadful comment about our world, but it is true. Maybe someday this condition will not exist. Until then, we must be thankful and continue to hope that others may someday enjoy our blessings.

CONGRATULATIONS to the cast of "Mrs. McThing!" The play certainly displayed the many hours of preparation that were necessary to present it.

PROVISO DEMOCRATS should feel elated over the outcome of the New Jersey election. In the race for governor, Richard J. Hughes, former Democratic judge, scored a "stunning surprise" victory over Republican James P. Mitchell, former Secretary of Labor in the Eisenhower administration.

This, along with other election results, tends to indicate approval of the New Frontier.

DR. PHILLIP M. HAUSER, world authority on population problems, estimates that within 800 years every square foot will contain a human being.

This is possibly already the case at various Proviso hall intersections.

Contemporary Review

Another Type of Record

by Ron Melnikoff

The United States flag flies in a blamy breeze. Around it lies a deeply foliaged tropical island. Yet, we could not call this island or several islands like it paradise. They may have been gardens of Eden once upon a time but not today. These islands are American Samoa.

History books tell us that we gained control of this postage stamp sized real estate when we needed a coaling station in the South Pacific. We bought the islands surrounding Pago Pago bay because they offered a good harbor.

Nevertheless, Pago Pago bay is no dreamy cove today. Instead of pearl shells, the tourist will find raw sewage and garbage in the bay. Likewise, thatched huts have been abandoned for wooden dwellings which look like transplants from a Chicago slum. Travelers have actually described Pago Pago as the slum of the South Pacific.

These are the obvious signs of neglect and decay, but there are others as well. Other signs are one rutted gravel road to serve the island's transportation, one contaminated building for the only hospital, a school system fifty years behind times, and as yet, no self-rule.

Why did we let this happen? We who wish to raise the living and political standards throughout the world, have flopped here because of neglect. Many administrators sent to Samoa received their jobs as political plums. These people did not go to Samoa to improve the islands' living standards. American Samoa should stand out like a sore thumb for here is a prime example of irresponsibility.

Nevertheless, some hope has finally arrived. Our government finally wishes to make amends for its neglect. Furthermore, the Samoans still like us. For some reason they still believe in us.

Vacation to Begin

Students and faculty will leave school at 2:35 p.m. on Wednesday, Nov. 22, to begin Thanksgiving vacation.

Period six will be from 1:40 to 2:05, while period seven will extend from 2:10 to 2:35.

Classes will resume on Monday, Nov. 27, at 8:20 as usual.

Proviso Pageant

International Honors, Quill and Scroll. Winner of George H. Gallup Award. National Scholastic Press association, All-American Honor rating.

Published weekly during the school year except for Thanksgiving, Christmas, Easter, summer vacation, and examination periods the latter part of January by the students of Proviso East high school, 807 South First avenue, Maywood, Ill. Second-class postage paid at Maywood, Illinois.

Subscription: $2 a school year.

EDITORIAL

Editor-in-chief: Henry Wessel
Managing editor: Janet Yench
Assistant managing editor: Di Ba
Associate editors: News, Beth Mul
Makeup, Barbara Giugliano
Sports editor: Paul Zilic
Assistant sports editor: John Tiefenthal
Co-advertising editors: Karen Vasos and Estelle Dravillas
Co-literary editors: Inge Schimo and Carol Schmidt
Adviser: Mr. Ronald S. Kozlowski
Columnists: Michelle Grimm, Nancy Robinson, Ron Melnikoff, Dan Novotnak, Betty Jane Nichols, Glenda Gord, Jacquie Durand, and Ruth Sheldon
Reporters: Nancy Robinson, Michelle Grimm, Ruth Sheldon, Betty Jane Nichols, and Betty Barajas
Head typist: Dace Roze

BUSINESS

Supervisor: Mr. Donald A. Millette
Comptroller: Sandra North
President: Dorothy Stewart
Mailing: Larry Kappesser

Fig. 10. Editorial page from *Pageant* of East Proviso (Cal.) High School.

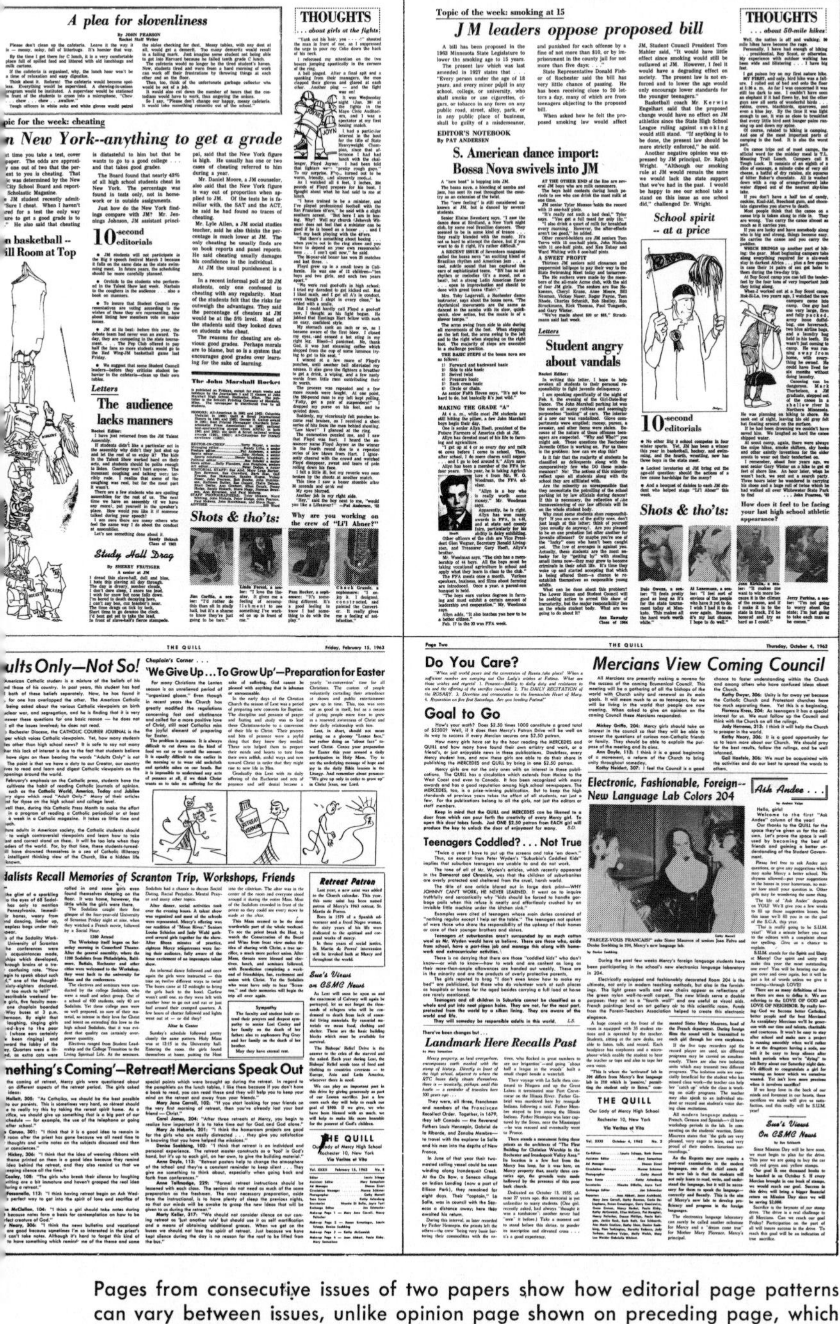

A plea for slovenliness

By JOHN PEARSON

THOUGHTS . . . about girls at the fights

Topic for the week: cheating

In New York--anything to get a grade

10-second editorials

Letters

The audience lacks manners

Shots & tho'ts:

Why are you working on the crew of "Li'l Abner?"

Study Hall Drag

By SHERRY FRUTIGER

The John Marshall Rocket

Topic of the week: smoking at 15

JM leaders oppose proposed bill

EDITOR'S NOTEBOOK

By PAT ANDERSEN

S. American dance import: Bossa Nova swivels into JM

MAKING THE GRADE "A"

School spirit -- at a price

Letters

Student angry about vandals

10-second editorials

THOUGHTS . . . about 50-mile hikes

Shots & tho'ts:

How does it feel to be facing your last high school athletic appearance?

THE QUILL Friday, February 15, 1963

Adults Only—Not So!

Chaplain's Corner . . .

'We Give Up . . . To Grow Up'—Preparation for Easter

Sodalists Recall Memories of Scranton Trip, Workshops, Friends

Retreat Patron

Sue's Views on CSMC News

Something's Coming'—Retreat! Mercians Speak Out

THE QUILL

Our Lady of Mercy High School

Rochester 10, New York

Page Two THE QUILL Thursday, October 4, 1962

Do You Care?

Goal to Go

Teenagers Coddled? . . . Not True

There've been changes but . . .

Landmark Here Recalls Past

Mercians View Coming Council

Electronic, Fashionable, Foreign-- New Language Lab Colors 204

Ask Andee . . .

THE QUILL

Our Lady of Mercy High School

Rochester 10, New York

Via Veritas et Vita

Sue's Views On CSMC News

Pages from consecutive issues of two papers show how editorial page patterns can vary between issues, unlike opinion page shown on preceding page, which retains same basic layout each issue.

From Rochester, Minn., the *Rocket* (above) of John Marshall High makes comparatively minor changes; right column and lower right feature are always in those positions.

From Rochester, New York, the *Quill* (below) of Our Lady of Mercy High changes its layout entirely; even masthead position varies.

involved student-school-parent relationships, with 29 editorials in this category urging support for forthcoming school bond issues.

How one school editor faced a national problem that came to his school and what he urged his classmates to do is told in the following award-winning editorial by Miles Morgan of "Fair Facts," Fairfax High School, Fairfax, Va.:

How Will You Accept Integration?

Integration has come to the public high schools of Virginia and will, as a matter of course, arrive at Fairfax High School.

We feel that this is a good thing. Many do not. However, the situation being what it is, integration of FHS is inevitable—the key question is how YOU will react to it.

Will YOU be among those who intentionally sit on the other side of him in an integrated classroom?

Will YOU laugh at him, or insult him in the halls?

Will YOU ignore him in group conversation or class discussion?

Just how will YOU act when he sits beside YOU in the cafeteria?

We believe that YOU, as a student of Fairfax High School, have the maturity and moral character to avoid a "Little Rock" or "Norfolk" or "New Orleans." We certainly cannot foresee FHS' closing because of blind prejudice and irresponsible action on YOUR part.

Yet Fairfax High School must do more than remain open. It must work through YOU and YOUR fellow students to create a harmonious situation, an atmosphere of willing acceptance of the inevitable: integration.

We would not ask YOU to look at integration's legal basis in the Declaration of Independence and the Fourteenth Amendment. We would merely suggest that YOU remember that all men have a heart—and that's all that really matters.

We know that YOU will not disappoint us when integration comes to Fairfax High School.

Not many school editorials confront such an emotion-laden topic for editorial comment. In fact, many concern tried-and-true subjects year after year. Here is a list of "old faithful" ideas that have appeared over and over again, but if you have something refreshing to say about them, try your hand:

1. School spirit.
2. Sportsmanship at games.
3. Class loyalty.
4. Preparing for examinations.
5. Good study habits.
6. Going on to college.
7. Interschool rivalry.
8. Respect for school property.
9. National honor societies.
10. Commencement and graduation.

★ An effective editorial is not limited to school affairs, but it will tie in with general student interests.

It is easy to write a bad editorial. In addition to selection of lifeless or vapid subject matter, editorial writers may present their facts so poorly that readers are repelled or lulled to inattention. Here are a few of the more common writing faults to be avoided in high school publication editorials:

1. Trite generalities and insipid comments.
2. Rambling comments padded to fill space.
3. Sermonizing in the "Father knows best" attitude.

Writing editorials for high school audiences offers a chance for responsible leadership of public opinion in keeping with the highest traditions of United States journalism. A worthwhile credo for such a performance was offered by Herbert Brucker, editor of the "Hartford (Conn.) Courant" and former assistant dean at Columbia University's Graduate School of Journalism. Here it is:

> A news story is made objective by reporting both sides of a controversy. An editorial is objective by weighing both sides of a controversy with a broad perspective and a deep understanding before deciding which side to fight for. Editorially, a newspaper should be objective only as to purpose. Once it has determined what is right in a given issue, it should pull no punches. . . . Too many newspapers now get too many of their opinions first, and then look for facts to bolster them. It is the deepest obligation of newspapers in a really free world to get the facts first and let these facts determine their opinions.

7. *The Copy Desk*

Preparing material for publication

A competent copyreader is a double-threat man who first edits copy and then writes a headline to pique the reader's interest.

Many a world-famous reporter owes part of his reputation to the quiet work of copyreaders who combed out clichés, substituted vigorous and graphic words, corrected mistakes, and made the language dance. Often a copy desk has shaped a dramatic and moving story out of the mediocre and trite.

One famous newspaper editor confessed frankly that he would rather acquire another able copyreader than add a brilliant reporter to his staff. Another called them the "anonymous heroes" of the press.

In this chapter, you will learn how the copyreader prepares copy for the composing room or for a commercial print shop; you will read about headline writing in the next.

Tools for Copyreading

After the typewritten news story has been completed by a reporter, the editor quickly evaluates it to get some idea of its news worth—what position and how much space it is entitled to. Now the copy goes to the *copy desk* for editing.

High school papers have a relatively simple editing setup; possibly one or two copyreaders behind a desk. In metropolitan dailies, however, the desk is semicircular or horseshoe-shaped with as many as a dozen men sitting on the outer side, the *rim*, and one man sitting inside, in the *slot*. This gives them their titles: those on the outside, *rim men;* the editor in the center, the *slot man.*

Some newspapers have one huge or *universal copy desk* to handle all news, regardless of whether it is local, national, foreign, sports, financial, women's page, or obituaries. But most dailies have at least a *city desk* for local news, a *telegraph desk* for press association and other wire copy, and usually a *sports desk* and a *women's page* (or *society news*) *desk.* On other papers, each major category of news

Spell out: N.Y. to New York

Abbreviate: New York to N.Y.

Join up: fo otball to football

Separate: trackman to track man

Insert: himslf to himself (e)

Insert: Thou shalt kill (not)

Lowercase: Capitals to capitals

Capitalize: states to States

Transpose: mikl to milk

Transpose: to slowly run becomes to run slowly

Delete: was ~~completely~~ destroyed becomes was destroyed

Delete and close up: leltters becomes letters

Let it stand: Leave ~~copy~~ as it was before being marked (Stet)

Boldface: Set underscored word in bold.

Italics: Set underscored word in Italics.

Emphasize period: So Linotyper doesn't overlook it.

Connect material:

This matter now connects ~~to speed reading~~ with this

or

sentence ends.

But no new paragraph

Paragraph: This mark calls attention of Linotyper

Paragraph: When we want a new paragraph here. ¶ This is

No paragraph: Sentence ends. Tells Linotyper.

no ¶ Disregard this indent.

Run in: Bob Smith,
John Miller,
Sam Jones, etc. (Run in)
becomes Bob Smith, John Miller, Sam Jones, etc.

Emphasize quotes: "This calls attention of Linotyper to quotation marks."

Follow copy: Set unusual copy yust the way Swede talks. (folo copy)

More copy: This story continues on a succeeding page. (more)

End mark: This is the end of the story.

(#) or —30—

Fig. 11. Copyreader's marks. Note their similarity to proofreader's marks (Fig. 13) but also the important differences and use of single marks only.

may have a *specialized copy desk* manned by copyreaders who are expert in the type of news story they will edit.

An elaborate copy desk with slot and rim are not necessary to do a competent job. A reporter may copy-edit his story in the press box at a baseball game or at a telegraph office counter.

JONES
PRANK

Victim 'Murdered' Twice;
2-5 Troopers Can't See Joke

Orangeburg, S. C., Jan. 4 (UP)--Juke Box Operator J. E. Hutto was driving peacefully into Orangeburg last night when he saw a car loaded with men careen to a halt in front of him.

A man leaped out of the car, dragged another struggling man behind him, whipped out a pistol and fired twice. The second man stopped struggling and slumped to the ground. The gunman picked up the limp form and shoved it back into the car, which drove away.

Hutto gave chase but lost the "death car" in Orangeburg. He stopped and reported the shooting to Sheriff George Reed, giving him the car's Florida license number. Reed quickly notified the State Highway Patrol.

The Patrol flashed the report to all stations by radio. Road blocks were set up all over the State.

Deputies meanwhile investigated the scene of the shooting. They found footprints but no blood.

Less than an hour later another flash came over the patrol radio net-work. Frightened witnesses reported another identical shooting at Summerton, S. C., 30 miles northeast of Orangeburg.

State troopers swiftly charted the course of the car and went into action. Minutes later they swooped down on the "death car" on the highway 15 miles south of Sumter, S.C.

(more)

Fig. 12. Edited copy. Tight copyreading has reduced length of this story and makes easier reading and comprehension. Note open area at top of first page left by reporter for headline. (Courtesy United Press International.)

★ Efficiency of the editing is what counts, not where it is done.

The copyreader uses a special written language, which instructs a printer with the precision of a mathematician working with another kind of symbols to express exactly what he means. Just as the alphabet has to be learned, so do the copyreading symbols in common use.

★ Everyone who edits copy must know the copyreader's marks.

How a professional puts his know-how into practice was demonstrated by Merton T. Akers, who held various executive positions with United Press and United Press International for well over a quarter century, in a memorandum to press association bureau managers. He described the copy as a "loosely-written story" that was too long, full of adjectives and clichés, and wandering out into "just words" toward the end. The original version and the editing done by Mr. Akers are shown in Fig. 12.

When a copyreader starts to edit a piece of copy, he needs a soft black lead pencil which will make heavy, yet easy-to-read marks or a ballpoint pen that will write without splattering ink if it catches in the cheap paper used for news copy. Most professional copyreaders favor a soft black pencil that is a bit thicker than the ordinary ones. Many publications supply copy pencils and their high school counterparts might do the same—unless staff members start making off with them for class use.

Take 2 of 2

At they found five laughing Duke University students--all very much alive.

The students said they were on their way back to school from Florida and only meant to enliven their trip with a few fake murders.

The "murder weapon" turned out to be an antique pistol, the ammunition firecrackers.

The troopers didn't think the "murders" were funny, but let the students go when they promised not to "shoot" anybody else.

#

Some student papers have found it good policy to use gray copy paper for working versions of news stories, captions, and yearbook text while they are polishing them for style, grammar, and space-fitting. Then when the staff has done most of this work the item is copied onto yellow paper which is edited for a final time before going to the printer. This allows any staff member to know just what stage the copy is in.

Many high school papers have found it useful insurance to make a carbon copy of the version typed on yellow paper. This means that, in the rare chance that something happens to the original copy on the way to or at the printer's, a carbon always is at hand. Professional reporters made copies of their stories, too, and the press associations use "*books*" with several two-faced carbons that provide as many as a dozen or more copies of the news on flimsy paper. Thus some of these are mirror copies read through the thin paper. This way an important story may be sent out on a large number of wires at the same time.

Some schools have a pool of typists who volunteer just for copying the edited news that goes to the print shop. This is especially valuable if the school has typing classes where the touch system is taught; the school paper provides a ready opportunity to put classroom knowledge into practice and a routine copying job is expertly done.

If a copyreader thinks there are still important changes to make in the version on yellow paper, he may use scissors and paste to incorporate revisions that have to be made at the last minute. He will cut and paste so that the copy going to the printer is easy to read and is neatly assembled.

This scissors and paste technique may be useful when an insert comes in after the original facts have been written. This avoids retyping the entire page yet makes it quite clear for the Linotype operator who has to set copy into type.

★ Always insure that copy can be easily read before sending it to the printer.

Library paste is recommended for paste pots, and the efficient student editor will insure that some junior staff member is responsible for seeing that the paste pots are kept filled. This same junior staff member might be assigned the additional responsibility for emptying wastepaper baskets at the end of working hours or for checking that a janitor has not missed any baskets. These jobs may not inspire a beginner but they will show whether he can be depended upon (a key requisite for future important appointments) and they permit a student to perform an assigned role which is needed in efficient operation of a publication.

If the edited copy is smudgy and heavily overwritten, it is best to retype it so that the printer will not be puzzled. Such copy opens the way to delays while the compositor tries to figure it out and to possible typographical errors which will require resetting of the slug of type later. In either case, the wasted time will be reflected in the printer's increased charges.

★ Sloppy editing will increase composition costs.

The copy desk must keep a *log* of all material it handles. Otherwise, embarrassment may set in along about press time when the editor finds he doesn't have enough type to fill all his pages or, more frequently, that he has too much *overset*. Unless this excess type is *time material* that can be used in some future issue, it must be thrown away. With typesetting costs running many dollars a galley, this is a luxury few student publications can afford.

The first step in keeping a copy log is to learn how much advertising has been sold for the issue and determine how much room is left for editorial matter, the *news hole*. Then, as each story, headline, and picture is edited, it is entered into the log:

Class play	5½″
2/2 Seniors choose	4 ″
PIC, Play 2x20 picas	6½″

Periodically, the copy editor will strike a subtotal and note how many more column inches are left vacant. As he gets down to the last few column inches, he can determine whether he will be overset. He can (1) edit late stories very tightly, (2) hold some feature material for later use, or (3) plan to prune a paragraph or two from stories already in type.

Accurate copy logging enables better planning and avoids the unconscionable waste of excessive overset. For a 5-column compact paper, overset should not run more than about an eighth of a galley a page. Good editing can keep it well below this maximum.

The chief copy editor, usually assisted by the editor-in-chief, will decide where news stories, features, and pictures are to be placed in the paper. This is done by marking their locations, sluglines, and estimated length on dummy pages or dummies, small-sized diagrams of the layout for each page. Ads are x-ed in and the various news items allocated to fill the remaining hole. (See section in Chapter 11 on dummies.)

Because reporters and especially copyreaders have to check so many facts, every reputable professional publication has its own library or, as the staff generally calls it, a *morgue*. This is where reference materials, clippings, and pictures are filed for possible future use. Some New York City metropolitan dailies have more than 2 million separate clippings, pictures, and charts about people, places, and things that already have been or may turn up in the news. The name "morgue" has a special appropriateness because it is here that you find biographies of individuals for publication when they die or when they achieve new distinctions. These write-ups are called obituaries or "*obits.*"

Student staff members should think about their own small library, although in many places they may choose to use the high school library, along the lines suggested in Chapter 25.

Regardless of whether the periodical or yearbook has a morgue of its own, the copy desk has certain reference books that will be needed repeatedly. Some of the more common references that should be easily available to copyreaders include:

1. Dictionary for checking spelling and a few historical or literary facts.

2. School directory, if one is published, or whatever official listing of students and teachers is available. This makes it possible to check spelling of proper names.

3. Publication's own *style sheet.* A must reference on any worthwhile publication.

4. Headline schedule with unit counts.

5. Map of your community to confirm street spellings and locations.

6. City telephone book. Like the school directory, this helps in checking proper names. But beware: If there are two "Joe Smiths" in the listings, you don't guess which one has a son in school. Check and make sure!

7. City directory. This also may aid in checking names.

8. Thesaurus which may help copy editors and headline writers to obtain synonyms.

Several single-volume references are especially useful, as you will learn in Chapter 25. However, a publication staff with a little extra money may want to purchase the annual "World Almanac," which is released each January and is a potpourri of assorted facts and figures, and a copy of "Columbia Encyclopedia," which ranks high on most librarians' reference listings. However, if the school library is constantly and conveniently available, the staff may want to use the school's copies of these two reference books along with many others.

Each student, whether he is gathering news or editing it, may set up his own personal morgue with clippings on previous stories he or other staff members have handled but which probably will be in the news again. While an individual scrapbook is highly desirable from a number of viewpoints, a personal morgue is kept for future reference and for your own use, not for display or exhibitionism. One of the authors found an excellent reason for having kept a scrapbook of clippings when he showed his to the editor of his home town newspaper and got a summer job while still in college.

A number of journalism publications will help high school newsmen and newswomen do better and more professional jobs.

All the national school journalism organizations have their own publications and so do many of the regional and state setups. Editors, business managers, and faculty advisors should consider joining those organizations that seem to be most appropriate for their needs. These were discussed in Chapter 2.

Among regular professional journals to which school publications might consider subscriptions are "Editor and Publisher," "Printers' Ink," and "Publishers' Auxiliary," all weekly publications for special aspects of the trade. All contain, from time to time, excellent articles with information that could be adapted to high school newspapers, magazines, and, less often, yearbooks. Practically all 50 states have a professional newspaper organization of publishers and editors, sometimes each separately. Most of them have monthly or quarterly publications to which school staff members might turn for special state or regional information.

A few schools report that they insure reading of professional journals to which their staffs subscribe by holding written tests on articles that were marked for reading. Some school publication staffs which subscribe to journalism periodicals, either for high schools or for professionals, have found it useful to develop routing slips to circulate them, thus insuring that all key personnel have a chance to benefit from valuable information.

The Copyreader's Art and Responsibility

Copyreading, it has been said, is both an art and a science. Certainly, it combines many responsibilities.

The copyreader searches for a whole variety of things when he *reads copy*. Here are some of the more important:

1. Typographical errors or *garbles in transmission.*
2. Mistakes in spelling, grammar, and punctuation.
3. Hackneyed and trite words and phrases.
4. Errors in facts.
5. Errors in interpretation, regardless of whether they arise from ignorance, partisanship, or faulty perspective.
6. Complicated and involved style, which—though correct in form—makes it difficult for readers to follow with ease.
7. Excess wordage, verbiage.
8. Faulty organization.
9. Inconsistencies in style.
10. *Libel* or statements which would harm an innocent person if they were printed.

★ A reporter should always edit his own typewritten version of a news story or feature.

Even so, he may fail to spot a typographical error. It may be a mental quirk that he just fails to see the mistake when he rereads his copy. So a second staff member should doublecheck for errors that might otherwise be missed. A copyreader may be this second reader and he watches for mistakes as he processes the reporter's copy.

On papers that subscribe for press association news services, copy editors keep a special eye out for mechanical garbles that sometimes creep into transmission by Teletype machines, telegraph, or cables. These are mechanical errors due to machine failure or breakdown in the relay circuit. Sometimes a wire service may have to repeat a whole paragraph or even several entire stories.

Mistakes in spelling, grammar, and punctuation are among the most common and most glaring today. Editors and publishers often bemoan the lack of competence of college graduates in these areas. In fact, some publications give preemployment tests to prospective staff members and much of the time is devoted to exercises that will expose deficiencies of these types. High school is none too soon to begin stressing proper usage.

A dictionary may be a reporter's best friend but, unfortunately for a bad speller, writing speed may be slowed excessively if a writer has to look up every tenth word to insure accuracy. Rules of grammar are becoming increasingly less rigid but they are not yet so loose as to permit some of the mistakes that appear in high school and college work. The more common errors are:

1. Subject-verb agreement. *Example:* The combination of English and social studies *were* a key part of the new program. Note: The subject "combination" is singular so the verb should be "was."

2. Pronoun-antecedent agreement. Example: "The New York Times" news columns filled many pages and *it* comprised mostly stories about Washington and foreign events. Note: The phrase "news columns" is plural so the pronoun should be "they."

3. Dangling participle. Example: A leading hero of the Space Age, the people turned out to acclaim him for his record-breaking orbital flight. Note: It was the astronaut, not the people, who was the hero. This might be rephrased, "The people turned out to acclaim this leading hero of the Space Age for his record-breaking orbital flight." Or it might be changed to, "A leading hero of the Space Age, the astronaut was acclaimed by a large crowd . . ."

Many of the more common mistakes in grammar and spelling are amusingly illustrated by the following "gag letter" adapted from the April, 1960, issue of "College English":

Dear Sir; you never past me in grammar because you was prejudice. but I got this here athaletic scholarship any way. Well, the other day I finely get to writing the rule's down so as I can always study it if they ever slip my mind.

1. Each pronoun agrees with their antecedent.
2. Just between you and I, case is important.
3. Verbs has to agree with their subjects.
4. Watch out for irregular verbs which has crope into our language.
5. Don't use no double negatives.
6. A writer mustn't shift your point of view.
7. When dangling, don't use participles.
8. Join clauses good like a conjunction should.
9. Don't write a run-on sentence you got to punctuate it.
10. About sentence fragments.

11. In letters themes reports articles and stuff like that we use commas to keep a string of items apart.
12. Don't use commas, which aren't necessary.
13. Its important to use apostrophe's right.
14. Don't abbrev.
15. Check to see if any words out.

Omission or insertion of punctuation may make a world of difference in meaning. Maxwell Nurnberg, who taught classes in the Division of General Education, New York University, worked out the following series of parallel sentences to prove this point:

(a) Thirteen girls knew the secret, all told.
(b) Thirteen girls knew the secret; all told.
Which is a libel on the female sex?

(a) I left him convinced he was a fool.
(b) I left him, convinced he was a fool.
Which sentence shows extraordinary powers of persuasion?

(a) What's the latest dope?
(b) What's the latest, dope?
Both are slang greetings, but which is insulting?

(a) Go slow, children.
(b) Go slow—children.
Which is the warning to drivers?

(a) A clever dog knows it's master.
(b) A clever dog knows its master.
In which case would the dog have the upper paw?

(a) The play ended, happily.
(b) The play ended happily.
Which is unflattering to the actors?

A small book, which is issued in both hard covers and paperback, will be most helpful in answering your questions about grammar and punctuation. It is "The Elements of Style" by William Strunk, Jr., and E. B. White (Macmillan, 1959).

After cautioning, "Do not overwrite," in the book just cited, E. B. White explains, "Rich, ornate prose is hard to digest, generally unwholesome, and sometimes nauseating." The same sad effects come from hackneyed words, trite phrases, and clichés. The first or even the tenth user of an expression may hope to achieve attention and interest; the millionth user is trying to pass a worn-out phrase or expression. He would do better telling the story in his own words.

One part of journalistic lore concerns a reporter who hated to use the same word twice in any story. Always he'd dig out synonyms, no matter how obscure. One day writing about bananas, he was reduced to "the yellow elongated fruit." So in many news rooms you will hear about "the yellow elongated fruit" if you strive for far-out synonyms.

Sports writers seem to have the greatest disinclination to call a ball by that name; they persist in writing about "hoghide," "horsehide," "pellet," "pigskin," or "pill."

But other reporters use stereotyped language, too. Here is a checklist of just a few of the more extreme examples that a competent copyreader would delete:

Acid test	News leaked out
Beat a hasty retreat	Nipped in the bud
Bolt from the blue	Per capita
Breakneck speed	Proud parents
Breathless silence	Round of applause
Crowded (or jammed) to capacity	Sadder but wiser
Fair sex	Select few
Goes without saying	Shrouded in mystery
Grim reaper	Sigh of relief
Hungry flames	Tender mercies
Long-felt need	Worse for wear

Regardless of whether he works on a weekly high school paper, a bimonthly magazine, or a metropolitan daily with six or eight daily editions, a newsman sometimes may be under the greatest of deadline pressures when he has to turn in his copy. The copyreader stands by to protect the writer, as much as he can, from errors that creep into his story. Is the name "John Q. Public" or is it "John P. Public"? Did the school win that championship in '43 or '44? Is the street address correct? Did that scientist receive the Nobel Prize in 1958 or was it 1948? All of these are hard factual background that can be checked. An appropriate reference book or file will tell. But should a writer halt to make the search if he might not be able to get his story in on time? Such is the dilemma of deadline copy and another reason for getting stories in early if possible.

Several years ago a New England managing editor sent out questionnaires to 1,000 persons whose names had been mentioned in local news stories. Of the 576 who replied, 411 reported they found no errors and 165 cited 183 inaccuracies. The errors were:

	Errors	*Percent of 165 responses*
Names	86	52%
Other factual	49	30%
Incomplete	24	15%
Headline errors	16	10%
Typographic errors	8	5%

Other studies have confirmed the same pattern. So if names, addresses, and other factual information are checked and double-checked, first by the reporter and then by the copyreader, chances are that most mistakes will tend to disappear. Only on Cloud Nine, it seems, would all errors be eliminated—but perfect accuracy is the goal sought by responsible journalists everywhere.

Interpretation, like hard factual material, may be in error. Sometimes this is due to failure to obtain the facts behind the news; reporters are not always told all of the truth and other times they do not try sufficiently hard to get it. Sometimes a reporter wears the colored glasses of his own prejudices, bias, and even enthusiasms. The best rule for reporters is the same that they give the umpires: "Call 'em as you see 'em!" If a reporter can't follow that advice, a copyreader can cut the bias from his story.

Not all the changes that a good copyreader makes are based on rules in a book; some are simply attempts to improve the writer's copy and to aid the reader. A copyreader should always seek to make a story more readable. And here are a few ways:

★ If one word will do the work of five or ten, substitute that one word in the copy.

★ If sentences are too long and complicated, split them into two or more complete parts.

★ If a phrase is potentially misleading, fix it.

★ If the general tone is lifeless and dull, strengthen it up to the proper pitch.

★ If there is excess wordage, cut it like a host carving a fish or a roast—with skill.

Sometimes, but not often if he is a professional, a reporter may misjudge the facts in his story and turn in copy that is faulty in organization. At worst, he may have missed the essential point for his summary lead (*leed*) paragraph; at least, he may have mangled the arrangement of facts in the body of his story. A copyreader may use scissors and paste to repair the defects or he may rewrite parts of the news story to give it greater unity.

As he edits copy, a copyreader insures that it conforms to the publication's style. Each efficient publication agrees on what its style should be and reporters and copyreaders are instructed to conform to it. A style sheet or *style book* sets a pattern for capitalization, punctuation, and spelling, where there may be a choice. In each case, it is a matter of personal—or publication—preference. "Street," "street," "St.," or "st." all are accepted ways of writing, but consistency in a paper speeds reading and reader comprehension.

Always, a copy editor is on the lookout for libel because damage to an individual's or institution's reputation may do great harm. While the civil and criminal penalties for libel are harsh, perhaps the greatest punishment that a reporter—and his copyreader, who is responsible, too—faces is the public exposure of the fact that he has failed in the essential task of his profession: to tell the truth.

There are two kinds of libel: civil and criminal. Civil libel is punished by making the guilty person or persons pay *damages. Actual damages* are for a wronged person suffering because of the inaccurate statement. For instance, actual damages would include all the money that he would have earned had he not lost his job because of the libel. *Punitive damages* are over and above actual losses and the courts levy them to punish the guilty party. Punitive damages may go many times higher than the actual damages.

Criminal libel carries heavy fines and, in some cases, jail terms. While civil libel action is brought by the aggrieved party, criminal libel cases are initiated by "the people," through their spokesman, the prosecuting attorney. In some cases actions for both could be brought against a person as a result of one libelous statement.

Laws of libel vary from state to state. That is why no book such as this can adequately explore the topic. But in almost every case, libel is defined as "false and malicious." In the legal sense, malicious means more than being mean and vicious; sheer carelessness is defined as malice in law books.

This brief description might make you think that every newsman goes about his business with a sharp sword hanging above his head. The sword is always there—but he has a stout shield against it.

★ Truth is the best defense against libel.

If it's true, a newspaper can call a person anything from a Communist to a dope peddler. But it must be true and it must be *provably true.* That means that it can be proved in court.

But what if a reporter makes an honest error? That does not wipe out the libel but it does *mitigate* the offense, make it less serious.

Another mitigation is to publish a *correction* or *retraction* as soon as possible after the error has been discovered. A newspaper would want to do this, even with a nonlibelous error, just to maintain its standards for accuracy. This is a pride-swallowing exercise, running a sorry-we-were-wrong item. But the man who acknowledges his own error is more respected than he who tries to ignore or make excuses for it.

Libel is nothing to be taken lightly, even by a high school journalist. But neither is the truth. Comparing them, remember the words of a poet:

"The truth is great, and shall prevail . . ."

All this brings us to the Eleven (one for good measure) Commandments for a good journalist:

1. Be accurate!
2. Be speedy!
3. Be accurate!
4. Be terse!
5. Be accurate!
6. Be clear!
7. Be accurate!
8. Be colorful!
9. Be accurate!
10. Be compassionate!
11. Be accurate!

Proofreading: Symbols and Practices

Newspapers pride themselves on accuracy. The final—and vitally important—insurance against mistakes is proofreading.

The official proofreader for a student publication should be a most conscientious person, well versed in spelling and grammar, with a keen mind that will question anything dubious to him.

The staff first sees its work in print in the form of galley proofs, printed on long strips of paper, 15 to 20 inches, a column wide. These must be proofread to detect and correct any errors that have been made in typesetting—typographical errors, or typos. It is assumed that editorial errors—those of fact or in typing—have already been corrected in the copy. But the proofreader must be alert for any that have slipped past the copy desk.

The best way to mark corrections is by the *book method.* This requires two marks for every error: One at the scene of the crime, in the copy, and one in the margin, to show how the correction should be made.

Three kinds of marks are used most frequently within the copy.

Words or letters to be removed are simply marked out, letters with a vertical line, words with a horizontal one. In the margin, lined up with the error line, the proofreader writes a *delete sign,* a stylized version of an old-fashioned d.

When a letter or word must be replaced by another, the error is circled and, in the margin, the correct letter is written. An underscore beneath a, u, and w and an overscore above o, n, and m, prevent confusion.

When something must be added, a *caret*—an inverted v—shows where the addition is to be placed. In the margin is written the proper material to be inserted. If it is space to be added, the marginal notation is a little tick-tack-toe diagram.

If the space is to be taken out—moving two letters side by side—a *closeup mark* is used both within the copy and in the margin. This looks like a pair of parentheses lying on their sides.

Occasionally the proofreader discovers that the "correction" he has made isn't a correction after all. Either he has just missed the point or the meaning has become clearer as he read farther. He will then put a dotted line under the copy where he erroneously noted the "error." In the margin, he writes *Stet* (let it stand); he thus tells the typesetter, "Just ignore this!"

Charts of proofreader's marks are available from the printer or one of his suppliers.

★ Note that proofreader's marks are not identical with those used by the copyreader.

Proofreader's marks have been developed because they are the easiest and quickest method of indicating errors. But if the proofreader can't remember the proper mark, he should just circle the error and write instructions in the margin. The object is to achieve accuracy; the method becomes secondary.

Proofreader's marks may vary in detail from one shop to another.

Fig. 13. Proofreader's marks. Note that two marks, one marginal, one within copy, are required for each correction.

But printers can read each other's marks and a student who masters the marks shown in Fig. 13 will be understood in any plant.

When an error occurs in a line of Linotype setting, the whole line must be reset. If this is done to correct the typesetter's error, the printer absorbs the cost. But if the customer—in this case, the staff—has made a mistake or changes his mind, it is called an *author's alteration* or *AA* and must be paid for by the customer. This can wreck a budget; recently a yearbook staff found itself with an unexpected—and unhappy—bill for $1,200 for AA's, most of which were unnecessary.

★ Author's alterations should not be made except for most compelling reasons.

Suppose the proofreader notes that John H. Carr has been identified as president of the junior class; actually it's John H. "Cann." To make this correction, the two n's can simply take the place of the rr and only one line need be reset. If this was the Linotype operator's error, there's no charge. If it was a staff mistake, the paper will be billed—somewhere between a quarter and a dollar.

But suppose the John H. "Carr" is really John H. "Carmichael." In order to find room to tuck in the six new letters, the operator may have to reset several lines. Often this means an entire paragraph has to be reset, with a substantial author's alteration charge.

★ Never "edit" on galley proof.

If the error is one of fact, it must be corrected whether it's a typo or an AA. But other editorial changes should never be made after type has been set. If a story has the word "car" and the editor belatedly decides that "vehicle" is better diction, it would again require resetting several lines to make a change that actually doesn't contribute anything to communication. It is highly doubtful whether any editorial changes are needed—or justified—after type has been set. If such a change has not seemed imperative on copy paper—where it can be made without cost—it is hard to understand why it should suddenly become essential when it bears a hefty price tag.

After the typesetter has made corrections on the galley proof, another proof—the *first revise* or just *revise*—is pulled. This should be checked carefully, first to note that every error has been corrected, then to make sure that no new error has been made in any reset line.

The next chance for checking comes in the form of page proofs, the first proofs made from a made-up page form.

By this time errors should be rare and the *guideline* method can be used by a proofreader. Now the error is circled and a line run from it to the nearest margin where the correction is written. Care should be taken that guidelines do not cross each other. It is best to have the guideline run off just a little higher than the error.

In either method, a soft pencil or ballpoint pen should be used. Fountain pens will blot into illegibility on newsprint.

Traditionally the proofreader initials each proof as he finishes reading it. This is his personal certification that he has done his job carefully and accepts responsibility for it. This is the only step in printing thus personalized; it emphasizes the importance of the job and the pride a good craftsman takes in accepting responsibility.

On student papers, more than one staffer usually reads proofs. The more proofreaders the better; typos are slippery characters and have amazing agility in escaping watchful eyes.

★ The advisor should always make the final check of galley and page proofs.

The best advice for a proofreader is: "Read with extreme care." But there are a few specifics which he should note.

The error easiest to overlook is one that produces an actual word. An error like "pzst" will almost leap off the page and into your eye. But when the eye sees "post" where it should see "past," there is a tendency to skim over it acceptingly.

Errors in headlines are conspicuous to the newspaper reader but easily overlooked by the proofreader. One staffer should be assigned specifically to make sure that the proper head runs with each story. It's all too easy to wind up with the "Class Prom" head over the "Class Play" story.

Some editors tack page proofs on the wall, then take three or four steps backward and read all the headlines. Errors in display type are more obvious at a slight distance, they claim. It's a method worth trying.

★ Unusual care should be taken in checking cutlines, especially under cuts of identical size.

At least one student editor has not forgotten—after 30 years—a sad experience. Cutline said: "This fine herd of Poland China swine won first place for James Jackson at the annual 4-H Fair." These lines were correct—except that they appeared under a picture of a committee that was planning a Hi-Y dance!

The printer, in making up the page, noticed that the dummy called for a 2-column, 4¼-inch cut. The first engraving he saw on the bank was the proper size; into the chase it went. Twoscore Hi-Y members did not direct their wrath at the printer, however; they beat back the ears of the editor. Quite properly so; it was his responsibility.

8. *Writing Headlines*

Summarizing for attention

Good headlines are as carefully constructed as ranch houses or skyscrapers.

They must conform to exacting standards. Flaws in headlines that fail to meet specifications are there for all to see. Editors who do faulty, inferior work receive booby prizes in public when readers laugh at their mishaps.

After a copyreader has edited a story, he must write a headline or *head.* A headline serves two functions: It grades the story according to importance and interest and it provides an element for creating a pleasant page pattern.

★ Headlines should be simple in form and large in size.

Heads are simplified by stripping away all nonessential elements. In post-Civil War days, headlines used to occupy almost as much space as the story. They usually started with a *stepped head* or *dropline:*

ROUGH RIDERS
STORM HEIGHTS
OF SAN JUAN

Then came an *inverted pyramid:*

Col. Teddy Roosevelt Leads
Charge of Cavalrymen
Against Spaniards

Then a *crossline:*

Casualties Said Light

And then more pyramids and crosslines till both the headline writer and readers were exhausted.

Today editors have found that if the main head doesn't lure the reader into the story, the second or third deck rarely does so. So decks are eliminated.

Occasionally editors will use a deck on a 1-column head at the top of page one just to "get more ink"—and emphasis—into a strategic area.

Another efficient use of a deck is as the *readout* from a banner. The banner, or streamer, is the large head that goes clear—or almost—across the page. The readout is a smaller, narrower deck that leads the eye into the story and acts as a kind of "decompression chamber" to take the eye from large banner type to body type with minimum discomfort.

Another simplification of headlines is to free them from artificial

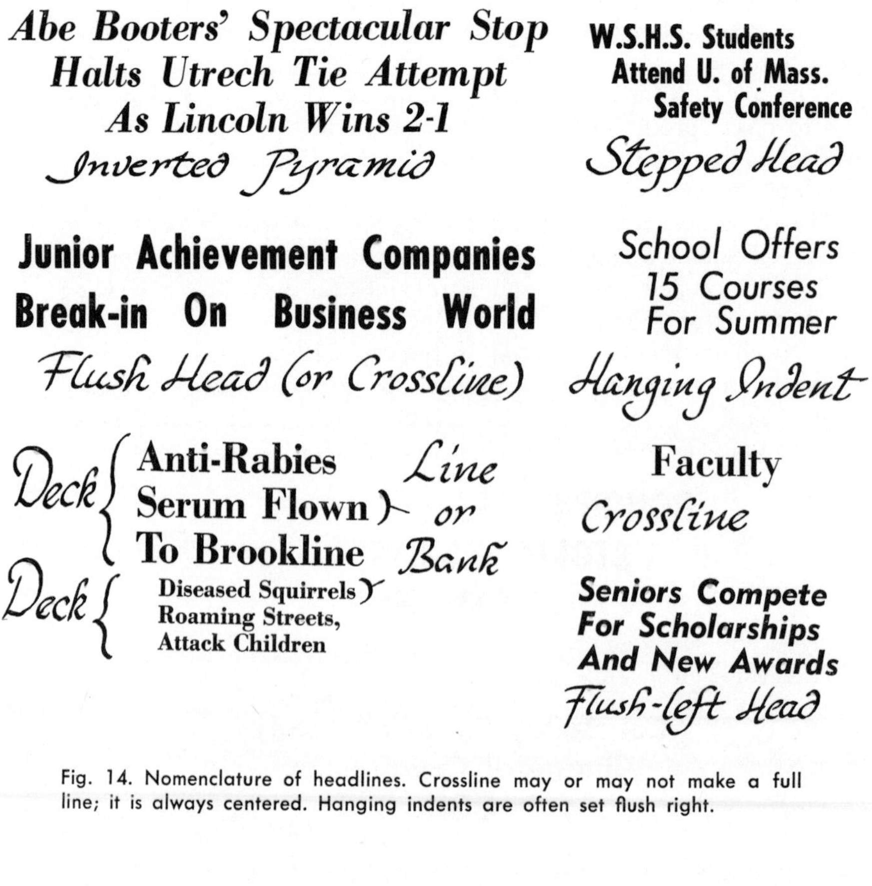

Abe Booters' Spectacular Stop
Halts Utrech Tie Attempt
As Lincoln Wins 2-1
Inverted Pyramid

W.S.H.S. Students
Attend U. of Mass.
Safety Conference
Stepped Head

Junior Achievement Companies
Break-in On Business World
Flush Head (or Crossline)

School Offers
15 Courses
For Summer
Hanging Indent

Deck { **Anti-Rabies**
Serum Flown } *Line or Bank*
To Brookline

Deck { **Diseased Squirrels**
Roaming Streets,
Attack Children

Faculty
Crossline

Seniors Compete
For Scholarships
And New Awards
Flush-left Head

Fig. 14. Nomenclature of headlines. Crossline may or may not make a full line; it is always centered. Hanging indents are often set flush right.

shapes such as the pyramid and steps. Modern heads are set *flush left,* like this:

This Headline
Is Modern
In Concept

★ Flush left heads are easiest to write and to set. More important, they are easiest to read.

The head writer need not worry about a *ragged* right-hand margin. As long as the type occupies more than half of the available width, it will be pleasing to the eye.

As the modern editor eliminates decks, he also minimizes the number of lines in a head.

★ One-column heads should never be deeper than three lines; multicolumn heads are most effective when no deeper than two lines.

If a head can be written in two lines instead of three, or one instead of two, this will afford room for larger type sizes. As one line of 24-point type has more impact than two lines of 12, the editor should always use the largest size possible.

★ All-capital headlines should be avoided.

Their legibility is far lower than that of the conventional *upper-and-lower* head. To gain even more legibility, many newspapers today are adopting *downstyle* heads.

In downstyle, capitalization is used exactly as—and only as—it is in body type. So this *u&lc head*

First Astronaut
Lands on Moon

becomes, in downstyle,

First astronaut
lands on moon

Or, if the head contains a proper noun, it is capped just as it is in the story:

Astronaut plants American flag
on moon's darkside mountain

Notice that only the first word of a sentence is capped; the first word on the second line is in lowercase.

Content of a headline contributes to its effectiveness. Research shows the most memorable heads are those with three words to a line. No professional would attempt to write every head in 3-word lines, nor should the student editor. The important thing to remember is that the rhythm of such a head:

Boom-boom-boom
boom-boom-boom

gives an immediacy and excitement that is essential.

Granted, it's difficult to get an earth-shaking headline when the Spanish Club decides to postpone its monthly meeting. Yet the head writer must make the headline alluring to the reader by implication, at least.

He must also make it easy for the reader to comprehend the meaning of the head as speedily as he reads it. One of the most famous American headlines was:

STIX NIX HIX PIX

This was clever—but it required an interpreter to tell many readers that it meant, "Small towns don't like movies with a rural setting."

★ Each line of a head should be as self-contained as possible.

★ Closely-knit phrases should not be broken between lines.

This is a poor head:

Explorers Find Abominable
Snowman in Himalayas

After the reader reads the first line, he proceeds to line 2. But as soon as he reads the first word he realizes that the phrase "abominable snowman" has been split. He then moves back up to the first line, rereads "abominable," and carries it down to link it to "snowman." While this hasn't taken a serious amount of time, it has annoyed the reader and has broken smooth reading rhythm.

"Don't end a line with a preposition!" This admonition isn't always true, of course.

It is perfectly okay to say:

Astronaut Takes Off
On Flight to Moon

Once in Swiss Tower

Ancient Church Carillon
To Find Home in Museum A

Once in Swiss Tower

Ancient Church Carillon
To Find Home in Museum B

Fig. 15. Kicker heads. A uses accent face (Poster Bodoni) over Bodoni Bold main head. B has Italics of the basic Bodoni as the kicker, which is underscored for emphasis. C shows a reverse kicker.

Fired! C

Charter Commission Works So Speedily
Job Ends Months Before Appointments

But it is a poor idea to write:

Football Team Travels to
Middletown for Big Game

Both these headlines have prepositions at the end of the first line but in only one case is a tight phrase broken.

★ The function of the headline is to lure the eye into body type as swiftly as possible.

Anything that slows down the eye, be it form or content, should be avoided.

The effect is that of traffic lights. It takes much longer to travel a mile on a local street than on a throughway. It is not the time spent in waiting for the green light that causes major delay, it's the time required to get back up to cruising speed. So with reading; any break of reading rhythm is less than desirable.

Two comparatively new headline forms add zest to modern newspaper pages.

The *kicker* is a small head that rides above a main head.

1-1 **Anti-Rabies Serum Flown To Brookline**
Diseased Squirrels Roaming Streets, Attack Children

1-2 **Quake Razes Chile Village**
Casualties Mounting As Fires Break Out

1-3 **Mayor Insists Police Chief 'Defied Me'**

1-4 ***Lonely Chimp Seeks Friends At Midnight***

1-5 **Schools Open For Fall Term**

1-6 ***May Flowers Bloom Late***

1-7 **Rain Forecast**

1-8 ***Dismiss Band***

1-9 **County's Swim Pools Overload Waterworks**

1-10 ***Church Council Elects Bennett as Moderator***

1-11 **Fog Delays Wharf Job**

1-12 ***Worm Turns; Car, Too***

Fig. 16. Portion of headline schedule of a daily newspaper. This includes only headlines set on Linotype and up to three-column widths. Note two-digit code. (Courtesy Mergenthaler Linotype Company)

2-1 **Seven File in Race For New Judgeship**
New State Law Calls For County Court To Open in June

No Panic
2-2 **False Fire Report Evacuates Schools**

Homer in 11th
2-3 ***Big Crowd Sees Tigers Win Game***

2-4 **Tax Increase Halts State Injunction**

2-5 ***Clergymen Take Message to Rioters***

New Bridge Open
2-6 **Traffic Jam Over**

Sheltered Lincoln
2-7 ***Storm Fells Elm***

2-8 **Snow Buries Valley**
Sneak Blizzard Takes Heavy Damage Toll On Budding Trees

Fired! R-2
Charter Commission Works So Speedily Job Ends Months Before Appointments

★ The kicker should be approximately half the point-size of the main head.

Customarily an Italic kicker is used over a Roman head and vice versa.

★ The kicker should be no wider than one-third the overall width of the entire head.

★ The kicker is set flush left. The main head is indented 1 pica per column.

Record Crops Seen

Storm Signals Up

Congressional Delegation
Sets Up Shop in County
Seeking Voters Views
On Army Engineers
Flood-Dike Plan

Hospital Maternity Ward
Rated Best in Midwest
Inspection Teams
Praise Records

No Sissies
Boys Find Hair Dressing
Very Manly Occupation

12 Minutes
Council Approves Budget
In Shortest Session Ever

New Factory Starts Hiring
For November Production

Massed Bands Beat Tempo
For Giant Knights Parade

Way for Road
Radio Tower Topples

Daylight Time
Police on New Hours

Fire Sweeps Shoe Warehouse

Reservoirs All Overflow

Final Testing Monday to Select
First American Man in Space
Choice Down
To Only Four
Rocket Men

Secretary of State Accepts
Invitation to Speak Here
Commencement Talk
Expected to Explain
Position on China

Once in Swiss Tower
Ancient Church Carillon
To Find Home in Museum

South Seas Ahoy!
Family Starts New Cruise
To Revisit Pacific Atolls

City Sales Tax at Record High
Barometer of Business Here

New Strain of Broom Straw
Rates High in Experiment

Onions on Menu
Now Strong Men Cry Too

Pheasants Plentiful
Game Bird Season Opens

Police Car Plunges over Cliff

Mayor Appoints City Clerk

So on a 3-column head the kicker would, ideally, be no wider than 1 column, and the main head would be indented 3 picas.

★ The kicker should be underscored by a rule approximately the thickness of the lowercase l of the kicker face.

Some unusually heavy kicker faces like Ultra Bodoni or Spartan Extra Black, will be strong enough to run without an underscore.

★ Kickers should be written independently of the main head.

No one knows yet whether the reader takes in the kicker before or after the main head; so the kicker should make sense either way. Kickers are an effective way to add explanation to the head:

After 18 Wins

Panthers Lose in Last Minute

Often they are used to attribute a quote, as:

Coach Jones

'Proud of Team Despite Loss'

Reverse kickers get their name because they reverse the size ratio; instead of being half the size of the main head, reverse kickers are twice as large.

The reverse should be kept short; that means that usually only one word can be used. The main head is indented as with a normal kicker.

Germs

Flu Bug Hits School;
Classes Called Off

A big asset that both kinds of kickers lend to a page is the white space that is "built in" at the right of the kicker and the left of the main head.

In the typographer's jargon, white space is *fresh air.* It's as welcome in a newspaper page as in a crowded classroom. We shall see many examples of how white space can be used effectively; a simple one concerns headlines.

★ One-column heads should be indented 6 points at the left; multicolumn heads, 1 pica.

This thin sliver of white at the left gives a fingerhold so the eye can more easily "lift the head off the page."

How to Write Headlines

Let's see how one would go about writing a headline.

Publications work up a *schedule* for their headlines, carefully indicating the maximum *unit count* for the typeface they are using. This count tells how many characters of varying width will fit into a column.

It's difficult at best to write a meaningful headline within a rigid maximum of characters. To impose other restrictions, including a minimum for the classic steps and pyramids, puts an almost unconscionable burden on a student headline writer. It must be pointed out that there are still some—and good—newspapers that use the older head patterns. But they are exceptions. A recent survey of newspapers in a Midwestern state showed that 97% of them were using flush left heads.

The standard unit for counting headlines is the regular lowercase letters such as a, b, c, and so forth. The i and l are smaller and count only ½ unit. In many other type styles, the lowercase f, j, and t also rate only ½ unit. The m and w count for 1½ units. The 1½ count also applies to all capital letters except M and W which are worth 2 units, and the capital I, valued at 1 unit.

One student staff worked out this memory aid and it may help you, too:

"All lowercase letters count 1 except the *flitjays,* which count only ½. (These ornithological halfpints are, of course, f, l, i, t, and j.) The *wammies* (w and m) take 1½."

Now let's take a headline and count it by this system, assuming our maximum unit count to be 20:

C l a y H i g h G r a d u a t e s

1½ ½ 1 1 ½ 1½ ½ 1 1 ½ 1½ 1 1 1 1 1 ½ 1 1 —18

H e l p i n M o o n F l i g h t

1½ 1 ½ 1 ½ ½ 1 ½ 2 1 1 1 ½ 1½ ½ ½ 1 1 ½ —17

From the above unit count, we see that the two lines are both well within the maximum of 20 units a line, and thus the headline is satisfactory. If a line occupies more than half of the width of the allotted space, it is acceptable. The ragged right margin actually adds interest for the reader when the head is set into type.

Writing headlines isn't quite as simple as it might seem. You have to switch and change words and ideas until they tell the story yet come down within the maximum allowed unit count. For instance, in the Clay High School story, you might first have thought of a top line that read:

Clay High School Graduates (24½)

Too long! So you reword it:

Clay High School Alumni (21½)

Still too long but closer. Then you decide to jump down to:

Clay Grads (10)

Too short this time. So you come up with the more acceptable idea that was cited earlier:

Clay High Graduates (18)

Students frequently are bothered about headlines on events that took place last week or last month. How do you make that appealing to your readers?

★ Use the historical present tense.

This rule makes it possible for headline writers to dress up news that might seem stale so that readers feel a sense of immediacy. Like a television film clip, this device (and that's all it really is) puts the reader at the scene—figuratively. But don't fall into the trap of writing, "Dies Last Week."

Stories about events in the future also present perplexities for student head writers. Here the problem is to indicate that it is a forthcoming event. This is done by using "will" or "to" before the verb: "Novelist Will Talk" or "Novelist To Talk."

After you have learned some of these basics, you will have to pay attention to some of the other rules.

★ Build the headline around the action or key idea in the news.

If these involve prominent people and places, refer to them. For stories with a summary lead paragraph, this may mean repeating substantially the same facts. In recent years increasing numbers of professional newsmen have complained about this duplication, but remember that prize-winning high school papers and many world-famous dailies go right ahead—and repeat.

★ Avoid headlines that lack facts, action, or color—*label heads,* or *deadheads* as some editors call them.

An example of what we mean is "Big Debate Today." Who will participate? What will be the topic? Why does it deserve space? Certainly nothing in that headline tells.

★ Stress strong active verbs; avoid the generally less appealing passive verb.

This is just the same rule as for newswriting.

★ Don't be afraid to use colorful words—but don't overdo it and become corny.

★ Avoid interpretations and editoralizing in headlines; just stick to the facts in the story.

★ Drop articles such as "a" and "the," and other short words like "and."

This is done to increase reading speed since the missing words will be supplied whether they are in the headline or not. A comma usually is used to replace "and," so that a headline might read:

Jones, Smith Hit Homers

★ Give the news exactly the play it merits but don't overplay it, either.

Remember the fable of the boy who cried, "Wolf!" too often. However, don't go to the other extreme. You can't have an interesting page if you speak in the typographic monotone of too-small heads. You need a change in pitch—in your voice or your newspaper page. Your readers will want to know the front page news at a glance but they will look inside, too, if you have done your job effectively.

★ How headlines are attached to regular news copy should be worked out in consultation with your printer.

What the headline writer does with his finished product depends primarily on what arrangements have been made with the printer who will handle typesetting and printing. Some request that all headlines be written on separate sheets of paper and attached to the copy which will be set in body type. Others ask that headlines be written in the blank space ahead of the lead paragraph on the first page. Still others desire to have headlines written on a separate sheet which is then pasted to the news story.

9. *Typography of a Newspaper*

Ingredients of the printed page

"First catch your rabbit!"

That was the initial step in the making of rabbit stew, according to a generations-old recipe.

The student editor who seeks to whip up a tasty typographic dish has several rabbits to catch. This chapter will discuss the ingredients that make up newspaper pages.

Body Type

The most important ingredient of a newspaper is so unobtrusive it is often overlooked: body type. American newspapers had been publishing for almost two hundred years before anyone really looked at body type and designed a face specifically to meet the needs of communication.

Body type conveys about 98% of all the information in a newspaper. The newspaper's primary function is to convey information. This adds up to a neat QED: Body type is mighty important.

The student editor usually has little choice in his body type; he must use the face his printer has available. The professional editor has the same problem; changing type faces on a daily newspaper is so expensive that it is done only at long intervals.

Because *newsprint*, the paper on which newspapers are printed, is of low quality and that of news ink is just as low, type used on newsprint should be chosen with these handicaps in mind. There are many good news faces; Corona, Ionic, Excelsior, Aurora, Imperial, and Regal are among those designed specifically for newspapers.

These faces are equally good for better-quality paper used by many student papers. *Slick paper* also marries well with *book faces* such as Baskerville, Bodoni, Caslon, and Caledonia.

These are all Roman faces; they have the highest readability, that quality which makes it easy and pleasant to read large quantities of type matter. Often a student editor—seeking variety—asks to have his paper set in a Sans Serif. Alas! The Sans have low readability and it becomes a bothersome chore to read them in masses.

Once the face itself has been chosen, the next decision is the size. Eight-point is probably the most efficient size for a high school paper, but even this simple statement must be taken with a grain of salt.

If you were asked to look at this diagram:

PRIN PRINTING

and answer: "Which is the larger cow, A or B?" you'd undoubtedly say B. (Now don't say A and mess up all our statistics!)

But the typographer would say, "A and B are both the same size because they're both in the same size pasture."

He'd be right—typographically speaking. For when he calls a face an "8-point type" he means that the "pasture"—the distance from the bottom of descenders to the top of ascenders—is eight points. If these "necks" and "tails" are unusually long, little of the "pasture" is left for the x-height. So we have the paradox of some 9-point type that is actually smaller than some 8-points because of its low x-height.

The two typefaces immediately under our bovine friends are both of the same type size. Yet one looks considerably larger than the other, doesn't it?

★ The choice of body type should be made on the size of its primary letters, not its numerical point size.

The printer's axiom "You can see a pumpkin better than a goose egg" means that a nicely rounded letterform is more readable than one which is squeezed from a circle into an oval.

Once the type has been chosen, there are three factors the editor can change to enhance its readability: length of line; spacing between lines; typographic color.

Measurement of a line of type is another case where two terms are used interchangeably and, because of their definition outside the printing world, can create confusion.

We customarily talk about *line length* but also say *column width*. Don't ask for a logical reason; why isn't it "meese" or "mouses"?

In this book we shall talk about the "length" of a line, be it of 8- or 48-point type. But we will—to conform with printers' custom—call it the "width" of a column and of a headline. (This is because newsmen measure headlines by columns. They speak of a "2-column head," not a "24-pica head.")

Today's standard newspaper line length in America is 11 picas, set in the early 1950's as an economic necessity.

If every newspaper in the country had a different column width, think of the plight of the national advertiser. Say Ford Motor Company wants to run an ad in every newspaper when the new models come out. It would be far too costly to prepare ads of different widths to meet various specifications. Yet if an arbitrary measurement were chosen by the advertiser, he might find his ad just wouldn't squeeze into the narrow columns of "The Slippery Rock Gazette," while it would float forlornly in the wider columns of "The East Inhabited Area Journal."

Student publications don't have to worry about national advertising. But they are wise to adopt the 11-pica column width. Local advertisers are used to preparing ads to this measure for the daily newspaper; readers are used to this width; student editors will learn to work in the pattern in which they'll operate as professional newsmen.

There is a neat mathematical formula for determining the *optimum line length,* that measure which assures maximum readability:

★ *Optimum = lowercase alphabet length × 1.5.*

The lowercase alphabet length (*lca*) is the total length of all the small letters from *a* through *z*.

The lca varies, of course, with the design of the face. But the optimum line length for most 8-point newspaper faces is about 16 picas.

An 11-pica line is obviously far below the optimum; in fact, it sits right at the dangerous minimum. So the reader is constantly faced with lines that are too short for comfort. The editor can give occasional relief by setting type 2 columns wide or setting it at 1½ columns and doubling it over to fill a 3-column area.

These three measures—1-, 1½- and 2-column—are the only ones that should be used. A composing room is like a factory; it must standardize to be efficient. These three lengths will meet all editorial needs without complicating the job of typesetting.

Printers have learned several rules of thumb by experience, and later scientific research has demonstrated that they are basically sound.

★ Never set body type narrower than 11 picas or wider than 24 picas.

Eight-point body type reads best when ledded 1 point. This is specified for the printer by the code: *8/9* or *8-on-9.*

This means that when type is set by hand an extra point of ledding is inserted between lines. On the Linotype, the operator adds that point of ledding by casting the 8-point type on a 9-point slug.

If ascenders and descenders are rather long, they separate the primary letters more widely and in this case a half-point of ledding is often adequate. This is easy on a Linotype, practically impossible in hand type.

Too much ledding defeats its own purpose; the lines may *fall apart* and the eye then "loses its way" as it travels from the end of one line to the beginning of the next.

Newspapermen use two kinds of color. *Flat color* comes from colored ink. Few student editors—in fact, few professional newspaper editors—have a chance to use flat color. But all of them can use *typographic color,* a variation of the gray tone produced by large masses of body type against white paper.

Look at this cartoon:

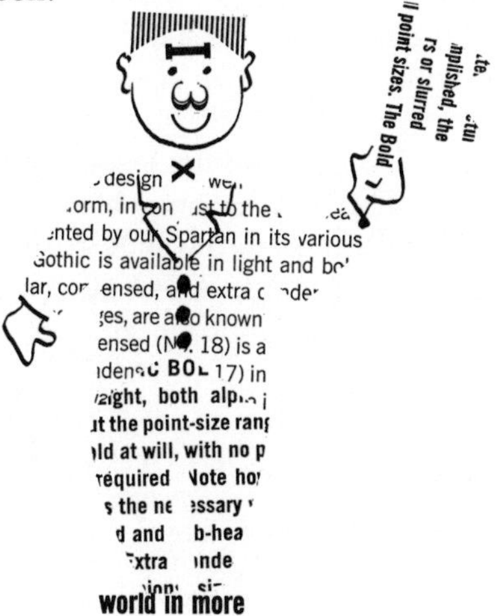

Note how the "color" of the man's trousers contrasts with that of his coat and hat. The editor seeks to get the same kind of contrast by manipulating the "color" of body type in his columns.

Color variation comes primarily from use of the *duplex* of your body type. Linotype matrices are made with two letter molds. One casts Roman—the regular body type; the other may cast Italic or, most commonly in newspaper faces, boldface, *bf.*

A common use of boldface is in *subheads.* These are a word or two, bf caps and centered, like this:

in the first quarter.
QUICK SCORE
But the Panthers struck back

The *boldline* serves the same function but eliminates the need to write or set a separate line. The first line of a paragraph is set boldface with the first or several words capped, like this:

the end's dramatic touchdown
run in the first quarter.

BUT THE PANTHERS struck
back soon to tie the score and

An entire paragraph may be set boldface. Such a *bold graf* should be very short. It is chosen solely by its position in the story—where color is needed—and not for emphasis.

To make sure that the bold type gets maximum contrast—against white paper instead of gray body type:

★ A slug should be dropped above a boldline and a slug goes above and below a bold graf.

Another good color device is the *box.* The conventional *4-sided box* takes considerable time and effort to produce. So contemporary style is to use a *sideless box* which gives the same typographic effect for only 20% of the effort needed for a 4-sided one. Elimination of even a few steps adds up to substantial savings in frequently recurring tasks.

To make a sideless box, the printer uses a *decorative rule* at the top and bottom only. This rule is not necessarily an ornate one; it need only be a distinct contrast to the simple, straight rules used elsewhere on the page. *Oxford rules,* a pair of parallel heavy and thin ones; *wave rules,* or those that appear gray are excellent for boxes.

Impact

Sideless boxes are so easy make that they add no co posing room expense. Yet th serve the same function a four-sided box. Body type is boldface, indented a full p at the left only. Rules are us only top and bottom. An cent face makes an ideal he

Fig. 17. Sideless box gives same effect as four-sided one but with only fraction of cost.

Body type bracketed between these rules is set boldface and indented 1 pica *at the left only.*

Boxes can be one or two columns wide. As they are most effective when not square, 1-column boxes should be at least 3 inches deep—but no deeper than 4 or 4½. Two-column boxes can be up to 3 inches deep as horizontal rectangles. They are not very effective as vertical shapes.

Gimcracks or *typographic spots* include asterisks, stars, ***bullets***—very large periods—or similar devices. These are very useful to separate items in a columnist's product or on editorial pages. Occasionally they are used for color within news stories.

★ Spots should be used sparingly.

Display initials—large capitals at the start of a paragraph—are seen less frequently in newspapers than in magazines or books. *Inset* or *sunken initials* are those dropped into the rectangle of type. They are handsome but create many problems for the printer. *Rising* or *stickup* initials are more easily set. These align with the first line of body type and project well above its mean line. If the student editor follows the practice of most professionals, he will use initials only rarely and then only on the editorial page or on a feature.

Porkchops are half-column portraits; they are usually considered —and used—as color spots rather than as photographs. Porkchops create problems; type running alongside these small cuts must be set well under the 11-pica minimum, and such short lines are not only unpleasant to read but difficult to set.

If porkchops must be used, the wise editor will leave the area next to them blank. This eliminates difficult reading and setting and gives greater emphasis to the picture by dramatic contrast with white paper.

Headlines

Editors love headlines. They like the exciting contents of heads; they like the startling effect of big *headletters.*

A collection of all the heads used by a newspaper is its *headline schedule.* The best-dressed papers make up their schedules from within only one family of type to assure typographic harmony.

If the student editor—who must make his schedule from type available at the printer's—can't find enough sizes within one family to complete his schedule, he can usually obtain good or acceptable results by filling in the blanks with other types within the same race.

★ Avoid mixing Romans and Sans.

For a typical student paper, a good schedule can be made from five fonts of type:

14-point Roman
18-point Italic
24-point Roman
30-point Italic
36-point Roman

If headlines are set on the Linotype, 14- through 24-point are usually duplexed; the schedule is thus expanded by three more faces.

Only under unusual circumstances will a student paper need a 48-point head, and 60 is probably the largest that will ever be required.

The schedule should be printed on a large piece of cardboard. It shows a sample of the head, its code number and the maximum letter count.

The *two-digit code* is the most convenient for designating heads. The first numeral refers to the number of columns, the second to the comparative weight of the head. So 1-1 means that this is a 1-column head and is the heaviest one in this width. A 2-3 would be the third heaviest 2-column head.

It's far easier for the copyreader to mark *1-7* on a head than it is to write *1-column, 14-point Bodoni Bold flush left*. The typesetter need only look at his copy of the schedule to know exactly what type to use and how to set it.

Newspaper Constants

Most material in a newspaper changes from issue to issue. A few elements appear in every issue and so are called *newspaper constants.*

The most conspicuous is the *flag* or *nameplate,* the formal, stylized name of the paper as it appears at the top of the front page. (This is *not* the masthead!) The flag is the newspaper's trademark.

★ The flag must be legible, distinctive, and attractive.

Nameplates may be set in type, handlettered and made into an engraving, or set by means of photo type.

The first factor in creating a flag is the name of the publication. Obviously "The Franklin Delano Roosevelt High School Gazette" can't use the same style as "The Clay High News" because of the difference in length.

Then the editor must decide on a plain or *decorated* flag. Decorated flags were popular in the early days of our country, became rare, today are making a healthy revival.

The most common decorations for student flags are maps (especially for consolidated schools), school or city insignia, a drawing of the school building or a landmark, athletic team mascot or symbol, or awards won by the publication or school.

Flags should not be overdecorated lest they lose legibility. For that reason, too, letters made from logs, ropes, ribbons, or similar materials should be designed with great care.

The easiest nameplate is set in type. If your printer doesn't have the proper faces, you can buy the few words in a flag from a commercial composition house or type foundry.

Black Letter is a favorite for daily newspaper flags. It has traditional dignity that is often appealing to the student staff.

Romans and Italics make sprightly flags. Often Roman initials are used with Italic small letters and vice versa. The effect is pleasant but there are some dangers. Some letter combinations, a Roman H with an Italic *a*, for instance, will not fit snugly and the flag will look as if it had been dropped and broken.

Scripts are available in a wide selection and often make striking nameplates.

If handlettering is used, it is particularly important to check it for legibility. Few student artists—indeed, few commercial artists—can successfully do nameplate lettering.

Photolettering shops, found in every larger city, will supply a flag in any chosen style, even some that look exactly like handlettering, at a low cost of around two dollars a word.

Artype letters, available at any art supply shop, can be used to create a pleasant flag.

Calligraphy, beautiful writing, grows in popularity. It is unique because the letterer can link letter combinations in a way impossible by other methods.

No matter how the flag is created, it is wise to have a cut made from it. Ask the engraver to file the negative. Then, if the plate is damaged, it is easy to replace it quickly and inexpensively.

The *masthead*—a term often but erroneously applied to the flag—is the formal statement that identifies the publication. In professional newspapers, it is required by postal regulations; student publications use it to recognize staff members.

The masthead usually appears on the editorial page.

In the masthead appear: name of the paper (preferably as a miniature of the page-one flag); name of school, address, and phone number; frequency of publication; names and/or insignia of scholastic press associations; emblems, or list, of awards won by the paper; and, most important, names and titles of all staff members.

★ Identification on the masthead should be a reward for good, loyal service to the newspaper.

So the masthead should never give only the name of editors or editorial staffers. The masthead should list the name of every worker who has met high standards of his job, whether he's a feature writer, a typist, or an ad salesman.

★ Establish—and put in writing—the qualifications for listing in the masthead.

A reporter should have a specified number of inches of published material. A copyreader or circulation man must have a certain number of hours on duty. Ad men's work can be gauged by the inches of space they sell, prepare, or service.

A cub reporter whose material must be extensively rewritten shouldn't be listed until he's won his spurs. The photographer who's irresponsible doesn't deserve the laurels.

Blue and Gold

"The Voice of Findlay High"

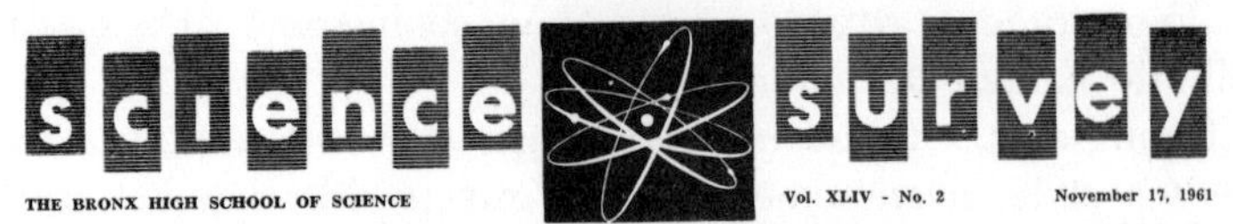

science survey
THE BRONX HIGH SCHOOL OF SCIENCE
Vol. XLIV - No. 2
November 17, 1961

Byrd HIGH LIFE

Catholic CENTRALITE

Fig. 18. High school newspaper nameplates. From top: Mastbaum Vocational Technical School, Philadelphia; Findlay (O.) High; Bronx (N.Y.) High School of Science; Topeka (Kans.) High; Byrd High, Shreveport, La.; Greensburg (Pa.) Catholic Central High; Abraham Lincoln High, Brooklyn; Sheepshead Bay High, Brooklyn.

Above all, in the words of an old newspaperman: "Kill off the glory guys who don't want to work."

Just as good work is rewarded by masthead listing, so poor work should be penalized by removing a name for one or more issues.

Neither bouquets nor brickbats should be bestowed by whim or whimsy. Written standards will assure every staffer of fair treatment.

BAY TIMES

Published by the students of
Sheepshead Bay High School
3000 Ave. X, B'klyn 35, N.Y.

William Friedman, *Principal*

Editorial Staff

NEWS EDITORS: Stephen H. Goodman, Joseph M. Trachtenb...
FEATURE EDITOR: Lowell A. Bodger
SPORTS EDITOR: Leonard Schulman
PHOTOGRAPHY EDITOR: Elliot Klein
ASST. SPORTS EDITOR: Sheldon Whitman
ASSOCIATE EDITORS: Enid Ber, Sharon Friedberg, Seymour Kupor.

Reporters

Leslie Berkowitz, Robert Greenfield, Jeri Kelman, Sher... Robert London, Jerrold Michaelson, Loretta Rabinowitz, ...port, Barbara Reis, Robert Trachtenberg
PHOTOGRAPHERS: Allan Press, Steven Prezant
TYPIST: Rhoda Goldsmith
BUSINESS MANAGER: Steven Peters

Faculty Adviser

Mr. Robert Fein

Vol. II, No. 5 March

Eastern Press, Inc., B'klyn 17, N.Y.

The north star

NORTH HIGH SCHOOL EVANSVILLE 11, INDIANA

THE NORTH STAR is published weekly throughout the school year by the journalism and vocational printing classes of North High School, 2319 Stringtown Road, Evansville 11, Ind. Subscription is by purchase of a North High School activity ticket or at 75 cents a semester for school delivery, plus 25 cents for copies mailed to subscribers. Single copies are 10 cents. Second class mailing privileges authorized at Evansville, Ind.
Founded Feb. 1, 1957, member of National Scholastic Press Association, Columbia Scholastic Press Association, Indiana High School Press Association, and Quill and Scroll.
EDITOR-IN-CHIEF .... LARRY STEPHENSON
MANAGING EDITOR .... JANET WALSH
NEWS EDITOR .... SHARON DODGE
ADVERTISING MANAGER .... ANN BARCLAY
CIRCULATION MANAGER .... JUDY CONNER
First Page Editor . . . Martha Geier; Second Page Editor . . . Anne Pampe; Third Page Editor . . . Cathy Rode; Sports Editor . . . John Mominee; Sixth Page Editor . . . Vicki Brewer; Editorial Assistants . . . Linda Nordhorn, Judy Shafer, Susan Stambaugh, Pat Theuerkauf, Dixie Turley, Larry Wildt, Kay Alldredge, Barbara Brooks, Kandy Kohlmeyer, Julie Kutlich, Danny Points, Janice Rowen, Anita Ruckman, Kathy Tromly, Karl Ralph, and Frances Sitton; Photographer . . . Dave Marshall; News Bureau Correspondents . . . Shirley Stucki, Librarian, Terry Noffsinger; Journalism Adviser . . . Miss Dorothy Teal; Printing Adviser . . . Mr. Bill Mace.

OLNEY HIGHLIGHTS
Published five times per term by and for
THE STUDENTS OF OLNEY HIGH SCHOOL
Philadelphia, Pennsylvania
Organized 1931

Vol. LX, No. 4 May 15, 1961

Member of
COLUMBIA SCHOLASTIC PRESS ASS'N
NATIONAL SCHOLASTIC PRESS ASS'N
QUILL AND SCROLL SOCIETY
PENNA. SCHOOL PRESS ASS'N

Editors ...... EDWARD LAMBERT
EDIE TANNENBAUM

PAGE EDITORS

...... Joan Steinberg
.... Linda Preiss
.... Andrea Fischer
... Howard Arkans
Samuel Pitluck
Mark Rubin
Paul Weisberg
.. Andrea Leerman
Eileen Mick

Photography .. Elliott Greenfield
Art .... Faith Alexander
Sue Stein
Exchange ..... Fredda Jenofsky
Sandra Hart
Lyn Berkowitz
Copy .... Phyllis Soltman
Sheldon Halpern
Adv. Mgrs. ... Larry Gershman
Anita Fellman

Writers .... Phyllis Dickter, Lenard Malish, ...illian Smith, Matthew Wartell
.... Eileen Tucker, Myrna Wallace
...NSOR .... MISS CLARE McCONNELL
.... Ilse Hofmanis, Phyllis Holden
ADVISER .... MR. MARTIN RUGG

...ureux.
Resumé du conte de Daudet
par Katherine Beale

realite.

Connie Rippere

as a practicing device." The ...
structor is able to speak or to
listen to the whole class or to

...nd after school, the
language lab is the scene of

an incr...
dents may benefit from this fine
set-up."

LINTON HI-LIGHTS ***November 22, 1961 — Published in the interests of students of Linton High School, Schenectady, New York. Editor-in-chief, Jo Ann Strom; Associate Editors, Royce Cohen, Barbara Baker, Joseph Ruzzo, and Winifred Cohn; Business Manager, Joseph Shuldiner; Advertising Manager, Michael Kussman; Exchange and Circulation Manager, Marion Bell; Reporters, Robert Binder, Barton Gipstein, Naomi Lasdon, Nan Lomasney, Kathy Monaco, and Beverly Shulman. Advisors: Photography, Mr. Ellis Thorp; Art, Miss Gilda Simiele; Staff, Mr. Stanley Solomon. Published September 29, October 27, November 22, December 19, January 26, March 2, March 30, and May 4.***

Fig. 19. Mastheads. Left, Sheepshead Bay High, Brooklyn; right, Olney High, Philadelphia; center, North High, Evansville, Ind.; bottom, Linton High, Schenectady, N.Y.

Folio lines number and identify pages. Folios should carry the name of the paper (and the name of the school if it isn't part of the title), its city and state, and the page number. Modern practice is to set folios one or two columns wide instead of clear across the page.

Folios should run as close as possible to the top outside corner. But if page makeup requires, they can run at the top of any column.

Folio lines under the flag are arranged differently from inside folios. On page one they are usually lengthened to run clear across the bottom of the nameplate, although they can be bunched up and made part of the nameplate design.

★ Do not separate page-one folios from the flag with a rule.

Folios are part of the nameplate complex; there is no need, or justification, for separating elements.

★ The editor-in-chief should personally check page proofs to make sure that the right date is used in folios.

It is difficult to earn a reputation for "newsiness" if your April 20 issue is dated April 6 because some printer forgot to replace old folio lines and no one caught the error.

(This happens occasionally on professional newspapers. When it does, heads roll like billiard balls in 3-cushion carom! This point is made not to condone the crime, but to preach the horrors of the punishment.)

Ears, those small blocks of copy which run alongside the nameplate, are usually a waste of space; few people read them. Student publications are wise to lop off the ears and let white space direct attention to the flag.

Familiar things grow so commonplace that they are often overlooked. Consequently there is constant danger that constants will become worn, broken, or dirty. Carelessness in such typographic details is as damaging to a good impression as carelessness in details of good grooming and manners.

The editor, advisor, and/or staffer specifically appointed should inspect all constants as soon as an edition is off the press. Those elements which show the slightest signs of wear should be replaced immediately.

Logos

Page logotypes, logos, are used by professional newspapers to identify departments and sections—especially women's and sports. Student papers do not need logos. If your readers can't identify the sports page by its contents, you need a new sports editor, not a logo.

Standing Heads

There is an antipathy among American newsmen against *standing,* or stereotyped, *heads.* But recurring features have high reader appeal and most editors want to capitalize upon that.

A good way is to use the name of the department or columnist as a kicker, then put a regular news head as the main head.

Art heads combine illustration and type and afford useful typographic color if well designed. Such heads are made by combining an engraving with type or by making a cut from a picture combined with a proof of type set by the printer or with Artype.

The name and subject of the column largely determines the style and decoration of an art head. For a school whose teams are called the Red Foxes, this head:

is a logical treatment of a logical name. Such visual puns are appealing to student readers.

Columns should be named so they are closely identified with your particular school. "Student Stuff" could run in any high school paper.

But "Currents in Three Rivers" is obviously a special possession of the Three Rivers High School.

Art heads should not be "cartoonists' dreams." Type must be legible, artwork good in taste and quality. If more than one art head is used, it will contribute to typographic harmony to create a family resemblance among them. This can be done by using the same style of type, the same technique for the pictures, or the same background or border.

★ Art heads should harmonize with the regular headline schedule.

The final ingredient of a newspaper page is *art,* pictures. This is so fascinating—and complex—a subject that it deserves, and gets, a chapter all its own.

10. *Photography and Art*

Pictures as tools of communication

When the Chinese said, "A picture is worth ten thousand words," they were wrong. Pictures alone do not have that high value. Most pictures require some words (we call them cutlines) to be effective communications. But illustrations can expand and sharpen the power of words alone, and so pictures—*pix* or a *pic*—are an essential tool for today's newspaperman.

The basic axiom for using illustrations:

★ Pictures should be cropped ruthlessly and enlarged generously.

Cropping

"I find the picture in the photograph," is the way the picture editor describes his job. That implies that picture and photograph are not synonymous.

A photograph is a chemical-optical reproduction of an actual scene. It is good if it has met technical standards of focus, lighting, angle, and composition.

A picture is a communication; its function is to convey information. A good picture may be a good photograph—or even a very poor one. A good photograph is not necessarily a good picture.

The picture editor must decide what the message is that is to be conveyed photographically. Then he removes all details that fail to contribute to, or might distract the reader from, that message. This process is comparable to the editor cutting excess verbiage from a written communication.

Suppose you have a photograph of the presentation of a citizenship award by the principal to a senior. The photo shows the stage, perhaps a glimpse of backstage at one side, and, of course, the two participants.

The picture editor asks, "What's the pic here?" It's the student, the principal, and the plaque. Everything else is excess baggage.

So the editor *crops* the photo to include only the three elements that tell a story.

★ Cropping must be done so purposefully that the reader will always know it was done on purpose.

If you want to crop into the head of a person, for instance, don't just slice off a thin layer of the skull. This will discomfort the reader; he'll think that the editor "just slipped." But if the cropping were done just above the eyebrows, the reader would rest easy; he'd know the effect was deliberate.

★ Don't crop at body joints.

Cropping at the wrist, elbow, shoulder, ankle, or knee is too reminiscent of amputation.

Cropping depends on the subject matter—the story—of the photo. If you have a portrait of a new class officer, you will crop somewhere below the shoulders in the conventional pose. But suppose the photo is of a biology student looking at a rare butterfly he caught. Here the insect and the student's eyes are the picture. The editor will crop away most of the student's head to direct attention to our little winged friend. The reader will recognize a person even if only a small portion of his head or face is visible.

★ To find the picture, use *cropper's L's.*

These are pieces of cardboard, about an inch wide, shaped like an L. By placing them over a photo, you can determine the rectangle that is the best picture.

When the picture has been found, the editor doesn't actually cut the photograph. He uses *crop marks* or an *overlay* to indicate to the engraver what portion he should use in making the printing plate.

★ Crop marks are never placed on the photo itself.

They are marked in the margin of the photo with a grease pencil as Fig. 20 illustrates.

At the bottom of the photo, (A) and (B), the editor indicates the sides of the engraving. In one of the side margins he marks (C) and (D), the top and bottom of the picture. If there are no crop marks, the engraver will shoot to the edge of the photo.

After the engraver has finished with the photo, crop marks can be wiped away with a tissue and the photograph filed for future use.

The size of the finished engraving (E) and the screen (F) are marked in the margin, too. Be sure that this is the dimension of the *finished engraving,* not of the photo or the cropped picture.

An overlay is a sheet of transparent tracing paper fastened to the

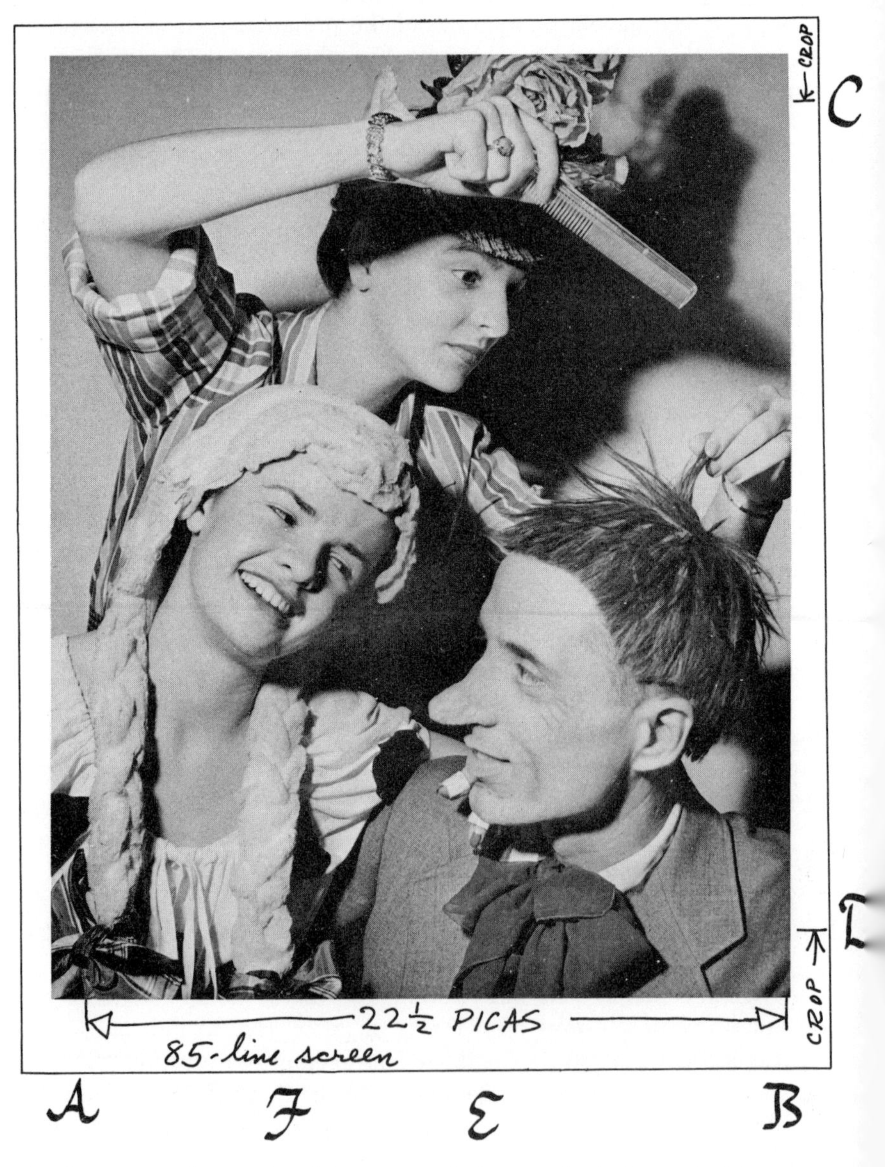

Fig. 20. Crop marks are placed in margins of glossy at A, B, C, and D. E indicates size of engraving to be made and F instructs on how fine the screen is to be. (Courtesy *San Diego Times*)

back of the photo, then folded over to cover the whole front. With a very soft pencil, the desired portion of the photo is indicated.

★ Photos are fragile; treat them accordingly.
★ Never use paper clips on photos.
★ Never roll a photo.
★ Handle photos with clean hands; avoid fingerprints on the face.

The surface of a photograph is a thin, soft emulsion. It can easily

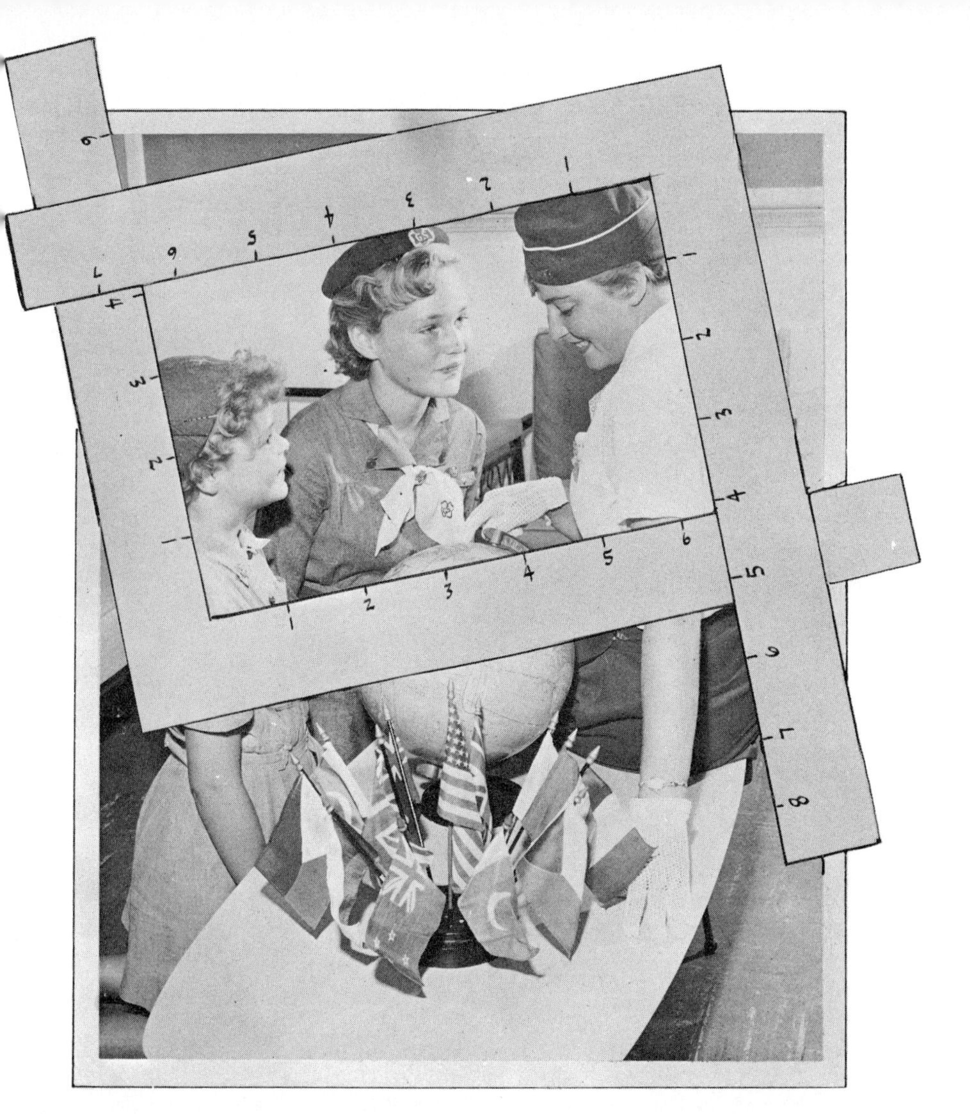

Fig. 21. Cropper's L's are moved to find rectangle within photograph that gives most interesting and informative picture.

be dented by writing on an overlay or the back of the photo. When the picture is placed under brilliant lights in the engraving process, each indentation will become as conspicuous as the Grand Canyon and will be reproduced in the engraving.

Usually pictures are printed as 8 x 10 *glossies,* with a very smooth surface that most engravers prefer to work with. When a *matte finish,* such as that of most studio portraits, is used, the tiny hills and valleys of the comparatively rough paper may be dangerously exaggerated in the cut. *Resisto* is a photographic paper with a semigloss finish that is excellent for engravings. It is a favorite of news photographers because it dries rapidly.

Most editors ask to have *contact prints*—the same size as the negatives—made of every shot that has been taken and then select those

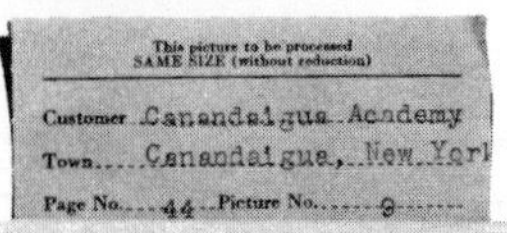

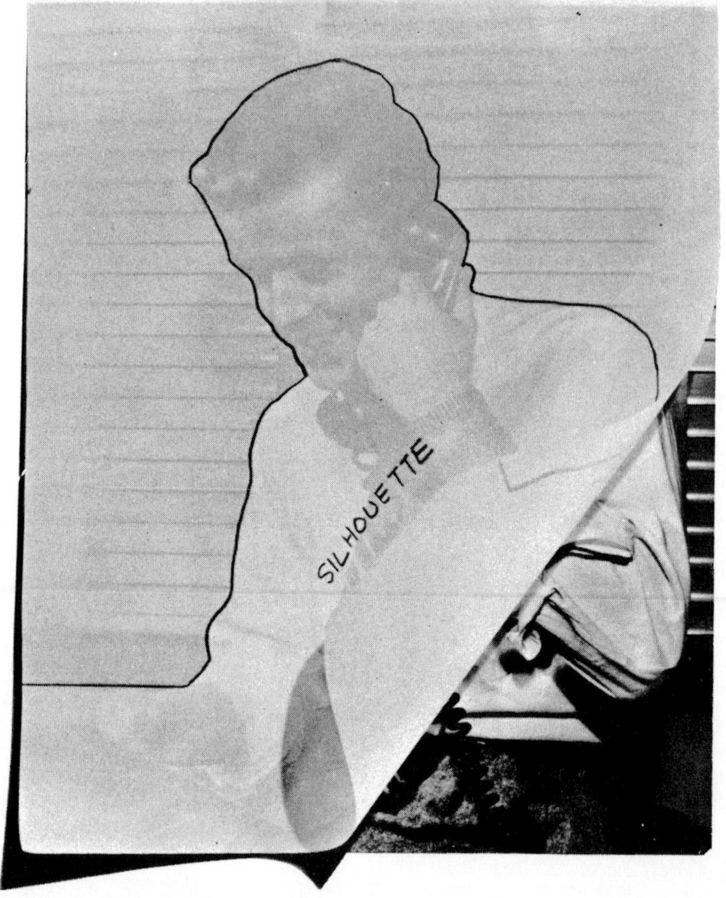

Fig. 22. Overlay used to indicate silhouetting of halftone. Overlays are also used for mechanical separations or for scaling pictures. (Courtesy Wm. J. Keller, Inc.)

they want printed as 8 x 10's. Sometimes an editor even indicates how the photographer should do preliminary cropping while making enlargements. This first cropping should not be too tight lest the editor lose opportunities for creative final cropping of his own.

Engravers prefer to *shoot down*, that is, make the engraving smaller than the glossy. This reduction also reduces flaws and errors in the photo or the engraving process.

Occasionally a cut will be made the same size as the photo with the instruction S/S (same size).

The engraver must also be told what kind of engraving he should make; there are several kinds.

The photoengraver is a magician; he makes much of his living by optical sleight of hand. Most of us are fascinated by magic; let's take a brief visit backstage and see how it's done. Our visit must be brief;

Fig. 23. Line engravings. A uses only black ink in drawing; B shows mechanical shading screens on skirt and sweater.

to learn all about photoengraving would take years—and a book far bigger than this one.

The engraver creates printing plates, also known as engravings, cuts, or zincs. (Most are of zinc but often copper or magnesium is used.)

The simplest engraving is a line cut. Grade schoolers often cut designs out of rubber erasers or potatoes and "print" with them. High school art classes cut "printing plates" out of wood or linoleum. These are all "line cuts," which print lines or masses of black.

Photoengraved line cuts are those made from original pen-and-ink drawings of which cartoons and diagrams are familiar examples. Fig. 23 in this book is a typical line cut.

But the engraver works his real magic with the halftone plates used to reproduce *continuous tone* originals, that is, photographs or art work that contain not only black and white areas but intermediate values of gray.

If you'll look at the picture of your friend in your wallet, you'll notice that the portrait has full black in the shadows, the teeth and collar are pure white, the skin is light gray, and the shadows around the eyes and nose are deeper gray. But the poor engraver has only black ink and white paper to work with. If he needs gray, he can't mix some white ink with the black; he must create an illusion of gray.

He does this by breaking down the continuous tone of a photo or painting into an overall pattern of tiny pure black dots. Where the dots are large and close to each other, the eye sees them as a mass of black. Where the dots are extremely small and widely dispersed, the eye sees white.

Where the dots cover half the area and the white paper the rest, the eye will see this as 50% gray. By changing the size and concentration of dots, the engraver can fool the eye into thinking it sees various tones of gray.

The engraver's screen looks like the screen on your back door except that it is made of fine black lines drawn on a sheet of glass. The finer and closer together the lines are, the finer the dot pattern. Screens are designated by the number of rows of openings per linear inch.

The engraver must be instructed as to what screen to use.

For newsprint, a *65-line* screen is the most common. With 65 rows of dots vertically and horizontally to the inch, there are 4,225 dots in a square inch. Smoother paper such as used by some student newspapers and most magazines will take engravings as fine as 120-line, and the dots are almost invisible to the naked eye.

The engraver—or the artist—can use some of this magic even with line engravings. Fig. 23-A is a normal line cut; it has only black-and-white lines and masses. But notice how the effect of gray is produced in 23-B. The girl's skirt and the boy's sweater look gray because of the many small dots that fill the area. His trousers are made of cross-hatching that produces another shade of gray.

The artist has done the cross-hatching himself; for the sweaters he used a mechanical shading sheet.

Shading sheets have many trade names; an early and still popular one is Zip-A-Tone. Shading sheets are thin, self-adhering transparent plastic on which is printed some pattern of lines or dots.

They are fun to use. After the artist has drawn his pen-and-ink picture, he lays a sheet of shading material over the art work. He *tacks it down* by rubbing a few spots with a smooth piece of wood or metal (or even his fingernail). Then with a *stylus*, a needle embedded in a pencil-like handle, he cuts around the area he wants shaded and lifts away the unwanted portion. The end of the stylus is smoothed off at an angle; with this he *burnishes*, polishes down the shading sheet so tightly it seems to be part of the original picture.

There are many available patterns and most of them can be used in combinations to create a vast range of effects. Shading sheets are available in black or white patterns. White ones can be used over black areas.

Similar shading can be applied by the engraver using the Ben Day process. In this case the artist does his black-and-white drawing as before. Those areas which he wants shaded are painted in a light blue (which is invisible to the engraver's camera). From a catalog the artist picks the Ben Day pattern he wants and tells the engraver which one to use. The engraver then applies the pattern directly to the printing plate.

Ben Day and shading sheets give exactly the same effect. The latter is less expensive as no extra labor is required of the engraver.

Scaling

The engraver does his work while the editor goes about his other chores, and cuts are usually delivered shortly before the printer starts the job of making up the paper.

But the editor must know what size the cuts will be as he dummies his pages, long before the engravings come back to him.

So he *scales* his pictures before sending them to the engraver.

Mathematics of scaling are simple. When a picture is reduced in the engraving process, its width and height grow smaller in the same ratio. If an 8 x 10 pic is reduced so it's only 4 inches wide, its height will be 5 inches. (In referring to the size of a picture, its width is always given first.)

The formula for scaling pictures is:

$$W : H = w : h$$

W is the width of the original photo and *H* its height; *w* and *h* are the width and height of the engraving.

Remember that in a simple equation like this all measurements must be in the same unit. It is wise to convert the dimensions of the glossy into picas before you start scaling.

Suppose you have a photograph that has been cropped to 5½ x 8 inches and you want to make a 2-column (22 picas) engraving. See how the formula works:

You remember from your math course that in an equation like this you must know three factors. You know the dimensions of the glossy and the width of the cut. Your unknown is *h*, the height of the cut.

Your equation looks like this:

$$\begin{aligned} W : H &= w : h \\ 5.5 \text{ inches} : 8 \text{ inches} &= 22 \text{ picas} : h \\ 33 \text{ picas} : 48 \text{ picas} &= 22 \text{ picas} : h \\ 33h &= 1056 \\ h &= 32 \text{ picas} \end{aligned}$$

(Remember that equations like this can be solved because the product of the means equals the product of the extremes. The two outside figures multiply to the same figure as the two nearest the equals sign do.)

The same results can be obtained without arithmetic (and the fractions that often result) by using the *common diagonal system.* This is based on the geometrical fact that if an engraving is laid on the glossy from which it's made, their diagonals will precisely coincide.

This simple method can best be learned by working out a couple of problems with the aid of Fig. 24. Let's assume in 24-A that the rectangle ABCD is the cropped area of a photo and we want to make an engraving 36 picas wide. How tall will it be?

Draw the diagonal AC. Along the bottom of the picture, on line AB, measure 36 picas, the width of the engraving, AE. At E raise a perpendicular to the diagonal at F. EF will be the height of the engraving. If you draw a line parallel to AB from F over to G, the area AEFG will be exactly the size of the engraving. There is no arithmetic to be done; just measure the unknown line and read the answer right from your ruler.

The same method finds an unknown width just as easily. Assume that in Fig. 24-B the area JKLM is the original photograph. We want to make a cut 5 inches high.

First draw the diagonal JL.

Along JM measure 5 inches, the height of the cut, JN. At N send a perpendicular out to the diagonal at O. NO is the width of the cut.

Only rarely will an engraving be larger than the photo. But the common diagonal still works as Fig. 24-C shows.

A small wallet-sized photo STUV must be blown up to make a cut 22 picas wide. Draw the diagonal SU and extend it way out to right field. Along ST measure 22 picas, SW. Raise a perpendicular here to the diagonal at X. WX is the height of the cut. Its area is SWXY.

Diagramming for scaling can be done on an overlay or by drawing the exact size of the *cropped* picture on a separate piece of paper.

★ Pictures on a newspaper page should be framed in white.

The pictures we hang in homes, offices, and classrooms are made more attractive by mats and frames. In the same way, the picture which is framed with a strip of white will be more attractive and dramatic in a newspaper page.

★ Pictures should be indented 1 pica per column.

If you have a 3-column cut, for instance, you will have 3 picas of white space. A pica-and-a-half will run at each side, and there should be a pica of white at the top and a generous strip at the bottom.

If this cut were to run at the edge of the page, it would be pushed way to the outside margin. In this case the 3 picas of white would be a strip at the inside, balanced by the margin of the page itself.

★ Cutlines should line up precisely with the edge of the engraving.

Explanatory type and the picture are a single integral unit. By making them exactly the same width, we tie them together more conveniently for the reader.

For the same reason many editors prefer to set cutlines in boldface. They think that the color of bold type is closer to the tone of the engraving and so reminds the reader that these two elements go together like audio and visual in television.

★ "Picture above type."

This is a printer's axiom that is used by the editor in two ways.

With a large picture, the editor will use a *catchline,* a line of display type between the engraving and the cutlines. This is far more effective than to run a display line above the cut as an *overline.*

The reading eye always wants to move downward. If it is attracted by a picture, it will either ignore an overline or read it with reluctance. But if the eye is attracted to the cut, then moves on its normal path downward, the catchline is a lure that draws it into the cutlines.

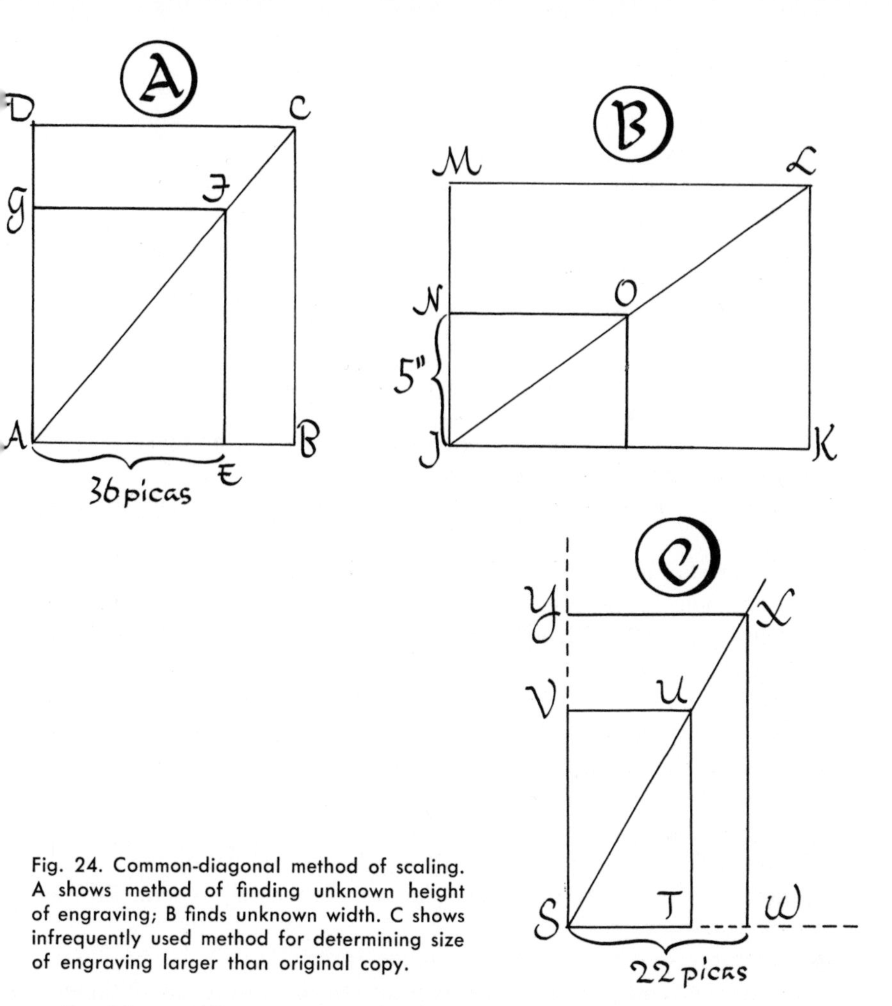

Fig. 24. Common-diagonal method of scaling. A shows method of finding unknown height of engraving; B finds unknown width. C shows infrequently used method for determining size of engraving larger than original copy.

Catchlines will increase readership of cutlines up to 25% over that when an overline is used.

An effective way to use a picture with a story is to run the headline the same width as, and directly under, the picture with its cutlines.

Or the picture can be *canopied* with the story by means of a headline that runs above both elements.

When a 1-column cut runs with a story carrying a 1-column head, the picture and its cutlines should run above the head.

★ Avoid dropping 1-column cuts into a story.

Occasionally it may be necessary to run a picture within a 1-column story. Such cases should be minimized—if not eliminated entirely. When it is imperative, the cut should be dropped *into* a paragraph, *never* between grafs.

If the reader comes to the end of a paragraph and sees a picture, he may well assume that he has reached the end of the story and quit reading.

★ Every picture must be identified.

The newspaperman operates on Murphy's Law: "If anything can go wrong, it will." Corollary 1 is, "If any picture can be misidentified by the reader, it will be." To avoid this, every picture must be properly labelled, even if it's of the star quarterback or the principal, whom "everybody knows."

One-column portraits are best identified by only the name, set boldface caps centered. If there are several people mentioned in a story but only one picture is used, a second explanatory line may be used:

JAMES C. COULTER
. . . named All-Conference end.

Writing cutlines is a specialized skill; the person who masters it is a valuable member of any staff.

★ Cutlines should never paraphrase the lead of the accompanying story.

Cutlines should say only: "This is why this picture is printed; these are the people in the picture; here is something interesting in the picture that you, Dear Reader, would probably overlook if we didn't point it out."

If cutlines are longer than this, they can only say the same thing the accompanying lead says. Then the reader is apt to forego reading the story. Thus the picture fails in its primary function, to attract the reader into body type.

★ Pictures are bait; the trap is body type.

Pictures should not be separated from their stories. It makes no more sense than to put a piece of cheese in one corner with a sign, "Mousetrap across the room."

★ Pictures should face into the page.

As the eye reads along, it is susceptible to inconspicuous influences that direct its movement. Any motion in a picture, either real or implied, has a tendency to move the eye along in that direction. If the eye is guided off the page by a picture, it will probably return to the page. But there has been an annoyance and a useless expenditure of energy that contribute to a loss of readership.

Real motion in a picture may be an athlete running, a debater pointing, or even a person gazing intently to the side. Implied motion is more subtle. It may be the profile of a person. It may be a pair of lines in a photograph that form—or only start to form—an arrow. It may be the sweep of fabric in a dress. No matter how subdued, such implied motion will carry the eye with it.

★ Harness motions in pictures to direct the eye to body type.

It is possible to create a mirror image of the original picture—so it faces in the opposite direction—during either the photoprinting or the engraving process.

Instruction to the engraver is: *Don't flop negative.* (Some people call the result a *flopped picture;* this is a confusing term because the negative is always flopped in the ordinary engraving procedure. Other

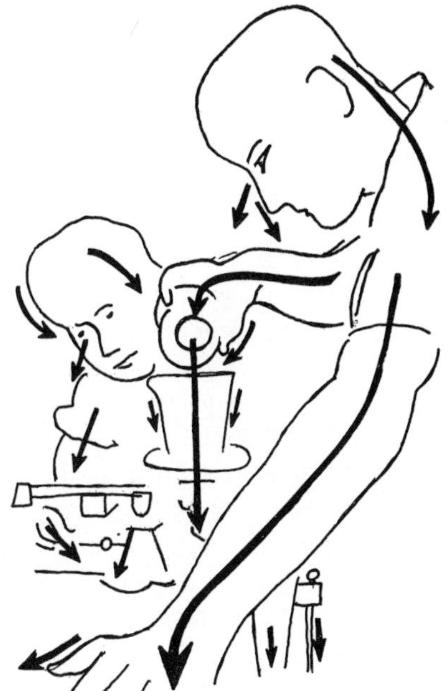

Fig. 25. Lines of force in photograph lead the reading eye as indicated in arrows of sketch.

people call the result a *reversed picture*. This is confusing because the term *reverse cut* refers to a plate that, in effect, prints white letters against a black background.)

Editors are often tempted to reverse the direction of a picture to make it fit more pleasantly or effectively into a layout—to avoid facing a picture off the page, for instance. But there is so much danger involved that this practice should be used only infrequently—about once in seventeen years.

You have perhaps seen pictures in newspapers where people are shaking left hands or the wedding ring or pocket handkerchief is on the wrong side of the body. The worst example is when signs read backward.

But even when it is not this conspicuous, there is a right- or left-handedness to most photos. Even though the reader may be unaware of the reason, he is made subconsciously uncomfortable because the unflopped picture is unnatural.

There are several special kinds of halftones that are becoming rare in newspaper usage but are worth noting in yearbooks and magazines.

Silhouetted halftones are those from which the entire background has been removed, leaving only the subject outlined against the white paper.

Vignetted halftones are those that blend, almost imperceptibly, from the black of the picture into the white of the paper. Vignettes are most difficult to print by letterpress, especially on newsprint, and therefore have been abandoned by newspapers.

A *modified silhouette* has at least one side trimmed off straight, with only a portion of the subject in outline. A modified vignette, also, has one or more straight edges.

Silhouettes, if used at all by newspapers, are usually confined to feature treatment.

Cuts may be *morticed* to make them more effective. Most common is the *notch* or *external mortice*. This is created by cutting a rectangle out of one corner of a picture. Into this space may be placed the cutlines or all or part of another engraving.

An *internal mortice* is an opening cut out so that the halftone completely surrounds the inserted material.

Mortices may be irregular in shape but most frequently are rectangular. Notches are least expensive, rectangular internals are next, and irregular mortices are most expensive.

Mortices are useful when there are large, uninteresting areas in a picture that cannot be removed by regular cropping. A dull gray sky alongside football goal posts or your school tower can detract from interest in a picture. If that dead area is morticed out and devoted to cutlines, impact of the picture can be enhanced.

★ Mortice only to remove nonfunctional areas in the picture.

★ Never mortice pictures only so they can be fitted together in an "artistic" effect.

Ordinary engravings are called *square halftones;* they need not be—and usually aren't—squares, but each corner of the rectangle is a 90-degree angle.

Half-column cuts are called porkchops or, when dropped into a column of type, *inserts* or *insets.*

Professional newspapers are reducing the use of porkchops. One objection is that unduly short lines of type are required to run alongside the picture. Such short measure is difficult to read and (hence expensive) to set.

School papers often are forced, by exigencies of space, to use such small pictures. A porkchop requires only 25% of the space of a regular 1-column cut.

It's most convenient to group porkchops by pairs and avoid the need for short lines of type. If a single half-columner must be used, there should be a minimum of 6 points of white space between the engraving and type, at the side and top and bottom.

Pictures are such an important tool for the newspaperman that he should constantly study ways to use this tool more effectively.

11. *Page Layout*

Packaging the news

Making up page one is one of the most interesting of an editor's jobs. It is a conspicuous test of ingenuity and ability, apparent the moment the reader's eye falls on a new edition.

Many newsmen think that the art of *layout* is one that a person must be born with. Others insist that it is a craft that can be taught. They're both right; layout ability can be learned as well as inherited.

The function of page layout is: (1) to attract the reader by a pleasant overall pattern; (2) to capture his attention by pictures and headlines; (3) to direct him into body type, and (4) to guide him from one story to another in such a way that he gains maximum information with a minimum of time and effort.

So the front page must be *functional.* Every element on it must do its own job and contribute to the total job of the whole page. And a good page must also be *organic;* it must "grow" from the material available.

The professional layout man says, "A good page lays itself out." He means that a page pattern will develop logically—almost by itself—from the *budget,* the assortment of news and pictures on hand for a specific issue.

Suppose the student editor has this budget for his November 5 edition:

Team wins conference football championship.
New principal appointed.
National Merit Scholarship semifinalists announced.
Senior play tryouts begin.

Suppose for his December 19 issue the budget is:

Senior play cast announced.
Spanish Club has party.
Wastebasket catches fire in cafeteria.
Vacation begins next Wednesday.

The two pages will look entirely different, won't they? Part of this is by design, of course.

★ Each front page should look as different as possible from all preceding ones.

The editor wants his reader to recognize immediately that this is a new edition. The worst thing a person could possibly say about a newspaper is, giving it a hasty glance, "Is this today's paper or last week's?"

The editor gets desirable variety by taking full advantage of his budget. His November issue might look like this, to play up his many hot stories:

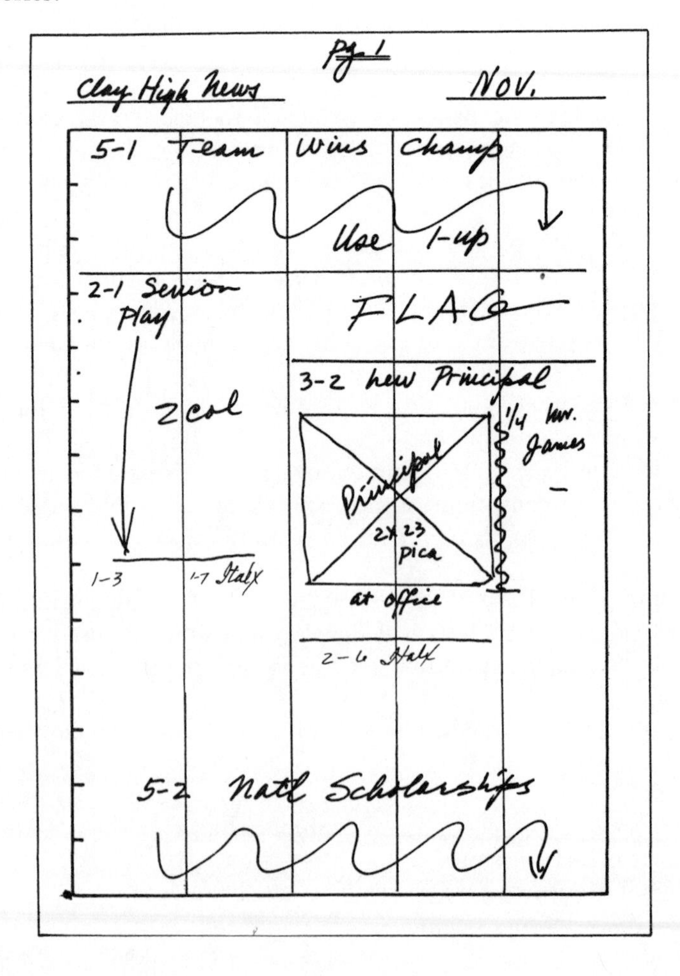

The next front page might look like this, using large pictures to create the interest that lackadaisical news events fail to provide:

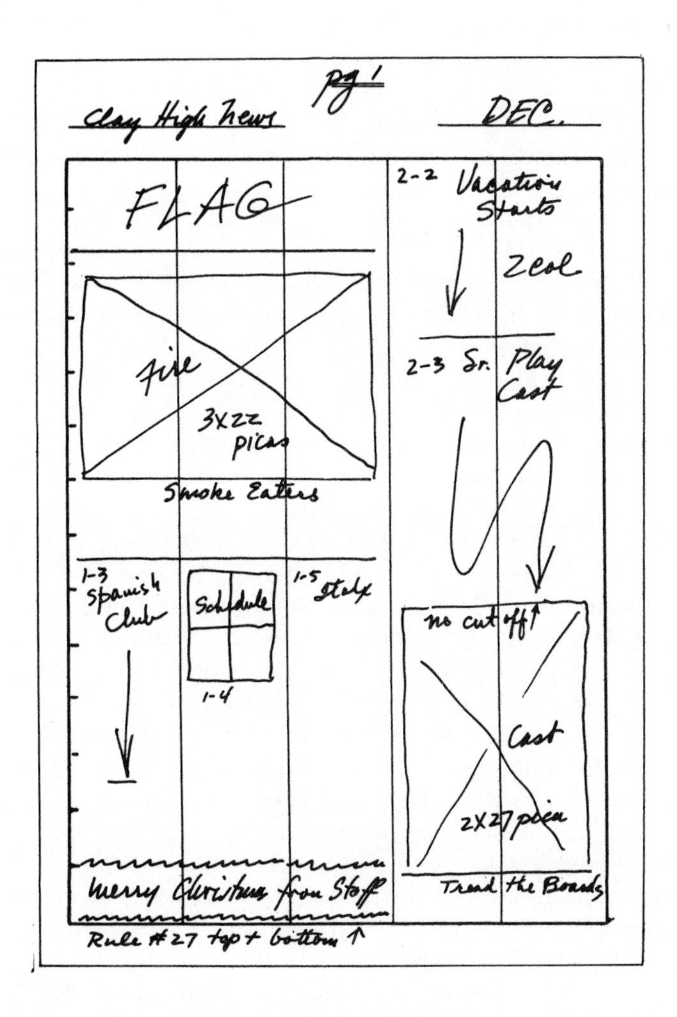

You'll notice that these two pages have five columns. Your daily paper has eight. This is a basic difference in *format*.

Format is the basic shape, size, and general appearance of a newspaper. *Full format* is a page of approximately 15 x 21 inches with six to nine columns and eight the most common. *Tabloid format* is a page of four or, most commonly, five columns, about 15 inches deep. This is approximately half the size of a full-format page.

The first tabloids were sensational newspapers that concentrated on all the news unfit to print. They used *poster layout,* in which the whole front page was devoted to one or two blaring headlines (with the stories on pages 2 or 3) and one large picture. They stressed sensational stories and handled them in *razzle-dazzle* style.

Especially after World War II, many new papers adopted the smaller page size because of economic reasons. Their makeup was a miniature of that used by full-format papers. Because they didn't want the connotation of "tabloid" content tacked to their papers, they used the term *compact*. It is not universally accepted today but its use grows because of a need to distinguish between the two kinds of layout and philosophy.

Most student publications are 5-column compacts. This is a useful size. Presses capable of printing compacts are numerous; in most smaller cities there are few that can handle full format. An 8-page compact makes a far more attractive package than its equivalent of four full-format pages.

The 11-pica column, as noted before, is the most practical for any newspaper, and five of such columns fit neatly into the compact page.

In our discussion on page layout, we will assume a 5-column compact page. But it should be kept in mind that the principles of typography are identical for pages of any size.

Another item to tuck away between your ears: Many laudable student papers have only three or four columns because that's the maximum capacity of available presses. But the more columns an editor has to work with, the more chances he has to create a pleasing page pattern, just as a basketball player can start more plays from the center of the floor than when he's jammed up against the sideline.

Because the news budget changes from issue to issue, it is impossible to set up a formula for a good front page. There are some basic, unchanging principles that will help, though.

Faced with a blank page in your notebook, where do you start writing? When you review that page, where do you start reading? On this page you're now on, where did you look first? In all cases the answer is: in the top left corner—the *primary optical area*.

On any written or printed page, this is where the eye instinctively looks first. There the editor must place some element that will immediately capture the reader's interest. This may be a picture, a box, or a strong headline.

★ Place a strong attention-compeller in the primary optical area.

Using the same examples of where you started to read first or write first, answer the next question: Where do you stop on a page? At the lower right corner.

Because the reader knows that this corner is his goal, his eye will instinctively seek it out; the basic motion of reading is a diagonal from top left to lower right.

★ Define the *reading diagonal* with strong display.

The eye doesn't zoom straight down as the proverbial crow flies; it

Mahler: 'I Want to Stimulate More School Spirit'

. . . STIMULATES SPIRIT
Mahler talks to reporter

"I want to welcome the entire student body to John Marshall. I want them to know that their Student Council is open to suggestions at any time," Tom Mahler, new Student Council president, said last week.

Mahler went on to list the many ideas planned for the coming year.

"I specifically want to stimulate more school spirit. We basically need more publicity for all school activities. We want to let all the students know what's going on.

"To raise more school spirit we are thinking of selling pennants with our school name on them," Mahler said. "Also we want to sell beanies to the seniors and to initiate senior beanie day."

He also hopes for better cooperation between the various clubs and the Council. "As a Council we want to know what they are doing and to aid them in any way possible."

Mahler said he would like to see a better turnout at the school dances. "In the extracurricular survey last year only a minority of the students were attending the dances. Since it was the majority that put us into office we want to please them.

"Therefore, this year we are cutting out the fall dance and changing it to a recreation night. This way we could have a better attendance at a school activity and at the same time please the majority."

Mahler concluded, "I'm looking forward to a good year. We have a fine student body and hard workers on our Council."

The John Marshall Rocket

VOL. V, NO. 1 — John Marshall High School, Rochester, Minn. — Friday, Sept. 14, 1962

First Play Is 'Far Out'

The first play of the year, "A Visit to a Small Planet," will be given at a student matinee Friday, Oct. 19.

According to Mr. Burdette Moeller, JM speech teacher in charge of the play, there are parts for nine men and two women.

The play was first presented in 1957 on Broadway.

It was later made into a motion picture which starred Jerry Lewis. Clague Hodgson a junior, will play that role for JM.

Cast members also include Jay Knox, Cheryl Winter, Rick Thorkelson, Bob Adler, Gary Winter. Jack Gross, Cindy Shick, and Dave Vale.

"You could call the play a comedy fantasy," Mr. Moeller said. "The world is the small planet as a visiting man from outer space sees it."

The play will also be staged for the public Saturday, Oct. 20.

Other plays planned at JM this year are as follows: "The Crucible," a drama to be given Nov. 16 and 17: a musical or an opera, probably Feb. 25. and 26: and "Charlie's Aunt," April 26 and 27.

Go Like Hot Bakes . . .

Hot potatoes may be sold at JM football games, according to Tom Mahler, Student Council president.

"I got the idea at the St. Olaf Workshop this summer. I think it would go over big. Most students like something hot at the cold games," Mahler said.

"We are hoping to try it Sept. 21. It would be sponsored by the Student Council. If successful, it would be given to other clubs.

"The potatoes would be served with butter and salt and would sell for 10 cents," he said.

India Exchange to Go Ahead

An exchange program between John Marshall and a high school in New Delhi, India, will continue for its second year this fall.

As a start, 10 JM students will soon be selected to begin a correspondence with students at the Modern School in New Delhi.

FOURTEEN juniors signed up last year to exchange letters. That group included Luann Rehling, Karen Sattre, Jon Thiem, Tove Frang, Sharon Lee, Sylvia Martig, Sue Scholer, Dianne Anderson, Lawrence Corbin, Narda Jensen, Lynn Johnson, Pat Andersen, Joyce Hill, and Elaine Swenberg.

A list of correspondents from New Delhi arrived recently at JM.

The "affiliation" between the two schools was started last year as part of a Peoples-to-Peoples program initiated by the Rochester chapter of the American Association for the United Nations.

MRS. HOWARD GRAY of Rochester, originator of the local affiliation, urges JM students to start early this year with their phase of the program.

"The JM students should tell the Indian students about their hobbies and school activities," Mrs. Gray said last week. "They should send pictures of themselves and their families. The students who are corresponding should read many books about India and conduct study groups and discussions about India's customs."

A SHIPMENT of materials is expected to arrive soon from the New Delhi school, said Dr. Ralph Wright, JM principal, last week. It will include copies of the school newspaper, Sandesh (The Message), and other literary materials.

Recently, Mrs. Gray received a letter from the mayor of Jabalpur, India, requesting a similar affiliation with that city.

Mrs. Gray also said that Bombay, India, has been suggested as another "affiliation" city.

Home-owned Assembly Slate to Include Four Speakers

The Homecoming coronation on Oct. 5 will be the next assembly to be presented at JM. It will be followed by 15 other assembly programs, including four by "toastmaster speakers."

The first speaker will be Ralph Nichols from the University of Minnesota. His topic: the art of listening.

Other speakers will include C. Mason Harvey who spoke at the state student council convention last year.

Pay for the speakers will come from the student activity fund.

THE JM BAND and the choir will present separate assemblies. The dates are not scheduled as yet.

Only one student matinee is planned by the dramatics department. "A Visit to a Small Planet," the first play of the year, is scheduled for an afternoon performance Oct. 19.

Career Day, held every other year, is scheduled Nov. 13. Local business and professional leaders will come to JM to speak to student groups.

THE SECOND annual Talent Show is slated Jan. 17.

University of Minnesota assemblies were again voted down for the second year in a row. All assemblies are produced by JM groups.

Here is a list of assembly programs:

Oct. 5—Homecoming, 1:15
Oct. 11—Ralph Nichols, 10:15
Oct. 19—Fall play, 1:15
Nov. 13—Career Day, 2:30
Nov. 20—Fall awards (tentative), 10:15
Dec. 19—Christmas, 1:15
Jan. 17—Talent Show, 10:15
Jan. 21—Robert Kazmayer: "Kazmayer Analyzes the Future"
Feb. 21—C. Mason Harvey, 10:15
March 28—Winter awards (tentative), 1:15
April 3—National Honor Society, 10:15
April 23—Student Council election, 10
May 1—Judge Philip Gilliam: "The Surge to Decency"
May 23—Cheerleading (tentative), 10:45
Senior awards
All-School awards

8 Sophomores Seek Offices

Eight students had filed for sophomore class officers by the close of school Wednesday.

Those who had filed for president were Ed Comartin, Gary Hill, Richard Field, and James Boyer.

Those who had filed for vice-president were Frank Firnschild, Dave Otto, Michael Bundy, and Tom Cranston.

No one had filed for the office of secretary-treasurer

The students could file, however, until yesterday at 3:15.

No primary will be held if other students did not file.

The final election will be held late next week.

Annual Big 9 Meeting Set for JM Monday

Administrators and special teachers from all Big 9 Conference schools will convene at JM Monday for their annual fall meeting.

On hand will be superintendents, principals and their assistants, athletic directors, and teachers responsible for band, choir, girls' athletics, orchestra, school paper, student council, yearbook, and speech at each school.

Meetings will begin at 5 p. m.

The Rocket Docket

After much study by the mailman, a letter was finally delivered last July to the library at John Marshall. The letter, an advertisement for a new magazine, was addressed to "John Marshall High, Rochester, Minn." and began with . . . .

"Dear Mr. High:"

* * *

The week's docket:

Tuesday, Sept. 18: sophomore class elections . . . Iowa tests (ITED) in afternoon, also morning of 19th and 21st, and afternoon of 20th.

Friday, Sept. 21: sophomore mixer from 9:15 to 11:30 p.m. . . . cross-country meet with Austin during halftime of the Northfield football game at the JM Stadium.

* * *

Inside this Rocket: serenading the President—page 2; seat belts save lives—page 4 (a report to teenagers); football mouth guards — page 3.

At the Summer Opera

Butterfly Stamps; Kids, Too

By SUE SCHOLER
Rocket Editorial Editor

It was Friday, July 20, at 2:05 p.m. "Solomon and Balkis," the first true opera at JM, was to begin in ten minutes. The 600 children from the recreational department were anxiously awaiting the performance.

A little girl rushed up to Sue Sauer, an usher, and said, "May I have another program, please? Tom has mine."

A little boy shouted at his mother, "Let's sit in the balcony. I want to sit in the balcony."

The impatient audience began to clap and stamp and to chant "We want the show; we want the show."

Mr. Sidney Suddendorf, the director, entered and a healthy applause greeted him. He explained the story to the audience to give them a better understanding. The orchestra played excerpts which indicated the quarreling butterflys, the storm, the djinns.

The lights dimmed. The performance started. The audience "ah—ed."

There was a whisper from behind. "Can you see?" And a quick reply. "Sure I can see; be quiet."

During the 40-minute performance the audience laughed heartily along with Solomon, played by Rick Thorkelson. They were fascinated by the nagging butterflys and the terrible storm.

During the storm a cymbol crashed. One little boy plugged his ears and shouted, "My ears hurt."

After the opera, a four-year-old girl was asked if she liked it. All she did was shake her head yes.

"Solomon and Balkis" or "The Butterfly that Stamped," by Randall Thompson, was adapted from the "Just So Stories" by Kipling.

The one male singing part was played by Rick Thorkelson, a JM senior. His wife, Balkis, was played by Marvel Kyle.

SCENE FROM SUMMER OPERA

The two quarreling butterflys were played by Alison Bach and Caroline Anderson.

No former senior took part in the opera. One-half of the cast was incoming sophomores.

Mr. Suddendorf was pleased with the result.

"It's something different, and I think the kids enjoyed it. I would like to see a one-act opera club develop at JM. It is good experience for the kids."

Mr. Suddendorf explained the possibility of having an opera next year.

"We wouldn't have one in place of the operetta, but we might have one in the Coffman Hall."

Mr. Robert Wise, JC theater director, served as technical director for the opera.

Fig. 26. The nameplate is floated on this page to allow feature to run above it. Note omission of column rules and use of sideless box in column 3. (Courtesy *Rocket*, John Marshall High, Rochester, Minn.)

meanders back and forth like an excited little boy at the zoo. He is attracted by interesting sights off the path and scurries over to enjoy them.

★ Lure the reader off the diagonal with interesting elements.

One of the techniques of doing this is:

★ *Anchor the corners.*

This is putting strong display elements near, or preferably in, the corners. No one knows just how the anchors do their job; but it is known that a well anchored page has high readership.

★ Don't forget the *basement*, the bottom half of the page.

In older days, editors placed all their big headlines at the top of the page and let the small ones settle *downstairs*. Some even made a rule that each head in a column must be smaller than any above it. The result was a page that just faded away. Today, with radio, TV, and a wealth of printed material competing for the reader's time, the editor can't allow even a small area of the page to fail in its job of attracting the reader.

★ Headlines should be well isolated from each other.

Each headline is, in effect, a barker on the midway, trying to draw a crowd into his tent. If a half-dozen pitchmen share the same platform, they'll make a lot of noise; but the poor listener will be so confused that chances are he'll hurry off to a quieter spot. So with many heads *jammed* into a small area.

★ Avoid *tombstoning*.

This, running a series of heads side by side, is a dangerous form of jamming. Pictures or boxes are useful for breaking tombstones. (But if the pic carries an overline, the tombstone remains; another good reason for using catchlines instead.)

When two heads must run side by side, they should vary as much as possible in form and size and should be written short to give some white space between heads.

★ Avoid *armpits*.

This inelegantly-named and ugly arrangement occurs when a narrower head rides right under a wider one. To avoid armpits, wise editors insist that there be body type in each column directly under a multicolumn head.

★ Use *horizontal makeup*.

When body type is flattened down into a shallow, wide unit it appears to be shorter than when it dangles in a long, single column. Horizontal makeup is more attractive to the reader who prefers short reading chores.

To gain the advantage of horizontal makeup, the editor will set body type double-column under a 2- or 4-column head. Or he can set it 1½ columns wide and run it under a 3-column headline.

Horizontal makeup also is a boon to the headline writer. It allows him to write better heads because he has more units to use.

17 Students Will Enter League Contests

Twelve speech students and five typing students from Pampa High will enter District Interscholastic League contests tomorrow in Canyon.

Mike Maguire, junior, and LaNell Riley, senior, will enter extemporaneous speaking, which is an impromptu speech given without previous meditation. Sherry Kotara and James Simpson, seniors, will enter persuasive speaking, in which one tries to induce someone to believe or do something, according to Miss Helen Schafer, head of the speech department.

Don Sears and Sue Price, juniors, will read poetry, and Mike Fort, senior, and Dana Taylor, sophomore, will read prose.

Debaters will discuss the pros and cons of federal aid to education. Girl debaters are Martha Price, senior, and Barbara Reeves, junior. Ray Wagner and John Graham, sophomores, compose the boys' team. They are coached by Miss Beverly Smith.

Five typists who will compete are Mary Ellen Cooper, Sue Ann Thompson and Joyce Prock, juniors, and Francine Green, and Drew Harvey, sophomores, according to Melvin Cardwell, typing teacher. Judging is based on the percentage of accuracy on two five-minute writings, Mr. Cardwell explained.

The top contestants in each division will enter the regional meet in Odessa April 14.

Journalism contestants, Linda Barker, senior, and Gail Cole, junior, will go directly to the regional contest in Odessa April 14. There is no district contest in journalism.

THE LITTLE HARVESTER

Vol. 14—No. 21 Pampa High School, Pampa, Texas Friday, March 23, 1962

MR. PRESIDENT — The student body of 1962-63 will be led by Keith Swanson, who was elected last week by juniors and sophomores. (See story on Page 8).
(Photo by Joe Barnett)

Three Romans Receive Honors In State Tests

Three Pampa High School Latin students won places in the Texas State Junior Classical League contests held in San Angelo March 16-17.

Russell Veal, sophomore, tied for first place in the first year mythology contest. Ray Wagner, sophomore, won second place in second year mythology, and Anna Jo Watson, senior, won third in third year mythology.

Vince Johnson, senior, was entered in third year derivatives. Contestants in the grammar contests were Carol Chase, sophomore, and Ed Albers, junior.

Pluto, god of the underworld, will be honored at the Latin-Junior Classical League banquet tomorrow at 6:30 p.m. in the cafeteria.

"The underworld" will be carried out in a theme of red. Gordon Bayless, JCL vice-president, and Ed Albers are in charge of decorations.

Suzanne Paden is head of all committees. Other committee members are Lanelle Emler, invitations; Ray Wagner and Sue Wiens, program; Tommy Thompson, food; Susan Watson, atrium; and Bill McKinney house committee.

Little Harvester Wins Medalist

The Little Harvester has received the top Medalist rating in the Columbia Scholastic Press Association, as results of judging were announced last Friday at the CSPA convention in New York.

The Medalist award is given to the top 10 per cent of the newspapers rated as first class. More than 1,700 entries from 47 states and some foreign countries were entered in the contest, according to information released by Joseph Murphy, CSPA director.

Edited by Linda Barker

Linda Barker is editor-in-chief of the Little Harvester this year. Bill Kidwell is managing editor; Connie Kuntz and Jan Porter, news editors; Gail Cole, feature editor; Ronnie Choat, sports editor; Linda Abbott, business manager; Joyce Young, advertising manager; Marilyn Lillienfeld and Jennifer Turner, circulation managers.

Miss Elizabeth Hurley, publications advisor, was scheduled to conduct two section meetings at the CSPA convention this year, on news coverage and advertising, but she was unable to attend because of the serious illness of her mother following surgery in Fort Worth.

Amarillo High School's Sandstorm received a first place rating in its class, and Tascosa High's Pioneer was rated second place. Third and fourth place ratings also are given.

Staffs to Attend Meet

Students on the Little Harvester and Harvester annual staffs and journalism class will attend the Panhandle High School Press Association convention in Canyon March 31. Melvin Munn of Pampa will be keynote speaker.

Gail Cole, junior, is a candidate for president.

After the general assembly, newspaper and yearbook workers will separate for sessions to be conducted by Miss Nancy Kaisner of Lubbock High School, newspaper, and Mrs. Norma Foreman

(See MEDALIST, Page 8)

Sophomores, Juniors Will Elect in April

Attention, juniors and sophomores! Class officer elections will be held the last of April, according to Miss Bernice Franklin, Student Council sponsor. A date has not yet been set.

According to the SC constitution, five nominees for each office will be chosen in free nominations in homerooms.

Senior Girl Wins Title, Irish Rose

Ruth Anne Guthrie, senior, was chosen "Miss Irish Rose" of the 16th annual St. Patrick's Day celebration at Shamrock last Saturday.

Seventeen-year-old Ruth, who was selected over 15 other candidates from the Texas and Oklahoma Panhandles, was crowned by U. S. Senator Mike Monroney of Oklahoma at the coronation ceremony held at the National Guard Armory.

Michelle LaMarca of Amarillo High School was first runner-up, and Jennifer Singley of Wellington was second runner-up.

The nine finalists were chosen by judges who observed their eating habits and walking posture and who asked them such ques-

(See IRISH ROSE, Page 7)

SPRING RETURNS — Chris Grayson and Jan Grady, juniors, enjoy the first signs of spring while fishing on a lazy afternoon.
(Photo by Joe Barnett)

Fig. 27. Four-column pages can be made up in interesting patterns such as this. Note use of Square Serif headlines, a face not common in American newspapers but an excellent headletter. (Courtesy *Little Harvester*, Pampa (Tex.) High)

Now he can say

Athletics Trounce Cleveland

instead of using the cryptic

A's TKO
Tribe

which is all that will fit into one column.

★ Minimize, if you can't eliminate, *jumps* off page one.

It is a nuisance for the reader, just as he gets engrossed in a story, to be ordered to proceed to an inside page. Often it is so much of a nuisance that he just refuses to do so. Many professional editors lay down a flat ukase: "No jumps!"

This can in itself create problems. What do you do when you have a story that's just too long to run on the front page and yet has been cut to the bone already?

Break it down into two or more stories.

Suppose you have a voluminous story on a Student Council meeting. Break it down into a story about plans for the Homecoming dance, another on where the gift painting of the senior class will be hung, a third on appointment of a new cafeteria committee. With a separate head on each, maybe all three stories can run on the front page. Perhaps the two smaller ones can be sidebars to the lead story.

★ Use the *one-up technique.*

This new makeup device was introduced in the early 60's. It gets its name from the fact that the editor *goes up* one column—uses one more column of space than of type. He may write a 4-column head but run just three columns of type under it. The equivalent of the fourth column is used as white space between columns.

He can use one-up under a 3-, 4- or 5-column head. Or he can have type set two columns wide and run it under a 3-column head or double it over under a 5-column head. Two 1½-column pillars of type can run under a 4-column head or three of them under a 5-columner.

★ Set leads in two-column measure.

This is a familiar device of the professional layout man. He'll set the first dozen lines at two columns, then break down to one. This automatically removes the danger of an armpit, and it also gives pleasant variety in line length for the reader.

Often a wider lead is set in 10-point type. This is a useful device although it does cause complications on the Linotype.

★ Ideally, the *measure* (line length) and point size should not be changed at the same time.

The first dozen or so lines should be set 10-point, 2-column; about six lines in 10-point, 1-column; the rest in 8-point, 1-column.

Or, after the dozen lines of 10-point, 2-column, there can be four or five lines in 8-point, 2-column, and then the rest in 8-in-1.

The student editor must remember that this is not always practical because of the changes required on the Linotype. If he cannot achieve the ideal, he shouldn't mope about it.

★ The whole business of producing a newspaper is a constant compromise between the ideal and the practical.

It does no good to prepare an ideal paper if you can't make your deadline. But when a newsman falls short of his goal, it should be because of circumstances beyond his control—not because he doesn't know better.

★ Never *pile rules* on top of each other.

This means that a box can't be placed atop another box or against a *cutoff rule,* a thin horizontal rule. Many newspapers are abandoning cutoffs because rarely do they serve a useful function.

★ The only time a cutoff is needed on page one is to separate a picture from an unrelated story immediately under it, or under a banner beneath which shorter heads must run.

On inside pages a cutoff is needed when a story *wraps* from one column to the next without going up to a multicolumn head. In this case cutoffs act like the side cushions on a billiard table to "carom" the eye in the desired path.

★ Wraps should overlap at least 1 inch—preferably 2 inches—or the eye is apt to become lost.

★ A wrap should never run higher in column two than the head on the story in column one.

★ Inject white space into the page.

When cutoffs are eliminated, they are replaced with white space. This is pleasant. Many papers eliminate the *30-dash,* the *end mark,* because it serves no useful purpose either. (When the reader gets to the end of the story he has little choice; he'll stop because he's run out of copy, not because he sees a little dash like this ———.) Again, fresh air takes the place of the 30's.

★ If vertical column rules are replaced with white space, at least a full pica of white space must separate columns.

If any smaller amount is used, often there will be lines that have more space between words than there is between columns. Then the eye will become confused.

Page Patterns

There are many "textbook patterns" for page-one makeup. They're valuable to know just as a carpenter likes to know the difference between a Georgian and a split-level house.

But for our immediate purpose, there are only two basic patterns, *formal* and *informal balance.*

In fact, there is only one that's practical; for formal balance is artificial and illogical. In this makeup pattern the page, when split down the middle, looks like half a page plus its image in a mirror. Each head and pic is balanced exactly by an equal unit across the page.

This presupposes that there will always be an exact equal for every story and cut you propose to use on a page. This just never happens. So, to create formal balance, stories and art must be arbitrarily cut with no regard to how much space is needed to communicate best.

Informal—or *dynamic*—balance acknowledges the fact that the world is not a neat, mathematically balanced thing. And if the newspaper is to be an accurate mirror of this world, it, too, must be fluid and dynamic. This doesn't mean a newspaper page can be sloppy and illogical. We can have some degree of logic in reporting even the most illogical happenings.

The editor imagines a pivot at the *optical center* of the page, about an inch and a half above the mathematical center. He places all his display elements on the page so it will "hang almost straight" on this pivot.

Note the adverb, "almost." In the first place, unless he uses formal makeup, he can't make the page hang perfectly perpendicular. More important, he knows that a little imbalance adds that dynamism which makes an interesting page.

Learning the optical "weight" of various display elements is a question of practice. There is no measurement—other than a trained eye—that will prove that this 2-column kickered head "weighs" as much as this 1-column cut.

Nor can we apply a formula that proves that this heavy cut close to the pivot will be balanced by a light headline farther away, just as a skinny little kid sitting at the very end of a teeter-totter can balance the chubby girl closer to the fulcrum.

But it is reasonably safe to assume that a page that pleases the critical editor will also please his readers. For, whether he's a student editor or an old pro, his taste and perception will usually be considerably keener than that of his audience.

Inside Pages

The makeup of inside pages is dictated, to varying degrees, by their advertising content. Student editors usually have more open space to work with than their professional counterparts. (But commercial newspapers need those towering stacks of ads; they're what bring in the revenue needed to produce a newspaper. The selling price of a paper covers little more than the cost of paper and ink.)

★ On any page, ads should be *pyramided* to the right and kept as low as possible on the page.

Such ad placement will always leave the primary optical area open for an attention-compeller. Ideally the whole top of the page should be kept open for editorial display. This is what stops the reader and creates an audience for the ads to address.

★ Make one headline dominate each inside page.

Friday, November 3, 1961 — The OPINION — Page Three

'Moo-oo-oo'

SUZI SWANSON, sophomore, is practicing for the cow-milking contest to be held at the PTA Fun Fair Nov. 18. What does it matter if Suzi is on the wrong side of the cow and is facing in the wrong direction? —Staff photo by Bob Drake

Mr. Wyeth Sees Counterfeit At Chicago Federal Reserve Bank

"The one thing I liked best was seeing all that money lying around," remarked Mr. Wyeth, PHS typing teacher, after touring the Federal Reserve Bank in Chicago.

Mr. Wyeth, along with five other teachers from Mid-State Eight schools, was chosen by the Commercial National Bank to make the trip. They went Thursday, Oct. 26, arriving at the bank at 10 p.m.

"We weren't more than 50 steps inside the door when twelve policemen boldly confronted us. The place was just swarming with them," relates Mr. Wyeth.

WE FIRST visited the clearing house where all checks are cleared. Continuing on our journey, we saw where checks are divided into separate groups.

"This room contained numerous IBM machines, sorters, and counting apparatus."

The entire trip was thrilling and rewarding to Mr. Wyeth, but in his opinion one of the most interesting parts was 'when we were able to see and compare counterfeit money to real bills.

"There is such a difference in their appearance when seen together; it is unbelievable that the counterfeit is not spotted immediately."

The main functions of the Federal Reserve Bank were explained to the teachers as they gained first-hand information about the complicated American economy.

Careers Begin For 11 At PHS

"I believe in boys and girls — the men and women of a great tomorrow. I believe in laughter, in love, and in faith, in all ideals and distant hopes that lure us on."

The above is part of the Teacher's Creed. Again this year Peoria High is a proving ground for 11 student teachers who believe in the creed and are now beginning to practice it.

Mr. Brown is assisting Miss Wood with a modern history class, Mrs. Easton, Miss Martin, and Miss Haltzman are practice teaching in English, and Mr. Wodka and Mr. Horwith are aiding the physical education instructors.

German and Spanish students are often taught by Miss Dickinson and Miss Perry; Mr. Gottschalk is assisting Mr. Martin in mechanical drawing classes.

Mr. Thompson is practice teaching shorthand, while Miss Smith instructs a clothing class.

The heart of the teacher education program is that student teachers practice under supervision. They spend at least one hour per day, three days a week at Peoria High until they have completed 40 clock-hours for each semester hour of college credit.

Ten of the 11 student teachers are Bradley University seniors. Miss Dickinson attends Illinois State Normal University.

Local AFS To Sell World Yule Cards

The Peoria High chapter of the American Field Service will sell Christmas cards and notepaper with an international motif to raise funds for the local program.

AFS students from Brazil, Chile, Equador, Finland, Indonesia, Italy, and Spain designed the stationery, which will sell for $1 per box.

It will be sold at the Fun Fair Nov. 18. Extra boxes may be obtained after that date from Mrs. Warren Bohner, telephone 688-3729.

'Central Cellar' Draws 320

"Central Cellar" attracted 320 students on Oct. 28. A profit of $160 was earned for the Committee of Forty, sponsor of the fall stag dance.

BRIDE'S LANE
710 West Main
Formals - Men's Rentals

The
Central National Bank
and Trust Company of Peoria

Moffitt's Jewelry
2600 N. Sheridan Rd. 685-8013
Hamilton Elgin, and Bulova Watches
Specializing in Diamonds and Diamond Settings

SAVE AT
A BANK YOU'LL LIKE!
Jefferson Trust and Savings Bank
Of Peoria
Phone 676-0831
Member Federal Deposit Insurance Corporation
one, two, three S.W. Jefferson Avenue

JACK AND BILL'S
Sports Shop
Distributors of
MacGregor Sports Equipment
325 Fulton 676-9068

Singer Jewelry Co.
GIFTS FOR ALL
OCCASIONS
420 Main, Ph. 673-8822

HERB HEINZ "66"
W. Loucks & N. Sheridan Rd.
Peoria, Ill. — Phone 685-986
We Give S & H Green Stamps

Nosin' Around

By BECKY BOURLAND

Senior Cisty Swain was honored on her birthday Oct. 22 with an all-class open house at her home from four to six. The open house was a surprise for Cisty, who is now 17.

Playing football on the Great Central Insurance Company lot, senior Mike Riddle suffered an injury to his leg. Luckily, it was not as serious as it appeared when the ambulance driver picked him up off the field, but I don't think Mike will be playing again for awhile.

Former Centralite Pam Herman was a candidate for Homecoming queen at Limestone High School. Congratulations, Pam.

For early morning entertainment, step into the cafeteria any morning after 8 a.m., where a quartet of sophomore boys try their luck on "Dream Lover," "Big John," "Who Put the Bop," and other masterpieces of today.

I wonder how it happened that George Bunchwell, a fictious freshman, received 12 votes in the election for class officers?

Key Club will be selling Peoria High book covers next Monday, Tuesday, and Wednesday in the homerooms.

The price is 15c for one and 25c for two.

So, show your school spirit by buying a book cover, and be sure to bring your money next week.

Colleen Cowan, Jeannie Hamner, and Charlynn Stonebock (alternate) will spend two weeks in July in Vermont with 8,500 other Girl Scouts from all over the country at the Girl Scout Junior Round-Up.

The three girls were chosen from a field of 25 from the Peoria-area. Each Scout received points on camping skills, a written test, and personal interviews. When the points were tallied, the girls with the highest scores were chosen to make the trip.

Four other girls from this area were also selected for this honor.

We're Having a Ball
and So Will You!
You're Invited!

Carson's
"Snow Ball"

Our Annual High School Holiday Party
Saturday, November 11
at 3:00 p.m.
in the Seventh Floor Skyline Room

There'll be music, fun, glamour and excitement! The "Snow Ball Room" will be jumping! SEE 15 lovely Homecoming Queens and junior attendants from Peoriarea High Schools model glamorous Holiday frocks from Carson's Bride's Room collection. SEE handsome judges from local High Schools choose Carson's "Snow Queen" and present her with a Traveling Silver Loving Cup for her school.

Come back your Queen Candidate. Join us for cokes and fun! And, be sure to register for the $25 formal we will give away after the Ball. FREE TICKETS available in the Young Peorian Shop and Bride's Room on Third Floor, or at the Skyline Room Door the day of the show.

COKES! All you want!

WATCH WEEK - TV's Hi-Fi Show for More News!

Fig. 28. Ads are pyramided to right to make sure of adequate room in primary optical area where here a strong picture has been placed. Page would be strengthened by moving two-column news head to upper right. (Courtesy *Opinion*, Peoria (Ill.) High)

Page 8 THE MERCURY April 27, 1961

Swainson Addresses Civil Rights Meeting

Thirteen Earn Poster Prizes

MUSE Announces Staff Changes; Accepts Articles for May Issue

Teens Inform Detroit Voters

Peace Corps Remain Imperfect See Page 2

The Mercury

Vol. 12, No. 8 MUMFORD HIGH SCHOOL, DETROIT, MICHIGAN April 27, 1961

IN THE SCHOOL'S METAL SHOP, vocational students Willie Lyles (center), 11A, and Melvin Turbow (at right), 9A, pour special sand into patterns used in the molding of aluminum castings. After packing the sand into the desired shape, the students will pour molten metal into the form. This process is used in the fabrication of various metal products. Mr. James Marshall, industrial mechanics instructor, supervises the operation.

Fig. 29. Unusual format is that of *Mercury* of Mumford High in Detroit. Full-page picture is first page reader sees; as he opens folded paper, conventional five-column page is revealed.

Something on each page should say to the reader: "Here's where you start reading!" If he stops for one story, chances are good that he'll read more on the page.

The *dominant head* should be definitely larger than any other on the page. When the reader must choose between two or more heads of nearly equal weight, he's apt to shrink from even such a minor decision and go to some other page where his mind is made up for him.

★ Every page should have a picture.

★ Pictures should be at the top of inside pages.

★ Pix should be well removed from the ad pyramid lest the reader mistake them for an advertisement and not give them the attention he would normally give to an editorial picture.

★ Avoid *naked columns.*

These are columns with no head or picture at the top. They look raw and unfinished.

Folio lines are sufficient to *dress* a column; their use, plus a box or picture, will usually avoid the need for a tombstone.

★ Tombstones should be avoided as zealously on inside pages as on the front page.

Sports Pages

Sports pages are usually designed an octave or so higher than other pages. This is appropriate for the vigorous, colorful actions they cover. Such makeup tends to approach the razzle-dazzle or *circus* makeup. The sports editor must exercise self-restraint; pages that are too "busy" tend to confuse the reader because he doesn't know where to start nor where to go once he has started.

Pictures are more important—if that's possible—on the sports page than anywhere else in the paper. Athletics are vivid and action-packed. Pictures that seek to report this bustling area cannot be static. Yet all too often, pix on sports pages—student or professional—are drab and stodgy.

★ The good sports editor insists on action pix.

If Johnnie Jones is awarded the Lettermen's plaque as outstanding athlete of the year, it is far better to dig a good action shot of him out of the file than to use a dull presentation shot.

★ Individual shots of team members should be action shots, even if they're posed action.

The sports editor needs a complete file of such pictures. Variety can be obtained by setting up a lend-lease program with other school papers in your athletic conference. School A loans its team shots to School B a week or so before the game, while B reciprocates by sending over pictures or cuts of its stars.

The sports editor shouldn't overlook pictures—or stories—of the so-called minor sports. Baseball may take the major spotlight, but a good shot of a golfer or cross-country runner gives pleasant contrast as well as more complete coverage. Girls' sports are all too frequently overlooked, especially when there is no interscholastic competition. But feminine athletes make interesting pictures and the unfamiliarity of the minor sports often has unusual novelty and appeal.

The Editorial Page

Unlike many professional newspapers, where editorial pages are making a comeback after years of scaring away readers by dull and vapid writing, student papers have always had popular edit pages. This may be because young people have strong ideas and the courage both to express them and to expose themselves to opposing viewpoints.

★ The function of editorial page typography is to distinguish this page of opinion from those pages which carry only hard facts.

At the same time, the editorial page must be attractive. This becomes difficult because the general tone of the edit page is "softer"—less spectacular or immediate—than that of news pages.

Eliminating column rules is a favorite device on this page. Even if the regular pages must carry column rules because there isn't room

FULLBACK RICH FIELD (28) BLASTS ON, DRAGGING TACKLERS WITH HIM
. . . end Ron Hawley (53) watches Field drive a few yards short of another Rocket touchdown

JERRY BUNDY (44) BLITZES WINGER BALLCARRIER
. . . teammate Chuck Eaton (47) moves in to assist

Rockets Stop Red Wing

Scholer: 'We Were Hungry'

By JOHN PEARSON
Rocket Staff Writer

After a decisive victory over Red Wing last Friday night, senior tackle Al Bierly summed the Rocket feelings with, "We sent THEM home with a 6 in their score, this time."

He was referring to the Rockets' defeat 7-6 in the last 22 seconds at Red Wing last year.

"We really wanted this one," pitched in senior Bill Scholer, who made his first start as guard. 'Last year they were hungry for it. This year we were."

Everyone in the noisy locker room agreed that it was a team victory. The players all talked about the game as they showered.

Chuck Field, senior halfback, said, "Team work, blocking, tackling, . . . that's all it takes."

Kit Monsrud who came in to replace Chuck Larson at halfback and scored three touchdowns, "It was a team effort." He was confident of the team's chances in the Big Nine this year.

The players were happy about their victory but cautious about what it showed, remembering last year's defeat after a good first game.

Coach John Drews said to the players as they took off their shoes, "We've got a long season." He told the sweating players not to get out of shape and to work hard next week.

Captain Roy Sutherland agreed quietly that it was a good start but warned, "Next week is just as important."

Dave Nelson, junior quarterback who made his varsity debut, said thoughtfully, "We won. That was one game. Next week's Owatonna; that's the big one."

★ ★ ★

JM Rookies Lead Team by Wingers

John Marshall's rookie backfield stayed close to the ground as the Rockets beat Red Wing 25 to 6 last Friday in the season's opener.

The backfield has been completely untried in varsity play.

In the starting backfield were wing-back Chuck Field, a senior; left-half Chuck Larson, also a senior; fullback Rich Field, a sophomore; and quarterback Dave Nelson, a junior.

Kit Monsrud, a junior, changed off with Larson and scored three touchdowns.

The Rockets took the kickoff and in nine plays bulldozed 67 yards to score. Rich Field went over from the one-yard line.

From then on the Rockets commanded the game.

Rich Field and Monsrud supplied most of the brawn. Field ran 92 yards in 19 plays without a loss. Monsrud scored the other three touchdowns, all from inside the ten. Both are underclassmen.

Quarterback Dave Nelson engineered most of the 20 Rocket first downs. He was in his first varsity start, replacing the graduated Dave Glasrud who ran the Rockets for two years.

Behind a strong line the team rushed a total of 342 yards on the ground. The Rockets attempted nine passes, but completed only two for 17 yards.

The new backfield didn't make many mistakes and behind an alert line turned in a team victory.

Only one Rocket was injured: starting end Tom Tervo, senior, with a bruised hip. He hopes to play in tonight's game with Owatonna.

Next Stop: Owatonna, a Big Nine Favorite

Despite Owatonna's loss to Albert Lea last week, JM football coach John Drews still feels they will be a major hurdle for the Rockets tonight at Owatonna.

"An awful lot depends on the first two games and we want to be ready for both of them. If we win them we might be well on our way." he said prior to the season opener. He still agrees.

Owatonna has seven returning lettermen, six of whom are linemen. One Big Nine coach has called their line "the best in the conference in several years." The average weight of their line is 206 pounds, 21 more than JM's.

Topping the Owatonna weight list are seniors Dale Nelson, 204-pound enter, Glenn Stoltz, 230 end, and Bob Bedney, 220-pound tackle.

However, the only returning back is converted quarterback Marc Reigel, who originally played halfback.

Owatonna coach Neal Davis said in a preseason interview, "We've got to find some backs." On that hunt hinges his success.

The Rockets will heavily depend on its line tonight. Drews feels that that is the key to the Rockets' success.

In its short history, JM has split four games with Owatonna. In 1959, however, a mistake on the part of the officials cost JM the game.

SERIES HISTORY

	JM	Owatonna
1958	0	28
1959	12	13
1960	26	7
1961	14	9

• • • • •

VARSITY FOOTBALL SCHEDULE
Sept. 7—Red Wing, here, 7:30
Sept. 14—Owatonna, there, 7:30
Sept. 21—Northfield, here, 7:30
Sept. 28—Mankato, there, 7:30
Oct. 5—Faribault, here, 7:30
Oct. 12—Austin, there, 7:30
Oct. 19—Albert Lea, here, 7:30
Oct. 26—La Crosse Logan, there, 7:30
Nov. 2—Winona, there, 7:30

HENRY WASHBURN'S

Bench Chatter

Monsruds at JM 20 Years

In 1964 Kit Monsrud, the last boy in a family of outstanding Rocket athletes; will graduate from JM.

Before Kit were his brothers Kim and Terry. And behind them all is their father, Cliff Monsrud, who has coached Rochester hockey and baseball teams for 20 years.

Mr. Monsrud, a JM industrial arts teacher, sat at his home near Simpson, Minn. With his wife beside him he discussed recently his family and athletics. "We're sports-minded," he said. "I like to see the kids play hard but I never pressure them into playing. They've learned to play hard to win. They're always good sports but never happy when they lose."

Coach Monsrud once captained the football and basketball team at Denfield High School in Duluth. He also played on the baseball team.

MRS. MONSRUD, who once was an ice skater and tap dancer, said her boys help one another in athletics. "They pull for each other. If one makes a mistake they tell each other about it. After every game they sit down and relive the whole thing, play by play, all over again."

Kim Monsrud, the oldest son, graduated in 1958. He captained the basketball team in his senior year and played baseball. Kim now lives in Rochester and works for IBM.

Terry was second in line and graduated in 1960. He played football, hockey, and baseball. He is presently in the Air Force stationed in Japan.

Kit, the youngest, plays football, hockey, and baseball. He is a junior at JM.

THE YOUNGEST in the Monsrud family, 13-year-old Linda, hopes to be a cheerleader.

As for the future of Monsruds in sports, Mr. Monsrud intends to continue coaching. And Kim now has a son that is a year and three months old. He may be the start of another generation of Monsruds in sports.

Rockets Aim for the Moon

By JOHN NICHOLS
Rocket Sports Editor

In a preseason interview, JM football coach John Drews was unwilling to predict the Rockets' success.

"There are too many big 'if's' to try to predict our success," he said.

At that time, one of the big if's was conditioning. "The boys didn't report in as tough condition as they did last year, but we hope to be in good condition for the first two games," he said.

According to Coach Drews, the Rockets will employ basically the same offense and defense as last year. The type of offense is a wing-T in which a flanker or wingback to either side is used. Senior Chuck Field has been running in that position.

Other backfield starters have been junior Dave Nelson, quarterback; senior Chuck Larson or junior Kit Monsrud, halfback; and sophomore Rich Field, fullback.

"We do lack the speed we had last year, so the offense is not as strong as the defense," Drews said before the season got underway.

Although the Rockets have lost speed, they have gained weight. "We're still not a big team, but we're bigger than last year."

The core of the offensive line is as follows: Tom Tervo, Dale Owens, Captain Roy Sutherland, Frank Borg, Chuck Eaton, Bill Scholer, and Craig Hoffman, all seniors.

DEFENSE LOOKS GOOD

"Right now, it looks like the defense is the strongest part of our play," Drews said. Much of the credit goes to linebackers, he said.

Assistant Coach Wayne Knipschield added, "We have a couple of guys who really like to hit hard and that makes a lot of difference."

Regular defensive specialists are Jerry Bundy, Ron Cady, and John Lillie, all juniors. Most of the offensive line doubles on defense.

Other specialists are as follows:

Punt and kickoff returns: Paul Klipsic, Lillie, and Monsrud, all juniors.

Placekicking: John Philo, a senior.

Punting: Philo and Frank Borg, a senior, Lillie, and Dave Sholwalter, a sophomore.

SOPHOMORES ON VARSITY SQUAD

This year there are four sophomores on the A-squad. "This is very unusual, but we feel that they can handle their position," Drews said. They are Tom Leonard, Dave Daugherty, Rich Field, and Sholwalter.

The most questionable part of the team is reserve strength. "With Robbinsdale in a preseason practice, our first team held its own, but the rest . . . well, that's another story. We're not overly endowed with reserves, and what we do have need a lot of work," Drews said.

Three players have changed positions from last year. They include Sutherland from guard to tackle, Scholer from tackle to guard, and Chuck Larson from quarterback to halfback.

DREWS'S SUMMARY

Coach Drews summarizes the season's prospects as follows:

"The team is in pretty good condition with no serious injuries. So far we have made normal, maybe above normal progress. If we win the first two, we're on our way."

He later added, "It'll take a real football team to beat us."

Mouthpieces Cut Injuries

By HENRY WASHBURN
Rocket Sports Writer

For the second consecutive year, mouth guards will be used to protect JM athletes.

Under a new ruling by the Minnesota State High School League, all athletes participating in football and hockey must be protected by mouth guards.

JM used mouth protectors last year although they were not mandatory. They paid off. The football team reported no tooth injuries.

The previous year there had been eight claims for teeth injuries.

A survey taken in Minnesota during the 1961 season among high school football players showed that 7,514 boys wore mouth guards. Eighty-nine percent fewer accidents were reported by that group.

Look magazine reported in its Aug. 19 edition that mouth guards not only protect the teeth and jaw but help to prevent brain damage resulting from impact in the region of the mouth.

The mouth guards last year were made of latex and fitted to the upper teeth of individual athletes by an adhesive gum on the inside of the guard. They cost four dollars apiece.

This year's mouth guards are being provided to the athletes of JM and Lourdes High School by the Dental Association.

The guards are made of a clear plastic and are stronger and more durable.

Guards this year are made from the personal impression of each individual mouth. That provides for a better fit and offers more protection. This year's guards cost fifteen dollars each.

On July 19, JM football players were fitted for the mouth protectors. Roy Sutherland, captain of the football team, commented at that time, "At first we gagged on them but we cut out the centers and now they fit okay."

Mr. John Drews, JM's football coach, was asked whether he could foresee any new protective equipment for football. "I think equipment will always be improved but if you take away the physical contact of the sport you lose a major feature of the game."

Fig. 30. Lively sports page from *Rocket* of John Marshall High, Rochester, Minn. Note use of stars to indicate a sidebar in column 1 and two-column setting of main story.

for adequate white space between columns, type on the editorial page can easily be manipulated to make this room.

Copy for the editorial page is written specifically for this page; editorials need not be interchangeable as news stories must be. So the editorials can be written to fit into a 21-pica column instead of the normal 22½ picas and so allow a full pica between columns.

Many an editor attempts to keep his editorial page entirely free of ads. If this can be done, he can get distinctive makeup by drastic changes in column widths. He can divide this page into 1½ columns, 1 column, 1½ and 1. Or he can use a 1½, 2, 1½ pattern or 2, 1½, 1½.

★ If advertising must run on the edit page, it should be light in color and dignified in tone.

It seems incongruous to have a serious editorial on the honor system run cheek-to-jowl with a loud, brassy ad for hillbilly records.

Editorial matter on the page can be best displayed if advertising can be placed to create a rectangle squared off across the bottom of the page, or to fill completely columns 4 and/or 5. The advantage of advertising position on this page is so great that no advertiser would object because his ad is not touched by reading matter.

Editorial pages don't need a logo to identify them. Yet many editors prefer to label their comment page; they hope it will help minimize the normal confusion between fact and opinion from which the typical reader seems to suffer. A favorite device is to reproduce the front-page flag in miniature and to continue the line in the same, or a radically different, type face saying "A Page of Opinion and Comment."

Editorials are the most important thing on this page and should be given the most important position.

★ The masthead should not occupy its traditional spot in the top left corner but should be dropped to the bottom of the page.

★ Ideally, editorials should be set wider than one column and in type larger than the regular news face.

★ Editorial heads should be large.

If we agree that editorials are important, then it seems logical that an edit deserves a head at least as large as a news story of the same length and importance.

Editorial cartoons are regular features on professional edit pages. They make attractive attention-compellers on student pages too. (The editor will find that editorial cartooning requires a rare skill that often can't be found in the student body.)

Columnists customarily find a home on this page. Care should be taken to avoid too many art heads, or too many styles of heads, lest the page look like an attic full of disparate junk.

One of the most popular elements of any editorial page—and a sure sign of vigorous readership—is the letters-to-the-editor column. These may be carried under a standing art or type head. Or "Letters to the Editor" may run as a kicker, with the main head carrying the theme

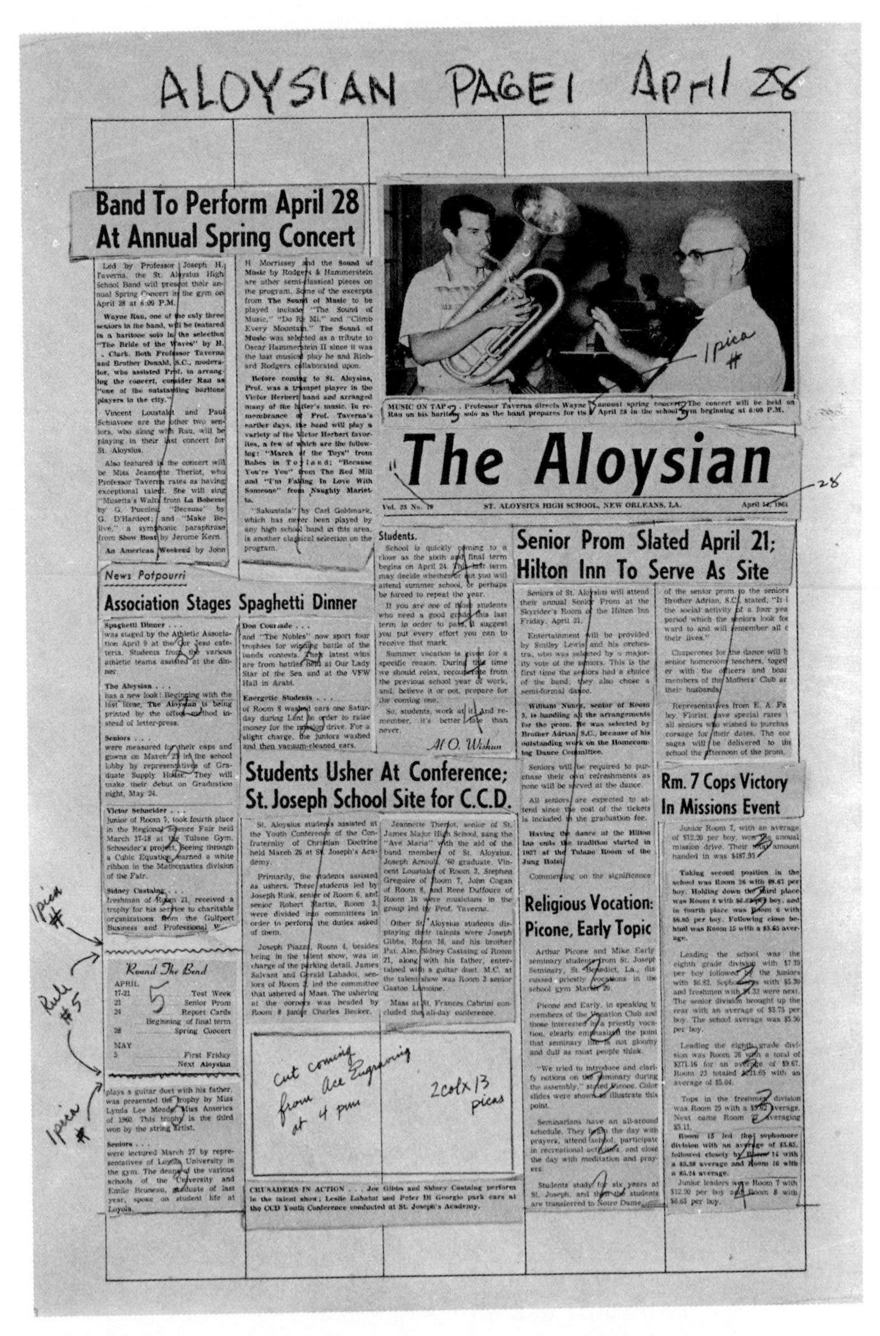

Band To Perform April 28 At Annual Spring Concert

Led by Professor Joseph H. Taverna, the St. Aloysius High School Band will present their annual Spring Concert in the gym on April 28 at 8:00 P.M.

Wayne Rau, one of the only three seniors in the band, will be featured in a baritone solo in the selection "The Bride of the Waves" by H. Clark. Both Professor Taverna and Brother Donald, S.C., moderator, who assisted Prof. in arranging the concert, consider Rau as "one of the outstanding baritone players in the city."

Vincent Loustalot and Paul Schiavone are the other two seniors, who along with Rau, will be playing in their last concert for St. Aloysius.

Also featured in the concert will be Miss Jeannette Theriot, who Professor Taverna rates as having exceptional talent. She will sing "Musetta's Waltz from **La Boheme** by G. Puccini; "Because" by G. D'Hardeot; and "Make Believe," a symphonic paraphrase from **Show Boat** by Jerome Kern.

An American Weekend by John H. Morrissey and the **Sound of Music** by Rodgers & Hammerstein are other semi-classical pieces on the program. Some of the excerpts from **The Sound of Music** to be played include "The Sound of Music," "Do Re Mi," and "Climb Every Mountain." **The Sound of Music** was selected as a tribute to Oscar Hammerstein II since it was the last musical play he and Richard Rodgers collaborated upon.

Before coming to St. Aloysius, Prof. was a trumpet player in the Victor Herbert band and arranged many of the latter's music. In remembrance of Prof. Taverna's earlier days, the band will play a variety of the Victor Herbert favorites, a few of which are the following: "March of the Toys" from Babes in Toyland; "Because You're You" from The Red Mill and "I'm Falling In Love With Someone" from Naughty Marietta.

"Sakuntala" by Carl Goldmark, which has never been played by any high school band in this area, is another classical selection on the program.

MUSIC ON TAP . . . Professor Taverna directs Wayne Rau on his baritone solo as the band prepares for its annual spring concert. The concert will be held on April 28 in the school gym beginning at 8:00 P.M.

The Aloysian

Vol. 33 No. 10 — ST. ALOYSIUS HIGH SCHOOL, NEW ORLEANS, LA. — April 14, 1961

News Potpourri

Association Stages Spaghetti Dinner

Spaghetti Dinner . . . was staged by the Athletic Association April 9 at the Cor Jesu cafeteria. Students from the various athletic teams assisted at the dinner.

The Aloysian . . . has a new look! Beginning with the last issue, **The Aloysian** is being printed by the offset method instead of letter-press.

Seniors . . . were measured for their caps and gowns on March 23 in the school lobby by representatives of Graduate Supply House. They will make their debut on Graduation night, May 24.

Victor Schneider . . . junior of Room 7, took fourth place in the Regional Science Fair held March 17-18 at the Tulane Gym. Schneider's project, Seeing through a Cubic Equation, earned a white ribbon in the Mathematics division of the Fair.

Sidney Castaing . . . freshman of Room 21, received a trophy for his service to charitable organizations from the Gulfport Business and Professional W...

Don Courade . . . and "The Nobles" now sport four trophies for winning battle of the bands contests. Their latest wins are from battles held at Our Lady Star of the Sea and at the VFW Hall in Arabi.

Energetic Students . . . of Room 8 washed cars one Saturday during Lent in order to raise money for the mission drive. For a slight charge, the juniors washed and then vacuum-cleaned cars.

Round The Bend

APRIL	
17-21	Test Week
21	Senior Prom
24	Report Cards
	Beginning of final term
28	Spring Concert
MAY	
5	First Friday
	Next **Aloysian**

plays a guitar duet with his father, was presented the trophy by Miss Lynda Lee Mead, Miss America of 1960. This trophy is the third won by the string artist.

Seniors . . . were lectured March 27 by representatives of Loyola University in the gym. The deans of the various schools of the University and Emile Bruneau, graduate of last year, spoke on student life at Loyola.

Students,

School is quickly coming to a close as the sixth and final term begins on April 24. This last term may decide whether or not you will attend summer school, or perhaps be forced to repeat the year.

If you are one of those students who need a good grade this last term in order to pass, I suggest you put every effort you can to receive that mark.

Summer vacation is given for a specific reason. During this time we should relax, recuperate from the previous school year of work, and, believe it or not, prepare for the coming one.

So, students, work at it! And remember, it's better late than never.

Al O. Wishun

Students Usher At Conference; St. Joseph School Site for C.C.D.

St. Aloysius students assisted at the Youth Conference of the Confraternity of Christian Doctrine held March 26 at St. Joseph's Academy.

Primarily, the students assisted as ushers. These students led by Joseph Rink, senior of Room 6, and senior Robert Martin, Room 3, were divided into committees in order to perform the duties asked of them.

Joseph Piazza, Room 4, besides being in the talent show, was in charge of the parking detail. James Salvant and Gerald Labadot, seniors of Room 3, led the committee that ushered at Mass. The ushering at the corners was headed by Room 8 junior Charles Becker.

Jeannette Theriot, senior of St. James Major High School, sang the "Ave Maria" with the aid of the band members of St. Aloysius. Joseph Arnoult, '60 graduate, Vincent Loustalot of Room 3, Stephen Gregoire of Room 7, John Cogan of Room 8, and Rene Duffourc of Room 16 were musicians in the group led by Prof. Taverna.

Other St. Aloysius students displaying their talents were Joseph Gibbs, Room 16, and his brother Pat. Also, Sidney Castaing of Room 21, along with his father, entertained with a guitar duet. M.C. at the talent show was Room 3 senior Gaston Lamoine.

Mass at St. Frances Cabrini concluded the all-day conference.

CRUSADERS IN ACTION . . . Joe Gibbs and Sidney Castaing perform in the talent show; Leslie Labatut and Peter Di Georgio park cars at the CCD Youth Conference conducted at St. Joseph's Academy.

Senior Prom Slated April 21; Hilton Inn To Serve As Site

Seniors of St. Aloysius will attend their annual Senior Prom at the Skyrider's Room of the Hilton Inn Friday, April 21.

Entertainment will be provided by Smiley Lewis and his orchestra, who was selected by a majority vote of the seniors. This is the first time the seniors had a choice of the band; they also chose a semi-formal dance.

William Nuney, senior of Room 3, is handling all the arrangements for the prom. He was selected by Brother Adrian, S.C., because of his outstanding work on the Homecoming Dance Committee.

Seniors will be required to purchase their own refreshments as none will be served at the dance.

All seniors are expected to attend since the cost of the tickets is included in the graduation fee.

Having the dance at the Hilton Inn ends the tradition started in 1937 of the Tulane Room of the Jung Hotel.

Commenting on the significance of the senior prom to the seniors Brother Adrian, S.C. stated, "It is the social activity of a four year period which the seniors look forward to and will remember all of their lives."

Chaperones for the dance will be senior homeroom teachers, together with the officers and board members of the Mothers' Club and their husbands.

Representatives from E. A. Farley, Florist, gave special rates to all seniors who wished to purchase corsage for their dates. The corsages will be delivered to the school the afternoon of the prom.

Religious Vocation: Picone, Early Topic

Arthur Picone and Mike Early seminary students from St. Joseph Seminary, St. Benedict, La., discussed priestly vocations in the school gym March 29.

Picone and Early, in speaking to members of the Vocation Club and those interested in a priestly vocation, clearly emphasized the point that seminary life is not gloomy and dull as most people think.

"We tried to introduce and clarify notions on the seminary during the assembly," stated Picone. Color slides were shown to illustrate this point.

Seminarians have an all-around schedule. They begin the day with prayers, attend school, participate in recreational activities, and close the day with meditation and prayers.

Students study for six years at St. Joseph, and then the students are transferred to Notre Dame...

Rm. 7 Cops Victory In Missions Event

Junior Room 7, with an average of $12.20 per boy, won the annual mission drive. Their total amount handed in was $487.93.

Taking second position in the school was Room 26 with $9.67 per boy. Holding down the third place was Room 8 with $6.63 per boy, and in fourth place was Room 6 with $6.05 per boy. Following close behind was Room 15 with a $5.65 average.

Leading the school was the eighth grade division with $7.35 per boy followed by the juniors with $6.82. Sophomores with $5.30 and freshmen with $4.32 were next. The senior division brought up the rear with an average of $3.75 per boy. The school average was $5.50 per boy.

Leading the eighth grade division was Room 26 with a total of $371.16 for an average of $9.67. Room 23 totaled $221.65 with an average of $5.04.

Tops in the freshmen division was Room 25 with a $5.62 average. Next came Room 27 averaging $5.11.

Room 15 led the sophomore division with an average of $5.65, followed closely by Room 14 with a $5.38 average and Room 16 with a $5.24 average.

Junior leaders were Room 7 with $12.20 per boy and Room 8 with $6.63 per boy.

Fig. 31. Pasteup dummy. Note that numbers of galleys are written on proofs to enable printer to find type more quickly. Long single lines indicate Galley #1. Engraver's proof is pasted in at top of page; at bottom, rectangle indicates late cut for which proof is not yet available. (Courtesy St. Aloysius High, New Orleans.)

of the first letter or a topic common to several letters.

Customarily the topic of a letter not covered by the main head is handled as a subhead. The writer's name is usually boldfaced to give it proper emphasis.

Departmentalization

Professional newspapers have, for many years, been attempting to *departmentalize* the news. They have succeeded to some extent. Local news is often concentrated on a specific page. Sports and society news occupy their own pages. But newspapers have been unable to departmentalize as much as "Time" and "Newsweek," for instance.

Student publications are usually able to run separate editorial and sports pages but beyond that point departments are usually more of a liability than an asset.

Dummies

The dummy is the "blueprint" the printer follows in making up a newspaper page. It may be a sketchy one, using a kind of "shorthand," or it may be a highly detailed *pasteup dummy*.

★ Every page of a newspaper should be dummied.

The *sketch dummy* is used almost exclusively by professional newspapers. Even for student papers that paste up their dummies, the sketch dummy is a useful preliminary.

Dummy sheets are usually printed or Mimeographed—or even drawn by hand—on 8½ x 11 sheet. The page is not drawn in proportion; columns are shown considerably wider than deep.

The editor indicates placement of a story by its headline style number and the slugline: 2-3 Commencement. A simple line shows how deep the story runs or where it wraps.

Pictures are shown by a rectangle crossed with an X; boxes by a plain rectangle.

On inside pages, the advertising department dummies in each ad. A duplicate—or carbon copy—is sent to the editorial department. Unless the duplicate is a carbon, ads are shown as a simple pyramid, the separate ones not identified. See Fig. 32.

The editor must know how much space a story will occupy in type so he can dummy it in accurately.

Type several lines from your newspaper to establish the average length of line. Double this and insist that all copy be typed at this measure. (One editor made sure there would be no exceptions. With a bottle of liquid solder, he just spiked down the margin indicators on every typewriter in the news room.)

Determine how many lines of type are in one column inch in your paper. If you're setting 8-on-9, there will be eight lines of type—the

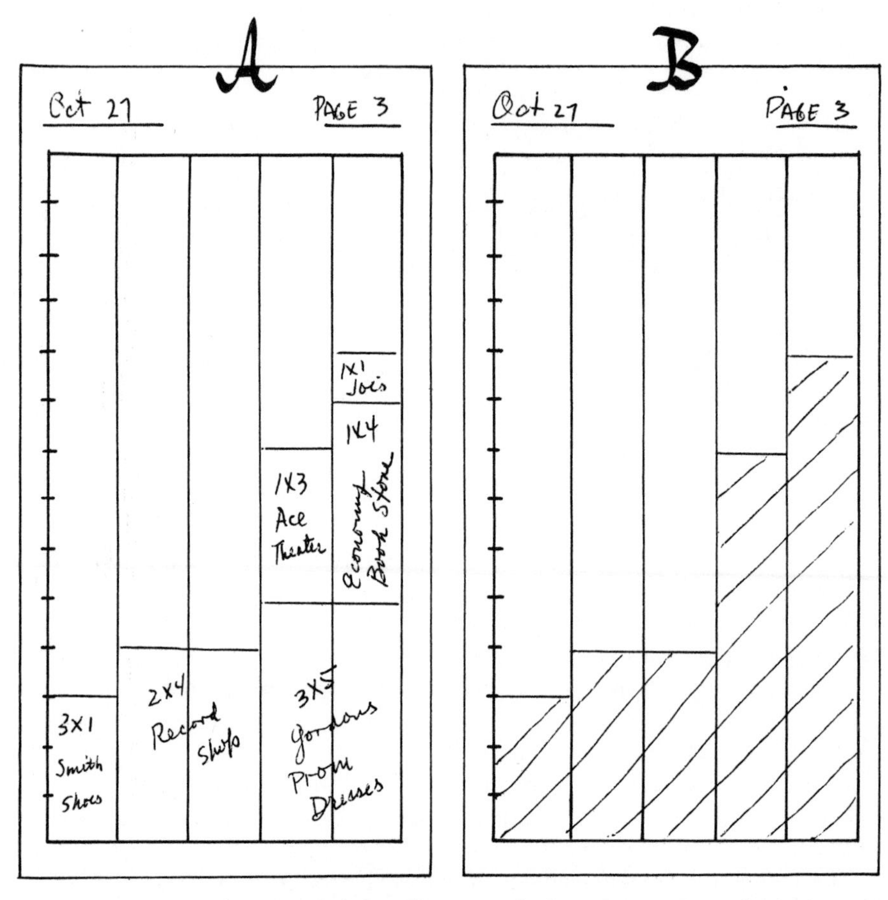

Fig. 32. Page dummies. A shows placement of ads, goes to printer. B merely indicates total area of advertising, goes to editorial department, which then places news matter. Note that dummies are not in true proportion; they are much longer in ratio to width.

equivalent of four typescript lines—per inch. Typed at standard double-space, the typewriter will get three lines in one inch of vertical space.

So all the editor needs to do is measure the length of a typewritten story and multiply it by .75, and he will have the column inches the story will make in type.

He figures cutlines the same way. Headlines can be measured from the schedule; pictures are scaled to show their size.

This method of dummying usually requires some slight manipulation on the stone. This is not always possible for the student staff. In this case, the staff must either allow the printer to make decisions or furnish him with a pasteup dummy.

The dummy sheet for pasting up is the exact size of the finished page. Sometimes columns are made a pica or two wider than actual ones to avoid overlapping of pasted material.

On these sheets are pasted proofs of every line of type, body or display, and each picture. The editor can then determine down to the last line just how his page will fit together.

Pasting up is done with a light coating of rubber cement which enables a proof to be lifted and repositioned without tearing.

Each proof must be identified by its galley number so the printer knows where to find a particular story. Usually the editor marks the galley number with a bright ink on every paragraph before he cuts it up.

When a paragraph is split from one column to another, each portion must be marked with the galley number.

Whole books have been written about newspaper typography and layout and obviously these few chapters have no more than lifted the lid on a fascinating subject. The student editor has much to learn in this area. But he also has pleasant rewards in store; there are few satisfactions in newspapering greater than those of producing a page with good layout.

And always the wise newspaperman—be he a student or a pro—realizes that type and its arrangement are his most important tool in communicating, which is his primary job.

12. *Selling Advertising*

Economic sinews of a free press

When you persuade your Dad to let you use the family car for your Prom date, when you campaign for your friend who's running for Student Council, when you present a term paper in a neat, attractive folder . . . you're advertising.

When you work on the advertising staff of your school paper, you use the same techniques.

Americans are surrounded by advertising all their lives. It influences their decisions and they use it to influence others'. It's an honorable vocation and one that is important to our country. The student who works on advertising for his paper will learn lessons that will be valuable in later life even if his work is far removed from professional advertising.

Advertising has been—and continues to be—attacked savagely by many critics. Some are motivated by selfish reasons, others by political reasons. Most critics are sincere; many are sophists. (It's interesting to note that recent best-seller books that violently castigated advertising were promoted by massive advertising campaigns. One cannot help but wonder at the motivation of a person who uses means he calls vile to attain an end he calls undesirable.)

It is not the function of this book to defend American advertising. But it is necessary to examine the nature of advertising so that the student advertising salesman can decide if the statement is true that:

★ Even at the student level, advertising is an important and praiseworthy activity.

Advertising is a method of persuading someone to do something, usually to buy something. But we may want him to vote for our candidate or for a new school bond issue. We may only want him to think something: that our state is a good place to spend a vacation, that a certain store is a friendly place to do business, that our school is the best in the world.

Advertising is not black magic. It cannot make people buy or do something they don't want to.

Advertising is not "well-phrased lies." Advertisers can, and do, tamper with the truth. So, unfortunately, do lawyers, baseball players, and students. But the bad apples in any basket are few, and there are laws to deal with those who do damage to their fellow citizens.

Advertising has made vast contributions to America. Why is it that in real value an automobile today actually costs less—in working hours—than when cars were first introduced some fifty years ago? Because advertising created a mass demand. That made it possible to use techniques of mass production. That, in turn, reduced the cost for each item.

By showing people what products are available, advertising has given incentives to Americans. If a man works harder because he wants to buy a college education for his son or an electric dishwasher for his wife, he contributes to the economic well-being of his community. That makes possible the fine schools, parks, hospitals, and other things on which your community prides itself.

Advertising is an absolute necessity to a professional newspaper. The cost of a paper to the reader just about pays for the materials. Some publishers estimate that revenue from the sale of newspapers is less than 20% of the manufacturing costs. The cost of gathering the news from all over the world, shooting pictures, preparing, printing, and distributing the paper is borne by revenues produced by ads.

Student publications do not depend this much on ad revenues. They are subsidized to varying extents by the school or student body. They have no payrolls to meet. Circulation costs are nil. But advertising revenues give the means of producing a better school publication.

Why do merchants advertise in daily papers? Advertising is an investment that pays good dividends. Advertising sells goods and that increases profits.

That is the reason why they advertise in student publications, too. At least that should be the reason.

Unfortunately, too many student publications ask the local merchant to "give us an ad." And all too often, that is what the merchant does. This is not a business transaction; it's charity.

★ The self-respecting student ad salesman will not accept a handout. He doesn't have to; he has a valuable commodity to sell on a strictly dollars-and-cents basis.

The high school market is a tremendous one. It is estimated that high school students in the United States annually spend 170 million dollars. Your school alone accounts for a substantial sum. It is well worth the investment of some ad dollars by a merchant to get his share of this market.

★ The first thing a student ad manager should do is estimate the size of the market his student body represents.

He can do this in several ways. Interviews with merchants often will bring out facts about teen-age business volume. Local banks have data on the size of this market. Polls and surveys of your student body will be even more accurate.

This is an interesting and valuable project that can be conducted by classes in economics, business, social studies, citizenship, or journalism.

Prepare a questionnaire along these lines:

I. How much spending money do you have per week?
- A. Allowance __________
- B. Earnings __________

II. How much money have you spent in the past week on:
- A. Clothing __________
- B. Food __________
- C. Recreation __________
  (include dates)
- D. Records __________
- E. Books __________
- F. Transportation
  1. Bus and train __________
  2. Automobile __________
  3. Scooter, motorbike, etc. __________
- G. Personal Items
  1. Haircuts __________
  2. Beauty parlors __________
  3. Shaving supplies __________
  4. Cosmetics __________
  5. Perfumes __________
  6. Gifts
     a. Christmas __________
     b. Birthdays __________
     c. Anniversaries __________
     d. Others __________
  7. Telephone __________
- H. Hobbies
  1. Record collecting __________
  2. Hi-fi, stereo __________
  3. Stamp collecting __________
  4. Model building __________
  5. Electronics __________

6. Others __________

H. Any other __________

TOTAL __________

III. How much do you estimate you have *personally* spent in:

A. The past semester __________

B. The past school year __________

C. The past calendar year __________

IV. What major item has your family purchased in the past year in which you had a voice in selection:

A. New home __________

B. New car __________

C. Television set __________

D. Vacation trip __________

E. Furniture __________

F. Others __________

This questionnaire can be condensed or elaborated to suit your needs. In any case, the answers will make formidable ammunition in persuading any merchant that your paper reaches a market important to him.

★ Whether it will be good business for a merchant to advertise with you then will depend on your ad rate.

Advertising is sold by the column inch—a space 1 column wide and 1 inch deep—or by the *agate line*—one-fourteenth of a column inch. National advertisers use the *milline rate;* they figure how much it costs, per agate line, to reach a million readers at a given rate for a given circulation.

The milline rate for a student newspaper is always considerably higher than for a daily newspaper. But the student salesman has a ready-made rebuttal to that: There is no waste in a student paper. Every copy—and presumably every ad—is read by every student; many a daily paper may be read only partially or maybe not beyond the headlines. Every student is a potential customer for the advertiser; many daily papers circulate in areas so far away that the reader won't even come close to many of the stores that advertise. Ads in student papers get high attention because the volume of advertising is low; in daily papers there are so many ads that many could be overlooked.

School papers offer a reader bonus, too. Many—if not most—student papers are read by the parents, brothers, and sisters of the student and they, too, represent a potential market.

Setting the rate for a student publication is difficult. Basically, ad space is worth what a merchant is willing to pay for it. The publication that gets results for an advertiser is worth purchasing at almost any reasonable rate. But what is reasonable?

Probably the best way is to determine the average rate used by school papers in your circulation and economic bracket. Obviously a paper in a school of 2,000 should have higher rates than one with 500 circulation. But it should also be noted that a school in a city, where students are close to stores, may have more immediate purchasing power than a consolidated rural school where the student body is scattered and does business in many towns. And a school body in a wealthy section of a large city may have more money to spend than one in a depressed or underdeveloped area.

The merchant is the final judge of equitable rates. If he does not protest, your rates are probably proper—if you have established a business relationship with him and he does not look on his advertising as a charitable gesture.

State, regional, and national school press associations have data available which will allow you to compare your rates with those of similar publications.

★ The student ad manager should have a well-laid selling plan.

First he must draw up a list of prospects. Current and past advertisers are the core of such a list. Then the manager should travel throughout the neighborhood and note those business places which are convenient to the student body and offer merchandise appealing to this group. He should check the yellow pages of the telephone book for the same factors.

A business place need not be across the road from school to be a prospect. A student may not go across town to buy a Coke after school; but he will travel a sizable distance to buy a hi-fi set. A hamburg hut may draw students for many miles after a game or dance. A boy won't mind going to the next town to a skating rink or a used-car dealer.

After the list has been drawn, student salesmen should be assigned to a group of prospects. Each one must practice the basic axioms of the salesman:

★ To make sales, you must make calls.

★ Each prospect should be called on regularly, preferably once before each issue or even once a week.

★ The student salesman should be neatly dressed and well groomed.

He (it may well be a girl, of course) represents not only his paper but his school; he owes it to his classmates to give a good impression.

★ He should be mannerly and polite.

He should give his sales talk, ask for the order, and depart. He should not act hurt if he is refused. Few people enjoy saying, "No!" The merchant means no personal rebuff if he turns down a business opportunity. If the answer is unfavorable, the student should say a smiling, friendly farewell and take off—but return next week, smiling.

Any successful salesman can tell many incidents of profitable sales and long-lasting business relations that came about only after uncounted fruitless calls.

It is hard to sell an intangible, and few things are as intangible as space in a newspaper. So the wise salesman will always have something tangible to show his prospect. This is a dummy of a proposed ad. The wise space salesman—student or professional—always takes along a new dummy to show the prospect on every call.

★ The salesman should always carry a copy of the latest issue of his paper.

Even if the merchant is familiar with the publication—and many businessmen will not be—it's advantageous for the salesman to have a "visual aid."

If the merchant advertises in another paper, an effective device is to clip his ad from that and paste it right onto a page of your paper. Then he can see exactly what his ad would look like in the form in which his student audience would be exposed to it.

If the prospect does buy space, the succeeding transaction should be conducted in a businesslike manner.

★ If the merchant has been promised a proof, it is the duty of the salesman to see that it is delivered promptly—and returned to the printer just as promptly.

★ The ad manager should keep a looseleaf *ad log.*

This may be a book or a clipboard with a list for each issue. When the salesman makes a sale, he should fill out a card similar to this:

> *Salesman:* Jimmy Brown
> *Account:* Campus Clothing
> *Issue:* November 5
> *Size of ad:* 2 x 5
> *Special Instructions:* On sports page if possible
> *Illustrations:* Mat to be cast

The manager transfers the data to his log. He keeps a separate sheet, or sheets, for each issue. If this ad for Campus Clothing is to run in two issues, the manager will mark it down on the sheet for each issue.

When the time comes for dummying up the paper, the manager will check off each ad as he dummies it into position. As closely as possible he will fill requests for special position. On his log he will note the page on which ad is dummied.

A carbon copy of this log goes along with the dummy to the printer. (The editorial department gets a carbon of the dummy so that page makeup can begin for news copy.) After each page has been locked up, the printer will check to see that every ad has been put in place. If any is missing, he will contact the manager and get instructions on whether he must remake the page or whether the ad can run elsewhere.

★ As soon as page proofs are ready, the ad staff must carefully check the proof against the log.

A *no-run*—failure to get an ad into the paper—is an insult to the merchant and no one can blame him if he refuses to do business with a carelessly operated organization.

As soon as the paper comes off the press, the bookkeeping department should enter each ad in the *journal.* Usually student publications send out statements immediately after each issue.

Each statement should be accompanied by a *proof of publication.* This is a tearsheet—a single page—or the entire paper. It is folded so the merchant's ad is on the outside, usually circled in red crayon.

Payments should be acknowledged at once with a form something like this:

> The Clay High News acknowledges with thanks receipt of your check for $_____.

After a specified time, charges are transferred from the journal to the *ledger.* Statements should be sent out monthly on unpaid bills. After a period, the student salesman should call on overdue accounts and collect. This is nothing to be embarrassed about.

★ It is neither good business nor kindness to let an account become overdue.

If the call is made in a friendly, businesslike manner, the merchant will not take umbrage.

The bookkeeping systems of student newspapers will vary as much as those of their professional counterparts. It's a good idea to ask a teacher of business arithmetic or accounting to help the staff set up an adequate but simple accounting system. Teach it to the business staff and insist that books be kept current and meticulous.

It helps build advertising linage to prepare cards which the merchant can place in his window to call attention to his ad in your paper. There are many other similar promotions which the student manager can borrow from the dailies.

Since almost everyone has a competitive spirit:

★ A good way to get a student ad staff to produce at its best is to keep a *performance chart.*

This graph should show the amount of advertising sold during the current and past—or several past—years.

Perhaps a similar graph can show the results of individual salesmen. Whether this is done or not, under all circumstances the list of prospects should be divided equitably among all salesmen. There is always a danger that the manager will take choice accounts for himself or give them to a close friend while some other person has only the marginal ones.

Every salesman should have one or two accounts that are reasonably sure of buying space regularly. He needs these successes to encourage him to call on prospects harder to sell.

Managing a sales staff takes diplomacy as well as leadership. The

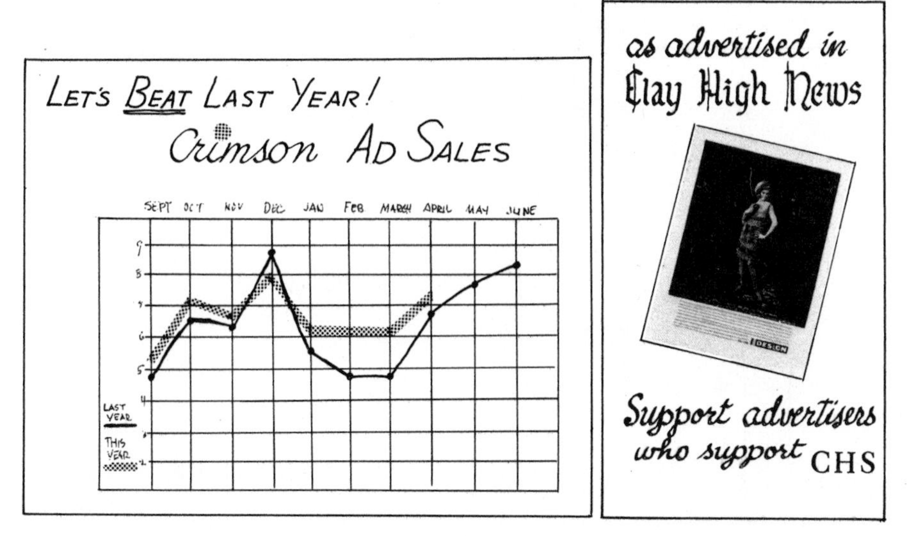

Fig. 33. Chart in ad manager's office shows performance of staff compared to last year. Window card displays ad from school paper for use in store.

student ad manager who gets the best performance from his staff has learned a lesson as valuable as any he'll ever get out of a textbook.

When it comes time to give recognition for staff work, don't forget those ad staffers who have worked backstage. The bookkeeper and the girl who sends out statements, the person who dummies the ads, and the one who takes charge of proofs are all valuable members of the team and deserve credit.

13. *Creating Advertising*

Serving the merchant and the reader

The most effective advertisement in a student publication is one directed specifically to a student audience and written in its idiom. So student-produced ads not only serve the merchant better, they appeal to the student body as much as editorial matter may and thus make the whole newspaper more interesting and readable.

Professional advertising uses many highly trained, highly experienced, highly specialized (and highly paid) talents. But any intelligent person can master the rudiments of advertising, and it is surprising how quickly high school students learn to produce advertising of high quality. While student work cannot be expected to be as good as that done on Madison Avenue, it can do its specified job in a workmanlike manner.

★ A newspaper ad is basically like a newspaper story; both convey information.

So the typography and layout of advertising have many things in common with that of the news columns. The only difference is that an ad seeks to motivate the reader by that information.

The editor tells his reporters that a news story must tell the 5 W's; so must an ad. Besides that, an ad must tell one more thing: the benefit the reader will obtain if he is motivated to the desired action.

Like a news story, an ad is most effective if its message is brief and interestingly told. Unlike a news story, an ad is personal; it is directly addressed to "you," the most important word in selling because it's the most important word to the reader.

When you prepare copy for an advertiser, write it as you would a letter to your best friend, telling him why he ought to go to Danny's Drive-In or why he should buy a new sport jacket.

★ Keep ad copy informal; speak in the language of the prospect; keep it honest; keep it brief.

Humor is especially appealing to a teen-age audience. Try for the light touch. But remember that while you can be humorous in your approach, never poke fun (even unintentionally) at the advertiser or his products.

★ The advisor should supervise all student advertising closely.

While this applies to any type of advertising, it is especially true in the case of humorous treatment. Immaturity, bad judgment, and questionable taste can be handicaps to a student publication in all areas. But in advertising, where the investment of a merchant may be destroyed by a distorted sense of humor, repercussions are swifter and bad effects last longer.

★ The simplest ad is the most effective one.

Ideally, the best ad is that which sells only one item. In practice, most advertisers want more items. At any rate, keep the list down. If the reader is drawn into a store, the ad has done its job just as well if one item was the attraction as if several tugged the customer in.

★ Eliminate everything from an ad that does not contribute to making the sales pitch.

You know how difficult it is to sell your mother on some idea if she is distracted by the telephone, doorbell, or kid brother. It is just as difficult to sell a reader through advertising, if his attention is divided among many elements in an ad.

★ Avoid diagonal lines in an ad.

They irritate the reader, who is used to reading on horizontal lines. (Besides, they're difficult to produce in the print shop.)

★ Avoid type that reads vertically.

Orientals love this; they're used to it. Occidentals just can't read up-and-down type.

★ Never run a line of type sideways.

The reader must turn the page—or almost twist his neck off—to read it. This is distracting at best, annoying most of the time.

★ Never run an ad sideways or upside down.

Even if the advertiser wants this unorthodox way to attract readers, most people will think it was a mistake. This reflects on the standards of your newspaper and its staff.

★ Avoid boxes within an ad, especially boxes within boxes.

Ads gain impact from size. Boxes fragment an effective area into smaller, far less useful ones. This is like breaking a strong football team into eleven individual players; they'll never make a touchdown.

When the advertiser insists on boxes, try sideless boxes (made just as for editorial use).

★ Avoid pictures that are used just to fill space.

The functions of illustrations in an ad are to expand upon written communication, attract attention, direct the eye to important copy blocks in the ad, and create an atmosphere that will make the reader more receptive to the sales message.

Unless a picture does at least one—and preferably several—of these functions, don't use it. This applies to decorative borders, too.

★ Pictures are one of the most potent selling tools.

Student ad men should learn to use effective art; for when an ad sells merchandise it is easy to sell ads.

There are three basic methods of obtaining pictures for ad use. Student photographers may take, and student artists draw, suitable pictures; stereotype matrices (*mats* or *flongs*) may be used to produce printing plates; or the staff may use cuts from its own, or its printer's, files.

Local photographs, using students as models or demonstrators, are probably the most effective of all advertising aids. The disadvantage, of course, is cost of photography and engraving. But often a merchant —after a trial period during which the paper pays this cost—is so convinced of the efficacy of local art that he is perfectly willing to take on the slight additional charge.

Using old engravings is the least satisfactory method. Many of them show signs of wear; many are dated; few are specific enough to do any good.

For papers printing by letterpress, the advertising *mat service* is the most satisfactory source of good art.

These services, periodically issued, can be purchased at low cost.

A stereotype mat is a mold of type and/or artwork made of a kind of papier-mâché. Molten metal is poured into the mold and the result is an exact replica of the original type or engraving, line or halftone.

Each collection of mats in a service package is accompanied by a *proof book* which shows all the illustrations in that issue. Mats and proofs are keyed by a simple code. The ad man looks through the current, and past, proof books until he finds just the picture he needs. Proofs and mats are identified by a simple code so it is easy to locate the proper mat.

Individual and cumulative indexes make it easy to find the general category of illustrations.

Manufacturers provide merchants with mats of specific merchandise. The student ad man should always ask the merchant if he has any of his own mats he'd like to use. Often this will result in the sale of larger space.

Mats are light and, if kept in a reasonably dry storage place, last almost indefinitely. So a student paper can accumulate matrices over a period of time and offer a wider selection.

Many small illustrations are contained on one large mat. The ad man cuts his desired mat out of the sheet. When he does this, he must use care to make sure that there is an adequate *shoulder* around the mold itself; otherwise the printer cannot cast it. If it is impossible to provide sufficient shoulder, the whole matrix should be sent to the printer with the desired one circled in grease pencil.

If only a portion of an illustration is to be used, this, too, should be indicated in grease pencil.

★ Never cut through a stereotype matrix; it will be ruined.

Two or more proof books are sent with each set of mats. One book is kept as a permanent record. When a picture is used, the name of the advertiser and the date used are written on the picture. (Mats can be reused; after they are cast they are returned and refiled. It would be embarrassing if the same picture appeared in the ads of competitors in the same issue.)

The second proof book is used to cut up. Clipped illustrations are used to make dummies.

In the case of offset papers, the proofs themselves are used in the pasteup from which the printing plates are made.

As in a news story, it's type that does the talking in an ad. The good advertising man makes sure that his printed "salesman" has the chance to talk fluently, clearly, and loudly enough.

★ Use only one family of type in an ad.

Just as a variety of dialects confuses a listener, so too many type faces confuse a reader. Sticking to one family assures the typographic harmony that is pleasant to the reader.

An *accent face* occasionally adds interest to an ad. This is a strikingly different type face used sparingly—for only one word, or perhaps a line.

★ Use the largest possible type.

The smallest body type in an ad should be 10-point.

★ Don't set type too wide or too narrow.

Never set type narrower than one column; never set it wider than 30 picas.

★ Avoid *runarounds*.

This is type set around a picture. It is more difficult to set—and to read—than type in neat rectangles.

★ Never set type into pictorial shapes.

It's always a temptation to set type in the form of a Christmas tree or a jack-o'-lantern or some seasonal symbol. Get Satan behind thee and don't succumb.

★ Avoid all-capitals.

The same lack of legibility that keeps editors from using all-cap headlines should keep the wise advertising man from using them. If you can't avoid such setting completely, at least minimize its use. If you must set all-cap, keep the words and lines extremely short; this takes away some of the curse.

The most effective way to set type is in a justified rectangle. Copy for such setting can be written normally on the typewriter. It is then *specced* (pronounced specked)—*specified*—by point size, ledding and line length: *10/12—14 picas.* The printer will automatically justify the lines and break them with no regard to how the lines were broken on the copy.

If you want the printer to follow the style in which you have typed copy, you tell him to *set line for line.* The result will be:

This is copy which has
been set in such a way that
each line of type
contains exactly the same
characters as the lines
of the typewritten copy.

If you want to align at the left, as the example above, draw two vertical parallel lines at the left of the paper and write: *set flush left.*

The same pair of lines at the right of the copy, plus the phrase *set flush right,* will result in type that looks like this:

This type is set
flush right,
a method that
is not very
effective.

Flush right copy is difficult to read because there is no constant point to which the eye returns after reading a line. Flush-right setting should be minimized—better yet, eliminated.

Type set in this way is
often pleasant in certain
layouts. This is stepped
type. It creates a pleasant
diagonal while keeping type
horizontal.

Specs for *stepped type* include the face and ledding, of course, plus the length of the line and the amount to be stepped down in each line:

Caledonia 12/14—18 picas
Step down 2 picas per line

When you use stepped type, remember that not only is each line longer than the preceding one by the width of the step but this difference increases with the number of lines involved. If you are stepping down six lines of type by two picas each, the last line will be 12 picas —2 inches—longer than the first line. Be sure there's enough room in the layout.

As a matter of fact, always be sure there is enough room for any type you specify.

There are highly scientific ways of determining how much space a block of copy will occupy when set in type or, conversely, how many words must be written to fill a specified area. This is *copyfitting.*

The student ad man can do the same thing in a far more simple manner.

Suppose you want to fill a 2½-inch by 4-inch area with 10-point Caledonia.

Find some specimen of this type and measure 2½ inches of several lines to determine the average number of characters in a line of that length.

Set your typewriter at that measure.

Then measure, on the block of type, how many lines, at the given ledding, will fit into a 4-inch depth. Measure only complete lines. If there's a fraction of a line, say 24½, drop the fraction. That extra half line will protrude beyond your available area and there may just not be room to tuck it in.

Then, with your typewriter set at the proper measure, just type off 24 lines and your copy block will be neatly filled. If a line is normally a character or two short, don't worry; there will undoubtedly be a couple that are a little long and they'll average out.

Headlines are handled the same way.

Suppose you have a head that says: *Come to the Prom.* Count the characters: 15½. Now look on the type specimen sheets or book that most printers furnish for their customers. If you decide that 36-point Garamond Bold is the face you'd like, count 15½ characters in that type. Measure them; you find they occupy about 18 picas in length. If you have 18 picas of open space for this line, you're in business. If your available area is shorter, look at 24-point, or even 18, and count them off until you find the size that will fit.

★ Always write advertising headlines a little short.

It is easy to make a line of type a little longer if necessary; it's practically impossible to make it shorter.

★ White space is one of the most effective typographic salesmen. Use plenty of it.

Every ad should have a generous frame of white within its outside dimensions. This will not only frame the message but will make sure that neighboring ads won't trespass on the reader's attention.

★ Keep white space at the outside, instead of at the center, of an ad.

An irregular silhouette in an ad is pleasant. But when there's a large hole in its center, the ad looks like a nebula about to explode.

Fig. 34. Thumbnails were drawn in small size before starred one was used to make layout for this ad.

Ad Dummies

Dummies are as important to student ad men as to student editors; more, indeed. For the ad dummy not only shows the printer how to make up the ad, it is a useful sales tool, as we've already noted.

Dummies range from the very rough to the most detailed.

Thumbnails are tiny, hasty sketches which indicate only the basic design of an ad. The layout man draws many of these until he develops the pattern he wants. Then he draws a *rough dummy*. This is done in the exact size of the finished ad. Pictures may be roughly sketched in or proofs may be pasted into position. Headlines are drawn in sketchily and blocks of body type are indicated by sets of parallel lines which by their proximity and weight indicate the size

Fig. 35. Dummy for ad. Illustration is clipped from ad-mat book; headline is lettered. Copy blocks are indicated for size and keyed to typewritten copy.

and typographic color of the type.

A *comprehensive dummy*—or *comp*—is a detailed, same-size plan of the finished ad. Proofs of all elements are pasted into exact position and the comp looks almost like the finished job.

The most finished dummy is the *mechanical.* This is an exact replica of the final ad as it is prepared for the platemaker. Only for offset papers do newspaper ad men use mechanicals.

Ad Layouts

There are many basic layout patterns for advertisements. We need not dig too deeply into most of them. Many are self-explanatory; many

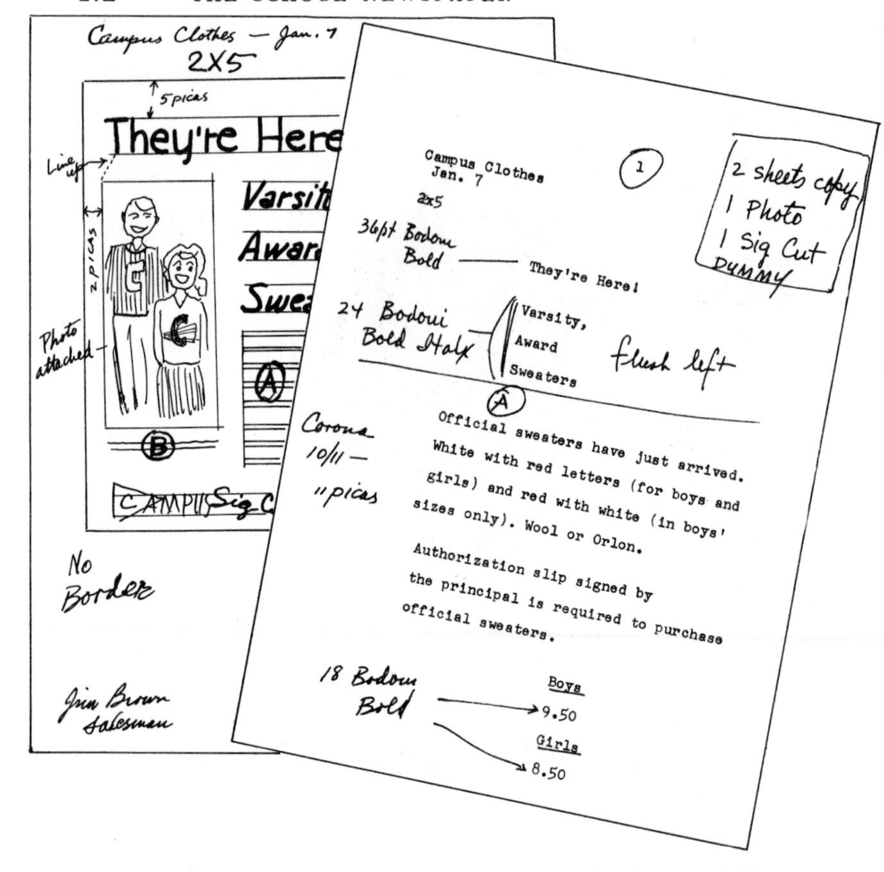

Fig. 36. Advertising "package" for printer. Note "inventory" in top right corner of copy, advertiser's name given on copy and layout sheets and how copy is keyed to dummy.

are academic. They are seen more often in modification than in their theoretical original form.

The *centered ad* is the oldest pattern. It is simple and attractive but can be stodgy and stiff. For ads where dignity and authority are required the centered ad has advantages. But its appeal to a teen-age audience is limited.

A *symmetrical* ad is a variation of the centered pattern. It combines, with centered elements, pairing of equal elements to create mirror halves either horizontally or vertically.

Classical and *geometrical* layouts are similar. Classic layouts arrange elements into patterns that were made famous by great artists of the past. The S or *reverse* S *pattern* is one of the favorites of all layouts because it leads the eye in graceful sweeps throughout the entire area of the ad.

Geometrical layouts arrange elements in well defined patterns such as a *frame*, L, or U.

Fig. 37. Some basic patterns of advertising layouts.

Rectangular layout owes a debt to the contemporary artist Piet Mondriaan. Large areas are broken into pleasantly related, harmonious forms. This is one exception to the "no-box" axiom we've discussed.

In a Mondriaan layout, no area should be the same size as any other. Lines of division should never be placed at the half, quarter or third mark of the whole ad.

These same principles are used in creating many kinds of layouts other than ads. They are discussed in Chapter 22 as they apply to yearbook pages, and the ad layout man ought to read that chapter as closely as he does this one.

The *jazz layout* is a pleasant one that's easy to create. It gets its name from the musicians who suggest—but never actually play—a familiar melody.

When an ad man does a jazz layout, he draws a light line inside the outer margin of the ad. This, first of all, gives him the necessary frame of white. It also creates a rectangle which will be suggested, but not defined, by elements of the ad. Each of the four sides must

Fig. 38. Jazz layouts. Note, in A, that picture suggests top and right side; copy blocks establish sides; signature suggests bottom and right.

In B, picture suggests top; headline sets both sides; signature shows bottom. In both layouts, notice how all elements are tied together by no-orphan system.

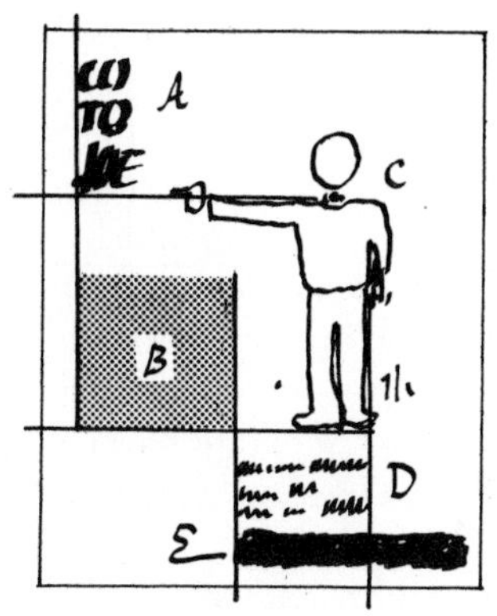

Fig. 39. Oriented ad layout. Sketch shows how each element buddies-up with at least one other. Headline (A) aligns with copy block (B) and with strong element of cut (C). B aligns with copy block (D) and signature (E). Note how elements are tied together horizontally and vertically.

be touched by at least one element. More than one element may touch any one side or a single element may touch more than one side. The whole rectangle is then "visible" only as a mental image of the reader.

Many contemporary ads do not fit neatly into any of these patterns. They are loosely defined as having dynamic or informal balance.

In laying out such a pattern, the ad man follows all the rules of the editor in laying out an informally balanced front page. (See Chapter 11.)

★ Dispose elements around the optical center so the ad hangs almost straight.

★ Place a strong attention-compeller in the primary optical area.

★ Define the diagonal along which the reading eye moves.

★ Use illustrations, and *lines of force* within them, to direct the eye to the copy blocks.

★ Keep the ad simple.

★ Keep the ad well oriented.

Orienting an ad means to position each element so it has a definite relation with at least one other element. This is also called the *no-orphan* or *buddy system,* because no element stands alone, as an orphan; each buddies up with at least one companion.

Figure 39 shows an oriented ad.

The headline (A) aligns with the top of the picture (C). The copy block (B) aligns with the left margin of the head and with the bottom of the cut. The subhead (D) buddies up with B and C, and the sig (E) aligns with the left margin of D.

There is no "orphan" in this layout and the reader's eye is pleased, just as we are all pleased with obvious neatness and order.

If you can orient an element horizontally as well as vertically and with as many other elements as possible, the sense of order is enhanced.

We haven't spoken about the *signature cut* (the *sig* or *logo*) because this is properly the concern of the advertiser. But the ad man must make sure that the sig appears in every ad. It is surprising how often the signature is left off an ad even in professional newspapers; great care should be taken to check on this vital element before each issue goes to press.

All material for an ad should go to the printer in a single package. Every word that will appear in the ad should be neatly typewritten on a separate sheet of paper, never on the dummy.

The copy sheet is headed with the name of your paper, the issue in which the ad is to appear, the size of the ad (given in column width and inches of depth, as 2 x 5—2 columns x 5 inches) and the name of the advertiser. All this goes in the top left corner.

In the top right is an "inventory" of the materials for the ad. The first sheet of copy is noted as *1 of 1*, if there is only a single sheet. If there are more than one sheet, the top page is *1 of 2* or *1 of 3*, etc. (The second sheet then becomes *2 of 2* or *2 of 3*.) The next item is: Dummy. Then list any engravings, photos, sig cuts, or stereotype matrices separately.

The object of the inventory is to enable the printer to determine if all the necessary material is on hand; if anything is missing it can be traced immediately and save the anguish of discovering a gap as the paper is ready to go to press.

All the copy is specced as to type face, size, ledding, and style to be used in setting.

The size of the ad is written on the dummy, too. This is to insure against mistakes the layout man may have made when he drew out the basic area.

Only rarely are individual proofs of ads furnished for student publications. The staff usually sees the made-up ad for the first time in page proofs. These, of course, come when time is getting short and pressure mounts. But ads should be proofread as zealously as the news.

★ Check first that the size is correct.

★ Then notice whether the layout is correct and whether the proper pictures have been used.

★ Then check the headlines for typos.

★ Now move down and read body type.

★ Check the price.

A mistake here is embarrassing to the merchant and a calamity to the staff.

★ Finally be sure that the sig cut is in the ad and properly placed.

Page 4 The Arthur Hill News, Saginaw, Michigan, Friday, September 29, 1961

Wiechmanns

PL 7-0461

FOOTBALL'S HERE!

Go Hillites! Support your Lumberjacks from season's start to end. Be prepared for coming games and look collegiate in top campus fashions from Wiechmann's.

"He's Out For An 80-Yard Pass!"

George is perfectly suited to any occasion in his dark olive green corduroy Campus Coat . . . with the warm sherpa pile lining, just right for football weather. ($35.00)

"Tonight After The Game? Sure!"

Sharon will look her best for the date in her plaid pleated skirt ($8.98) with a classic shetland type cardigan to match. ($7.98)

The striped cardigan sweater by Jantzen ($14.95) looks great on George, co-ordinated with Rambl-Top slacks ($5.98) by Farah.

Fig. 40. Full-page ad directed to students' tastes and needs and tied in with opening of football season. Students model garments. (Courtesy *Arthur Hill News,* Arthur Hill High, Saginaw, Mich.)

CALDWELL'S

salutes

WILLETTA TUCKER

Willetta, senior, works after school and on weekends at the Capri Theater. Willetta is business manager of the Little Harvester paper.

WELL'S

BUFFETERIA
2014 N. HOBART

AL BURGER
HOBART

Soon each senior will be walking the last mile to receive a diploma, his key to the future.

To Carol Frazer, one of the seniors this year, it was a great year of games, parties, and exams . . . truly a perfect year to climax school days.

Some of the activities which Carol has enjoyed this year are annual staff, Spanish Club, Future Teachers, Quill and Scroll, Junior Red Cross, and advertising for the Little Harves-

D R

110 North Cuyler

presents

Fashion Model

WILLETA LOWTHER

Willeta, senior, is wearing a white organza formal designed by Nat Cantor. The fitted bodice is made up of tiny pleats. The full, flowing skirt has a lavender over-skirt which is sprinkled with white butterflies.

Willeta is a twirler in the Harvester Band, a member of All-Regional Band, and a member of Who's Who in Pampa High School.

113 North Cuyler MO 5-5715

Fig. 41. Advertisers salute seniors and use students as models for garments in these ad campaigns in *Little Harvester* of Pampa (Tex.) High.

If there is corollary material with the sig—address, phone, shopping hours, etc.—check them with particular care.

Because elements in ads are pretty well separated from each other, it's all too easy to overlook some of them.

★ It is wise to tick off every line with a red pencil as you read proof on it.

Then have someone else check first of all whether you have read everything and then to see if there are any errors you overlooked.

Advertising is interesting work. It is an opportunity for service and for creativity. It is important work. It should be tackled just as any other responsible task is. The rewards are many and the greatest of these is the satisfaction that comes from doing a big job well.

14. *Circulation*

The lifeblood of a newspaper

The title of this chapter would be as appropriate in a book on physiology as this one on journalism—for circulation means life in both subjects.

The finest news coverage and writing, pictures, editorials, and advertising are literally useless unless and until read. It is the job of the circulation department to make sure there are readers.

There are three basic kinds of circulation of professional newspapers; student publications use the same, although often with variations.

Free circulation is just that; it delivers papers without charge to everyone within a specified area. In the professional field, free-circulation papers are usually anathema. In many instances they are *shoppers,* filled completely with advertising. Professional newspapers despise shoppers; they consider it unfair competition to sell advertising without any overhead for the news department. They feel the shopper is riding, undeservedly, on the reputation of legitimate newspapers.

But many a real newspaper has begun as a free-circulation publication until it gained reader acceptance and could establish a paid circulation list.

Forced circulation isn't quite as ruthless as it may sound. This is the system whereby the price of a subscription is included in some other fee. A person who joins the National Forbisider Association automatically receives a subscription to the "Forbisider Journal" and part of his dues are earmarked for that purpose.

Paid circulation is the most highly desired. It is a prerequisite for a publication to receive second-class mail privileges, the official cachet, as it were, of a real newspaper. Newspaper advertising salesmen stress that those publications with paid circulation are best read because the reader obviously wants them and welcomes them into his home or office.

Circulation for professional newspapers is further broken down into home delivery, street sales, and mail subscriptions.

Let's see how the three basic categories are used by student staffs.

Obviously there is no such thing as "free" circulation. Someone has to pay for producing a newspaper. The professional paper has to raise its advertising rates; the student paper usually has to be subsidized by the school.

Most administrators are happy to provide such a subsidy. They know that a good student paper is invaluable in informing the student body —and its parents and public—and in creating a wholesome school spirit. Many credit the paper highly for helping establish and maintain high standards of scholarship, citizenship, and service.

Free circulation enables 100% circulation. This is a potent asset to advertising salesmen.

It also simplifies the job of circulation. The simplest way to circulate a free paper is to distribute piles of them at strategic points in the building. A more effective way is to deliver proper quantities to each home room. Then an absent student is assured of getting a copy on his return.

In case of subsidized circulation, advertising revenues are used to reduce the subsidy or to provide a fund for acquiring certain "luxuries" —new typewriters, furnishings for the newspaper office, keys for staff recognition, or an annual picnic or party.

If the school is working on a tight budget and the principal just can't find funds to support the paper, the staff may seek help from the PTA, the lettermen's or alumni association, local service clubs, or similar civic-minded groups.

★ Free circulation is ideal for the student paper; it is worth a great deal of effort to achieve.

Forced circulation is frequent in schools. The price of the paper is included in the student activity ticket, which is sold under many names. Sometimes the student becomes a member of the general organization and obtains a subscription automatically. In most schools, membership in the GO—or SO or SU, or whatever it's called—is so close to 100% that forced subscriptions give practically the same coverage as free circulation.

Paid circulation is the greatest challenge to the student staff. To get adequate coverage, the circulation department must plan and perform a man-sized job.

Circulation campaigns may be conducted at the start of each semester or at the beginning of the school year. It is wise to make the big effort as school starts in the fall and to sell as many yearly subscriptions as possible. If your school has a midyear graduating class, then provisions must be made, of course, for those students who will be leaving at the end of the first semester and want a subscription only until that time.

★ Subscriptions are best handled through home rooms.

A popular circulation device is to shoot for 100% home room coverage. A circulation quota is set—one subscription per student with allowances for those who have brothers or sisters in school; usually one subscription a family is counted as all that's necessary. The home room pays for the total subscription cost in any way it likes. Some rooms have a treasury which they maintain through parties or group projects. It's easy to pay the lump subscription sum from such a source.

Some home rooms ask each student to pay the price of his own subscription. Some accept contributions beyond this sum in order to furnish subscriptions for those students who cannot afford to pay for their own.

Ours is an "affluent society," we are constantly told. Most of us need not really worry about the wherewithal to buy our family's necessities—and most of us have something left over for luxuries. So we tend to forget—or not even understand—that for some students a dollar, or even a half-dollar, is a staggering sum.

It is embarrassing to the student who just can't buy his own subscription. He is too proud to say that his father is sick and that his mother's meager earnings are too small to support a family. Often unthinking classmates may chide him for failing his home room in making a 100% record. The result is a hurt, resentful person whose school days may be clouded by such an unhappy experience. Any arrangement so such a student will not be left out—nor made to feel like a charity case—is one to be sought.

The reward for a 100% room is a reduction in the price, usually 25%.

The same inducement can be offered to individual subscribers who buy their subscription before a specified deadline.

A well-planned subscription campaign can be a lot of fun for the staff and for the whole school. Plans should be well in hand before school closes in the spring so things can open with a bang in the fall.

The best way to sell any merchandise is to give the prospect a sample. So many staffs try to have the first edition of their paper available free to all students on the first day of school.

Organize the circulation staff so that every home room will be covered at the same time. This usually means enlisting the help of editorial and advertising staffers and other student leaders.

At a pep meeting for these solicitors, explain in detail—and with enthusiasm—what their duties are. Give them a list of the sales points that will convince their classmates to subscribe.

Each solicitor is given a receipt book, usually one that provides duplicate copies. Each subscriber is given a receipt; the carbon goes to the circulation manager.

★ Have solicitors report daily.

This not only minimizes chances for errors, it removes the temptation of having newspaper money in a solicitor's pocket. Your students are honest; they're not going to misappropriate funds. But it is easy to spend money inadvertently and then, when the delayed day for settling accounts comes around, the solicitor finds himself short of cash.

Often it is possible to give added inducements—beyond a price reduction—to subscribers. In some communities, merchants are happy to offer some special deal to subscribers. In several places, operators of movie theaters give a dime reduction on tickets when the subscriber presents his receipt.

Lapel buttons that identify subscribers are an excellent sales gimmick. Some schools allow subscribers to vote for Homecoming Queen or in other popularity contests.

Rivalry between home rooms or organizations is a wholesome spur. The first room to turn in a 100% record may be given a trophy or allowed to name a queen or even (if the principal is particularly sympathetic) skip an afternoon of classes without penalty.

Competition among solicitors is equally effective. The winning salesman may receive a free activities ticket or a season's pass for basketball. Or his feat may give him extra points in meeting Quill and Scroll Society requirements or toward earning a school letter or key.

★ Concentrate the campaign to one week—and make that a week of constant ballyhoo.

School rooms and corridors should be filled with posters. The smart circulation manager enlists the aid of the art teacher who may assign such posters as class projects the previous spring.

Arrange a special assembly early during the sale week. As your guest speaker ask a local newspaperman; no one can sell a student publication with as much enthusiasm and authority as a professional in the field.

Your school band probably won't be at concert peak this early in the year. But there are always instrumental groups that will be pleased to play at the main entrance as school closes or in the cafeteria during lunch hour to keep the carnival atmosphere.

While most soliciting will be done in home rooms, there should be other times and places where students can subscribe. A table in the lunch room and at main entrances will attract many subscribers.

Such a campaign, obviously, requires the cooperation of the principal and faculty members. This is usually proffered willingly. But the wise circulation manager will make formal—and early—request. The principal should be approached in the spring. Perhaps the faculty can be addressed at a meeting before school opens.

★ The student body should be kept informed on the progress of the subscription campaign.

The most common device is a thermometer in the main hall or entrance that shows results approaching the quota. Some students think this is too corny and dream up amusing variations; but the basic graph idea is the same—and good.

During the campaign, record-keeping must be meticulous. After the campaign, it is essential.

Long before the big push begins, lists should be compiled of every student in school, grouped by home rooms. (The school office, politely approached, will be happy to help make such lists.)

Solicitors report at a given time each day. They turn in their money and are given their own receipt. From the carbon copies of subscribers' receipts, names are checked off the master list. Many circulation managers keep two such masters; with two persons checking names, errors can be minimized, they believe.

The circulation manager keeps a ledger in which he enters the amount each solicitor has turned in.

All these records are invaluable; a safe storage space should be provided for them and an inflexible rule established that they never be taken from the room.

After the campaign is over, and all rewards have been given, the circulation department has the responsibility of delivering papers to subscribers.

At a specific time on publication day, delivery should be made to home rooms. If the room has 100% subscription, the job is easy; just give the teacher or president the necessary number of copies.

Otherwise the messenger should have a list of subscribers in each room. As each student receives his copy, a check is made after his name.

★ If a student is absent, his name should be written on a copy which is given to the teacher to await the absentee's return.

Some schools have experimented with central distribution points and the check-off system. The subscriber is given a card—or it may be his student organization card—with designated areas to be punched or inked when he receives his paper. This takes time, results in traffic jams, and is generally unpopular.

If there is a sizable segment of the student body which is not covered by subscriptions, sales stands for individual copies should be set up at convenient points in the school.

Individual copies may also be sold at stores near the school. The merchant is allowed a small commission. The circulation department delivers a specified number to the merchant who signs a receipt for them. At the end of the week, the unsold copies are picked up, the cost of the sold copies is figured, the merchant's commission is deducted, and payment is made. A receipt is given at this time by the student.

The circulation man should check such sales outlets frequently and replenish exhausted supplies.

It is usually the job of the circulation department to pick up papers from the printer. Often this department takes on the responsibility of delivering copy to the printer as well.

All this discussion has been directed to circulation within the student body. But there is another body of prospective readers that should not be overlooked.

Teachers are as interested in the school paper as the students are. Many staffs provide complimentary subscriptions to the faculty, administration—at the school and at higher levels—and members of the service staffs, secretaries, custodians, cafeteria workers, etc. This is tendered as a token of appreciation for the cooperation these people give so willingly and frequently to the student staff.

Sometimes teachers insist on buying subscriptions. These may be at regular rates or ones set especially for such helpful personnel.

Alumni, especially recent ones, like to read the school paper to keep track of old friends and acquaintances. Graduates who go on to college are especially eager to maintain ties with their old school. The wise circulation manager will sell mail subscriptions to seniors (or their parents) in the spring.

Other alumni can be contacted by letters in the fall. Such mailings should contain a simple order blank and an envelope in which to return the order and money. Members of civic organizations that have a special interest in schools should also be contacted.

The best prospect list, of course, is current mail subscribers. A letter should remind them of the approaching expiration of their subscription and invite them to renew it.

It is, of course, the duty of the circulation department to mail copies as soon as the paper is printed. For most schools, the best way to mail single copies is in envelopes. Very inexpensive ones are now available from almost any paper merchant, and the printer himself probably has a supply.

If papers are *single-wrapped*, care should be taken that copies are not rolled into tight little cylinders. When the subscriber opens his copy, it fairly explodes in his face and he doesn't know if he's supposed to be reading a newspaper or playing an accordion. Paste should be applied carefully to the wrapper so it doesn't stick to the paper and perhaps tear the copy as the wrapper is removed.

The free list, complimentary and exchange subscriptions, serves the useful purpose discussed in Chapter 3. But this list has a tendency to grow like Jack's beanstalk. It should be inspected regularly and pruned frequently. Each copy of your paper costs money to produce; too many frees may become a bothersome financial burden.

It is usually a function of the circulation department to decide—or help decide—the price of subscriptions or single copies. This is always a pesky decision for any publication to have to make.

The selling price of any item is determined primarily by the cost to manufacture it. The financing of a student paper has a major bearing on the setting of rates. Normally a staff tries to obtain one-third of its production cost from circulation, with the other two-thirds from advertising and/or subsidies.

To determine this sum, the staff must know the cost of an issue, or, better yet, of a page. Remember that there are many costs that are easy to overlook.

The major expense is typesetting, makeup, and printing. This is usually covered in a single bill from the printer. Engravings are a sizable cost; are they covered in your printer's bill or does the engraver charge the staff directly? Photography costs are easy to overlook although they are substantial.

Also included in your costs are paper and other supplies (if not furnished by the school); transportation of copy, proofs, and people to and from the print shop; postage and telephone, and—don't overlook this—your free list.

An average subscription price is 75¢ a year or 45¢ a semester. Single copies usually sell for a nickel or, most frequently, a dime.

Frequency of issue determines subscription price; a monthly can't charge as much as a bi-weekly, unless it delivers an equal number of pages during the year. The size of the page has some, but usually only minor, bearing on the price. The major determinant is always the quality of the paper. If the staff does a good job, the circulation manager's job becomes easy.

It is wise to enlist the counsel of the advisor, the printer, the business arithmetic teacher, and the principal in establishing subscription prices.

The experienced circulation manager knows that he can get best coverage when the paper appears regularly. So he will keep in close touch with the editorial staff and encourage it to meet deadlines so press day will become established in the mind of the student body as something to look forward to with anticipation—and assurance that the paper will be out when they expect it.

This is just another example of the fact that a newspaper cannot operate with several independent departments doing their jobs in hermetically sealed areas. On a newspaper, student or professional, everybody's job depends upon another person's. Few organizations demand the close and harmonious cooperation of people of so many disparate talents and skills. The circulation staff is the final, and indispensable, link in a long and intricate progression. It deserves the best people and their best performance.

BOOK THREE

The School Magazine

15. *The Creative Magazine*

Showcase of student work

While the "literary" magazine was the first scholastic publication in American schools, its popularity has waned since the past century. According to records of the Columbia Scholastic Press Association, there are approximately 16,000 newspapers published by schools but less than 2,000 magazines.

More's the pity!

A school magazine serves a useful purpose. It is the showcase of creativity. Every creative person works for an audience; he needs the stimulus of public exposure of his work. Sure, some literary works have lain in attic trunks, locked by the creator's admonition, "Don't publish this!" But, in most instances, the tone of such writings—and the care with which they were copyread—hints strongly that the author had high hopes his orders would be disobeyed.

School magazines can raise the level of all creative activity in a school. They should concern themselves not only with literary creations in all its varieties, but with fine arts, drama, speech, and science projects.

Many student "newspapers" that appear only at long intervals might serve their schools and readers better if they added a magazine format to their magazine publication schedule.

Each high school magazine grows out of its accumulated traditions and its special environment. This is as it should be.

In some schools, the magazines grow almost exclusively from courses in creative writing and are showplaces for the exceptionally good class work. Short stories, essays, opinion articles, and poems written as school assignments are screened for eventual publication. This is good as far as it goes, but it excludes both nonliterary achievements and writing done outside of class.

In other places, the magazine serves as both a repository for good creative work and a channel for reporting news happenings. This combines the traditional newspaper and the literary magazine into a single publication.

In still other schools, the magazine serves as an installment of a yearbook and tells the unfolding story of the academic year as it takes place. If bound together at the end of the school year, magazines of this type might replace an annual. In some localities where this is done, the yearbook has been discontinued.

Each of these variations requires a different staff organization and method for handling copy. If the publication prints predominantly material from creative writing classes, editors have to work closely with teachers of these sections and, if at all possible, have the faculty make assignments that follow requirements for a diversified table of contents. Such close relationships with appropriate teachers keep the editor from being as free-wheeling as his colleague on a school newspaper. However, if students and faculty are successful in obtaining superior yet varied work, then the resulting publication will reflect favorably on all concerned: school, administration, magazine, teachers, editorial staff, and authors.

The staff on a literary magazine may be much smaller than that on a student newspaper. Much of the material in a paper has to be staff-written, while generally only part of the contents of a literary publication is done by staff members. This corresponds with the prevailing practices of professionals in these two fields. Newspapers cover and edit news as it happens; most magazines select much of their material from outside sources.

Art for a school literary magazine may be drawings, paintings, or photographs. A newer trend in mass circulation magazines is to use photographs rather than conventional drawings and sketches to illustrate short stories and articles; high school editors should study leading magazines and adapt for their purposes any attractive ideas that they find. Certainly they should always keep in mind that a good photograph is far more satisfactory than bad fiction, inferior drawings, or poor poems.

Editors also should remember that the good school magazine depicts three-dimensional creativity. A clay sculpture is as worthy of recording as a short story. A well-made piece of furniture from the woodshop is as much a work of art as a sonnet. A skillful stage set is as noteworthy as an essay.

If a school magazine properly performs its function, there will be constant need for *documentary photography* of creative work in three dimensions: sculpture and mobiles, wood and metal objects, stage miniatures and sets, anything that cannot be recorded in type.

We must digress here for a moment to discuss student cartoons. They have great appeal but they also have inherent booby traps. Student humor is rather primitive; it constantly verges on cruelty and poor taste. More school magazines—and their staffs—have been immersed in hot water because of cartoons than for any other reason. Cartoonists often think it's uproariously funny to sneak some questionable gag past the editor and advisor. They must be taught to concentrate their humor in their work, not on practical jokes. The editor must always be alert to assure that all cartoons are legitimately funny and that there is no ill-considered innuendo that might escape casual notice.

Art work will be determined chiefly by the available excellence. If you have good photographers and few, if any, artists for sketches and drawings, then use photographs. If you have good artists but no good photographers, then use drawings and sketches. If your school produces superior nonliterary accomplishments, then emphasize them rather than stories, articles, and poems.

★ Like the written portions of a school magazine, art work should be geared to the ideas conveyed and to student resources.

Planning the Contents

The *progression* of a magazine, the way its contents are placed, contributes much to the pleasure of the reader.

A professional magazine editor once gave this formula:

> A magazine must be arranged like a symphony. There are many motifs and movements, but each, as well as being a pleasant thing in itself, must be woven into every other.
>
> Each issue must have something to make you mad and to make you sad; something to annoy you and something to inspire you; something to make you think and something to make you relax.

Another editor said:

> I edit my magazine for a couple I know well. While I know that Walt and Thelma won't both like everything in the *book* [the trade's name for a magazine], I want one or the other of them to like every piece. If Walt or Thelma—or Walt and Thelma—don't like a piece, I can't find room for it.

The student editor will find it useful to edit his magazine for two students, a boy and a girl whom he knows well. He must make sure, of course, that Sam is interested in things other than sports and Daisy other than boys. They must be typical, not longhairs or juvenile delinquents.

When one of the authors edited a service magazine, his formula was: The first story is about the whole division; then comes one on an individual; then one on a regiment (the largest subdivision of a division), one on a squad (15 men), one on a company (125 men), an individual again, and finally a strong piece that should interest and involve all the readers.

Remember, though, that no editing can be done strictly by formula. The editor must constantly make judgments on what to use and what to discard. Few editors—including those of school magazines—have to worry about filling space; the problem usually is an overload of material.

Two things that these "magic recipes" all stress are:

★ Involve the reader, "hit him where he lives."

★ Use the widest variety of subject, style, length, and layout to attract as many readers as possible.

Opening and closing sections of a magazine require unusual care. If an interesting cover has attracted the reader to open the magazine, he immediately ought to find an equally interesting story to arrest his attention. Too often he finds the Table of Contents. For school magazines, this index isn't needed at all; almost no one reads or uses it.

★ Get a smash story on your first spread.

★ Get a strong feature on your last spread.

To use our symphonic analogy again, a good musical composition comes to a definite end. But too many magazines just peter out. The reader must be left on the "upbeat." He must have a feeling that the symphony ended in a blare of trumpets and a rich chord. This requires a good story, well displayed, for the last spread, not just the tails of stories that have been jumped from earlier pages.

Selecting a good short story, feature article, or poem from those submitted for publication always presents problems. For instance, how do you know it's good? Well, the first thing is to ask: Do YOU like it? This is not the only criterion that an editor should use in making his choices but it may be an important one. This assumes, of course, that you are not too different from your classmates. If you like judo and all the rest like baseball and football, maybe your reactions can't be trusted too far. Ditto if you rave about Chaucer while all the rest of your literature class like Ernest Hemingway, J. D. Salinger, or T. S. Eliot.

Personal whims of an editor should not be the sole qualifying ground for acceptance. As we said earlier, an editor may visualize a typical boy and girl (or maybe a cross-section of his classmates) and ask himself: Will THEY like it? In trying to ascertain his answer, he should be just as objective as a judge on a state supreme court. His personal bias and prejudices should be kept well under control. If the work passes this test, then it should be printed with the hope that it will give the public (readers) what they want. This is one justification heard in professional circles for printing some materials.

Still another test should be the effectiveness of the work under consideration. Does it do what it sets out to do? If it is a suspense story, does it hold the reader's attention to the end—or can you guess the solution before you are halfway through? If it is a sonnet, are the internal and external poetic patterns preserved—or is it just a sloppy jingle in masquerade? If it is a feature, is the research accurate and complete—or are many questions in the reader's mind left unanswered?

These same basic qualifying standards apply to visual work as well as written copy.

To answer some of these questions about excellence, a student editor may wish to consult his staff colleagues or faculty members. This is a good idea, especially if he is not quite sure in his own mind. There is nothing wrong with this cooperative effort—unless the editor uses it to avoid his own responsibility for decision. As he talks over various points about style and structure with others, an editor will be adding to his own set of standards and preparing himself for better decisions in the future.

Now let's look at some of the problems for each kind of copy in a high school literary magazine. Each offers its own particular questions, so generalizations are not too common.

Essays and opinion articles have a noble and honorable history that may appeal to a minority of student writers who have something to say and can say it exceptionally well. Editors should keep in mind, however, that high school students, in most cases, are not experts on the complexities of the United Nations or the intricate techniques of modern advances in science or medicine. Students are experts on teenage problems and their own adjustments to living in the second half of the mixed-up 20th century.

The late Heywood Broun, sports writer, columnist, and first president of the American Newspaper Guild, was asked once why he wrote so many columns about himself and his opinions. He replied, "On these, I am the world's greatest living authority." High school students might well follow his example.

★ Write essays and comments about subjects on which you have background, experience, and knowledge.

In essays and opinion features, students should not try to ape the historically interesting but antiquated styles of essayists of hundreds of years ago as found in English literature textbooks. Remember that if these essayists were living in the 1960's they, too, would write differently.

★ Always keep your audience in mind and write for it.

A few English teachers may want their students to pattern their initial essays along the patterns of long ago. If so, there is little reason why a literary publication is compelled to print them. They are like finger exercises of a great musician—necessary but not great art. If class work is restricted to this type during the initial weeks before the first issue of a magazine, an editor may (1) save some juniors' work from the spring semester, (2) get the teacher to permit a few exceptions to the general assignments by exceptionally gifted students, or (3) request articles written outside of class assignments.

One variation on the opinion article is a round-up of what a cross section of typical or prominent students in your high school think about a certain topic of importance. For instance, you might consider printing an article on "going steady" or on preparing for college entrance exams. These would be deeper than a series of "inquiring reporter" answers and could reflect the high school students' thinking as a whole. Among the adult population, a number of agencies conduct polls regularly and their findings are followed with interest, especially during an election year. All efforts to gather information for an opinion feature require considerable time. In this case, you would be doing research in the field by interviewing fellow students instead of seeking out books, records, or individual experts.

Conventional feature articles certainly are entitled to considerable space in high school writing curricula and in school magazines. Increasingly in recent decades, mass circulation magazines have turned over more and more space to nonfiction, and most of these articles have been the traditional features.

Among the features, which were discussed in Chapter 6, are the interviews, historical or anniversary pieces, news interpretations, personality sketches or profiles, and seasonal articles. Practically everything that was said about features in the discussion under high school newspapers applies for magazine editors. One difficulty is that some teachers and students feel that feature articles are not entitled to a place in a "literary" magazine. This is unfortunate because it runs counter to what is happening in professional journalism.

Short stories are almost exclusively the province of literary magazines because of their absence from newspapers and yearbooks due to space limitations and philosophies of publication. However, some schools discover talented fiction writers, and they deserve a chance to see their work in print just as do writers of facts, features, and editorial comments. But quality and supply vary from year to year. Some editors have solved this difficulty by shifting the ratio of fiction, nonfiction, and poetry to fit the supply of excellence. While this precludes constant table of contents from issue to issue, it does gear the magazine to a high quality of material.

What plot and what locale should school short story writers select and their editors favor? Ones with which they are familiar.

What was said a little while ago about picking a topic for an essay or opinion article applies with equal force to fiction. There is no sense in a high school student in Minnesota writing a short story about a soldier's experience in the Korean War unless he has captured the real feeling of the situation from his father, older brother, uncle, or garrulous neighbor. (Of course, there are just enough exceptions to this generalization to prohibit making it an absolute injunction.)

★ A high school audience is most interested in fiction which relates to what most students have experienced.

Successful short stories, like effective feature articles, may help readers to discover things about themselves that they never before saw in quite such sharp focus. Ezra Pound, the poet, once described literature as "news that stays news." He meant that effective writing provides new insights for readers because it tells the truth with literary lighting effects just a bit different from those used previously; this gives the writing and reality a new link. Tribute of a rare sort is reflected in the comment, "Gee, I wish I had thought of that."

Good poetry, always elusive, is hard to find and even harder to measure. Archibald MacLeish, who should know since he is one of the United States widely respected poets, once wrote:

> A poem should be wordless
> As the flight of birds
> . . .
> A poem should not mean
> But be.

The young in heart (and that means, sometimes, the young in age, too) are our best poets. William Cullen Bryant wrote his memorable and most famous poem, "Thanatopsis," when he was 17 and long before he became a famous New York City newspaper editor.

In view of the admitted difficulty in finding superior short stories and poems, some editors have printed poor and sloppy work because it was the best they had on hand. This is a matter of conscience as well as expediency, and compromises should be kept to a minimum.

Some high schools blend a news magazine and literary publication into a single effort. If the two parts can be kept separated and without a clash of interests, then the editors have achieved their exacting assignment. Staff members have to keep in mind constantly that they have a dual function to perform. If they try too hard to kill two birds with one stone, they may have an editorial mixture that is a real "mix." Most editors will do well to allocate a special section of their magazine as a literary supplement to the news coverage of the rest of the publication.

Guidance given earlier in this chapter about a literary publication and that given in Chapters 5 and 6 about general newspaper coverage and philosophy apply to this combined magazine.

Regardless of the basic editorial philosophy, however, magazine editors face different problems in editing and makeup than their colleagues on school papers. One thing they share, though: They must be familiar with copyreading symbols and principles. These are basic for anyone who handles copy prepared for a printer. (See Chapter 7.)

What are some of these differences?

Editing a poem, for instance, is sacrilege. An editor's choice lies in accepting the writing intact or rejecting it. He may change not even a word or two—but he can suggest changes to the writer.

Editing a short story can be done—sparingly. But here, again, staff members are not permitted the same editorial privileges of rewriting allowed to newspaper copyreaders. Suggested changes in emphasis or length may be passed on to the author for his guidance in revising and cutting.

In essays or opinion articles, copyreaders and editors on a magazine have to insure that they are really polishing the writer's ideas and not changing his meanings. This may become a matter of editorial integrity, and, especially if a by-line is used, a writer has a quite proper complaint if substantial changes are made without his prior agreement.

Feature articles are closest to straight news stories in regard to editorial changes during copyreading, but even here caution should be exercised to make sure that proposed polishing or tailoring to space are almost the only reasons for extensive editing. This caution is especially required if the feature carries a by-line.

News stories to be printed in a magazine format may be handled exactly the same way as those edited for a newspaper format. Cutting to fit is done here as readily as for school papers.

Since magazine staff members have to visualize facing pages or even whole sections as single units rather than to concentrate just on makeup of a single page, copyreaders and editors have to be especially careful to keep track of how much space an article, poem, or essay will take. In most cases, they will select a filler to complete a page. This problem varies from that of a newspaper makeup man, who may jump stories from column to column and from front page to inside.

★ Final editorial responsibility always rests with the copy editor or his superior. But they have to abide by the rules.

Headings on material in a literary magazine serve a different function from those in a newspaper. For news copy, the headline writer seeks, in almost all cases, to give a capsule of the highlight of the story, to capture the essence of the news. For features, he tries to lure the reader into the article. This latter is the general rule for heads or titles on short stories, features, and poems. A magazine audience, it is assumed, will read material if it is interested; few readers scan the titles for fundamentals of current events, as is often done with news items, and then go on to others with the feeling that they know what the contents are.

An alluring magazine title will stop the readers' eyes, tempting them to dip into the piece and, hopefully, to complete it. But a title has to be more than attractive; it has to be accurate as well as in keeping with both the article's content and the magazine's general style.

★ Keep magazine titles attractive, accurate, and in harmony.

A whole array of headings may be used. Here is one breakdown for titles of features and opinion articles that may be helpful to an editor who feels that he must substitute a better one for the author's own *working title:*

1. Label heads.

The Problems of Going Steady

Things to Be Thankful For This Thanksgiving

2. Summary statements.

Why We Should Schedule Central High in Football

The Agonies of Being an Honor Student Frighten Me

3. Striking statements or phrases.

The Right to Talk Back

How to Get A's on All Your Exams

4. Descriptive phrases.

Those Hybrid Science Courses

Questionnaires for Teachers

5. Quotations.

I Wanted to Be Alone

The Lord Helps Those Who Help Themselves

6. Parodies and literary allusions.

The Fine Art of Class-Cutting

What This Country Needs Is . . .

7. Questions.

Curfew for Teen-agers?

WHAT MAKES A GOOD STUDENT GOOD?
National Honor Society Candidates Tell
What They Think the Answers Are

8. Direct Address.

You Should Stay in High School,
President and Principal Agree

You Were There

Titles on short stories and poems are designed to attract attention with a phrase or sentence, and about the only limitation is whether they are effective in explanation or in connotation.

Regardless of all the authors' right to have their works appear virtually as they wrote them, the copyreaders and editors bear the blame or praise for putting together an effective and respected publication. A high school publication is not the place for a writer to work out his neurotic symptoms or to get his revenge upon a classmate or teacher. If there are questions about poor taste, libel, irresponsible journalism, or similar problems, students should consult the chief editor or, if he is uncertain, the faculty advisor.

A poem, no matter how well it scans, may be in poor taste or libelous. So may any work, including pictures and other art. But these problems do not arise often.

As a showpiece of student creativity, the school magazine should always strive to attain the highest standards in all the fields it covers—literary work, three-dimensionally art, drawings, and photography. People on a successful staff will be helping all their classmates to put their best foot forward.

16. *Magazine Makeup and Art*

Attractive pages build readership

Letterpress, which dates back at least to the 15th Century, produces some excellent high school magazines. But a far newer method, *offset lithography,* has unusual advantages for this type of publication, and so this is an excellent occasion to explore the rudiments of the process.

Offset lithography (more commonly just *offset*) was invented in 1799—not very long ago in the history of the world. It is based on a much older axiom: "Oil and water won't mix."

Lithography, its original form, means "writing with a stone." Lithography is still used to print fine art; if we watch the lithographer at work, we can easily learn the principles involved.

On a smooth piece of stone, he draws his picture with greasy crayon or paint. Then he sloshes water all over the surface. The water wets the stone thoroughly, but the oily surface of the crayon repels the water.

With a little hand roller, a *brayer,* he now rolls ink across the face of the stone. The water repels the ink and keeps it away from the stone. But that greasy crayon welcomes the oily ink like kinfolk.

So now there is a layer of ink on top of the crayon image—and nowhere else. When a piece of paper is laid on the stone and pressed down, it picks up the ink and reproduces the original drawing.

The artist adds more water, then more ink, and is ready to print the second copy. This is lithography.

Offset lithography adds a new element: the first word in its name.

Instead of lithographing the image directly to the paper, as in the basic process, the newer method lithographs it onto a rubber blanket.

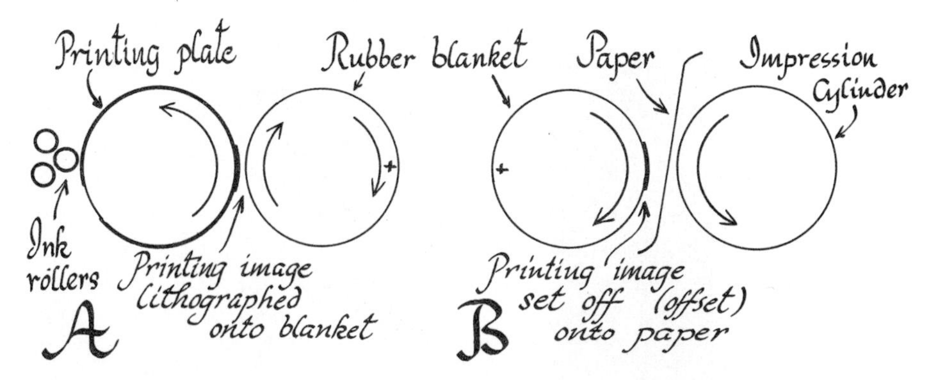

Fig. 42. Schematic of offset lithography. In A the image is lithographed from printing plate to rubber blanket. In B image is set-off from blanket to paper.

From here the image is *set off*—or offset—to the paper.

This explanation has been greatly simplified. But, no matter how deep into detail you plunge, the basis remains unchanged: Oil and water don't mix, and by utilizing this principle you can produce a good school magazine.

No longer does the printer use a slab of stone; he uses thin plates of aluminum, or even cardboard. The artist needn't draw the image by hand; it is put on the plate photographically (by almost the same methods of photoengraving discussed in Chapter 10).

Offset presses come in many sizes, from those that print on letterhead-size sheets to those that print for billboards. The metal plate is wrapped around one cylinder, the paper around another; the press buzzes along with the great speed of any rotary press.

A major advantage of offset is that the student staff can do most of the work of preparing a plate. This cuts down costs and also affords opportunity for fascinating creative work for the student.

Offset Production

There are several methods for preparing copy for offset plates. Let's examine the simplest.

Type is set by hand, by Linotype, or by typewriter (of which more in the next chapter). The printer furnishes a *reproduction proof,* a *repro,* which is printed, with great care, on special paper.

Art—hand or photo—is prepared in the customary manner (which is discussed in Chapter 10). This is sent to the platemaker who prepares line or halftone negatives. From these he makes *blueprints* which will be used in pasting up.

When all materials are on hand, the staff artist—or whoever else is charged with this job—begins the makeup process.

On a sheet of smooth drawing paper or Bristol board, he marks the outside dimensions, margins, and column areas with a light blue pencil. This blue is invisible to the camera's eye during platemaking and so

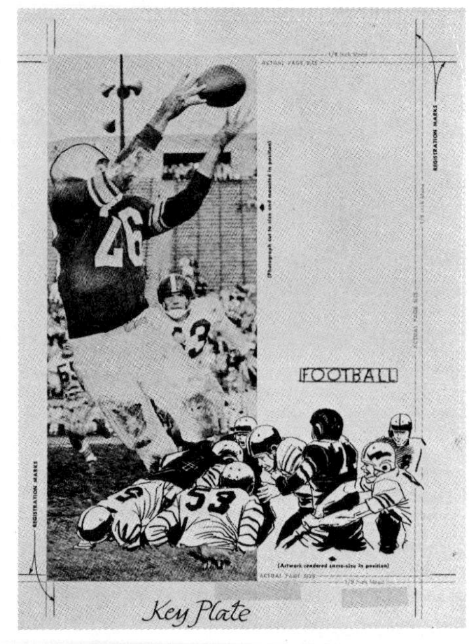

Fig. 43. Mechanical separation for two-color printing. Key plate is printed in black and combines halftone and line art.

Overlay is drawn in black ink but the plate made from this art is printed in blue.

On opposite page is the printed result. Area in gray here was printed in bright blue. Note how headline type has been placed according to instructions given on key plate. (Courtesy Wm. J. Keller, Inc.)

doesn't have to be erased.

With great care, especially to keep lines horizontal, he pastes down the repro proofs where they are to appear on the finished job. Where pictures are to appear, he pastes the blueprints. But these—the *blues*—are just tacked down, pasted lightly. The platemaker will use them only for instructions on positioning; he will *strip in* the negatives, from which the blues were made, into a negative that he makes of the rest of the page.

When line art is used, it can be drawn same-size and pasted down with the type.

When the entire page has been pasted up, the result is a *pasteup* (logically enough) or a *mechanical.* From this is made the printing plate.

In commercial plants, repros are coated with a thin layer of wax as an adhesive. The student pasteup man uses rubber cement. If this is applied thinly, the paper can be removed and repasted if it must be moved. A permanent bond is made when both the paper and the drawing board are coated with cement. This is allowed to dry so it is just barely tacky. When the two cemented surfaces are placed together, they stick like Damon to Pythias. So you'd better be sure to get the

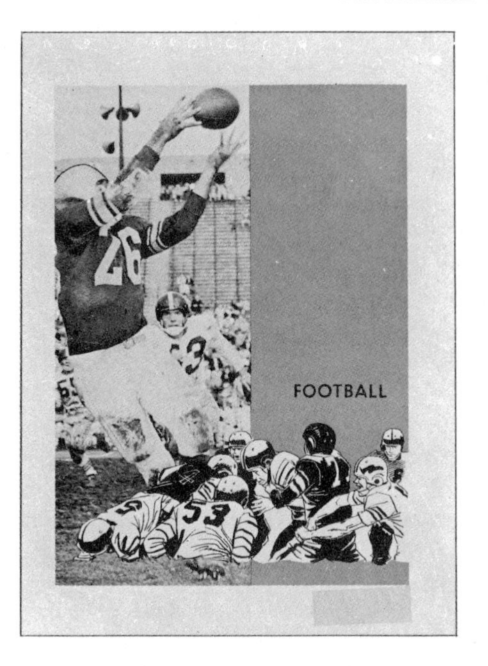

paper in the right place; there's no opportunity for second guessing.

The pasteup man works on a drawing board or table and uses a T-square and triangle constantly to be sure his work is in horizontal and vertical alignment. This procedure takes time but it is of the utmost importance.

The printer is asked to furnish two or three copies of repro proofs. In case of calamity there will be a spare. Proofs are protected by a *fixative*, a clear plastic coating applied from a "bomb" container.

All elements should be pasted down as flat as possible. A lifted edge casts a shadow which must be painted out—*opaqued*—from the negative. This takes time and money. When elements are cut up, prior to pasting, they should have a margin of at least an eighth of an inch all around. This is to make sure that during the opaquing—if any—there is enough room so the paint doesn't inadvertently cover some of the type.

Many offset houses furnish *pasteup sheets*. These show the page dimensions and are covered by a grid of lines one pica apart, all in "invisible" light blue. These sheets enable a constant check that elements are positioned properly and squarely. Such sheets are so useful that it is a good investment to have some printed up for your magazine if the printer doesn't furnish them.

Small pages are always pasted up in pairs. But remember that only at the center fold do two companion pages face each other. Page 2, for instance, will be pasted up—just as it is printed—with the second-last page of the magazine. Page 3 goes with the third-last, and so on.

Larger pages are often pasted up separately; the platemaker pairs them up with the proper buddy as he makes the offset plate.

Color can be used inexpensively in offset. This requires *mechanical separations.*

Fig. 43 shows a typical magazine cover in two colors, black and blue. Here's how the artist prepared the copy.

On a drawing board he drew those elements which print in black, the *key copy*. Then he placed an overlay, of clear acetate, over the first drawing. On this overlay he drew those elements which print in blue. He used black ink on the overlay; the plate is made just as any other one, and doesn't become a "blue" plate until it is printed in blue ink (indicated by gray in our reproduction).

To make sure that the plates will print in proper positions, the artist puts a *register mark* on both the key and the overlay. These must superimpose precisely. During printing the pressman must make the blue and black register marks fit just as exactly. When they do overprint precisely, he knows all the other elements will be *in register*. If the marks don't fit, it is easy to see how much higher or lower and/or how far to either side the blue plate must be moved to obtain true register. Register marks are so placed that they are trimmed off the final product or hidden in the fold.

The same technique is used for adding color to inside pages.

Color should be used in such a way that it can be several points out of register without spoiling the effect.

Color is useful as a *tint block* on magazine pages. Large areas of color provide a background on which type is *overprinted, surprinted.* Magazine use is identical with that in yearbooks as discussed in Chapter 22.

Colors can be combined to create intermediate hues. In the cover (Fig. 43) we've just discussed, the artist could have put small dots or fine lines in certain areas of both the blue and black plates. The printed results would appear as dark blue. The ratio of density of the two colors would determine the shade of blue.

Offset also produces particularly fine *process color* (discussed in Chapter 22) but usually this is too expensive for school magazines. It is possible, though, to buy preprinted full-color magazine covers at low cost or to obtain color work which the Chamber of Commerce or some other organization has had printed, then adapt this material as a magazine cover.

Occasionally a staff will print the cover on gift wrappings or wall paper, thus obtaining color at a fraction of the cost of regular color work.

But we are getting ahead of ourselves. Before we can make plates, we must have the components of the pages. Let's look at them.

Body type is as important to a magazine as to any publication. The same qualities of readability discussed in Chapter 9 are essential in magazine as well as newspaper work. There is a tendency to use larger type—9- or 10-point—for magazines. The size of the page and the width of the column of your magazine are determining factors; the larger the page, the larger the type.

Headlines can be set on the Linotype or Ludlow as for newspapers, with Artype or similar *stick-on letters;* or handlettering can be used—if it's good.

Much of the art in a magazine will be the creative work the publication displays, the product of art classes, hobby clubs, photographers, and the like.

It is best if hand art is done with a *monochromatic palette.* The artist uses only one color; black, blue, and brown are favorites although it can be any. He darkens or lightens the basic color by adding black or white to it. The result will reproduce well in the black-white-gray "palette" of the printer.

If full-color work is to be reproduced in black-and-white, the original art can be sent to the platemaker. But it's a better idea to take a *b & w* photograph and send that. The photo will show whether the original colors will reproduce with enough tonal variation in black-and-white to give the effect of the painting.

If paintings are photographed, care must be taken that glossy oils do not reflect a *hot spot,* a burst of light that hides detail.

Offset is ideally suited to watercolors and wash drawings, to original lithographs, etchings, woodblocks, linoleum prints, or, in fact, any medium used by any student artist.

Photographs reproduce well, too. The screen used in offset is at least 144-line, much finer than that normally used for letterpress.

Line drawings reproduce well and have many uses in a magazine. Student cartoons are always favorites of the reader. *Spots,* little decorative elements that may or may not be related to adjacent copy, add interest to the page. "The New Yorker" uses spots admirably; look at them.

Line work is done in India ink for any process.

If the school magazine properly performs its function, there will be constant need for documentary photography of creative work in three dimensions, as was pointed out in the previous chapter. Documentary pictures, which record in detail, need sacrifice no artistic quality. Indeed, the greatest documentaries combine a factual record with superlative esthetics. The student photographer assigned to this task will need complete mastery of lighting, focus, and composition.

Magazine Layout

Layout of magazine pages is similar to that of the yearbook. (The magazine art editor should read Chapter 22 with care.)

Like a yearbook, magazines are laid out in two-page units. The same principles of design apply to both publications, with two noteworthy differences. The magazine page is more closely tied to regular columns than is the yearbook; this is primarily because more copy must be carried in the magazine.

Jumping the gutter is more tricky in magazines. The gutter is the inside margins of two facing pages. This is a chasm that separates the pages, and the designer's job is to tie them into a single unit.

But the designer cannot, practically, jump the gutter by running a headline across both pages. Take a look at Fig. 44; it shows how a 16-page magazine is printed in a single *signature*. Suppose you were working on the page 4–5 spread. (A *spread* is a unit of two facing pages.) The pages are printed far apart and, if there is even a slight variation in folding or cutting to make the final magazine, the headline might not match up where it breaks from page 4 to 5.

If, as is the case in smaller magazines, printing is done two or four pages at a time, the possibility for misalignment becomes greater.

So the designer will use a headline which has a single line of large type on one page and a line or two of smaller type on the facing page. Then, if alignment is not perfect, it is not so obvious.

Improper lineup is even more apparent when a picture runs across the gutter. This practice should be avoided except on the center spread, which is printed as a single unit.

Using the buddy system, discussed in Chapter 13, for all the elements on both pages and making sure that elements orient to those on the facing page is the best way of jumping the gutter.

★ Always start a good story with a 2-page spread.

The impact of a spread is more than twice that of a single page. If a story takes two or more pages, use the spread to catch the reader. Too many magazines—including professional ones—start with a single page and then go to a spread. This is like shooting at a deer with a BB gun and then, only after he's running like mad, using a rifle.

The wooing of the reader starts with the cover, which may be done in one of three basic styles.

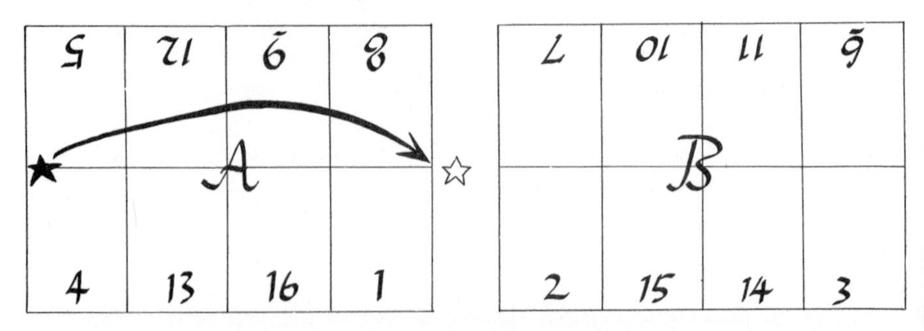

Fig. 44. Imposition chart for printing 16-page signature or magazine. Eight pages are printed at one time; then page is turned sideways so the star on left of A lies, face downward, at outline star. Then second form is printed so Page 2, on B, is on back of Page 1, etc.

FOOTBALL

The Season: Part I

In late August and early September of each year, an amazing phenomenon sweeps schools throughout the land: the football season. On the Hilltop, the good old American game of football has held a prominent place for many years. Marquette High has always been the team to beat in Catholic conference play; changed ball club. Time and again the hard running Maroon backs tore for five and six yard gains through the center of a hapless defense. This combination of running and a heat-wilted Hilltop resistance netted one touchdown and threatened another when Marquette seemed to stiffen. But a 21-yard touchdown pass broke its back. Behind, but not down, the Toppers drove twice within scoring range and twice their own mistakes wiped out the chance of a TD. It appears that the Chicago jinx, still quite in effect, would have to wait for St. George to be broken.

The Hilltoppers fared better against another Jesuit rival as they soundly spanked Campion 20-0. Marquette's Tom Fox and Mike Harrington ran Campion into the turf with a display of fine running. The "Fox" outlegged a pack of pursuers for a 67-yard TD and the "Hare" scampered through an opening to touchdown-land, 27 yards away. The renowned "Rough Rocks", mainstay of the last two title winning teams, threatened at times to crumble to soft sand, but again managed to look like concrete whenever the enemy got within scoring range. Shades of Tim Graf! Just when he showed real head crushing capabilities and had rumbled to a 15-yard touchdown, P. J. Pfannerstill was carried off the field with a sprained ankle. "Fuzz" recovered and Marquette had a victory under its belt.

SPORTS

Against St. George
Deflating the Dragon . . .

Photo—James Conklin of the Journal.
The Hare
With a Loyola hound in pursuit . . .

The third game was all Marquette. While holding newcomer Jordan scoreless, the Hilltoppers ran wild for 54 points. The "Fox" got two of his patented long ones on jaunts of 92 and 62 yards. The "Hare" got his two TD's on 2- and 22-yard plunges. Scallon smashed over, around, and through the Jordan defense to two touchdowns and the ground gainingest afternoon of his illustrious career. Brian Moffat got his first of the season on a 25-yarder, and Chuck Hausmann, only underclassman to score, slanted off tackle for six points.

St. George of Evanston came into town riding the crest of an undefeated season and a national ranking. They returned home a bunch of awfully deflated dragons. Marquette entered and left roaring like the proverbial lion. They were up for this game and from the first play of the game it showed. The Hilltopper backers cheered and chanted themselves to near delirium as their boys smashed St. George into a state of shock. Fox churned through the opposition's secondary for a 27-yard touchdown. Sheer beef and a hole in the Hilltop defense led to St. George's TD in the second half which knotted it at 7-all. They were on their way again, only to be rudely bounced back three consecutive times by a surprisingly powerful Marquette resistance. The teams engaged in a to-and-fro shoving match for the last eight minutes, leaving the final score: Milwaukee 7, Chicago 7.

The game represented the finest exhibition of defensive line play, crushing blocks, elusive running, desire, and rock 'em-sock 'em football that has graced M.U. stadium in many a year. St. George showed sparks of fine running in the person of Paul Camstrano and Marquette possesed a defense solid enough to stop him and his teammates.

This is the Marquette team picked to win the Catholic championship this year. St. George represented the biggest challenge to this rating so far. Coming through as they did, the Hilltoppers promise to be a mighty formidable opponent for anything the conference can dig up. Their assignments are carried out with precision, the blocking is crisp and effective, the line hits fast and hard, and the running is superb. In the Jordan game the team began to jell and the George game showed the depth and exciting, driving play Marquette is noted for. The non-conference "season" ended with M.U.H.S. 2-1-1. The Hilltoppers' vast improvement leaves them odds-on favorites to grab their third straight Catholic Conference crown.

—John Frey

7

Fig. 45. Typical page of news magazine. Gray panel at top of page was royal blue in original. (Courtesy *Flambeau Monthly* of Marquette University High, Milwaukee)

The *gallery cover* presents a picture for its own sake. "Saturday Evening Post" has made a tradition of its self-contained cover pictures.

The *mousetrap cover* is used by "Life" and "Look." It uses a picture (or more than one) to lure the reader directly to the main story. While the picture must be good and have much appeal in itself, its main job is to "sell" a specific story.

The *billboard cover* is used by "Harper's" and other magazines of that genre. It presents the titles of stories in that issue, depending on

I WONDERED HOW

I wondered how to love,
And then I saw the sun and earth
Communicate their love,
Rapturous beyond words.
Green trees grew
In its fire,
Flowers burst,
Melting rainbow rivers flowed
On new-warmed earth;
And tears of many autumns
Washed my watching eyes.

—SUE ELLEN SCOTT

Fig. 46. Literary magazine page combining pen-and-ink drawing and copy, short poem. (Courtesy *Acorn*, Jefferson Senior High, Roanoke, Va.)

the intellectual background of the reader to motivate him to enter and read.

Of course, always the cover has a fundamental job: to identify the magazine.

The nameplate or logo is the basic trademark of a magazine. It must meet the same requirements as those of a newspaper flag.

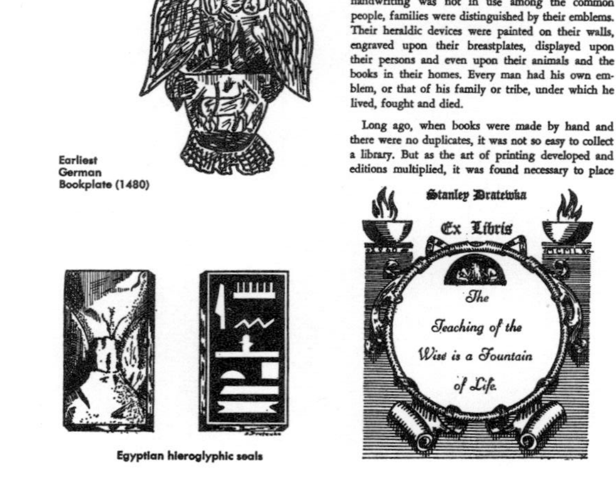

Ex Libris: The World of Bookplates

STANLEY DRATEWKA

A MAN'S signature is a personal thing— no less personal than the reflection of his face in a mirror. It therefore took me some time before I could bring myself to realize that signing my name on the fly-leaf was not exactly an ornament to a beautiful volume . . . but when I did come to this realization, I was ready to cross the threshold of *"Ex Libris"*: the world of bookplates.

Bookplates are rather rare these days, although the item itself is simple enough: merely a piece of paper, stamped with a name and a design, to indicate ownership of a volume. In this age of modern developments in every field, this small bookish art has been somewhat overlooked by bibliophiles, art lovers and collectors in general.

In entering the world of *"Ex Libris,"* I found that I was reaching back to a beautiful tradition of fine craftsmanship, to an idea that is much older than any book. It first appeared in Egypt, where men, cherishing their few hieroglyphic tablets, had their own seals pressed into the soft clay as a mark of ownership. These small seals, signatures, autographs, stamps of many crafts and trademarks in commerce were identifications that have an important place in the history of man.

In the early days, before the schoolmaster was aborad in the land, when learning was the possession of the aristocrats and the churchmen only and when handwriting was not in use among the common people, families were distinguished by their emblems. Their heraldic devices were painted on their walls, engraved upon their breastplates, displayed upon their persons and even upon their animals and the books in their homes. Every man had his own emblem, or that of his family or tribe, under which he lived, fought and died.

Long ago, when books were made by hand and there were no duplicates, it was not so easy to collect a library. But as the art of printing developed and editions multiplied, it was found necessary to place upon them some distinguishing mark of ownership. So, in Germany, the home of printing and bookbinding, the first bookplates were made.

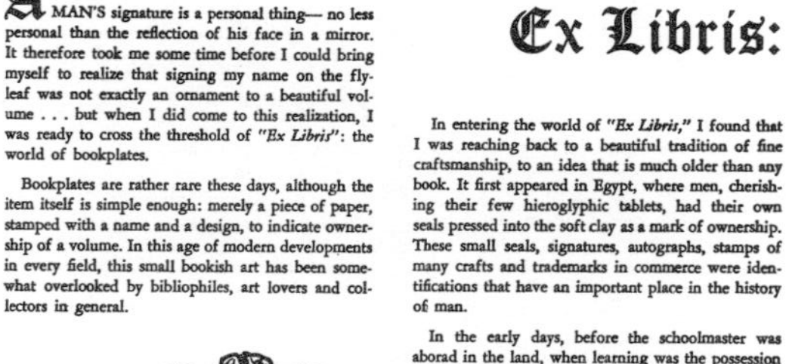

In browsing through a German volume on this subject, my eye was caught by a plate representing a coat of arms supported by an angel. The original of this bookplate, a woodcut, is believed to be the earliest movable *ex libris* and was pasted in a book presented to the monastery of Buxheim, Germany, in 1480. During the next fifty years German bookplates reached a high degree of artistic excellence. Among the designers were no lesser personages than the old masters Albrecht Duerer, Lucas Cranach and Hans Holbein.

The great exodus from England had a sobering effect upon the development of bookplates in America. American bookplates are poor specimens when compared with the rich foreign examples of the same period. The colonists, when they came from England, brought books and with them also bookplates. Their descendants, who continued the connection with the mother country, used plates. But the fashion never became very general and was confined to those of gentle birth: the lawyers, the clergy and the men of education.

The earliest American plate was a plain printed label with the owner's name, "John Cotton, His Book," and the date 1674. Paul Revere was well known for his bookplate engravings.

Among the rare American bookplates are those of John Franklin (Benjamin's brother) and Thomas Dering. But most valuable of our plates is the *ex libris* of George Washington, with his arms engraved on the seal and made between the years 1777 and 1781.

The essential parts of the bookplate are (1) the name of the owner and (2) the old Latin inscription *"Ex Libris,"* meaning "from the books of." The obsolete Latin words continue to be used both for their conciseness and the antiquity of their orgin.

The first mission of a bookplate is to be distinctive and clearly to assert ownership. The second mission seems to have originated in one of man's weaknesses: namely, that of remembering to borrow but forgetting to return. *(Continued on Page 18)*

Fig. 47. Center spread from *Shrdlu*, New York School of Printing, Manhattan. Headline and bookplates at top of column 1, bottom of column 2, and lower right are printed in brilliant red.

Impressions

Mood

BARBARA LUBINSKI, '61

YOU yawn and stretch, aware of the comfortably drowsy feeling which permeates the atmosphere. Music from the radio seems to sift through the room like filtered sunbeams; only the prettiest strains pass through. Dreamily, its fingers clasp at your being in perfect harmony with your equally dreamy mood.

It's strange how they come there—the fantasies, the hopes, the castles built on pink clouds. Your room is now a menagerie of dreams, each crystallizing in the air, but disappearing at your clutch, leaving behind only their magic.

The phone rings, bringing you shatteringly back to reality. After a short conversation you return to your room. Only, it's different now. The drowsiness has turned to fatigue. The music has the same melody but it no longer carries you with it. That intangible mood is gone and, try as you may, it won't come back. At least not tonight.

So you open a book and start to study.

Sundown

SUSAN MATTHEWS, '61

A FIERY red ball glows in the west, reflecting its glory in the leaves above my head, turning their green into bright autumn hues. The western sky above the sharp outline of purple mountains shades from a brilliant red to pink and finally softens into blue. As I turn away from this glorious sight, I see the windows of my house transformed into stained glass.

Looking upward through the trees again, I see that the glow has softened. A second later a chill pervades the air as the last golden ray filters through the leaves and the sun sets on another day.

Visitor Uninvited

ALICE KAVANAUGH, '61

DO YOU know the feeling of loneliness when a train whistle sounds in the still hush of the night or early morning? The feeling of near panic when the melancholy sound floats over the city, drifting into your room uninvited, telling of busy people, strangers who are visiting your city for one brief moment, people whom you do not know and yet are longing to know?

Or perhaps you were wandering through the vast steel city of coils and wires and heard it screaming louder and louder, urging you to come and travel with it . . . away . . . away from your own little world.

But perhaps, as I, you just smiled and said . . . some other time, some other place, for I'm not lonely . . . yet.

Tranquillity

REBECCA MULLEN, '62

THE wind swept its way through the forest of pines, bending the taller ones over in protection of the younger, smaller trees. These older pines had grown tall and straight through the years, in which petrifying cold, torrential rains, and snow sleeping on their branches only served to strengthen them more. It was this strength, as well as the solitude of this cool, green haven, that invited worried minds and heavy hearts to ease their burdens by walking and meditating beneath the sheltering limbs. Here even the most perplexed and heavy-hearted were aware of the beauties of nature and the wonders of God.

Interlude

ROY NELSON, '61

I WONDER how it feels sitting there, waiting for someone to come. Then someone does come and all its cold metal parts go into action. I wonder how it feels to go speeding down a road, not knowing which way it will turn next, not knowing if it will make the next turn.

I get into my small car and it is a part of me. We take the turns together only for a few moments of peace. Then I must return to life.

26 27

Fig. 48. White space is used well to display five separate items on this spread from *Acorn* of Jefferson Senior High, Roanoke, Va.

Some magazines reinforce the logo by using an unvarying design, changing only the color. Within the constant "frame" of the cover, changing art or type is used for variety.

Because a school magazine doesn't appear frequently enough to create a strong image, it is wise to:

★ Keep the design fairly constant.

★ Keep the nameplate and its position unvaried.

The cover of the student magazine may be of heavier stock than inside pages. This depends on the budget, of course, because such a cover—on a more expensive stock—must go through the press all by itself instead of being ganged up with several other pages.

Self covers, those of the same paper as the rest of the magazine, are adequate for magazines up to 32 pages, at least.

The choice of paper has possibilities as wide as the choice of a phonograph record. The most inexpensive is newsprint; the most expensive is coated stock. Many student staffs equate "slick" paper with quality. Actually, too-glossy paper is hard to read; light reflects glaringly and irritatingly from it. The method of printing and the kind of pictures you use are major factors in the choice. Letterpress requires a coated paper with a smooth surface if fine-screen halftones are to be used. This need not be glossy; dull finish is also available in coated stocks. Offset can reproduce fine detail on rougher paper.

Antique papers have much *bulk;* the sheets are thick in comparison to their weight. This has advantages; it makes the magazine seem bigger—and better?—because the reader has a bulkier package in his hands.

Offset papers are available in many *textures,* or *finishes.* Among the most popular are *pebble* and *rippletone.* Student staffs should withstand temptation to use too marked a texture; often it draws more attention to itself than to the information it bears.

Paper should be chosen by four criteria:

1. It must be adaptable to the printing method used.
2. It must be available in economical sizes.
3. It must be pleasant and comfortable to the eye.
4. It must give pleasant tactile sensation—feel nice in the reader's fingers as he peruses the magazine.

The most popular sizes for student magazines are:

8½ x 11, the size of a standard business letterhead.

6 x 9, a little larger than "Reader's Digest."

5½ x 8½, half the size of the letterhead.

9 x 12.

These sizes *cut without waste.* Printing papers come in large sheets which are multiples of the above dimensions. If the magazine is of an odd size, there will be long, useless strips of paper left over when the big sheet is cut down to page size. Although no one gets any use from this waste, the staff must pay for it, for paper is sold by weight and

Fig. 49. Cover design, used on magazine of Empire State School Press Assn., maintains identification by using the L-shaped panels at top and left every issue. Artwork changes, may be line or halftone. Panels are in color, which changes each issue. Here it was bright yellow.

it is weighed before trimming, like lambchops.

Bleeds are pictures that extend to the very edge of the paper. When pictures are bled to any but the inside edge, a quarter or eighth inch larger sheet must be used and excess trimmed away after binding. (Cuts must be made that much larger, too, to allow for the trim.)

The capacity of available printing presses is an economic factor in choosing a page size. Often a press can print many 8½ x 11 pages at one time. But if the page size is 9 x 12, fewer pages can be printed in one signature, a number of pages on a single sheet which is then folded and cut to proper size. Larger pages then require more press time—and more money.

So it is always wise to consult with your printer before choosing paper or page size. He can show you many ways in which your choice

Fig. 50. *Acorn* of Roanoke, Va., has a completely new cover design each issue. Here, deep blue and Rembrandt brown are used.

can save money or give you more for the same amount.

Many colors are available in paper and ink. But good old black and white are still the best. If colored stock is used, it should be in a light tint to afford maximum tonal contrast between paper and ink. If colored ink is used, it should be rich and deep. Type is illegible in yellow and in the lighter tones of green, blue, and orange.

Colored inks may be used on colored stock if they harmonize. A rich brown is pleasant on a buff paper. But blue on green is not good and the too-frequent choice of red on green for the Christmas issue is horrible.

Red ink should never be used to carry type; it irritates the eye. Colored inks rarely do a good job on halftones.

The 8½ x 11 and 9 x 12 formats usually have a two-column page with columns from 19 to 21 picas. These pages can also be broken into three columns of 13 picas.

The 5½ x 8½ and 6 x 9 formats have two columns of 13 to 14 picas.

Any three-column page can be divided into two columns, 1½ times the width of the normal one; into a single column and a double column; or, on rare occasions, into only one column. In the last case, care must be taken to use a larger body type or to set that single column into wider margins so the line isn't too long for comfort.

The basic function and principles of good typography and layout apply to magazines just as to newspapers and yearbooks. So the magazine designer ought to read the chapters in this book that discuss those subjects. He ought to read other good books in the field. Most of all, he should read all the magazines he can get his hands on—if not to read them, at least to look at them and analyze how they use the unfailing principles that contribute to easy, pleasant reading.

17. *The Mimeographed Publication*

When the budget is limited

A Mimeograph machine, it has been said (we hope facetiously), is more important to a government than a Constitution. Surely every administrative unit from the White House to the school board keeps this ubiquitous machine at full production. Fortunately there are enough machines left over that school magazines can be produced on them.

Just in case any reader of this book is newly arrived from Mars, let's see how a Mimeograph operates.

An image is *cut*, actually pressed, into a *stencil*—a sheet of impregnated cellulose whose fibers spread to allow ink to pass through. All areas of the stencil remain attached to the main body. (If that weren't true, we couldn't use letters like a, b, d, e, which have bowls; the center portion of the round letters would be cut entirely out of the stencil. We see this happening to the o on poorly cut stencils.)

The stencil is placed around a hollow cylinder. Ink is squeezed by centrifugal force from the back and through the stencil onto a sheet of paper.

So the Mimeograph is a refined and mechanized version of the stencils that little children play with and that shipping clerks use to paint addresses on cartons.

There are many stencil-printing machines. The Mimeograph is the oldest and best known and has become almost a generic term. When we use it in this chapter, the word can mean any such machine.

The limitations of the machine allow little choice in page size or format. The sheet may be 8½ x 11 (letter size) or 8½ x 14 (legal size). The sheet may be used for a single page or folded to create pages 5½ x 8½ or 4¼ x 7. If the sheet is not folded, the page may have three 2-inch columns or two 3½-inch ones, or a 4- and a 2-inch column. The folded, smaller page, 5½ inches wide, can have a single column of 4 inches, or two of 2 inches. The 7-inch-wide page can have two or three columns, each a quarter inch narrower than those used on the 8½-inch pages.

Mimeograph paper—a special grade made specifically for such use—is available in many colors. Mimeo inks are, too.

When colored inks are used, they must be full-bodied and strong in tone. Type printed in light inks is almost illegible.

Black ink has the highest legibility. It is wise to do your printing in black and get variety from colored paper. This should be in light, pastel tones. Some combinations of colored ink with colored paper create pleasant effects. Again, there must be maximum contrast between the two; the paper must be very light, the ink as dark as possible.

Monochromatic color harmony is best, using paper in a light tint of the color of the ink. Colored inks on paper of a different color rarely produce satisfactory results.

Typewritten composition is the simplest kind of *cold type,* that kind of typesetting which does not use the hot metal of regular foundry type or Linotype slugs. The finest cold type is produced on machines that use photography to place the images of letters on paper and film. Such machines are comparatively new and the authors have not found any high school publication set in photographic type. But undoubtedly it will not be too long before such cold type becomes available.

The techniques of preparing attractive typography for Mimeographed publications can be those of offset publications using typewritten composition.

Content of a Mimeographed publication is similar to that produced by any other method. But because typewritten copy takes more space than typeset copy, condensation becomes more important.

After the story has been edited, it is retyped by a *production typist,* usually a girl because they're generally the best typists. She types each line carefully to make it as close as possible to the desired column width. She will hyphenate far more frequently than when typing ordinary copy. When she comes near the end of the line but cannot fill it because the next word or syllable is too long to fit in, she fills the line exactly with ****** or ///////.

If the line is too long, she will type the number of excess characters in the right margin.

As she is copying this last version onto the stencil and notices a short line, she puts extra spacing between as many sets of words as is required to justify the line, make it align at the right. If she has extra letters to squeeze in, she'll put two letters into one space by pushing down the backspace key halfway but not releasing it till she's typed the second letter.

New typewriters, especially electric models, can put half-spacing between words. This simplifies justification. If letters have to be squeezed together, they should be narrow characters: t, i, f, j, l, and the punctuation marks. Usually only two—or at the most three—extra letters can be tucked into a line. This depends on the line length, of course, and the typist must determine what is the maximum excess as she types her trial draft.

Headlines can be placed on the stencil by typewriter if a large enough size is available. The two standard faces on typewriters are *elite,* with 12 characters per inch, and *pica,* with 10. The smaller should be used for body type. Another fairly common face has only eight characters to the inch; some, available only in all-capitals, are even larger. These make good headlines.

If heads must be set in the same "type" as the body, there are several variations which add interest to a page.

THIS HEAD IS INSET When the *inset head* is used, there must be a generous margin between the head and the copy block. Note, too, that there is one more short line than the lines of the head. This is to insure that the head will be framed at the bottom as well as at the side.

HANGING INDENT. This head is misnamed; actually the head is neither hung nor indented; the body type is. This is effective for a short, one-line head. The indent must be marked; three spaces is the minimum and with wider columns it may have to be increased to five or six.

Variations of the *hanging indent* are:

HANGING INDENT IN TWO LINES. This builds a strip of white alongside the top line of the head and injects that much more fresh air into the page.

HANGING INDENT; NO RUN-IN Notice that in this style the body type does not start on the same line—*run in*—with the headline.

The big advantage of these four heads is the white space that surrounds them. This is also their major weakness. With space always at a premium, many editors hate to use this much unprinted paper. Though white space should never be considered wasted space, there are some small stories that do not need quite so much display.

RUNNING IN THE HEAD is the way this style is designated.

It is the simplest form and most conservative of space.

The run-in head may be a separate phrase or it may be the opening of a story. In the latter case, the story must begin with key words.

WINS SCIENCE AWARD.
Sophomore John L. Smith today
was notified that he is one of
10 state winners in the . . .

This separate head does its job well. So does this one which is an integral part of the story:

A STATE SCIENCE AWARD
went to John L. Smith, a Clay
High School sophomore, this
week. He was . . .

But notice how ineffective the run-in is if the lead is not strong:

NOTIFICATION THAT HE is
one of 10 winners of a state
science award was received this
week by John L. Smith . . .

★ Vary the normal column width as another way of opening up the page and displaying type to advantage.

Notice how this paragraph
stands out from those above and
below it because of its nar-
rowed measure. When this device
is used, the indention on each
side must be generous, at least
four spaces.

A common practice is to underscore words in typewritten headlines. ★ Underscoring should be used only on one-line heads and preferably not with capitals.

There are several devices on standard typewriters that can be used as paragraph starters or as gimcracks to separate unheaded items.

The *, £, #, + (which becomes more common on machines), and even the *ampersand* (&) can be used. But don't overdo this; too many of these special characters will make your pages look like a commercial invoice.

These characters can also be used, alone or in combination, to make borders for the same sideless boxes discussed in Chapter 9.

Heads may also be cut in the stencil, either free-hand or with the use of *lettering guides*. These are plastic sheets with grooves, corresponding to the strokes of the letters, cut through. Letters are traced through this into the stencil with a stylus, a pencil-like holder with a wire, like a heavy, dull needle, projecting from one end.

Guides are available in many styles of letters. Usually complex letterforms are divided in two for easier manipulation of the stylus. To make an R, for instance, the stencil cutter will make the vertical stroke by using the guideline for I. He'll then bring the second guide, containing the bowl and the diagonal tail, into proper position and draw those two elements.

Unlike other publications, Mimeographed ones will use many all-cap heads. These have low legibility (as we said in Chapter 8) but their bulk is needed to afford adequate typographic color.

★ Never use Script or Cursive letters in all-caps.

In these lettering styles, the low legibility of all-caps becomes absolute illegibility.

Pictures can be cut into the stencil by hand, or photographically prepared illustrations can be inserted into the stencil.

Original drawings are done first in the conventional manner in India ink but on *bond* or *tracing* paper. (Bond is the common letterhead paper.)

The artist places the original on a *light table,* a sheet of sturdy frosted glass with an electric bulb under it. He folds back the stout kraft-paper protective sheet from the stencil and lays only the stencil, in the proper position, over the drawing.

The most useful drawing stylus—there are several varieties—is one made of a loop of wire. This goes around corners smoothly with minimum danger of tearing. To reduce the danger still more, the artist may place a sheet of raw silk or cellophane over the stencil and work over that. Silk sheets are obtainable from Mimeograph suppliers; any kind of cellophane can be used providing it is not too heavy. Take it off a box of cookies or a hosiery package.

The stencil will cut only lines, of course, but the artist can get shading effects by crosshatching (as was discussed in Chapter 10).

★ You can never—and shouldn't try to—get areas of solid black in a stencil.

There are devices for laying in mechanical shading, similar to the Ben Day and Zip-A-Tone processes. A plastic sheet, on which a regular pattern has been raised in relief, is placed under the stencil which is then rubbed with the blunt end of the stylus or a special instrument which looks like a little flat spoon. You've no doubt done something like this when you've laid a piece of paper over the textured cover of a book and, by rubbing the flat edge of a soft pencil over the paper, transferred the pattern of the fabric.

Many patterns are available in such screens. You can also make your own. A piece of ordinary keep-out-the-flies wire screening works nicely. Sandpaper makes interesting effects. Leather, or plastic simulations of it, can be used.

There are also ingenious toothed wheels that make shaded or dotted lines.

If original art is not available, line drawings from many sources may be used for tracing. The A. B. Dick Company, manufacturers of Mimeographs, offers a fat book of drawings done especially for tracing on stencils. Or you may clip drawings from magazines and catalogs and store them in a *swipe file*, where you classify them under any convenient headings: boys, girls, couples, adults, sports, seasonal, decorative—these are a few good major groupings.

Stencils prepared by photography are available at slight cost from your supplier, or for nothing from several sources. These, too, are classified by major groupings. In your own stencil, cut out an opening just large enough for the prepared stencil. Then that photostencil is cut out of the large sheet—often several such pictures are on one sheet—with a margin of at least a half inch. The precut stencil is pasted onto the back of yours by means of a special adhesive. (In an emergency you can use ordinary correction fluid.)

Care must be taken that the margin of the pasted-on stencil doesn't hide any lines in your regular stencil. The adhesive must fasten down all the edges of the prepared stencil; otherwise ink may seep under, accumulate, and eventually deposit ugly gobs on your paper.

As soon as all the elements have been prepared, the editor draws a dummy of his page. This is same-size and should be done very carefully. All artwork is copied on tracing paper. This need not carry detail but must be accurate in outline or, in the case of heads, in height and width. Tracings are pasted or retraced into proper position. Stories are indicated by parallel lines of which only the top and bottom ones must be accurately placed.

Now the actual stencil cutting begins.

Typing is done first; drawings would tear as the stencil rolls into the typewriter.

Typing stencils is such a familiar chore that it isn't necessary to detail those steps. But a few admonitions must be emphasized.

★ The typewriter must be carefully cleaned before each stencil is cut.

★ The typist must maintain an even stroke so all characters are cut deeply enough yet no bowls completely cut out.

Typographical errors are corrected by covering the error thinly with *correction fluid*, allowing it to dry and then carefully striking in the correct letter.

★ Be sure to wait until correction fluid has dried thoroughly.

Impatient typists find that the seconds they save by anticipating the drying process are wasted—and many more, too—when the correction turns out fuzzy.

★ Strike the correction character with a sharp, crisp blow—but not too hard.

★ The typed stencil is fragile. It must be handled with care.

If your magazine is folded, either the stencil must be cut on a wide-carriage typewriter (which can accommodate the stencil turned lengthwise) or the stencil must be cut in two. After two halves are typed, they are pasted together with stencil cement; so an overlap of a quarter inch must be allowed for applying the adhesive.

Before you start pasting stencil halves together, it is wise to make a rough *pagination dummy*. Fold small pieces of paper together to make the proper number of pages for your magazine. Number them conspicuously. As you take the dummy apart, you'll see how stencil pages must be matched up. If you have a 16-page magazine, for instance, page 2 will be on the same stencil as page 15; the front cover pairs with 16, page 3 with 14, 4 with 13, and so on. Only the center spread—in this case pages 8 and 9—has consecutive, facing pages on the same stencil.

As the second step, headlines are drawn in. Then artwork is either drawn or pasted in.

The stencil is now ready to run, another operation too familiar to require detailed discussion. But some old advice is worth repeating:

★ Make sure the Mimeograph is clean and in good operating order *before* you start the job.

★ If *slipsheeting* is necessary, be sure to have the needed paper on hand.

Slipsheets are pieces of waste paper that are inserted between printed sheets to keep the ink from setting-off from one page to the back of the other.

★ Allow plenty of time for the ink to dry.

Usually a half hour is sufficient time to wait before you begin *backing up*, printing the other side. Check drying before you back up; humid conditions slow down drying.

After printing, binding begins.

If your magazine has folded pages, they may be *gathered*, slipped inside each other, without any binding. Most frequently such pages are *saddle stapled*, with staples driven through the fold from the outside. This requires a stapler with an arm longer than that of a desk model. Most school offices have such long-armed staplers; if yours doesn't, the investment is not too large for the staff to buy its own.

Two staples are sufficient to bind a magazine of up to 32 pages, which is just about the maximum that can be saddle stapled.

If pages occupy an entire sheet, they must be bound by *side stapling*, the staples driven, from top to bottom, along the edge of the page. When this binding is used, sufficient margin must be left for the staples.

A single staple in the top left corner may be adequate to hold pages together but it does not create a pleasant package.

Stapling is not a glamorous job but it should be done carefully. If the staple doesn't penetrate exactly on the fold, pages will not open properly and the reader will be justifiably annoyed.

Now, that wasn't a hard process—putting out a Mimeoed magazine—was it? Always the key to success is taking pains.

The Mimeograph process requires the skill of many people. If anyone in the long chain does his work poorly, without pride or care, the efforts of everyone else are destroyed—or sadly depreciated.

There are several machines that make production easier and better.

Electric typewriters are a boon to the stencil cutter. While they're not exactly dime-store merchandise, they're well worth their cost. The staff ought to start a kitty to accumulate funds to buy one for the magazine's exclusive use.

A great virtue of an electric machine is the uniformity of the stroke. Each letter will hit the stencil with the same crisp pressure whether the key has been hit by a weak left-hand pinky or a sturdy right-hand index finger.

The simplest "compact" electric typewriter offers this advantage though its cost is no more than most standard models.

More expensive electrics offer *proportional spacing,* which contributes greatly to the readability. On an ordinary typewriter, each character occupies the same amount of space as any other. This means that the M and W must be crowded up to fit into their little acre while the l looks like a telephone pole in the middle of a pasture. Proportional spacing gives more room to wide letters, less space to the skinny ones.

The Varityper and IBM Selectric make a variety of type faces available on one typewriter.

The Varityper does not have conventional arms, connected to the keys and bearing a character at the end. Instead, all characters are raised on a small curved metal plate. When a key is struck, the proper character moves into printing position and smacks against the ribbon.

Each *type bar* of the Varityper has a complete alphabet. When the typist wants a new face, say an Italic, she simply removes the bar with Roman letters and replaces it with an Italic bar. She can type one word, a paragraph, or a whole page, before returning the original bar to the machine. It takes only two seconds to change bars and the cost of extra bars is not excessive.

The Selectric carries all its characters on a metal sphere about the size of a golf ball. Alphabets can be changed in seconds on this machine, too. The machine has another innovation that is fascinating to watch. Instead of the carriage moving past a constant impact point where the keys hit, the type ball moves along on a stationary platen. As it moves across the page, it also spins in two directions simultaneously to bring the proper character into printing position. The result is just as much fun—and far less expensive—to watch as the ball on a roulette table.

Very new on the American scene is a European invention, the Gestafax. This device opens striking opportunities for the staff with a Mimeograph machine.

The Gestafax makes a stencil, electronically, from *hard copy,* normal typewriting, drawings, etc.

The copy for a page is prepared as it is for offset, as we discussed in the previous chapter. The only difference is that copy must be same-size; it cannot be reduced as for an offset plate.

An electric eye scans this copy and reproduces it on a stencil that is used just like any other.

Now the staff can use even halftone pictures, and other art work need not be traced; the original is pasted into position on the hard copy and can carry much finer detail than is possible to produce with a stylus. If pasted-on material casts a shadow which is duplicated on the stencil, it is removed with correction fluid.

Obviously this machine is expensive. But its applications are so many for school use that the staff will be doing the principal a favor to bring this to his attention. He would, of course—being a redblooded American—reciprocate the favor by letting the staff use the machine to make its stencils.

Mimeographing can effectively be combined with letterpress or offset printing.

Some staffs can afford to have their covers printed each month; thus they can use a variety of pictures as well as of paper and ink.

Some staffs have only the nameplate printed. If a whole year's supply is printed at one time, the cost is slight. A different color of paper can be used for each issue without increasing the cost, at least by more than a few cents.

Mimeographing can produce printing in two colors, or even more.

For regular two-color work, a separate stencil is required for each color. This is prepared by the same mechanical separation we talked about in the previous chapter.

Unless the run is very long—an unusual occurrence with Mimeographed magazines—the color of ink can be changed without trouble. A sheet of oil-resistant paper is placed around the ink drum to keep the regular black ink in there where it belongs. A piece of absorbent cloth is placed over the protective paper and saturated with the new color ink.

When this method is used, the "pressman" must keep a close eye on the finished job. For fresh ink is not fed from the hollow cylinder as in normal operation. If inking becomes light, he must lift the stencil and replenish the *pad*.

With this pad, two or more colors can be printed at the same time. Dabs of various colors are placed in proper positions on a single pad. This requires, of course, that the various elements in the stencil be widely separated.

A rainbow effect is obtained by placing dabs of ink close to each other. As printing goes on, the colors run into each other and create many new shades. This effect is accidental, however; it can't be controlled. So it should be used only with artwork. You can't print type in intermediate colors that are often hard to read.

Layout

The same layout principles that apply to any publication also apply to Mimeographed ones. The smaller pages and comparatively larger type required in Mimeographing restricts the layout man's opportunities to maneuver his elements. But he has the same useful tool as his opposite numbers on the other publications: white space.

The struggle to find room for copy on a Mimeographed page brings constant temptation to skimp on white space. But the value of fresh air to Mimeoed magazines is so great that the layout man must steel himself to battle with temptation, Satan, and the editor who just has to get in these ten extra lines of type.

A fair number of student newspapers are produced by Mimeograph. The staff works under handicaps, though. It is difficult to design a pleasant newspaper page in three columns; it verges on the impossible when halftones can't be used.

Staffs of such papers ought to consider publishing a news magazine. They can report current school events but don't have to display the news so boldly or make up pages with so much display.

While it's highly improbable that a student staff can duplicate "Time" or "Newsweek" on a Mimeograph, close study of these news magazines will acquaint the student staff with a set of basic principles of organization and typography, a style which is far easier to follow in stencil printing than is the style of the newspaper.

Because Mimeographed publications are entirely student-produced, their quality varies more widely than those produced by letterpress or offset by professional craftsmen. Anyone who examines a large number of such publications comes to the same inevitable conclusion:

Most student staffs don't get maximum quality from the Mimeograph process.

Some of this failure is undoubtedly due to the machines themselves. Many schools have Mimeographs that came over on the Mayflower. But most often the fault is that of the operator. If he lacks skill, patience, pride of craftsmanship, and reliability, results are obvious. Fortunately, the reverse is also true; a conscientious, able operator almost always produces work the whole staff—and school—can be proud of.

Most companies that sell stencil machines are eager to send a representative to instruct the student staff. These men will not only demonstrate the processes discussed in this chapter but will show you many tricks of the trade that will make your magazine better.

We might as well face the fact that Mimeographed publications rarely have the professional quality of printed ones. But there are two consolations:

1. The content of a publication is far more important than its pack-

aging. Good copy would be worth while if it were handwritten and tacked on a bulletin board (as "newspapers" are in many of the new nations).

2. It is better to have a publication of lesser mechanical quality than to have none at all.

This is a basic American philosophy. Our people decided long ago that it is better to make a less-than-perfect newspaper, magazine, or book available, at low cost, to a great many people than it is to produce a mechanically perfect publication at a price that restricts it to a few readers.

Our country was built by inexpensive written communications; the inspiring pamphlets of Thomas Paine were not sterling examples of fine printing. Mimeographing can be the 20th century counterpart of Colonial broadside printing.

BOOK FOUR

The School Yearbook

18. *Yearbook Planning and Editing*

Working for twenty years from now

Confucius wasn't the only fast man with a proverb; the Arabs coined a few of their own and one makes a perfect introduction to this chapter:

"Every man in his lifetime must do three things—plant a tree, beget a son, and write a book."

The sage Bedouin knew that each of us wants to leave some kind of monument. He knew that these three things—a new generation, a growing tree, and a book—are the most permanent mementos anyone can create.

Because a school yearbook is so permanent, it deserves only the best efforts of everyone on the staff. Your classmates will soon forget the winning basket in the championship game or the performance of the leading lady in the senior play. They will never forget your work on your yearbook; for it will be a cherished possession for the rest of their lives.

The fact that a book endures influences the work of the staff in two ways.

Accuracy must be impeccable. The book will be used as a record as well as a preserver of memory.

Quality must be beyond fad and foible. A book that has a "modern" gloss because it follows the vagarious style of the moment will look dated and artificial by the time your readers have children of their own in high school.

Information must be specific. On the morning when the book is delivered to your readers, text is unimportant. Everyone recognizes that picture as the point-after-touchdown that nipped your deadliest rivals in the closing seconds of the Homecoming game. Old Joe, our dearest friend, doesn't have to be labeled. We can pick out our favorite teacher from a dozen faces.

But memories fade quickly; ask your parents. Twenty years from now most yearbook pictures become meaningless without complete and accurate captions.

★ The yearbook must be written for a reader who will look at it 20 years from now.

Producing a yearbook is as big a job as any student can be assigned. It means long, hard hours and, usually, a sacrifice of other, less arduous activities. But rewards are great and they grow with the years.

Proper planning can eliminate most of the tears and not a little of the sweat.

★ Staff organization is the first key to success.

The staff should be organized early in the spring of the year preceding publication. The editor-in-chief is the most important person; his selection should be one made only with deliberation.

He must be familiar with all phases of yearbook production. For that reason most schools insist that the editor have previous experience, and almost all reserve this important position for a senior.

The business manager may be appointed by the editor-in-chief or the publication board. Usually, if the editor makes appointments they must be ratified by the board.

The business manager is responsible for the financial well-being of the book. He heads the advertising and circulation staffs and keeps all records. His work is second in importance—and that only by a nose—to the editor's.

Organization of the yearbook staff may follow any one of several successful plans. The important thing is to make sure every job is filled and that there is a clearcut and invariable channel up to the editor and then the printer.

Fig. 51-A shows one logical arrangement. It breaks the job of producing a book into the major components: copy, art, production, and business.

Note that such a chart is concerned with jobs, not people. One person may do more than one job; in some cases, two persons may be required to cope with all the duties shown by a simple square on the chart.

Another logical division of duties is shown in Fig. 51-B.

The board of editors is made up of the editor-in-chief and those senior editors (this does not designate their class year) who make up the second row in the table of organization. The faculty advisor is also a member—and a mighty important one.

There should be several all-staff meetings in the spring. A good yearbook is a team effort and every member should be aware of the goal

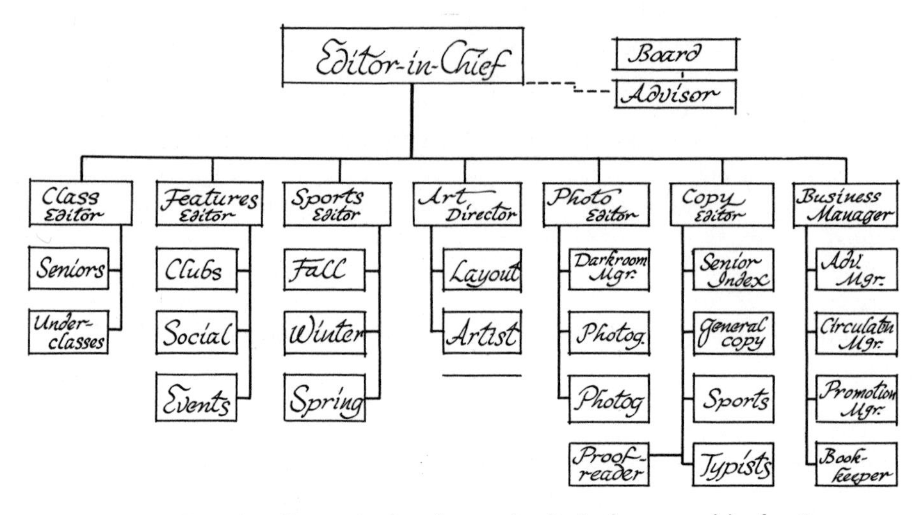

Fig. 51. Typical staff organizations for yearbooks, both arranged by functions. Above, division is according to sections of yearbook. Below, division is by general contents.

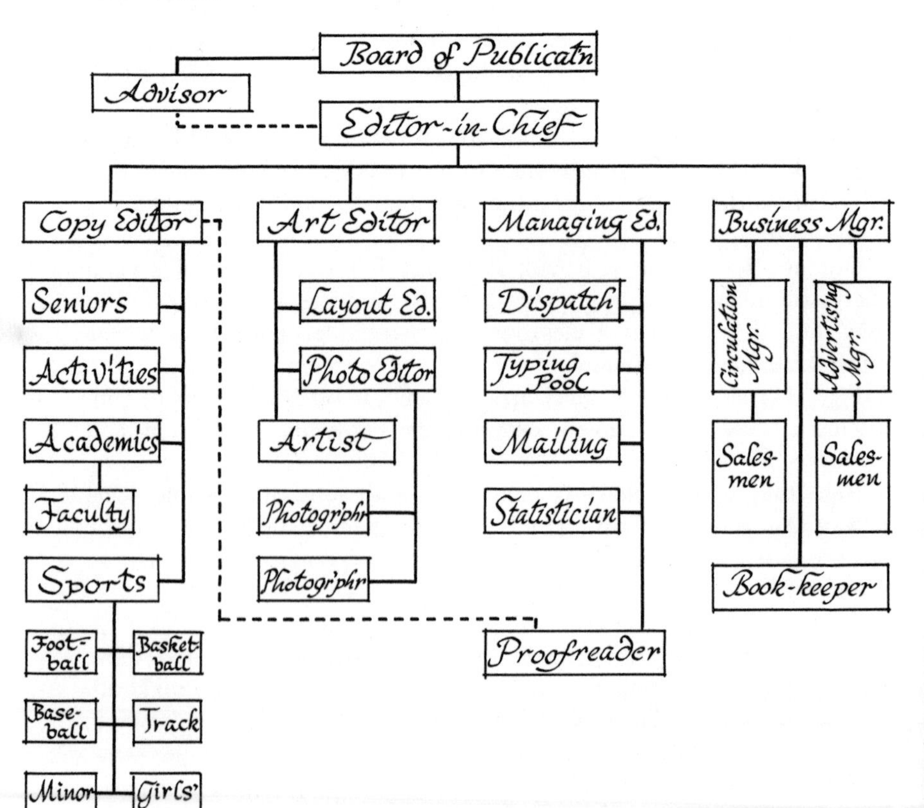

of the team as well as his personal one.

The board of editors should meet frequently in the spring, at least weekly; many editors have daily sessions then. In the fall and winter, staff meetings are almost continuous, if informal.

The staff needs an adequate workshop. Most school administrators provide an office that can be locked and used exclusively by the yearbook staff.

Quarters need not be elaborate. One of your authors shared a tower room with assorted furry and feathered friends—as well as the staff, of course—and those memories are pleasantly interleaved in the pages of the book produced.

The workshop needs as many large tables as can be squeezed into the area. A four-drawer file cabinet is a necessity. The editor, business manager, and copy editor get one drawer each; the fourth is for general staff use.

There must be storage cabinets—or at least shelves—for bulky art material.

★ All working papers must be properly filed at the end of each day.

Papers allowed to accumulate will get worn and/or lost. It comes as a shock to find a photograph dog-eared beyond use or a sheet of the senior directory lost beyond recall—especially when, as usual, discovery is deferred until the moment the material is due at the printer's.

A paper cutter is a valuable tool. Don't succumb to false economy here; a cheap cutter will soon get out of square and its blade will bow so it cuts arcs instead of straight lines.

Cutters are dangerous; they can nip off a finger. They should be treated with respect.

The artist will usually prefer to work elsewhere. But if he is unusually gregarious, a drawing board may be provided here for his use.

Some schools provide office space during the summer. If not, the editor will set up an adequate working area in his home. For he will be involved in his important job all during the between-school months.

Basic plans should be made in the spring; it is best to have the production contract signed at this time so that services of the printer can be used in the crucial early stages.

Since before he was selected, the editor has been pondering the *theme* of the book. But in late spring, in close unity with the copy and art editors, he will make a firm decision.

Occasionally an editor will dismiss the use of a theme as "corny." What he fails to realize is that every creative work must have a theme whether or not it's obvious or even apparent.

Without a theme, a yearbook will be a collection of several "books," bound by happenstance into one cover.

The theme is the single thread that ties together such disparate elements as baseball pictures, senior portraits, and a report of the debating team's record into a well-integrated logical whole.

Every yearbook has a theme it shares with all others: the events of the school year and their influence on students and the school. The more obvious theme is merely a device to present the basic material in the most pleasant and logical manner.

The obvious theme should be appropriate and logical—but these are so dependent upon the treatment that it allows immeasurable scope.

The theme should be lasting. The 1962 yearbook that chose the Twist as its theme is already old-fashioned; the one that took space exploration will be timely as long as there are unexplored outer reaches.

The theme should be one that can be pleasingly developed in words and art. Themes that can be summarized by a favorite quotation are usually inherently sound. "All the world's a stage," for instance, can be developed in two parallel strands. The stage itself allows for interesting pictorial treatment. And the continuation of Shakespeare's fancy—the growth of the individual—can be easily translated into the advance of a student through school.

The background of the school—historical, economic, social, or cultural—should play a major part in selecting a theme. A school in New Bedford, Massachusetts, would more logically choose the theme of whaling ships than one in Des Moines, Iowa. One in Bucks County, Pennsylvania, could do a delightful exposition on Amish folk art but one in Iron Mountain, Michigan, would do far better with that of the Finns who settled that area.

Yet each of these themes can be adapted to any school. The landlocked editor may take the familiar quotation, "There is no frigate like a book" and create a perfectly logical theme that enables him to use all the nautical symbolism he wants.

An editor in Palo Alto, California, might choose to weave into his book the many and varied cultural backgrounds of his classmates' ancestry. Then he could use Pennsylvania Dutch, New England Yankee, California Spanish, and countless other art forms.

The Civil War Centennial made that era of our history a popular theme for countless books in the early 60's. The editor at Richmond, Virginia, could tie it closely to local history; his counterpart in Oregon could use the theme on a broader basis.

Local centennials (or semi-, sesqui-, bi- or tricentennials) are always good themes. History becomes more important to Americans each year. But current events—handled in perspective—can be equally effective. Our concern with the United Nations, the growth of student exchange programs, the quest for peace and human dignity, the enduring search for knowledge, harnessing of the atom, man's tentative probes into space, all these are rich theme possibilities.

Schools are not—if they ever were—ivory towers today. The student lives in a large world as well as in his smaller academic sphere. A good yearbook should not only say "This is how it was at Central High in this year." It should also say "This is how the world around Central High was in this year."

So a theme should be evocative; in itself it should recreate the year in memory. Few things will do this as readily and completely as music. Every class has "Our Song," and merely the title of a favorite ballad will transport the reader back in time. Daily newspaper headlines are just as efficacious.

Humor, if it is subtle, can be pleasant but most student editorial boards are afraid to try it, or feel they will lose authority, importance, or dignity thereby. They feel that levity is beneath their dignity. (Shades of Abe Lincoln's jokes!)

A theme is effective if it can develop in successive stages. One school used the theme, "Unity from diversity." This was illustrated by a bouquet of markedly different flowers.

The first section was introduced by a single flower. For the second section, that flower was grayed down while another, in full black, was added. One by one, flowers were added, the new one always in black, the previous ones in gray. Finally the bouquet—a single, integrated whole—was produced.

Copy stressed the diversity of the student body, of courses of study, of activities, and showed how these many elements were united into a common goal and so created a uniquely whole student body.

Whatever the theme, it must represent the school—and in a favorable manner. It cannot glorify any single group, nor poke ridicule at any individuals.

★ The theme must be handled in a fresh, imaginative manner. Clichés are as deadly in yearbook themes as in English themes.

With the theme chosen, each senior editor plans on how he can develop it in his section. This development must be logical and unobtrusive.

★ The theme must always be subordinate.

It might be likened to the few gold threads that run through fine Oriental silk. They enhance the pattern but never hide it. The yearbook theme should never be important in itself; it should be an almost invisible thread that knits the book into a single unit.

The basic techniques of writing and editing for the yearbook are essentially those for a newspaper and magazine that have been discussed in Chapters 5 and 15. There are some noteworthy differences, however.

Writing in periodicals is ephemeral. While its short life does not condone poor writing in such publications, the much longer life of yearbook writing should be a spur to the highest quality possible.

Fortunately, yearbook deadlines are not as pressing as those of other publications. Writers and editors should use the extra time to give their product a very high gloss.

★ The yearbook writer must avoid the clichés and slang of the moment.

They age quickly—and not gracefully. His allusions cannot be to minor passing events; the reader two decades away will find them unintelligible. Identifications must be explicit; it will be difficult for the reader to recall whether Miss Smith taught English or history.

★ Write yearbook copy as if it were for a stranger in Europe.

This does not mean that there can be no easy comfort of the familiar. A homey flavor is possible with the most explicit copy.

There is time to write, rewrite—and then do it over again.

★ Don't be afraid to rewrite copy.

The giants of literature are rarely satisfied with their first attempt, or second, or fifth. If a great novelist can do seven drafts of his book, the student writer ought not grow weary at least until he has done his work that many times.

★ Avoid using "purple prose."

It is a great temptation to use Mr. Roget's "Thesaurus" to find sonorous and rolling phrases to replace simple statements. But no truer axiom was ever coined than "Beauty is simplicity."

★ There should be continuity in yearbook copy.

The difference in style between copy blocks in the academics section and in the sports pages should never be so great that the reader is aware of a change. Ideally, the whole yearbook should read as if it were written by one person.

★ Accuracy is of the first importance.

★ Accuracy is of the first importance.

This admonition is so essential that it has been repeated. We have stressed the importance of accuracy in all journalistic work. It is not at all a deprecation of accuracy in newspapers and magazines to emphasize that accuracy is even more important in a book.

Your yearbook will be a reference book for many people for many years. It must be as accurate as humanly possible.

★ Copy should be read by several people. Proofs by just as many.

It is the responsibility of the section editor, and ultimately the editor-in-chief, to attain high standards of quality and accuracy.

★ The editor-in-chief should read every word of copy before it goes to the printer.

Preferably, he should read copy in continuity as it will appear in the book. Because copy goes to the printer piecemeal, the editor should keep carbons. When he reads copy for pages 82 to 97, he should also read that preceding and following this section. If either has already been set in type, he must make necessary changes in the live copy to make it blend into the others.

Yearbook copyreaders have a much more rigid copy-control job than their opposite numbers on periodicals. For the space allotted to copy on the typical spread is inflexible.

Many printers furnish copy sheets on which finished copy is typed. This has vertical rules to show how wide to type copy to produce desired line lengths in various type sizes and faces. If your printer doesn't have such sheets, it's easy to make your own.

Your printer will furnish you with sample blocks of your body type. If you have, say, a block on a sports page that measures 18 picas wide by 4 inches deep, measure 18 picas on the specimen. Type several lines to determine the average number of characters per line. Then set your typewriter to that count. Type each line as close to full as possible without breaking words unduly.

Measure 4 inches on the specimen block to determine how many lines will fit into the available area on the spread. Remember that only full lines should be counted; if a fraction of a line extends beyond the specified area, it may bump into a picture.

Many staffs like to have every copy block written so the last line is full. Short lines are called *widows* and a generation ago typographers labored mightily to "kill the widow." Today's tendency is to ignore widows if they are longer than one-third of a whole line.

The function of type is to carry a message. If copy has been properly written, it is not sound to change it just so the type comes out in a neat square. Usually the addition or elimination of words in well-written copy destroys the rhythm of the composition.

If widows bother you, you can instruct your printer to *center the last line*. This mitigates the pain that widows bring to some critical eyes.

The editor will use common sense in handling widows. He wouldn't let only *es* stand in the last line or even a whole word if it's as short as *I* or *all*. Eliminating extremely short widows doesn't require massive surgery on the copy.

Remember, though, that killing widows comes under the heading of author's alterations, discussed in Chapter 7, and you must pay for each demise.

Yearbook staffs have a tendency to abuse "downstyle." This is the practice of minimizing the use of capitals (and is also discussed in Chapter 8). They carry it to such an extreme that they use "june" and "middletown" instead of "June" and "Middletown." Worse yet, they will even down proper names. This is wrong, it is insulting, and it is stupid.

e. e. cummings, the late poet, gained notoriety by insisting that his name be set downstyle. But the principal of your school—or anyone else whose name appears in your yearbook—is not "principal john h. smith" or "quarterback james brown." They are individuals; their names are proper nouns and not generic terms.

★ Proper nouns are capped.

Most contemporary yearbooks have too little copy. There ought to be a good, complete story of the school year in words as well as pictures. Effective as they are as communicators and pleasant as they are to the reader, pictures alone cannot tell the whole story adequately.

★ In planning your book, be sure to allow enough space for such a written record.

Yearbooks started out as "literary reviews," a showcase for student writing which the creative magazine has since become. While a yearbook would not be acceptable to most students if most of its contents were essays and similar compositions, the written word must always be an integral part of the yearbook, not just something to fill up space around pictures.

Words wear well. Your reader some 20 years hence will enjoy well-written copy just as much as he does the art in your yearbook. You are writing and editing for posterity; do this important job so you'll be as proud of it in 1980 as you are the day the book comes off the press.

19. *Yearbook Production*

The highest-priced student responsibility

Producing a yearbook requires close meshing of many gears. It is too much to expect human memory to cope with the many details involved. So a good production control system is an absolute necessity.

While the editor may want to keep his own private progress chart in a notebook, wall charts serve two good purposes. They enable everyone on the staff to tell the status of any page in a moment and they are a spur and a morale-builder.

The chart may be such a simple one as Fig. 52. The first column lists the initials of the editor in charge. The second gives the page number and brief description of its contents. Note that there are two columns each for layout, art, photos, and copy. The due date is entered early in the cycle in one column; in the other are the initials of the staffer assigned to that duty. When an assignment is completed, the square in the date column is filled in. A red square shows that deadline has been met; a blue square, that this phase was late. The last two columns show the date the page is due at the printer's and the final column the date of mailing.

A hasty glance will detect blanks that show unfinished jobs. The editor then can start prodding. Blue squares are danger signals; someone will have to work at forced draft to gain back lost time.

Some charts have another column to show when proofs are received, by whom read, and when returned.

A more elaborate system is shown in Fig. 53. Here pages are grouped in spreads and signatures.

Work Progress Chart ACADEMICS

Publisher's Deadlines 1st. NOV. 15
2nd. DEC. 19
3rd. JAN. 10
4th. FEB. 10

	Ed.	DESCRIPTION OF PAGE	Layout	Due	Art	Due	Photo	Due	Copy	Due	Deadline	Sent
35	FD	Divider	FD	9/17	BB	9/15			FD	9/20	9/30	
36	NM	Classroom Pix	BB	9/24			KT	9/17	KA	9/20	↑	
37	"	" "	"	"			"	"	"	"		
38	"	" "	"	"			"	"	"	"		
39	"	Honor Roll	"	"			"		"	"		
40	"	Natl Honor Society	"	"			JO		"	9/16		
41	"	" " "	"	"			"		"	"		
42	"	NSF Winners	"	"			"		JB	9/22		
43	"	Science Fair	"	"			"		"	"		
44	"	Key Winners	"	9/25			KT		"	"		
45	"	" "	"	"			"		"	"		
46		" "	"	"			"		"	"		
47	EL	Awards Assembly	"	"			"		"	"		
48	EF	Crucible Club	"	9/22			JO		KA	9/16	↓	
49	SJ	Athena Soc.	"	"			KT		"	"	9/30	
50	NM	Best Teacher Award	"	10/7	BB	10/1	S		"	10/1	10/12	
51	"	" " Pix	"	"		"	S		"	"	"	
52	"	Lantern Night	AS	9/22			KT	9/15	NM	9/18	9/30	
53	FD	Students' Creed	AS	"	AS	9/18		"			"	

Fig. 52. Work progress chart. Note that pages are always paired, except first page of the book or section, which, because it is on a righthand page, does not have facing one. (Courtesy Wm. J. Keller, Inc.)

No systems or charts given in this chapter have the force of legislation. They can and should be changed to meet the needs of the individual staff. The important thing to remember is:

★ Yearbook work should be well planned, well controlled, and well recorded.

★ The yearbook production schedule must be both detailed and inviolate.

The starting point of the schedule is the printer's deadlines. These are sacred. All other deadlines are only milestones en route to publication day.

The editor apportions time and effort so that signatures can be completed at the pace the printer's schedule requires.

Here is a typical schedule:

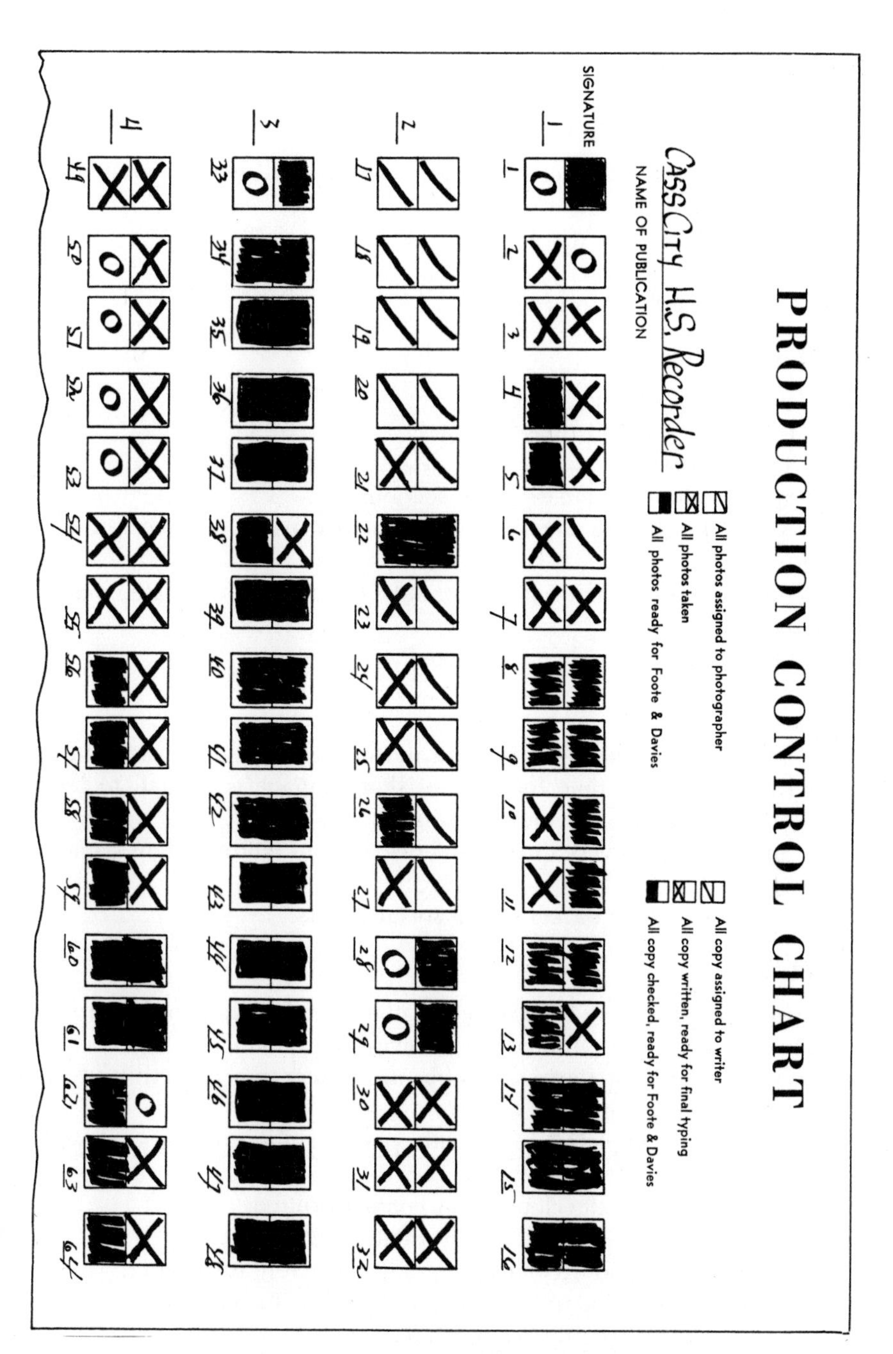

Fig. 53. Portion of production control chart. (Whole sheet shows 10 signatures, 160 pages.) Top square indicates photos and art; lower portion, copy. Diagonal stroke shows that assignment has been made; cross, that assignment is completed; black squares, that material is ready for printer. Zeros show that no material is needed on that page.

Note that first signature requires art work for Page 6 and final check for nine pages. Second signature has just been started; but third signature is ready for the printer as soon as art for page 38 is checked. Signatures need not be sent to printer in order, but each must be complete. (Courtesy Foote & Davies)

APRIL (year before publication)

Editor-in-chief, business manager, and editorial board chosen.
Budget prepared.
Staff meetings held.
Theme selected.
Contract with printer signed.

MAY

Budget approved.
Rough pagination done.
Type selected.
Senior editors paginate their sections.

Art editor begins layout of introductory pages and section dividers.

Business staff begins plans for advertising and circulation campaigns.

Outside photographer contracted.

Photo editor works with school administration in scheduling group pictures.

Evergreen pictures—those with no time element—are shot. Early spring is an ideal time for campus shots; foliage is enough to lend charm, not so heavy it hides details.

Sports editor covers spring athletics. (Photo editor assigns camera coverage.)

Activities editor covers spring social events.

JUNE

Many staffs prefer to have senior photographs taken in the spring. This creates a few problems but solves many more.

Business staff prepares and addresses letters to prospective advertisers, perhaps subscribers also.

Schedules completed for outside photographer and cleared with him.

Spring pictures developed and contact-printed.
Copy editor writes introductory matter.
Introductory and divider pages laid out, ready for printer.
Pages on Spring activities completed, ready for printer.
First advertising sales calls made.

JULY AND AUGUST

No formal schedule. Editors use this time to finish incomplete spring duties; wise ones allow plenty of time for just plain thinking.

SEPTEMBER (start of academic year of publication)

Staff meeting first week of school. Staffers who haven't been involved during the summer are brought up to date on progress, and schedule for the months ahead is presented and explained. This is the meeting for a rousing pep talk; ask your printer to suggest a good speaker, one who is brief and inspiring.

Fill vacancies caused by staffers moving or becoming involved in jobs or other activities.

Review duties of each staffer.

Announce schedule of meetings and working hours.

Circulation campaign starts at once.

Material for senior section compiled.

Copy and photo assignments made for the rest of the year.

Advertising salesmen resume making calls.

OCTOBER

Class, faculty, and group photographs taken.

Cover material, style, and design chosen.

Layouts on fall activities, most of football pages and academics finished.

Senior layouts well under way.

Business manager reviews finances. If there is need for outside fund-raising affairs, now is the time to stage them.

Review budget. Must size of book be cut down? Or can you afford extra pages or extra color?

Before the leaves fall, get any necessary outdoor shots.

NOVEMBER

First shipment to printer. (Only complete two-page spreads should be sent. Hold single pages.)

Choose paper for *end leaves*. Prepare necessary art work for them.

Prepare all advertising copy, art, and layouts.

Lay out all pages for which material is complete.

Work to fill vacant spots in signatures.

DECEMBER

Order covers.

Second shipment to printer. (By this time, only senior section, clubs and organizations, activities, and sports are left to cover.)

JANUARY

Third shipment to printer. (This is usually the senior section.)

Complete layouts of all other pages. (Again fill the holes in signatures; the printer wants to get forms on the press.)

Give final print quantities to printer and cover-maker.

FEBRUARY

The b-i-g month!

All copy to printer! (If there are activities which you can't cover yet, now is the time to arrange an extension on one or two signatures, if that is possible. Perhaps you will need to prepare some emergency pages that can be used in case it becomes impossible to get late material in on time.)

MARCH

Proofs starting coming in. Read them carefully and return them promptly. (A whole crew at the printer's is waiting for you now.)

Stage your final subscription campaign.

Collect all outstanding money.

APRIL

Have a postmortem. Jot down ideas for next year's staff.

Tidy up the workshop. Get files in shape for next year's staff. Check all records to make sure they're accurate and up to date.

Help the new staff organize.

MAY

If you have a supplement, you will have been working on it since March. Finish the job and send it to printer.

JUNE

Here it is!

Distribute books to subscribers.

Arrange sale of individual copies if you have any to sell.

Distribute books to advertisers if this is part of the contract.

Collect all advertising accounts.

Pay all bills.

Use a fine-tooth comb on the yearbook. Again jot down ideas for new staff and point out pitfalls that you avoided—or didn't.

Senior editors should meet with their successors and pass along paternal wisdom about their jobs.

Check for errors. If any have crept past your vigilant eyes, correct them now and place marked copy in school archives. Yearbooks are often used for reference; inaccuracies can be costly.

Relax and enjoy your well-deserved plaudits.

The editor's first major production decision is the format of the book. The three page sizes that are most economical and practical are based on how pages cut out of the large sheets of paper the printer uses. Odd page sizes mean that much paper will be wasted because thin slices trimmed off a large sheet cannot be used for other jobs. The yearbook is charged for the entire raw sheet; staff members should make sure they use all of it.

When the page size has been selected, margins should be established. This chart shows the three economical page sizes and suitable margins:

BOOK SIZE	GUTTER MARGIN	OUTSIDE MARGIN	TOP MARGIN	BOTTOM MARGIN
9 x 12	1⅛	1	1	1¼
8½ x 11	⅞	⅝	¾	⅞
7¾ x 10½	¾	⅝	⅝	⅞

The next decision is the progression of the book, the order in which topics will be presented. This is a typical progression:

- Introduction
  - Title pages
  - Dedication
  - Theme explanation
- Administration
  - School heads
  - Faculty
  - School superintendent
  - School board
- Activities
  - Clubs
  - Traditional events
    - Homecoming
    - Class proms
    - Class plays, etc.
- Academics
  - Scholastic honors
    - Honor societies
    - Scholarship winners
    - Competition winners
    - National Merit Scholarships
    - Science Talent Search
  - Classroom activities
- Sports
  - Football
  - Basketball
  - Baseball
  - Track
  - Swimming
  - "Minor" sports
  - Girls' sports
- Classes
  - Freshman
  - Sophomore
  - Junior
- Seniors
  - Commencement
  - Honors
  - Officers
  - Directory
- Advertising

There is no preferred sequence for these topics. The introduction will logically come first; seniors traditionally close the book even as they close their high school careers. But any topic may appear where it contributes to telling an orderly, pleasing story of the school year.

The wise editor remembers that the function of a school is education. He will make sure that this facet of student life is given its deserved importance. Plays and sports are pleasant dessert but the reader will demand the meat-and-potatoes of the more substantial elements of his academic career.

As long as all the important aspects of the school year are included, they may be grouped into many different categories.

Some yearbooks have successfully handled topics in chronological order. All things that happened in the fall are grouped into one section; winter and spring account for two others.

Once the progression has been set, *rough pagination* is determined. This establishes—at least approximately—how many, and which, pages will be devoted to each section.

This presupposes, of course, that the editor knows how many pages his book will have and, within flexible limits, how many of those will be devoted to advertising.

Yearbooks are printed with from 4 to 36—and sometimes even more—pages on a single large sheet of paper, a signature. *Imposition charts* show which pages make up a signature. The editor will work to complete signatures; until every page on a signature is ready, the printing job is as stymied as if no pages had been made up.

We'll discuss signature planning a little later, especially when color is involved. At this time the editor is concerned only with avoiding placing topics on a signature in such a way that early pages might have to be held up awaiting one or two pages that, by their very nature, must be among the last to be produced.

A device so new that many staffs are unaware it exists is the *insert,* or *supplement,* a 16-page signature that is printed after the rest of the book is completed. This is used to cover spring events, such as sports, social affairs, baccalaureate, and commencement, which happen after the book has been printed, maybe even delivered.

This enables a record that otherwise could never be included in a yearbook.

Inserts are provided with an adhesive from which a protective cover is peeled away as the signature is placed into the book. The cover is made so the insert will fit properly; if ordinary care is used in pasting the insert in place, it is bound in almost as securely as the sewn signature.

Sixteen pages is the maximum for an insert; that is all the extra room that can be allowed in binding operations.

Usually inserts are mailed to yearbook buyers during the summer. In this case the budget must allow for mailing envelopes and postage.

Some schools mail inserts to graduates and allow undergrads to pick up the addition in the fall.

If inserts are to be mailed during the summer, all arrangements must be made before school closes for vacation.

Some responsible person at the school must accept delivery. He should then notify the students who will do the mailing.

(Because many students will be away during the summer or will have vacation jobs, the business manager and/or the editor-in-chief must be sure that one or more responsible students will be available.)

The mailers must have a place to work and have access to it. This is not always as simple as it sounds, as you well know if you have tried to get into a school or one of its rooms during vacation.

The mailers must have an adequate supply of stamps. Before school lets out, ask the printer to send you a blank signature in the same paper as your insert will be on. Put it into the same envelope in which mailing will be done. Have the post office weigh the package and tell you what the postage will be. Inserts can be mailed at book rate or as educational material, which also goes at a favorable rate.

Your student body will know about the insert; it should be a major sales point. On the last days of school, inform them, by all possible communications methods in your school, approximately when they can expect the mailing.

Identify the envelope plainly. You can have envelopes imprinted with proper material or you can have special labels printed. In either case, these can be obtained well in advance so that addressing can be done before school closes.

A covering letter gives instructions for pasting in the insert tightly and permanently.

Some inserts will be lost, that's for sure. So it's wise to have the printer run a few extras; one to two per cent of the total number of books should be adequate. The cost is low.

Then, come autumn, you can give these extras—or sell them for a dime or quarter—to those people who didn't receive theirs or threw the envelope unopened into a wastebasket.

Any left over can be used for displays during the sales campaign. Or they can be given to students who are pictured as they delivered the valedictory or received scholarships and other honors. They'll be glad to have them to send to relatives and friends.

If you have even vague plans for an insert, discuss it with your printer. The insert may be 16 of the pages originally planned for. Or it may be an extra. The printer need not know until late in winter whether you'll have an insert. But the binder must know before he starts work on the cover so he can allow room for the extra pages.

Inserts mean a little extra effort and cost. But their advantages are so many and obvious that every staff ought to consider their use.

The components of an insert are handled just as those for regular pages. Procedures are identical except that the staff works under new deadlines. These will be included in the contract or a letter from the printer.

Several psychological factors complicate insert deadlines. There is a natural let-down when the deadline for the book itself has been met. Term papers, exams, and graduation activities take lots of time, especially of graduating seniors. Incentive is not so intense. The staff knows that if the books themselves aren't delivered before the end of school all varieties of complications will set in, but if the insert is mailed August 4 or 14 it doesn't seem to make much difference.

The staff should be well aware of the real incentives. An insert makes a much better book. Seniors, especially, will be happy that they have a complete record of their most important school year.

The procedure outlined in this chapter looks like a big job. It is. But any job is made easier by good planning and familiarity with the task.

The fact that countless student editors are producing excellent yearbooks can be both a consolation and a challenge to you and your staff.

20. *Yearbook Art*

School years captured in pictures

It is interesting to compare yearbooks of the Gay 90's (yes, they had them then!) and those of today. Old books were basically word books; pictures were few because cuts were expensive. Today's yearbooks are basically picture books.

While type is not to be deprecated, certainly pictures are an important part of a book—if only by the area they occupy. But they must communicate well to reach their maximum effectiveness. No one would say that a tackle is more important than an end on a football team, and no one would draw comparisons between staff members of a yearbook. Sufficient to say that the art editor has a key job that demands the utmost from him.

Two kinds of pictures are used in yearbooks: photography and hand art. The former, as the documentary medium, is the most important.

Photography

There are so many good books on photography that this one will not dwell on technical details other than those that require special attention from the staff. This chapter will devote itself to the use of photography.

★ Good photographic coverage demands good planning.

One of your authors edited a picture magazine during World War II. Photographic material was in such short supply that literally every shot had to be preplanned; there was just no film for *insurance shots* or photopaper for darkroom experimenting. A typical issue had 56 pictures which came from only 58 negatives. Such economy is not as necessary today, but the lesson is that planning is as essential as tripping the shutter.

The staff's first decision: Do we use professional or student photographers?

Professionals produce technically excellent work. Their skill, experience, and facilities assure you of good pictures produced with a minimum of headaches.

A student cameraman is more closely involved with his school and the yearbook. He can often get to the heart of a story more directly because of his familiarity.

In either case, the choice of photographers is not to be taken lightly. Insist on samples from the professional and letters of recommendation. Ask your printer for advice; he has undoubtedly worked with photographers of the area and knows the ability and reliability of the applicants. The mere fact that a man hangs out his shingle as a photographer doesn't make him a real pro. Many an excellent studio just isn't geared to the demands of yearbook work.

★ Choose student photographers with great care.

Many a camera bug "talks a good picture." Examine his work; don't be impressed by his glib references to cameras, lenses, and exposures. Above all consider his reliability. Too many staffs have grown prematurely old because a cameraman neglected to *soup up*—develop—his negatives or decided a date was more important than a session at the enlarger.

Does the student cameraman have adequate facilities? He'll need a good camera (or maybe two), access to a proper darkroom, and good enlargers. If the yearbook is furnished such facilities by the school, breathe a prayer of thanksgiving! Most often the student cameraman has to find his own.

The most satisfactory arrangement is to combine professional and amateur talents. The pro can take formal portraits, shots of large organizations, and some of the news pictures that pose unusual technical problems. The student concentrates on informal pictures. Often he'll shoot the same subjects as the professional just to afford some variety for the art editor.

A growing custom is to hire a professional to do the developing and printing of student photos. Usually this effects substantial economies in time and cost. Often this arrangement is modified so the student develops his own film and makes contact prints, with the pro doing the final printing. Often the professional will allow the student to use his darkroom or maybe even cameras. (Many a young person has moved from this "apprenticeship" right into the studio as a paid assistant.)

★ Photographic assignments must be planned several weeks in advance.

After the professional has been chosen, set up a series of workable deadlines with him. He will need two or three weeks, sometimes longer, to deliver prints. (If you have large classes with individual portraits, this may be a task of many weeks.) If he delivers contacts, time must be allowed for the staff to select those to be printed. The professional has other jobs; he can't devote all his time to your book. Nor can he interrupt other work to get immediately to yours.

Remember, too, that one late or forgotten photo can delay an entire signature or even a section.

Establish photo deadlines by working backward from your printer's deadline. Let's say the deadline for club group photos to go to the printer is December 15. The staff needs two weeks to do the page layouts; that brings us to Dec. 1. The photographer needs two weeks for processing film and making prints; we're now back to November 17. Actual shooting will take 10 days; it's now Nov. 7. Add four days for insurance; shooting must begin Nov. 3. If the Thanksgiving holiday cuts down work days, the schedule must be moved back.

A detailed photography schedule should be begun the previous spring, checked, and, if necessary, revised constantly.

Individual portraits and formal group shots are the greatest problems. Not only the schedules of staff and photographer but those of the subjects, too, must be considered.

★ Establish a policy on postponing group shots. Many staffs require an organization to give 48 hours' notice to change appointments for group photographs. Twenty-four hours is usually satisfactory for individuals. If you establish such a policy, enforce it.

If you have the cameraman come back two or three times to catch all the Lettermen, the Spanish Club will have the right to demand that he wait for the absent secretary to show up. (She forgot all about it and is right now enjoying a soda at the Snack Shop!) But if you shoot the Lettermen despite Shortstop Joe's absence, you'll find the word quickly gets around and other groups will be at full strength and on time.

★ Instruct your cameraman definitely on how long to wait for latecomers.

Ten minutes is long enough to wait for any group. Tardy Timothy will quickly learn the error of his ways when he finds the picture of his club was taken on schedule. Tim's friends will get the message, too.

School administrators are invaluable in helping you set up a shooting schedule and find adequate space.

★ Group pictures, especially larger ones, are best shot against a plain background.

Often it is possible to erect screens or hang draperies. Some staffs find it efficient to place rings or hooks on the molding of the shooting room. From these they can hang draperies onto which fasteners have been sewn.

Ordinary bedsheets, preferably in pastel colors rather than white,

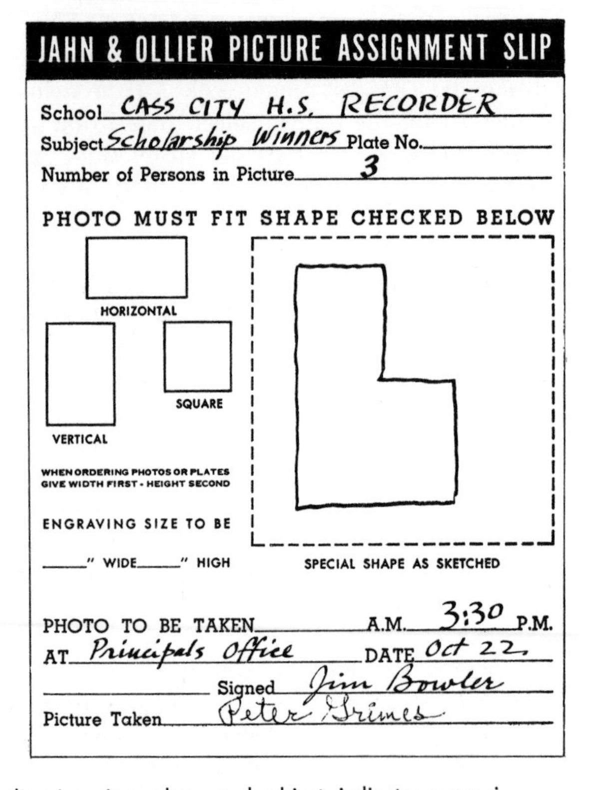
JAHN & OLLIER PICTURE ASSIGNMENT SLIP

School CASS CITY H.S. RECORDER
Subject Scholarship Winners Plate No.
Number of Persons in Picture 3

PHOTO MUST FIT SHAPE CHECKED BELOW

HORIZONTAL
SQUARE
VERTICAL

WHEN ORDERING PHOTOS OR PLATES GIVE WIDTH FIRST - HEIGHT SECOND

ENGRAVING SIZE TO BE

" WIDE " HIGH

SPECIAL SHAPE AS SKETCHED

PHOTO TO BE TAKEN A.M. 3:30 P.M.
AT Principals Office DATE Oct 22,
Signed Jim Bowler
Picture Taken Peter Grimes

Fig. 54. Photo assignment slip gives time, place, and subject, indicates approximate shape of picture desired to fit layout and approximate size of picture in print. If picture is to be very small, cameraman will avoid minute details that might be lost in extreme reduction. (Courtesy Jahn & Ollier Engraving Co.)

make inexpensive but adequate backgrounds.

Senior portraits are often taken in the preceding spring. Groups should be taken as soon after fall organization as possible. Other shots are tied to the calendar.

Other major categories of photographs are special events, sports events, and candid shots.

Section editors should assign coverage of events as soon as dates are set. For important stories, assign two cameramen. It's impossible to re-stage a Homecoming parade; have some insurance shots.

★ Candid shots should be scheduled, not left to chance.

Continuing events need not have insurance coverage. If shots of the lunchroom turn out unusable, you can shoot them over next week. But be sure your schedule allows for such repeat work.

★ Senior editors should meet weekly to check photo coverage and up-date assignments.

All assignments should be made on *photo order cards*. Their form may vary but they must contain: content of the picture, approximate size in which it will be used, horizontal or vertical composition, tonal value (dark or light) and effect which is sought, right or left lines of force.

It is wise to reinforce these instructions with verbal ones.

★ The editor and photographer should discuss every major shot beforehand.

The cameraman must follow instructions. If, when he has arrived at the scene, he sees that a better picture can be shot, he should do that alternate only after the original assignment has been filled.

Order cards are made out in duplicate. The second copy is a handy way to check performance of the cameraman.

A simple but effective method is to place nine hooks on a wall or bulletin board. These are labelled "Future," "Next Week," "Sunday," "Monday," and so on. As soon as an order card is filled out, it is entered on the master schedule and the card goes on the "Future" or "Next Week" hook. Each evening, before closing shop, the photo editor transfers the appropriate cards from "Next Week" to the specific day of the week. Thus on Monday night the board will have assignments for Tuesday through Saturday on the proper hooks as well as those for next Monday on the "Monday" hook.

As the assignment is filled, the cameraman takes the carbon card off the hook and places it in a designated basket (or on the tenth hook).

Each day the photo editor checks the assignment cards and reminds the cameraman, who has also checked them as a daily routine.

It is inexcusable to miss an assignment. It is a discourtesy to the subjects involved; it may leave a fatal gap that cannot be filled.

As assignments are made and performed, editors and photographers must keep in mind the needs of the layout man. These are: *harmony, contrast,* and *lines of force.*

Harmony is a pleasant repetition of forms and patterns.

The simplest example is the so-called *pattern shot.* This may be a row of similar flags atop the football stands, stacks of textbooks awaiting first-day classes, neat rows of chairs or tables taken from an unusual angle. Opportunities for pattern shots abound and they're always pleasant on the yearbook page.

Harmony can come from similar poses of subjects under different surroundings. You might, for instance, see that a substitute on the bench assumes the same pose as a girl waiting on the front steps for her ride home. Or a teacher may gesture during a lecture just the way Cyrano de Bergerac does in the class play. Or three students may be lying prone; one has tripped on a high hurdle, another is a subject in a first aid class, the third is just snoozin'.

Harmony can come from a common subject matter. You might shoot students studying in class, at home, in a car, or under a tree.

Harmony may be more far-fetched. At one school, the flight of front steps was a favorite perching place for students. The cameraman shot a long row of students and the picture ran opposite a page which showed a line of birds sitting on a telephone wire.

An interesting study in harmony is to shoot many recurring scenes in differing techniques. If there is statuary in your hallways, shoot it in soft and sharp focus, starkly alone or with students around it, with natural light or harsh flash.

Contrast can be accented in many ways, too.

Contrast can be in tonal value. A shot of students in the noonday sun can be contrasted by a night shot of the same scene. Seasonal differences can make good shots in themselves or as backgrounds.

Contrast can come from obvious differences. A hulking fullback with a tiny cheerleader will bring smiles if they're in the same or adjacent pictures. Or you can show the same section of the grandstand after your team has scored and after the opponents have. Or show a student all bundled up for a heavy winter and a swimmer in briefs.

Contrast comes from differing shapes. Most pictures are rectangles of about 3 x 5 ratio. Long vertical or horizontal shapes are always welcome. Tall, skinny pictures are hardest to obtain; the cameraman must always be alert for them.

Contrast comes from the position of the camera. A good yearbook requires long, medium, and close-up shots. Many of these variations can be planned. You know that the divider-page shot of the school will be a long-range one. The portrait of the Homecoming Queen will be a semicloseup. But look for the contrasting varying focus that will lend sparkle. Perhaps the shadows in the main doorway will make a pleasant frame for a candid shot of departing students in medium range. Or you may shoot the queen from the stands across the field—or come in for a tight closeup of a friend placing the crown on her head.

Series of shots are always pleasing. They can provide harmony and contrast at the same time. Take bulletin boards, for instance. The one in the art room will be far different from that in the physics lab. Yet the common subject ties them into a pleasant, integrated whole.

Or shoot a series of architectural fragments. Especially if your school has a modern addition to an older building, there may be an interesting difference in cornices, window sills, door frames, or flooring. Or show the various kinds of lighting fixtures: the pattern of lights in the gym, the lamp on the principal's desk, the spotlight in the lab, the misted light in the shower.

The layout man must "face the picture into the page." This gets sticky if the cameraman provides only shots moving in the same direction. That's why it's wise to have two photographers covering nonrepetitive events. If they shoot from opposite sides of the field, the editor will have a choice of the winning touchdown moving either right or left as his layout demands.

Ideally, no picture should stand alone. It should have some definite relationship to all other pix on the spread. And, always, pictures should contribute to developing the basic theme—"This is the way it was in our school this year"—as well as the specific theme of the book.

★ Pictures must communicate.

Every shot in the yearbook must tell a story. It may be as simple as "Spring has come," two students conversing under a tree. Or it may be as momentous as the visit of the President of the United States to your school.

Always the editor, in assigning a shot, and the cameraman, in making it, must ask, "What's the story here? Just what is this picture supposed to tell?"

But, no matter how well the shot has been planned, no matter how well it has been composed or cropped or placed in the layout, it must be a good photograph as well as a good picture.

It must not only be functional and pleasing in its original glossy form, it must have those qualities which will insure good reproduction. After all, your readers aren't going to look at glossies; all they'll see is a reproduction on the page of the book.

As soon as the photographer has delivered his finished print, check it for technical specifications. By this time you know whether the assignment has been properly fulfilled, that the story has been told, that the picture will fit into the layout properly.

Now the yardstick is *density*, the range of tones in the glossy.

Photos range from the pure white of the paper to the pure black of an impenetrable layer of silver salts. (This range has been broken into units of 10% variation in the Kodak Gray Scale, which can be purchased at any photo shop to use to evaluate your pictures.)

The best photograph will have no "whites" darker than the tone in the first, 10% block. Its deepest tones will be no lighter than 90%. There will also be good *middle tones.* Any photo that does not have a full 80% range of tones, from 10% to 90%, will reproduce poorly. It will be *washed out* or *muddy.*

There are obvious exceptions. In fact, a cameraman may deliberately shoot so that there are no middle tones at all; the result will be a line cut, in effect. Or, for dramatic effect, he may shoot in *high key* with no dense blacks or in *low key,* for a dark and gloomy effect. But these are exceptions, and quite rare ones.

The experienced editor can judge the density of a photo with a hasty glance. The student editor is wise to lay the gray scale on the shadow and highlight areas of a glossy to determine if the range is proper.

Check all portraits against deep shadows, especially along the cheek bones and under the nose and mouth. They make the subject look like the villain in the late, late show. All shadows must show detail. Highlights—the whites of eyes and teeth—should be brilliant, with plenty of "snap." Highlights on the skin should not be quite so bright but must be definite. White clothing must be whiter than the highest flesh tones.

In addition to proper density, a good photo must have detail, in both the light and shadow areas. A *hazy* or *fuzzy* picture will be as out of focus on the printed page as it is in the original.

Again there are exceptions. Occasionally a photographer will shoot *soft focus*, creating a vaporous effect which may be pleasant. (Too many "soft focus" pictures are, alas, only the result of poor focus.) Or the cameraman may deliberately shoot the fore- or background far out of focus to avoid distractions. But these are exceptions. Good pictures are sharp and sparkling.

If a picture doesn't meet necessary quality for reproduction, return it to the photographer and have him do it over. This may produce migraine. Student cameramen often develop temperament at this stage of proceedings; they feel their ability has been questioned. But there is no place on the table of organization for a prima donna. If a cameraman can't—or, worse yet, won't—do an adequate job, he should be replaced immediately.

Often student editors are reluctant to ask a professional photographer to reprint a glossy. They distrust their own ability to criticize a pro's work. But the typical portrait photographer is producing prints to display in a frame. There's a vast difference between a photo that looks perfect on your parents' mantelpiece and that which will make a good printing plate.

A photo always looks better than the reproduction which your reader will see. If there is any doubt about the quality of a print, reject it. At any rate, question it closely. Remember that the final judge of reproductive quality is the platemaker. Don't hesitate to ask him for a final OK.

Long before the shooting starts, the staff must set standards for photography.

Portraits

Individual portraits are the most important part of the book to the individuals involved. (Watch how a reader, as soon as he gets his book, turns to his own picture. Only when he has laved it with loving scrutiny does he look at the other contents.)

Good portraits depend on posing, lighting, printing, and cropping—plus the care with which the subject prepares himself.

Many staffs prepare a simple Mimeographed instruction sheet for seniors, especially, and those who will have individual portraits. This will include such basics as:

1. Wear plain and appropriate clothing.

For boys this is a coat and necktie. For girls a sweater or blouse is desirable. Avoid too "dressy" clothing. Avoid large patterns; loud plaid jackets and print dresses with huge flowers will look like circus posters.

"Sorority drapes," fabric dropping off the shoulders in a deep V-

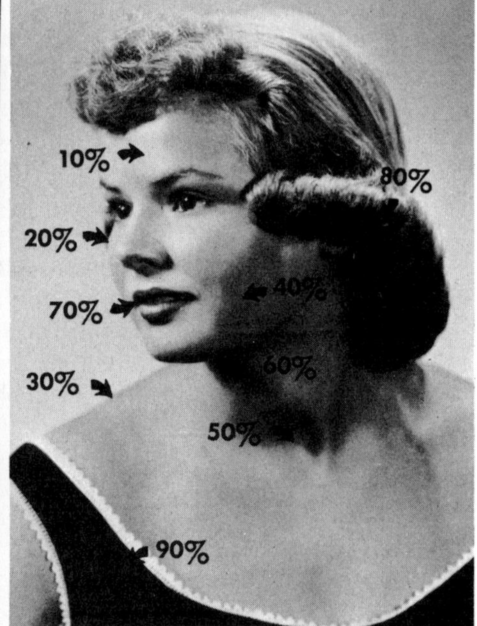

Fig. 55. Photograph above shows excellent gradations of tones. Three pictures at left show variations of densities. A is too contrasty; shadows are too dark, highlights chalky. C is too flat; there is not adequate contrast and all tones seem to run together, losing lifelike crispness. B has proper range of densities for good reproduction.

neckline, are not in good taste. Often they fail to set off the feminine face to its best advantage. Thin girls and especially those with poetic, swanlike necks, are anything but flattered. Usually this extreme style is a matter of a fad of the moment; the wise staff will prevent classmates from succumbing to a momentary whimsy that they'll be sure to regret in a few months.

Blondes look better in dark clothing; brunettes in light.

2. Avoid heavy makeup. (Lipstick should be kept to a minimum and be in a light shade. Eye makeup should be avoided. This is fine for a movie *femme fatale;* for a high school girl it verges on the ridiculous.)

3. Avoid flashy jewelry. (Heavy earrings and giant economy-sized necklaces focus attention on themselves and the subject is overshadowed. Boys should notice their lapel pins; they'll look like Cuban medals if they're anything but unobtrusive.)

4. Pay attention to your hair. (Boys should have a haircut about a week before their sitting. Fresh haircuts make the subject look like a victim of Custer's last scalping. Girls should not have a permanent or a set just before their sitting; their hair will look like a cheap wig.)

The photographer must be warned against profile or semiprofile shots. They can kill a layout if alphabetical arrangement makes the picture face off the page. He should also avoid "glamor" photos where the head is tilted at an extreme angle or where the body is turned in an artificial, come-hither pose.

There will be a few students who insist on such Hollywoodish portraits. They don't know any better; you do. Refuse to use such pictures—and let your students know beforehand that you insist on good portraits.

The conventional straight-on or three-quarter pose is the best for the individual and works best in a layout.

All backgrounds should be the same and definitely on the light side. As lighting changes are made to bring out the best features of every individual, the background value will change. But the photographer should be instructed to avoid extremes of light or dark lest one picture stand out, a la sore thumb, in a layout.

★ The photographer should also be instructed to shoot in sharp focus.

Diffused focus saves in retouching but results are far from happy.

Insist, too, that all portraits be retouched.

Precise instructions should be given on the head sizes and cropping of portraits. All head sizes should be the same to avoid a page that looks like an illustration for Gulliver and the Lilliputians.

The portrait should be cropped so the nose is slightly above the center of the picture. There should be a generous halo of background; too-tight cropping makes your classmate look like a shrunken head in a gift box.

When these specifications are met, it is possible to mount pictures in groups with no additional preparatory work and with the assurance of a pleasant spread.

Group pictures require high skill from the photographer.

If possible, the background should be appropriate to the group. But often all group shots must be made in the same room. Two or three backgrounds of different tonal values are required to give proper separation between them and the subjects. Light clothing and uniforms are best against a dark background and vice versa. This is easiest to achieve by using drapery.

If natural backgrounds are used, be sure they are plain. Wallpaper and drapery that look pleasant to the human eye often undergo horrible metamorphoses under the camera's eye. It is disconcerting to have wallpaper shrubbery grow out of a subject's ears or a lighting fixture protrude like horns from his head. Be especially wary of painted portraits in the background. The oils on the portrait of the Hon. Lucius Thrumporton will reflect the light so much that his will be the most conspicuous face in the group.

In posing a group, avoid the photographic cliché of the "Gangster Massacre." This is named for the technique of the hoods of the Roaring 20's who lined their victims against a wall and . . . brrrrrrrr!, shot 'em dead. (This is also known as the "picket fence" cliché.)

It is necessary to group the subjects so they can easily be identified. Try to arrange heads so they make a recognizable "row" but vary a little on the horizontal plane. Stairways and terraces make convenient posing platforms.

Don't overlook the rich possibilities of outdoor settings for groups, especially those which are in any way connected with outside activities.

Lighting is an important factor. In all group shots, there must be two sources of front lighting to avoid highlighting the center of the group and subordinating the other members. Backgrounds must be well lighted.

For outside groups, the best light source is in "open shade," away from direct and strong sunlight which casts deep shadows. "Fill-in flash" should be used on all outside shots.

Groups of less than 15 may be posed more informally than larger ones.

In all cases, a group picture should be of "only one group." That means that all members must look at the same spot; right at the camera is best. Two points of interest mean two "pictures." Don't let half the group look at a poster for the Spring Prom while the rest gaze upon one of the decorations. Don't pose the subjects so there is far more space between two people than between any others; this will fracture the picture into two smaller ones.

Many editors insist that, in reproduction, heads be as large as a dime. This is a fair gauge, although actually heads can be as small as a quarter-inch and be recognizable with good printing.

B

Fig. 56. Proper posing spells difference between good and horrible. A is typical "massacre shot" cliché; poor cropping has scalped tall faculty member. In B grouping is logical and interesting although care would have avoided hiding part of face of teacher at right.

When two or more groups of the same size appear on the same page, head sizes of both should be identical.

Group pictures are subject to the basic rule of picture editing: Crop tight, blow up big.

Sport shots require unusually expert cropping. Action shots are split-second affairs; the cameraman has little, if any, time to compose in his viewfinder. The editor must find the picture in the photo.

Other candid shots may come under the same category of targets-of-opportunity. Semicandids can be composed more tightly on the

Fig. 57. Sketch shows how improper grouping results in four separate "pictures" because there is no common focus of attention of models.

negative but still require skillful cropping.

As much as possible, pictures for a yearbook should be handled on a same-size basis. This does not mean much extra darkroom work; it does speed production at the printer's.

Hand Art

Hand art is mostly used to develop the theme and create a mood. Rarely is there a sketch artist on the staff who is skillful enough to communicate as well in drawings as photographs do.

Yet, used as an accent, hand art adds a pleasant flavor to your pages. *Divider pages*—those that introduce major sections—are especially striking in hand art.

The varieties of hand art are almost limitless. Even the relatively unskilled—or at least inexperienced—student artist can handle many of them well.

Pen-and-ink, or brush-and-ink, is a perennial favorite. Ink should be pure black, preferably India; paper should be white or have a slight bluish tone.

Original art is usually drawn 50% larger—by horizontal linear measurement—than the finished reproduction, although many sketches can be drawn same-size for editorial convenience.

If cross-hatching is used, take care that the lines are not too fine or close together; in reduction they may blend together and look black.

Pen-and-ink may be combined with photography as in Fig. 58. Notice that the photographed subject must be shot against a plain background or cut out of the photo and pasted onto white paper before the drawing is done.

Spatterwork is fun. It's easy to do and creates a pleasant effect. To make Fig. 58, the artist cut out the paper masks for the snowman, the sign and the foreground. After he had laid them into position, he dipped a toothbrush into India ink. Holding the brush about 4 inches above the paper and 4 inches horizontally from the mask, he ran his

Fig. 58. Spatterwork, favorite art form for yearbooks, is shown in A. B is traditional pen-and-ink. C combines photograph and line drawing; model is photographed against white background, then artwork is drawn on glossy. (Courtesy Wm. J. Keller, Inc.)

finger, a pencil, or a knife blade across the bristles toward himself. As the bent bristles snapped into place, they flipped tiny particles of ink onto the paper.

The area around the masks was the primary target. After he had created the concentration of dots there, he removed the mask from the foreground and laid a fine mist of ink upon that area.

By varying the position at which the brush is held, different effects can be obtained. Poster paint can be used instead of ink. The resulting picture must be protected with an overflap and/or fixative.

Silhouettes are another pen-and-ink technique. The subject is placed between a stretched sheet or piece of paper and a strong light. His shadow is traced or drawn free-hand. The result is pleasant. Individuals can usually be identified only in profile; details must be eliminated. They only tend to confuse the reader.

Watercolors and oil paintings can make good yearbook art. But unless they are done in monochrome—using only one color—they will often not reproduce well in black-and-white. They should be tested by photographing them. The resultant glossy or the original painting may be sent to the platemaker.

Pencil drawings are costly to reproduce. If they're shot as a halftone, there will be a gray background. If you want a white background, the

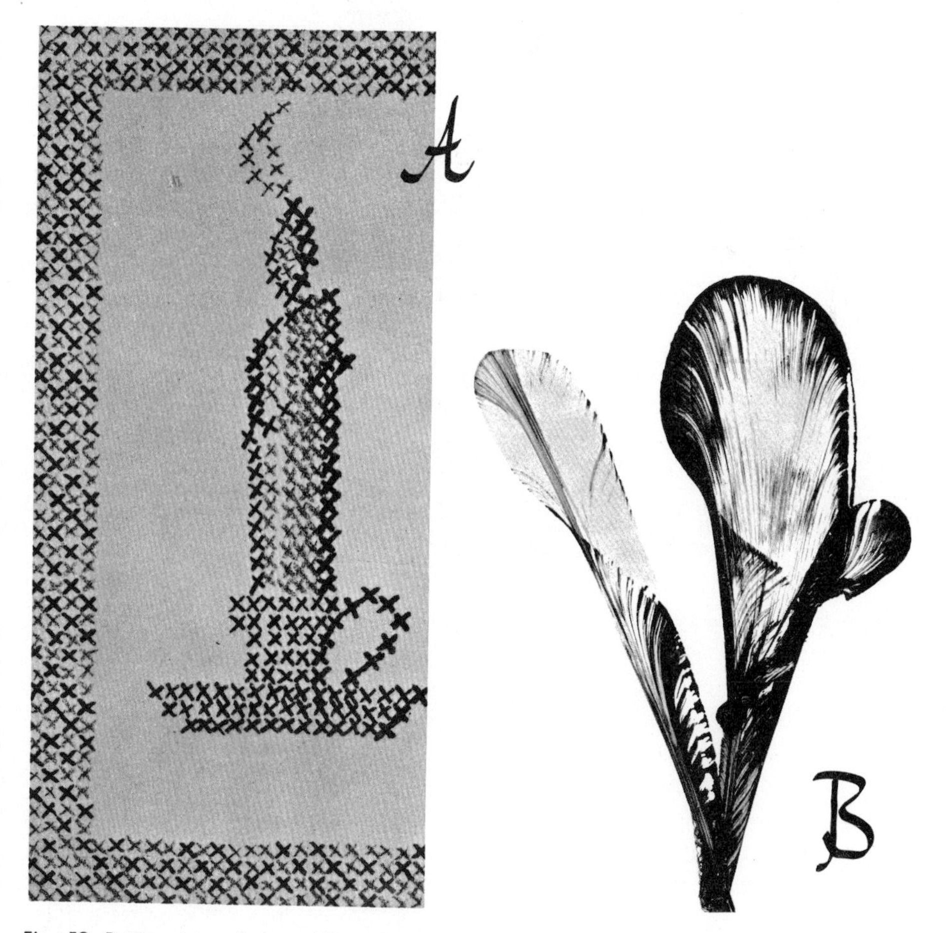

Fig. 59. Petit point technique (A) is a pleasant way to develop old-fashioned theme. String technique (B), as explained in text, creates crisp, modern effect. (Courtesy Wm. J. Keller, Inc.)

platemaker must use the expensive dropout process.

Petit point mixes pencil and pen. A design is drawn on grid paper. Then tracing paper is laid over the sketch and X's are drawn in the proper places. Each X should occupy one square of the grid. Mixing pen and pencil or pencils of various colors will give variations in tonal values. The original or a photograph of it may be sent to the platemaker. It is usually best to send a photograph; it is less fragile and the editor can better visualize how the black-and-white reproduction will appear.

If your book is an extreme contemporary style, *string* drawings make striking abstracts. A string is dipped into ink or poster paint. After the

Fig. 60. Collage produced by pasting together various toned materials; face is Zip-a-Tone, shirt is spatterwork. Inset is thumbnail of finished design. (Courtesy Wm. J. Keller, Inc.)

excess pigment has drained off, the string is coiled onto a sheet of drawing paper. A sheet of heavier paper is placed upon it and pressed lightly. While that pressure continues, the string is drawn out. As it unwinds it creates a pattern such as those in Fig. 59.

These "drawings" can be done with black on white or white on black. Again, the original or a photo of it can be sent to the printer.

Collages are interesting. They are made by pasting materials of strongly varying texture into realistic or abstract forms. The collage must be photographed and the glossy sent to the printer. The light source for the camera should be high and to one side to emphasize textural differences. Collages must be assembled with great care so they don't become a hodgepodge.

Collages can also be made from Zip-A-Tone or other toned material. Spatterwork in various intensities can provide interesting effects, or an overall pattern can be "printed" by using a sponge, fabric, or a sliced-off potato with ink or poster paint.

This toned material is cut out and pasted into the desired pattern as in Fig. 60.

Outlining can be done with brush or pen to enhance the effect.

Three-dimensional art adds a distinctly professional touch to a yearbook. Sculpture may be serious or light. The skilled sculptor is rare at scholastic levels, but many a student can create humorous figures.

Clay sculpture is a favorite. Lines should be kept simple; the exaggeration of a good caricature will be easier to achieve than absolute accuracy of proportion.

The figures should be photographed, preferably against a plain background. Often the background includes a pen-and-ink sketch.

Papier-mâché sculpture is effective. A wire skeleton is built for each figure; in Fig. 61, the heads are old light bulbs. Around the armature—the wire frame—are wound pasted strips of paper, ¼ or ½ inch wide. Old newspapers can be used to build up the form and white paper for the final layers.

Like clay figures, papier-mâché sculptures must be photographed. Either kind of sculpture may be painted; but, if simple planes and proper lighting are used, unpainted figures can be effective.

Paper sculpture is simple but it can be highly sophisticated. Paper is cut, torn, bent, twisted, folded, or curled into desired shapes. Dramatic lighting while photographing the sculpture can give effects as striking as that of Fig. 61.

There are many *photographic variations* that add interest to a yearbook.

Photograms are most useful in developing a theme. On regular photo paper in darkness or under a safelight, lay suitable objects in a pleasant composition. Then turn on the ceiling light or shine a flashlight on the paper. The result will be a white silhouette of the object. Or you can expose the objects—they must be small ones—onto a piece of film

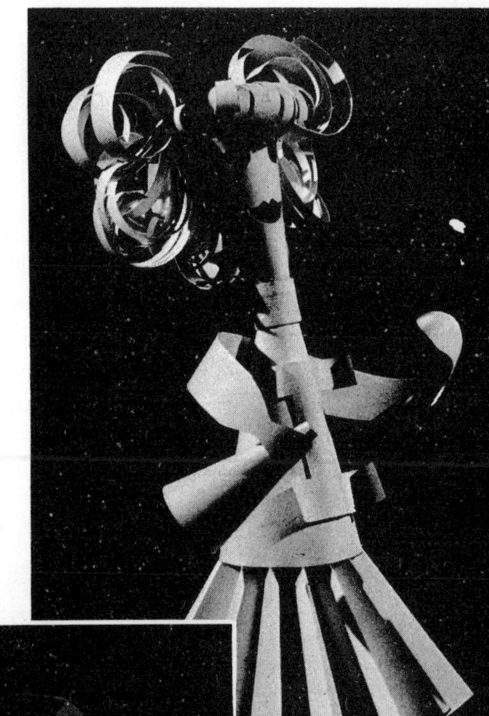

Fig. 61. Sculpture makes striking yearbook illustration. Top is paper sculpture; lower is papier-mâché. (Courtesy Wm. J. Keller, Inc.)

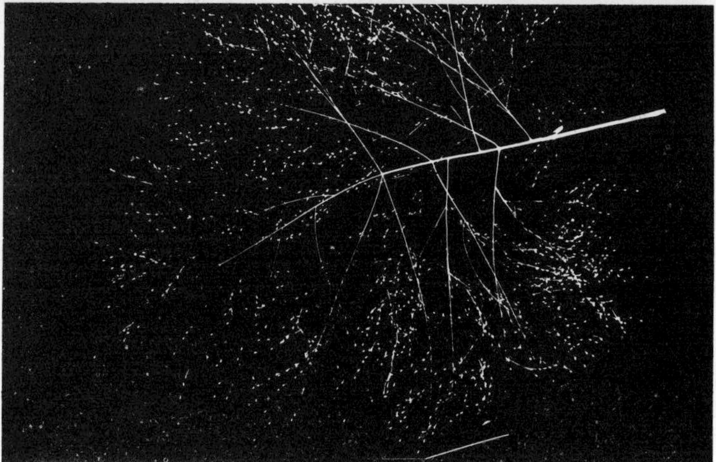

Fig. 62. Photograms made by placing three-dimensional objects on photographic paper and exposing to light. (Courtesy Wm. J. Keller, Inc.)

and use that to make black shapes on photo paper.

Interesting variations can be made by shining the light from various angles or by moving or adding objects between successive exposures.

The light source must be weak and the artist must experiment to obtain the proper exposure times.

The two examples in Fig. 62 are both floral. Fig. 62-A is a sprig of grass exposed only once. Fig. 62-B was exposed to light from three

Fig. 63. Continuous tone photograph, shot and printed for maximum contrast, is made into line engraving. Architectural subjects, and those with well-defined lines and planes, are better adapted to this technique than portraits. (Courtesy Fred A. Demarest.)

different angles. Notice how the center of the rose allowed no light to pass and is pure white. Other parts of the flower allowed light to pass through thin petals or to diffuse under a raised leaf.

Normal appurtenances of student life make good photograms: pens, pencils, class pins or rings, slide rules, paper clips, test tubes, brushes, scissors, erasers—the list could go on and on.

Bas reliefs can be made photographically and are especially good for architectural subjects. This method requires two negatives, the regular one and a *reverse,* or *positive transparency.* (The latter is made by exposing the normal negative onto a piece of film instead of photo paper.)

The two negatives, slightly out of register, are taped together and used as a single negative to print a glossy.

Line art can be created by using a contrasty negative and printing it onto *orthochromatic paper* that will eliminate intermediate tones.

Interesting effects are obtained by laying a piece of loosely-woven fabric over the photo paper before exposing it.

Solorization is done by exposing photo paper to a negative in the normal way, then turning on the top lights for an instant. The result is a reversal of tones. This is a tricky process that requires much experimentation.

Reverses are striking if the subject is properly chosen. Reverses are made by printing from a positive transparency or by having the platemaker make a reverse plate from a normal photograph. The effect is that of viewing a negative lying on a piece of white paper.

There are many commercial photo houses that will, for a slight cost, transform regular photos into crayon-like mezzotints. Special engraver's screens also create dramatic effects. These use parallel lines instead of crossed ones in the halftone process. Lines may be horizontal or vertical or in concentric circles.

If good student talent is not available, *clip books* are a source of hand art. These are collections of pictures, in various black-and-white techniques, arranged by categories. There are many clip books on sports, for instance, that give a wide selection of drawings in various shapes, sizes and techniques.

Clip books are sold at low prices. Their obvious disadvantage is that they are available to anyone who wishes to buy them. It might be embarrassing to find two yearbooks in the same city using the same pen-and-ink drawing of, let's say, a cheerleader.

Handling of Art Work

★ Whatever the art, hand or photo, it's fragile and should be handled with care.

★ Avoid fingerprints on photographs.

★ Never write on the front of a photo, or on the back of any art, with anything harder than a grease pencil.

★ Don't try to smooth warped photos; the emulsion is sure to crack. (If a glossy is curled too tightly, rewash it and put it through the dryer again.)

★ Keep paper clips far away from art.

★ Be sure unwanted pencil lines are erased from hand art.

★ Continue your care when you ship artwork to the printer. It must be packed flat, never rolled.

★ Use heavy corrugated board, *top and bottom,* and stout Manila envelopes.

★ Be sure to mark the package PHOTOGRAPHS—DO NOT BEND. Conspicuous red labels with this copy can be bought at any stationery store; they're a good investment.

It takes lots of work to produce and edit the art in a yearbook. But the rewards are great.

Your readers are exposed to the finest contemporary photography in the periodicals they read. They know good photography when they see it, and they expect it in their yearbook. They're as generous with their praise as they are with criticism. The finest reward any staffer in the art department could wish for is the smiles of satisfied readers as they admire the art in their yearbook.

21. *Yearbook Typography*

Few words but important ones

Because yearbooks use so many pictures, some editors look upon type as a minor nuisance, the excelsior that keeps the photos from bumping into each other. But the function of type is always important and in the yearbook, because a little type must do a big job, its selection is of the utmost importance.

Body Type

The editor's first decision is body type. The printer will show specimen books of available type faces. The editor should choose one that is big on the slug and of pleasant, round form, as has been discussed in Chapters 9 and 16.

Body type should be Roman for its high readability. Periodically a fad for Sans Serif flares up in schools. It should be quenched zealously; the Sans have dismally low readability.

Among the most popular and most useful body types are Bodoni, Caledonia, Electra, Fairfield, Garamond, Primer, Century Schoolbook, and Times Roman. This is by no means a complete list; there are many other good faces available.

Ten-point is the most useful size, and this should be ledded 1 point except when descenders or ascenders are extremely long.

Captions are explanatory text that runs with a picture; in newspaper usage they are called cutlines.

Captions should be set in a contrasting face. The boldface of body type can be used, but don't use its Italics; the color variation between picture and type is too great. Sans Serifs make excellent caption faces; they have the high legibility we seek when copy is short.

There is a wide variation in the x-height of Sans Serifs and so their selection should be made only after careful examination. Don't choose only by the point-size designation; the face may be disappointingly small.

Often a different size of the caption face is used for the senior directory. Here again the Sans are a wise choice.

★ Body type should never be set narrower than 12 picas or wider than 24.

It is wise to establish basic column measures for your yearbook even though that restriction is not as tight as on a newspaper page.

Concentrating settings into three measures makes for a more efficient and economical manufacturing operation. Sometimes editors scorn this advice. "We have a contract with a firm price," they'll say. "It isn't going to cost me a penny more if I change the measure on every line of type."

This may be true but only to some extent. It may not cost you more money this year. But the printer must show a profit, and you can bet a Coke-bottle cap that his quotation next year will reflect the bad habits of the editor this year.

But more important than money is time. Variations in type setting always take time; that means that if too many hours have been wasted while setting type, that time will have to be made up somewhere else along the route and the quality of your book is bound to suffer.

For a 7¾ x 10½-inch page, three settings would be: 12 picas (three columns per page), 18 picas (two columns) and 24 picas (which would be a single column).

For 8½ x 11 and 9 x 12 pages, the settings are: 13 picas (three columns per page), 18 picas (for two-column pages), and 24 picas.

Settings on senior pages and for captions will be different, of course; smaller type allows shorter lines but also reduces the maximum length. But good planning can keep the need down to three measures in this type, too.

Captions need not be the exact width of the picture. Set in one of the three standards, captions then can be centered or set flush left or flush right to the picture.

★ If captions don't align perfectly with the picture, they must be markedly narrower.

Set flush left or right, they must be at least 3 picas narrower; centered, they must have at least a 2-pica indent on each side.

The question of *typographic style* must be decided in close cooperation with the copy editors. Some questions to be decided are:

How much will paragraph openings be indented? A usual method is to indent 1 em—the same number of points as that of the type size; thus 10-point type would be indented 10 points. Often the first paragraph is not indented while succeeding ones are.

Sometimes no paragraphs are indented; extra white space separates them. This is pleasant but also dangerous. It's easy to forget to drop in the necessary space.

Will initials be used?

Will emphasized words be set in *Italics* (preferred) or all CAPITALS (far less desirable)?

Handling of captions requires other decisions:

Will there be a period at the end of each caption? (This is most vexing when captions are only one sentence or a fragment thereof.)

How will position be designated?

★ Captions should designate the top row, or standing subjects. Then comes the second one and so on. Thus the reader reads from top to bottom and left to right.

Will it be *Row One, Row 1* or *Top Row*?

Will it be *Left to Right, (left to right)* or *l. to r.*?

What will the punctuation be at the end of a row—dash, colon, semi-colon, comma, or none?

If titles are given in captions, will they be set in Italics, spelled out or abbreviated? *Pres.*, Pres., *President*, president?

How will senior directory type be set? *John H. Jones* or *Jones, John H.*?

Will you use middle initials in names?

Any of these styles is proper. But style must be consistent. The staff must consciously adopt a style and make all copyreaders and typesetters well aware of it. That means there must be written directives for easy reference.

Headline Type

Headline type contributes conspicuously to the personality of a yearbook. It should be chosen with that factor in mind as well as for legibility and beauty.

In Sans Serif, the most popular are Spartan, Tempo, and Vogue. In Modern Romans, the most popular are Bodoni, Bulmer, Caledonia, Garamond, and Times Roman. Memphis, a Square Serif, is also popular and good.

The choice will depend mainly upon the resources of your printer.

Handlettering may also be used in offset books, but too often student lettering lacks both beauty and legibility.

Photolettering can be used if the printer does not have the type of your choice. The cost is not excessive and the printing contract can be revised to provide type from sources other than the printer's.

★ All headletters should be from the same type family.

Five sizes of display type are all that are needed.

Divider pages will use between 36- and 72-point. This may be

Fig. 64. These two pages show the most common violations of good typographic principles in yearbooks. (Courtesy Wm. J. Keller, Inc.)

Type set too wide →

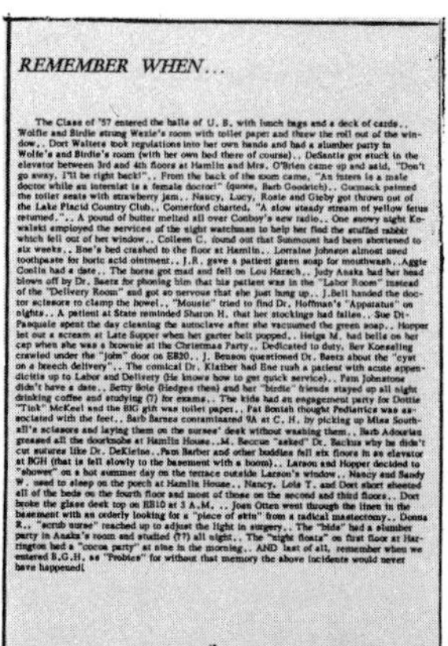

REMEMBER WHEN...

The Class of '57 entered the halls of U. B. with lunch bags and a deck of cards.. Wolfie and Birdie strung Wezie's room with toilet paper and threw the roll out of the window.. Dort Walters took regulations into her own hands and had a slumber party in Wolfe's and Birdie's room (with her own bed there of course).. DeSantis got stuck in the elevator between 3rd and 4th floors at Hamlin and Mrs. O'Brien came up and said, "Don't go away, I'll be right back!".. From the back of the room came, "An intern is a male doctor while an internist is a female doctor!" (quote, Barb Goodrich).. Cormack painted the toilet seats with strawberry jam.. Nancy, Lucy, Rosie and Gieby got thrown out of the Lake Placid Country Club.. Comerford charted, "A slow steady stream of yellow fetus returned.".. A pound of butter melted all over Conboy's new radio.. One snowy night Kowalski employed the services of the night watchman to help her find the stuffed rabbit which fell out of her window.. Colleen C. found out that Sunmount had been shortened to six weeks.. Bne's bed crashed to the floor at Hamlin.. Lorraine Johnson almost used toothpaste for boric acid ointment.. J.R. gave a patient green soap for mouthwash..Aggie Conlin had a date.. The horse got mad and fell on Lou Harach.. Judy Anaka had her head blown off by Dr. Baetz for phoning him that his patient was in the "Labor Room" instead of the "Delivery Room" and got so nervous that she just hung up.. J.Bell handed the doctor scissors to clamp the bowel.. "Mousie" tried to find Dr. Hoffman's "Apparatus" on nights.. A patient at State reminded Sharon H. that her stockings had fallen.. Sue DiPasquale spent the day cleaning the autoclave after she vacuumed the green soap.. Hopper let out a scream at Late Supper when her garter belt popped.. Helga M. had bells on her cap when she was a brownie at the Christmas Party.. Dedicated to duty, Bev Koesseling crawled under the "john" door on EB20.. J. Benson questioned Dr. Baetz about the "cyst on a breech delivery".. The comical Dr. Klatber had Bne rush a patient with acute appendicitis up to Labor and Delivery (He knows how to get quick service).. Pam Johnstone didn't have a date.. Betty Bole (Hedges then) and her "birdie" friends stayed up all night drinking coffee and studying (?) for exams.. The kids had an engagement party for Dottie "Tink" McKeel and the BIG gift was toilet paper.. Pat Bonish thought Pediatrics was associated with the feet.. Barb Barnes contaminated 9A at C. H. by picking up Miss Southall's scissors and laying them on the nurses' desk without washing them.. Barb Adourian greased all the doorknobs at Hamlin House..M. Beccue "asked" Dr. Backus why he didn't cut sutures like Dr. DeKleine..Pam Barber and other buddies fell six floors in an elevator at BGH (that is fell slowly to the basement with a boom).. Larson and Hopper decided to "shower" on a hot summer day on the terrace outside Larson's window.. Nancy and Sandy W. used to sleep on the porch at Hamlin House.. Nancy, Lois T. and Dort short sheeted all of the beds on the fourth floor and most of those on the second and third floors.. Dort broke the glass desk top on EB10 at 3 A.M. .. Joan Otten went through the linen in the basement with an orderly looking for a "piece of skin" from a radical mastectomy.. Donna R., "scrub nurse" reached up to adjust the light in surgery.. The "bids" had a slumber party in Anaka's room and studied (??) all night.. The "night floats" on first floor at Harrington had a "cocoa party" at nine in the morning.. AND last of all, remember when we entered B.G.H. as "Probies" for without that memory the above incidents would never have happened!

48

margins too scant →

too narrow ←

vertically →

and at too many measures ←

Type gets lost in tint block →

← Poor cropping

foundry type, photolettering, handlettering, or blowups from type proofs.

Subdividers, for departments within a large division of the book, will use 24- to 36-point.

For the main head on a 2-page spread, an 18- or 24-point is used and subheads on such a spread should be markedly smaller, 12- to 18-point.

The size of headlines depends on the type face selected; lighter faces normally will be used in larger sizes. Overall typographic color will also determine how much of that color should come from heads.

★ Don't use too-large headlines.

There is a tendency for student editors to choose larger sizes than are required or desirable.

The fifth face is used, when needed, for *running heads,* a comparatively new but most interesting development. A running head is a continuous piece of copy that continues from one page to another. So, if a reader were to read only that element on a page, he would have a smooth-flowing commentary as he proceeded from the front to the back of the book.

★ Running heads should be set in a face that contrasts to that used for headlines.

An Italic version of the regular headletter is popular and effective. A good Script can add interest. If the running face is not a member of the headletter family, it should be in marked contrast so it is never confused with the heads.

Fig. 65. Running heads carry continuous copy from one page or spread to another. (Courtesy *Onondagan,* Syracuse University)

The running head should be divided in such a way that the portion that appears on each spread is reasonably self-contained and logical.

Here is a typical progression in the Sports section:

Hail our athletes, wearers of the gold and blue, . . .

(This is on the divider page with a football action shot.)

. . . They have brought honor to Clay High . . .

(Picture of championship baseball team and trophies won during year.)

. . . the excitement of victory and the pain of defeat. . . .

(Picture of exploding stands with scoreboard showing winning touchdown and one of a weeping girl cheerleader.)

. . . They battled in the golden Autumn . . .

(Many football shots.)

. . . and in the bite of winter. . . .

(More football.)

. . . They triumphed as individuals . . .

(Shots of individual football and basketball plays.)

. . . but found greatest satisfaction in teamwork. . . .

(More basketball shots.)

And so the running head goes, tying preceding and following pages and sections.

Literary quality of the running head must be high because it's so conspicuous. It is a useful device for developing the theme.

Often the *running technique* is used for captions too:

While Thespians posture before the footlights . . .

. . . unseen but essential workers toil backstage . . .

. . . as the audience sits entranced . . .

. . . by the perennial magic of "Our Town."

★ Running captions should not be used when identifications are necessary.

If such *idents* are needed, they should be set separately and run under the running caption. Usually running captions are set in Italic and idents in the normal caption face.

★ Headlines are guideposts for the reader.

Heads shouldn't stop the reader but lead his eye through the spread. Heads should appear at the beginning of a story whenever possible. If the head is placed in such a way that the eye will not normally proceed from head to copy, there must be a strong *paragraph starter* to lead the eye into the copy block.

An effective paragraph starter is an *initial, rising* or *inset*. Inset initials are specified as *two-line* or *three-line* initials, depending upon their depth.

★ Inset initials should align precisely with the lowest line of body type.

This alignment is difficult and therefore rising initials are the most popular and efficient.

School Best School

Page No. 82

Copy Sheet For WRITE-UPS

10 Point Type

All type copy must be
TYPEWRITER DOUBLE-SPACED
on these sheets

INSTRUCTIONS: This sheet provides a s
amount of type to space allotted in layout.
denote *width of write-up in printer's type*. T
desired width, staying as close to the line as
words unnecessarily. *Length or Depth of Wri*
copy will make 1 inch of type. If you want
your copy to the vertical line under 1¾" a
lines of copy. To avoid delays due to type
not type more than the layout space will ac
side of sheet only. Please follow style chose
Do not type beyond width of copy block

Figures show width of copy block on layout when typing is set in 10 pt. printers type. → 1¾" 2½" 3¼" 4⅛" 5"

Copy B

Coached by Robert Thomas, the varsity ended the basketball season with an 8-10 record. Lack of ability to win on the road and the loss of men through injuries hampered them from having a successful season. Captain Roger Baker was instrumental in leading the team to important victories. Tom Wallace and Joe Raes sparked the B. S. cagers by aver- aging 16.2 points per game.

The courtsters started the season by losing the opener to Painsville High 87-74. They were then upset by R. P. M. 77-39 and then by S. L. O. 86-69. The team finally began to show some promise by beating A. S. Tech 87-53 and T. U. 65-59. They were defeated in the final game by H. H. S. 78-75. A very thrilling game.

Having weathered this rugged season, next year should be more promising for Coach Thomas. His line-up will in- clude ball-hawk Fred Day, shooting ace Norman Maynard, and high-scoring Joe Raes, all veterans of at least one season. While B.S. will be more experienced, next year's competi- tion should be keener. The new schedule will include strong V. I. P. and undefeated T. Tech. Whatever the outcome, B. S. will again receive the enthusiastic support from the student body and faculty and cheer "Let's go, B. S." will ring loudly through the annex.

IMPORTANT: 6 lines of typewritten copy double spaced equals 1" depth of printers type.

I have personally read and correcte
the above copy for accurate spellin
and good grammar. SIGNED.

Fig. 66. Copy written to fit specific area. This sheet (only a portion of which is reproduced) is designed for 10-point type. Typewritten line as wide as those here will make line of type 3¼ inches wide. Ordinary copy paper can be ruled to fill specified line length in any given type face. (Courtesy Wm. J. Keller, Inc.)

Operational Staff

com

june 9

the eighty-fifth annual

mence

ment

Fig. 67. Common abuses of typographic principles result in illegible headlines such as these. (Courtesy Wm. J. Keller, Inc.)

Avoid layout trickery with headings. It is seldom in good taste, more often adds confusion to a good layout.

MUSIC

FACULTY

Other paragraph starters are bullets (large periods), stars, arrows, triangles, check marks, and the stylized paragraph mark such as those which are part of most body-type fonts.

Special characters can often be found to harmonize with the theme. *Florets*—stylized flowers—are favorites and come in as many varieties as real flowers.

★ Headlines should be set only in horizontal lines.

Headline styles shown in Fig. 67 result only in unhappy pages.

Note the word MUSIC in Script capitals. It can be deciphered only after diligent effort.

★ Never use all-caps in Script, Cursive, Text, or decorative initials.

All-cap setting is always poor; with ornate faces it's suicidal.

Typography has been called "the symphony of printing." Its mastery requires many years. But even the most gifted typographers seek to learn from the masters. So the wise student editor will seek, and accept, the advice of his printer. The printer has devoted himself to his art, and he is just as concerned as the staff that the yearbook be a true work of art.

22. *Yearbook Layout*

Pleasing the eye to reach the mind

No coach can tell every man on the football team what to do under all circumstances. Twenty-two players moving freely on the gridiron create so many situations that the total number possible is beyond estimating. So he drills the team in fundamentals and each man must adapt those principles to the varying occurrences on the field.

Yearbook layouts can, and do, vary just as much. Potential combinations of pictures and type blocks in various sizes are unlimited. The editor must solve a new problem each time he starts work.

★ Layout must be functional.

Layout has three major purposes:

1. To create a pattern that is pleasant and will attract the eye;
2. To lead the eye through all the elements of the spread, two facing pages;
3. To help communicate by presenting a logical knitting of words and pictures.

★ Layout must be organic.

It must grow from the materials the designer has to work with. Just as those materials change from spread to spread, so must the layouts change.

The first thing the designer does is decide which element best expresses the most important idea on the spread. This element—art, head or copy—is spotlighted, with all other elements focusing reader attention on it.

★ Layout must be invisible.

Many student staffers learn with surprise that books are designed.

Although we all have lived with books since our first fairy tales, we are unaware of the artistry that created those pages. This is the mark of a great designer, to make his work look as if it isn't work, as if the book just grew like a tulip from a bulb.

★ Avoid gimmicks.

A beginning designer seems to think that a page must be razzle-dazzle to demonstrate his skill. He's like the amateur actor who postures and gesticulates. But not the professional actor; the best one never seems to be acting at all.

The overuse of fancy backgrounds, circles, silhouettes, photos cocked at an angle, color elements—this is like applying several coats of brilliant paint to hide poor carpentry.

Note that this admonition says the "overuse" of such devices. Used sparingly—very sparingly—these techniques can add variety and interest. But temptation to excess is always present and too often is overpowering.

★ Never place an element anywhere in the margin—that is, between the normal type area and the edge of the page.

Before a musician can play variations on a theme, he must make the theme familiar to his audience. So with the editor.

He must establish a basic page size and shape. This means that on every page, each margin must be touched, and thus defined, by one or more element. Pictures may break out of the basic rectangle. But when they do, they must bleed, go all the way off the page.

★ The basic tone of each spread should be the same as of other spreads.

This doesn't mean that all pictures and type blocks must be the same size. But the total area covered by ink on each spread should be approximately the same.

Obviously there will be exceptions. The title page may have very little type or art; another page may be completely covered by a picture. But these are accent pages. They must be the exception; the rule must be the norm.

★ Only one added color should be used throughout the book.

Not every yearbook can afford color (which will be discussed later in this chapter). This is not a handicap. A good book will be good in black-and-white. Color can add to a good book; it can't make a poor book good.

★ All art work should be done in the same medium.

It is possible to mix pen-and-ink, charcoal, and wash drawings in a single volume. But it is far easier to create overall harmony if only one technique is used.

The designer begins his work by gathering all available art for a spread. He will have copy and heads or he will discuss with the section editor how they will be handled so he can allow sufficient space and position it properly.

He then draws thumbnails, small, rough, hasty sketches that suggest

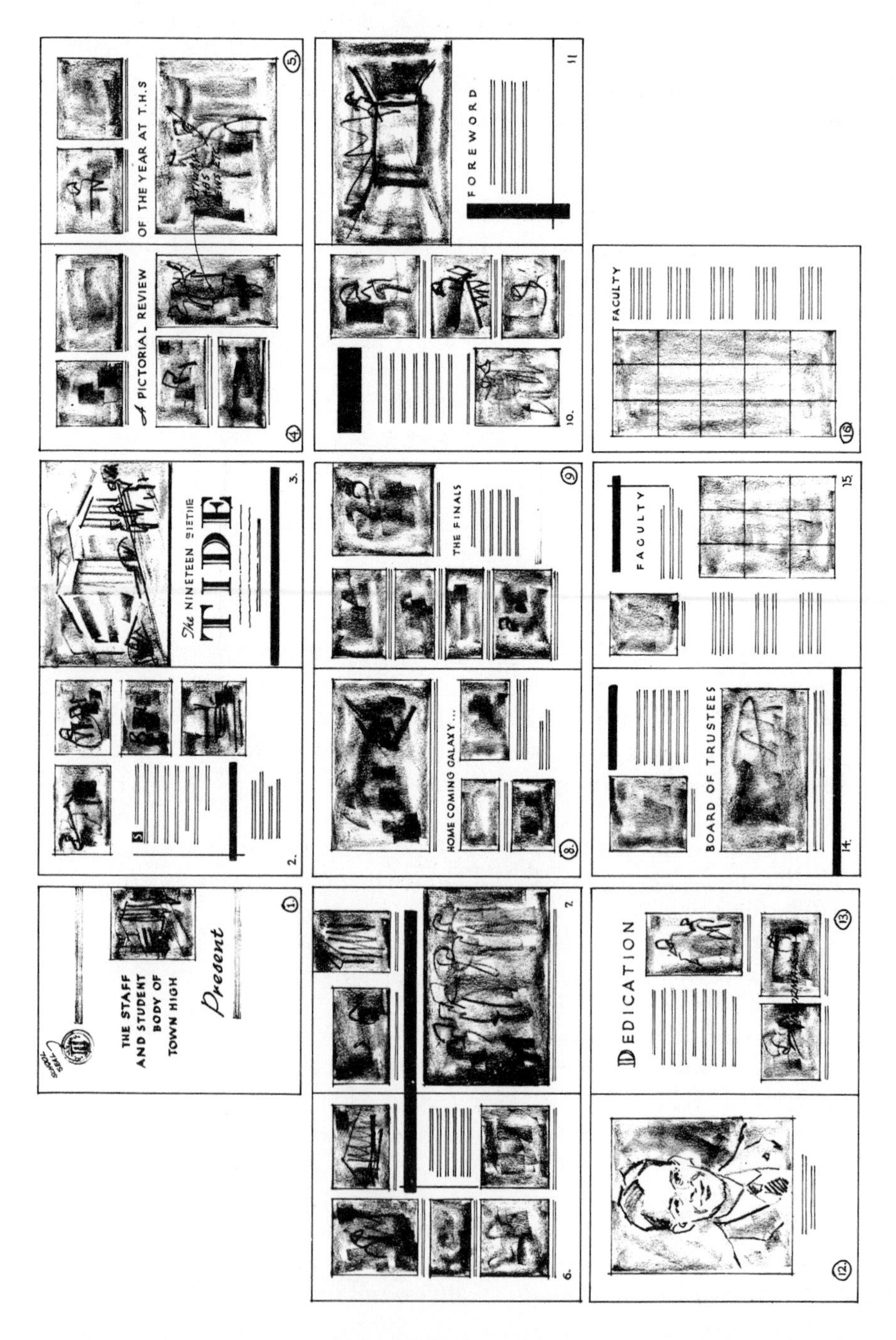

Fig. 68. Miniature dummies enable editor to study progression and assure both harmony and contrast. Gray areas indicate use of color. Note that all pages with circled numbers are printed on front side of press sheet; all others, on back. If color is available on either side of the sheet, all pages on that side can use color at no extra charge. (Courtesy Foote & Davies)

how the various elements can be placed in harmonious relationship to each other.

★ Yearbook pages are designed in facing pairs, as a spread.

Just like his colleague on the school newspaper, he has two basic layout patterns he can use: formal or informal balance.

Formal balance can be achieved by centered or symmetrical layout. Centered layouts are self-explanatory; every element is centered on a vertical axis running down the middle of the page. Symmetrical layout arranges elements so that if the page, or the spread, is split down the middle, each half will be a mirror image of the other.

Formal balance is too static to appeal to high school readers, or, in large quantities, to any reader. But it has dignity, stability, and authority, and there are places where such layout pattern is appropriate.

Formal balance can be modified to make it more dynamic by having the balance between halves of a page or pages of a spread only approximate and not a mirror arrangement.

Formal balance is the easiest for the inexperienced designer to achieve, and so we often find formal pages interspersed with informal ones. The effect is pleasing.

Informal balance is harder to create. In fact, many a beginning designer is scared by the apparent anarchy of such pages. But the fact that the laws aren't obvious doesn't mean that there is no discipline under which the designer must work.

First the designer imagines a pivot at the optical center of the spread, about an inch above the mathematical center. Then he disposes all elements on the pages so the spread hangs almost, but not quite, perpendicular.

★ A little imbalance is pleasant on a spread.

If you'll look at a favorite picture in your home or at school, you'll notice that almost invariably there are strong diagonal lines that make the picture "lean" a little to one side. This imbalance lends a nice dynamic motion.

Balancing an informal, or dynamic, layout is something like balancing two little kids on a teeter-totter. The lighter one has to move far out to the end of the plank, or the little fatso closer to the fulcrum. Or two tiny folks may balance their Daddy.

Of course, a page is more like a Ferris wheel; we have several elements that must balance each other. There are no scales or balances to measure the "optical weight" of an element; for this the designer must trust his eye.

A few rough rules of thumb:

★ Pictures with dark backgrounds outweigh equal-sized but lighter pictures.

★ A picture at the top of the page will outweigh an equal-sized one at the bottom.

★ Circles outweigh squares.

★ Vertical pictures outweigh horizontal ones of the same area.

★ Elements on the right half of a page or spread will outweigh their mathematical equals on the left. This is because of the left-to-right movement of the reading eye.

★ Headlines and copy blocks weigh about half as much as a halftone of the same area. The color of the type, of course, can change this ratio.

As he draws his thumbnails—and the good designer will do up to a dozen, or even more, for every spread—he can use some basic layout patterns as a starting point.

Classical layout is so named because the great artists of all ages have utilized it so often. Here elements are placed to form basic patterns, such as the triangle with the point at top or bottom; L-shapes with the juncture at any corner of the spread; T's or U's pointing in any direction, or, the most beloved of all, the S or particularly the reverse S.

The frame, a band of strong display elements along any one, or any combination of sides, is easy and attractive.

Rectangular layout is sometimes called the Mondriaan technique, for Piet Mondriaan, the contemporary painter. It is discussed in Chapter 13. It applies to yearbook spreads as well as ads.

The *expanding layout* is created by defining the basic page, within margins, to capacity. Then in one corner—usually an upper one and, more often than not, the top left corner of the spread—a picture is expanded by bleeding it off the top and side. As the picture expands out of the rectangle, it seems to enlarge the entire page.

Another useful layout pattern of several names—oriented layout or the buddy or no-orphan system—is discussed in Chapter 13, too.

The more buddying-up on a yearbook page, the more agreeable it is to the reader. He likes things neat and orderly. He is more pleased by a picture that obviously has been placed with care than by one that just floats around on the page.

The buddy system can be used to advantage to unify any other layout pattern, too.

Once a thumbnail has been sketched, the designer works with a rough dummy. This is a full-sized duplicate of the finished page.

An easy way to visualize what the final page will look like is to cut pieces of construction paper to the size of the scaled cuts (discussed in Chapter 10), headlines and copy blocks. Black and two tones of gray can represent halftones; copy can be clipped from a magazine. By moving these same-size elements around, the designer can actually see and determine the most pleasing and functional pattern.

When the pattern has been decided upon, it is rendered in pencil as the rough. This dummy, along with the art work, is submitted to the art editor and/or the editor-in-chief for approval.

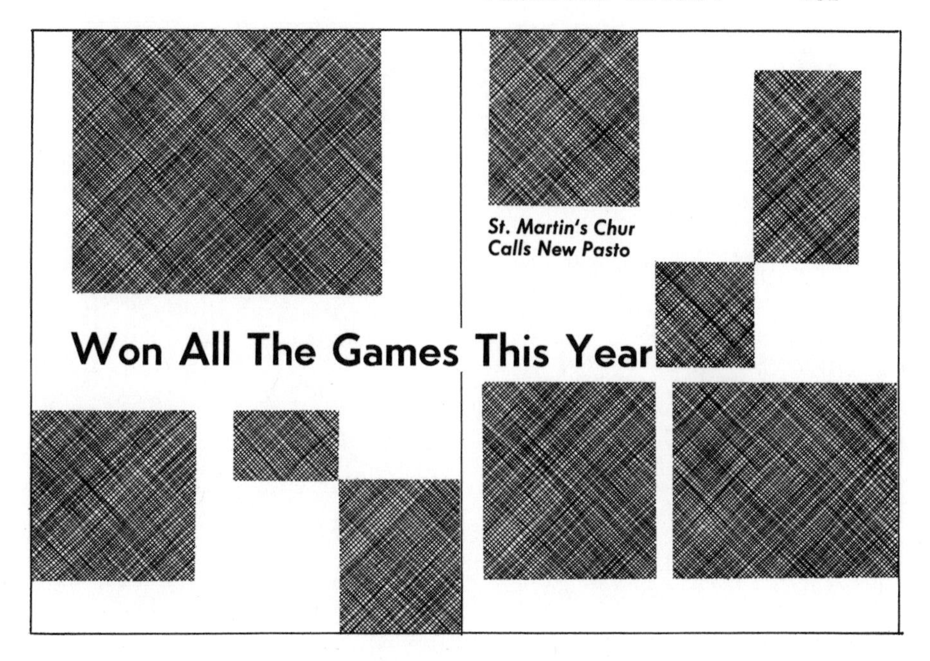
St. Martin's Chur
Calls New Pasto
Won All The Games This Year

Fig. 69. Placement of pictures determined by manipulating rectangles of material of same size and tone as photos. Any appropriate type face, no matter what its copy, is used to indicate headlines.

Then the *final* or *working dummy* is drawn with great care. Usually this is done on printed sheets which are covered with a grid of light blue lines one pica apart. (If the book is in offset, the pasteup man at the printer's uses a similar sheet to prepare the page for the platemaker's camera. Using the grid as reference points, he can duplicate the dummy to the most minute detail.)

Margins must be carefully shown. The area for each picture—as it will be scaled down—is shown precisely. Copy must be properly fitted and the block positioned.

These dummies, or layouts, are the plans from which the printer builds each page. He will follow the plans as carefully as a carpenter; any changes made by the staff are costly and, if they require an inordinate amount of time, will be charged for as author's alterations, such as those discussed in Chapter 7.

It is convenient—and smart—to have a checklist to remind you to give all necessary instructions:

1. Are all pictures and type blocks in proper size and position?

It's embarrassing to have a picture marked for the top 22 square inches on a page and then find out that the halftone is 28 square inches. Does the printer trim it and perhaps destroy the effect? Does he reduce the photo and perhaps crop further than you had intended? These gaffes are expensive in time if not always in money.

2. Are all elements properly keyed?

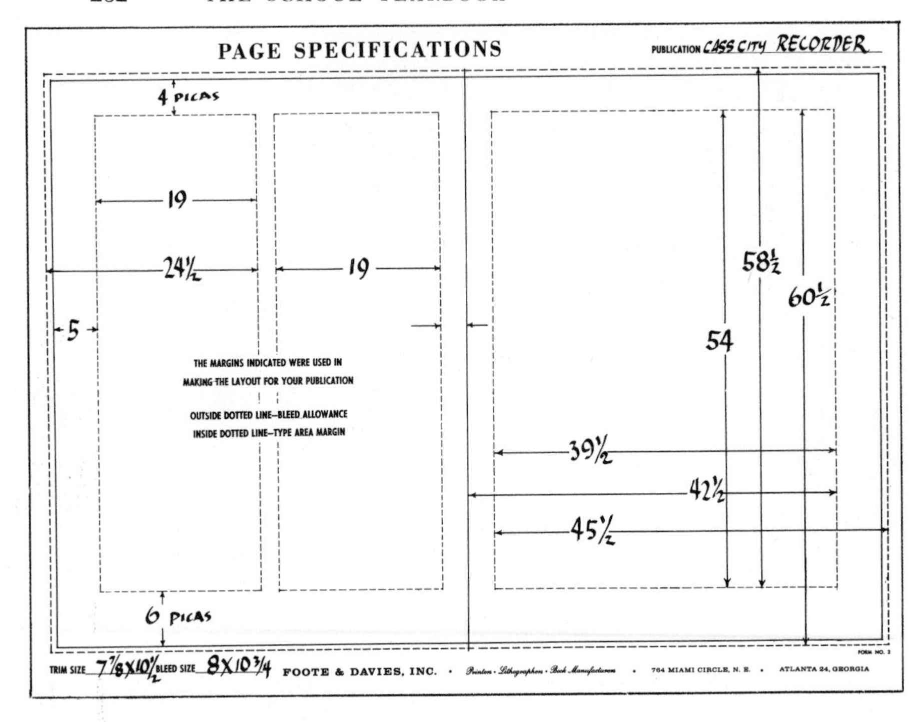

Fig. 70. Specification sheet. Layout man uses chart like this as constant reference to determine that margins, columns, and bleeds are consistent. (Courtesy Foote & Davies)

Pictures are indicated by an outline on the dummy and there are marked "Photo #1," "Art #3," and the like. "Art" refers to any nonphotographic illustration. The corresponding picture is labeled by both that number and the page on which it appears: "Photo #4, Pg. 27." This key is written lightly on the back of the photo with a blue grease pencil or onto a projecting flap.

Copy blocks are designated by letters—"A," "B," "C," and so on—to avoid confusion with pictures. Copy is usually shown on the dummy by pairs of parallel lines, although here, too, a rectangle may be drawn. It is plainly marked "Copy A" and the original typescript as "Copy A, Pg. 27."

3. Are the folios indicated?

The folio is the page number plus, sometimes, the name of the book. These should always be in the same position, usually at the bottom of the page. Numbers go to the outside corners, the name at the inside margin. If a picture bleeds into that position, the folio is just omitted. But it should never be omitted by sheer oversight.

4. Are color areas and screens clearly indicated?

These are additional instructions to the basic keys. A picture might be marked "Photo #2, green duotone" or "Copy A, green."

Tint blocks and reverses are marked in the same fashion.

5. Is the name of your school on every dummy?

Most printers work on many books at the same time. Unidentified layouts can bring deadly confusion.

The dispatch department should check carefully to be sure that each layout sheet is accompanied by the proper number of pictures and by all the copy that goes on the page. It is much easier to find a missing photo or headline in the yearbook office at that time than at the printer's, or some weeks later when everyone involved is engrossed in new duties.

Remember that three different departments will be working on the material you send. The composing room will set the type, the camera room will make halftone and line negatives, and the makeup department will put them all together. They don't even see each other's copy.

★ Place instructions on the proper copy.

There is no point in writing the typeface or size on the dummy; the typesetter never sees it there. He needs this information on the typescript. Nor will it help the cameraman to have a notation "Reduce to 18 picas wide" on the dummy which is in someone else's hands; he needs it with the art.

Conversely, all instructions on makeup should be written on the dummy, nowhere else.

Once a spread has left the designer's and art editor's bailiwick, they begin immediately on another pair of pages. The new layout must have some family resemblance to all previous ones but will vary in detail as much as the elements therein do.

The designer may use the same basic layout pattern or he may inject a totally different look for variety. He may use a formally balanced spread; he may have a very heavy or light one. But always he will remember that, if this is a variation, he will make it dramatically contrasting, and he will use such variations sparingly.

He is much like the composer of music. You'll notice that when the school band prances onto the football field, it chooses a stirring march. The tempo remains constant. But after the brasses have played several bars or several choruses the piccolo gets a solo spot. Its clean, sharp tone is as delightful as a glass of water after a bag of potato chips.

The designer tries for the same contrast.

He may have several square or nearly square pictures in a layout, then introduce a long horizontal or vertical photo. Or he may use a black picture to contrast with a pageful of light ones.

He may introduce a silhouette halftone or a line drawing as an accent to square halftones. But always he remembers that the piccolo wouldn't be nearly so exciting if it dominated the band's music all the time.

★ Avoid collages.

A collage is a large picture made by pasting together many small

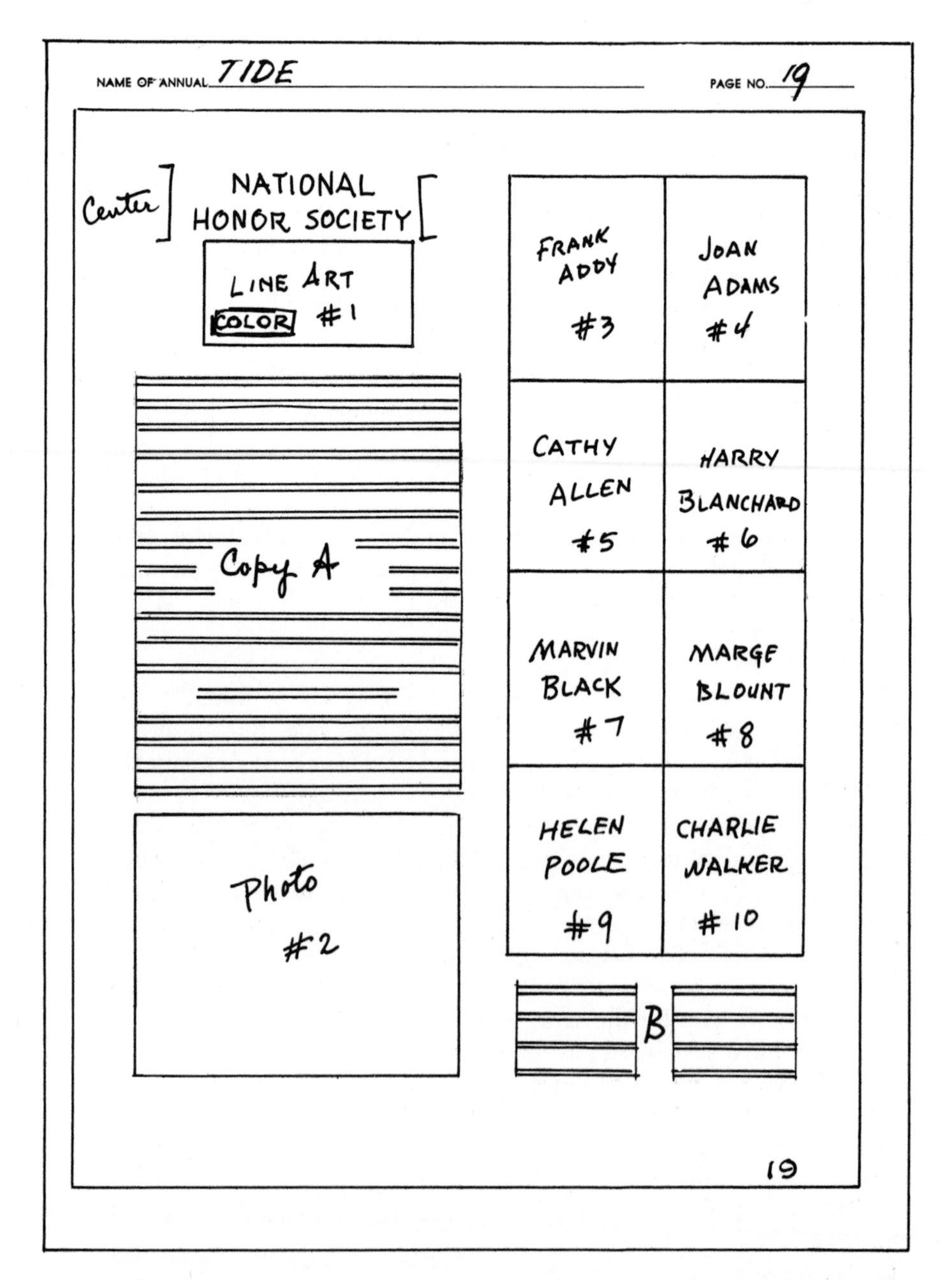

Fig. 71. Dummy shows copy by alphabetical designation and art by numbers. The printer converted this dummy . . .

NATIONAL HONOR SOCIETY

Membership in the Senior National Honor Society is the Highest Honor a Junior or Senior at Newton can receive. To be eligible for membership, a student must be in the eleventh or twelfth grades, have an "A" average if he is a Senior, and never have made below a "C" at any time. In addition to this, a student must have shown enthusiasm, leadership, and service and be recommended for membership. This year thirty-three new members were taken in, the most ever taken in at one time. The main project of the Honor Society is to help with the schedules before and during Christmas holidays. The meetings are held on the second and fourth Thursdays of every month.

Each year members sell popcorn to raise money, some of which goes to provide a medal awarded by the society to the most outstanding achievement during the year.

OFFICERS

Mary Jones . . . . *President*
Marvin Brooks . . . . *Vice President*
Patrick Keel . . . . *Treasurer*
David Harper . . . . *Secretary*

FRANK ADDY
CATHY ALLEN
MARVIN BLACK
HELEN POOLE

JOAN ADAMS
HARRY BLANCHARD
MARGE BLOUNT
CHARLIE WALKER

19

Fig. 72. . . . into this printed page. Line art on original is printed in deep red. (Courtesy Foote & Davies) photos. Collages have a peculiar fascination for student staffs but rarely is there a designer with skill enough to create a good one. Even among professional artists, he who can assemble a good collage is rare. The odds of a good one just happening are far longer than those of Russian roulette and the results can be just as fatal.

★ The best spread is one that is dominated by one picture that is definitely larger than any other.

Pictures gain impact from size. Just as an ordinary man looks like a giant in a bunch of pygmies, so a large picture looks even larger—and has more punch—when all its companions are definitely smaller.

One of the peskiest layout problems is that of the senior section, or that of any other class which carries many individual portraits. It is the mass of pictures that creates the problem. For we can use none of the techniques of obtaining variety in subject or size or by silhouetting; each portrait must be exactly like every other.

A useful device is to combine the academic section with that of the seniors. Most schools find that academics combine most pleasantly with the portrait gallery, although presumably any other section could be used.

Combining two sections enables the layout man to use larger pictures, even full-page ones, to contrast with the small head shots.

The vexing problem, though, is breaking the monotony of the rectangular masses of portraits. This can be done by using pictures in rows of varying lengths to create ragged edges on the mass. Or an occasional portrait can be removed from a row and the space left blank or filled with a small line cut, often a device related to the theme of the yearbook.

Even such a simple device as running the identification above, rather than below, an occasional portrait, will break up the monotonous lines of head shots. In offset books, this adds no cost; in letterpress books, the printer must saw out those portraits which will not align. This imposes an extra cost but it is slight and is worth the expenditure.

Portraits of class advisors or other faculty members may be made larger than the senior portraits and inserted into the block of smaller pictures. Student pictures, even of class officers, should not be used in this way; to avoid even the suspicion of favoritism, all senior portraits should be identical in size.

Running heads are useful in the senior section. Line art gives pleasant contrast to masses of halftone. If color is available in only one or two signatures, the editor should consider its use in the senior section.

Disposition of the *senior index* also has a bearing on the attractiveness of senior pages. In some books, only the identifying name is used with the picture; the information about the courses, activities and personality of the senior is given in another section, the index.

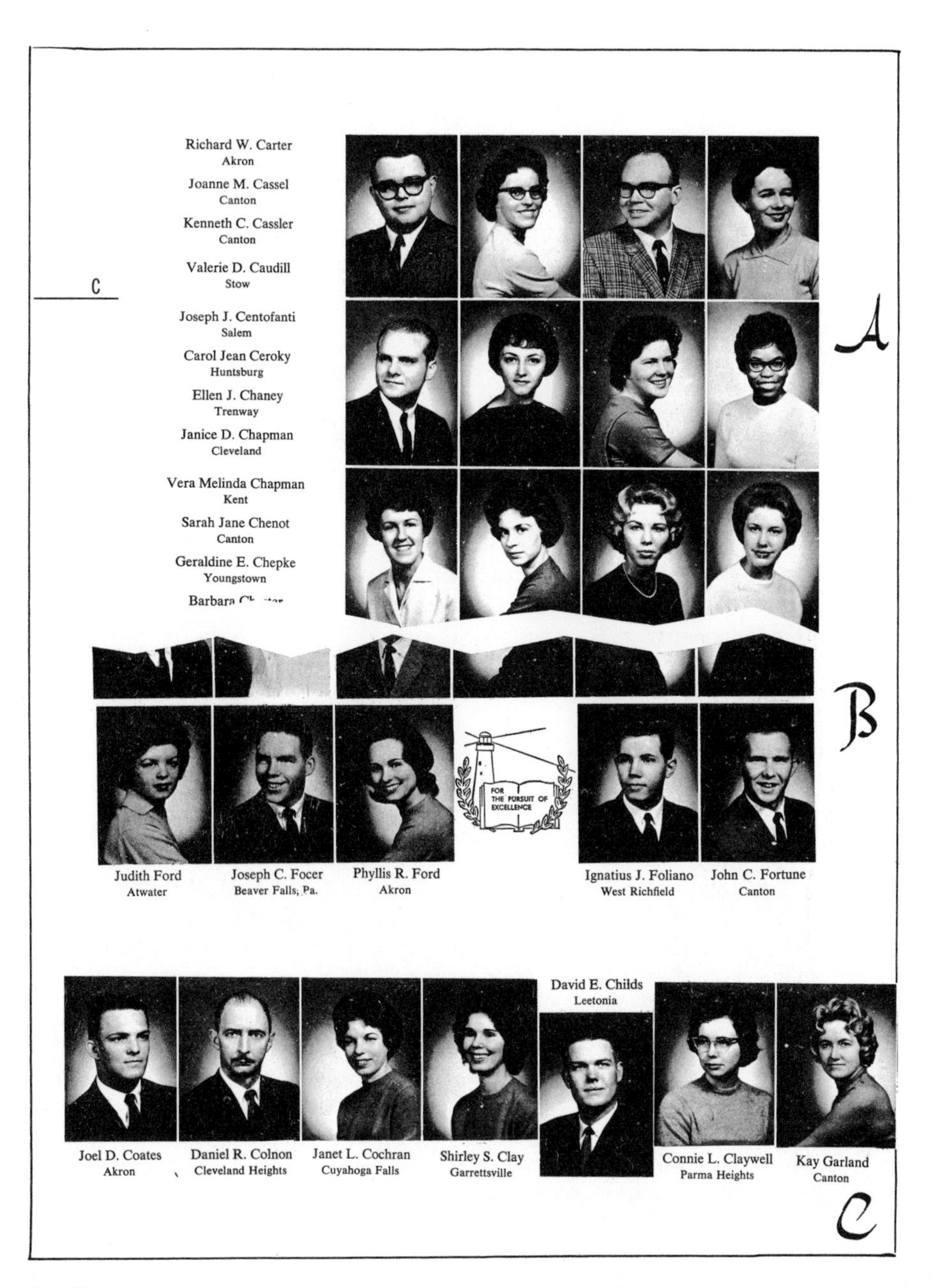

Fig. 73. Senior pages. A shows conventional method for handling many individual pictures. B breaks up masses of portraits by inserting seal or similar line art. C breaks up monotony of horizontal line by dropping one picture and running identification above it.

This practice aggravates the problem of disposition of portraits because it forces more pictures onto a page.

From the designer's point of view, it is better to include this index material with the portraits. This requires more space, unfortunately, because usually the areas of type have to be tailored to the number of lines required for the most active senior on the page and there will be blank areas where a senior has few extracurricular interests. But this white space helps to break up the page, if you can afford it.

Interesting treatment of senior pages will, perhaps more than any other single thing, raise the visual quality of your book. So the wise editor will experiment diligently. He should cut out, from light gray paper, the exact number of rectangles which he will have to work with as portraits. He will move them around on his layout sheets until he creates a pleasant pattern.

While he is doing this, he must remember that it is most economical in terms of engraving and makeup to gang portraits into groups. If each picture must be handled individually, costs will soar. But if his layout calls for an occasional single head shot, the editor can still gang it for the engraver if he places it at the end of a group so it can be sawed off with a minimum of effort.

Color

Color is a luxury but a most peculiar one. It costs extra money to use color in a yearbook (although not as much as many staffs think). But once the initial cost has been contracted for, there's little limit to the amount of color that can be used.

Most student designers, and many a professional, react as they might at a restaurant where the proprietor offers to serve a customer all he can eat. The unwise person will gorge himself and suffer stomachache all night. Overindulgence of color has the same bad aftereffects—although this time it's the reader's eye that suffers.

The mark of the good designer is how he does not use color.

The typical student staff may say: "We've paid for the color on this page and it won't cost us a penny more if we print the headlines in red as well as using color in a duotone. And while we're at it, why not run the captions in red? Won't cost us a cent more. And John's idea of running some red lines through the layout won't increase our cost any." And so they finally wind up with a red-and-white spread with black added rather than a black-and-white with added red.

★ Color must be used functionally.

Color has three functions. It enhances communication; it helps lead the eye through the page; it creates a mood that makes the reader more receptive. Unless color performs at least one (and preferably two or three) of these jobs, it shouldn't be used—even if "it doesn't cost a cent more!"

Color expands upon the written word by emphasizing a picture or making it more lifelike. *Full color* or *four-color process* duplicates the full spectrum of nature. The platemaker prepares a plate for each of the primary colors: red, blue, and yellow. These are halftones, composed of dots just as a black-and-white is. But when they are printed, the eye "mixes" these dots. Just as an artist mixes yellow and blue paint to make green, so the eye mixes blue and yellow dots on the paper and "sees" green.

Black adds strength and detail to four-color printing. But *three-color process* has been perfected so that, in many cases, it can create a lifelike picture on the printed page. Eliminating the black plate also eliminates a healthy part of the cost.

Process plates are made from colored slides, color photographs, or hand art in oil, watercolor, or any other medium. Color negatives cannot be retouched as their simple black-and-white cousins can, so the quality of the original must be high.

The fine points of choosing art for color are far too fine to learn in any other way than to have an expert discuss a specific picture with the art editor. So those staffs fortunate enough to be able to use full color should work very closely with their printer, long before the pictures are even taken or painted.

Two-color process can produce realistic pictures but within definite limitations. An artist can paint a picture with only two colors in his palette. Using red and blue, he can paint in those two colors and in all their various tints and shades as well as in all the variations of purple or violet obtained by mixing. But he can never create greens or oranges because they require the missing yellow.

So the art chosen for two-color process must be one in which the third primary—it can be any one of the three—is not necessary.

A simpler use of two colors is the *duotone*. This uses two colors to create a new, third one. Original art for a duotone is a black-and-white, usually a photo although any continuous tone picture can be used. Two plates are made from this original. One plate is printed in a dark ink (usually black) and the other in a lighter, brighter color.

The eye does not see the original two colors; it sees only the mixture of them. The result is a picture that has an illusion of depth and great richness in its tonal value. The cost of a duotone is only a fraction of that of two-color process and far lower than four-color.

A favorite and inexpensive use of color is as a tint block. This is also erroneously called a *screen* because the plate is broken down into small dots so the color will appear as a tint rather than in its full value. Tint blocks are used as a background for pictures or type.

The contrast between the tint block background and the material surprinted over it must be pronounced or readability will fall off dangerously. The darker the color, the more the block must be screened.

Yellow, for instance, can be printed in a solid area if the surprinting is black or the deeper browns and blues. But a red tint block must be screened down to only 20 or 30 per cent of its value—a pink—or it will overpower the surprinting.

Tint blocks can be silhouetted for interesting effects. If you have a picture of your school, for instance, you can lay tint behind only the building, leaving the sky and foreground in just black-and-white. Or you can use an *internal silhouette* which will leave the building in black-and-white with all the rest of the photo carrying a colored tint behind it.

The simplest use of color is to print a picture. But this is rarely satisfactory. Only the deepest of colors have enough body to print a halftone and even they may lose detail. Line work will reproduce well in all but the lightest values of yellow and green.

There are many variations possible in the use of color. As always, the best person to advise you on this is your printer.

All these uses of color enhance communication.

Color catches the eye, especially if there is only a little on a page. This ability can be utilized to direct the eye through a layout.

Headlines and paragraph starters—as well as art, of course—gain impact from color. You can direct the eye from a large head or picture to a smaller one, and a new area of the page, by printing the small element in color.

But again it must be emphasized that only with sparing use of color can it be a good guide. You can hardly see a red traffic light against a background of red neon signs. Too much color on a page confuses the reader more than it helps him.

"A happy reader is a thorough reader." All the elements in a yearbook are directed to giving the reader satisfaction, making him happy. Color can be effective, also, in creating a mood of pleasure.

Color itself is a "happy-maker." We enjoy spring and its flowers more than the drab monochrome of winter and we enjoy the brilliance of autumn foliage as a happy contrast to the sunburned brown lawns of late summer.

So the addition of color elements on a page lifts the heart of the reader. Therefore the temptation to overuse color rears its ugly head. But remember: Through a dinner guest is happy with dessert, he prefers to get most of his calories from the entree—your black-and-white page.

A well-chosen theme is often more effectively developed through color elements. And color can be another unifying thread that gives family resemblance to all spreads.

If the budget doesn't allow color on all pages, it may permit its use on one or more signatures. So, when you prepare your progress chart, show those pages where color is available at no extra cost. Many a staff has paid for color on the title and divider pages and then neglected to use it on other pages in the signature.

Pages using color are laid out just as black-and-white pages. Unless the layout is basically sound, color will not improve it.

If the designer uses the system of cutting out his elements from paper and moving them around on the dummy, he should use colored paper of the same intensity as the ink will be. Color adds weight to elements. If the designer doesn't take this into account, he may find some of his spreads unpleasantly different from the way he had visualized them.

Layout is the packaging of the editorial content of your yearbook. A good product deserves the best packaging; we wouldn't sell a platinum watch in a paper bag.

So layout is second in importance only to the quality of the content. It deserves and requires skill, imagination, and painstaking care. The staff of a large university reported in 1960 that it had devoted almost 41 man-hours to each page in its yearbook. A tidy portion of this was spent on layout. This may be more than your manpower resources will allow; but it points up the importance of a conscientious, craftsmanlike job.

In all layout problems you are fortunate in having an able mentor, your printer. He himself, and many in his organization, are not only superior typographers and layout men; they are always eager to help you. Layout is one of the most interesting aspects of their job as well as of the student staff's. We all like to share a pleasant assignment; so do they.

23. *Yearbook Covers*

You *can* tell a book by . . .

Maybe you can't tell a book by its cover, but, at least in the case of a yearbook, you can get a good idea of the contents from the final packaging.

Selecting and designing a cover is influenced by three factors. (1) The cover must protect the book, not only during the first few readings but throughout the many years that it will be a cherished possession. (2) It must be handsome and an integral part of the book. (3) It must fit the budget; the cover represents up to 20% of the total cost of your book. It is important to make all decisions only after considered thought.

The kind of cover—usually determined by the budget—must be chosen before design can begin, although the design must always be kept in mind during decision-making.

Materials

There are many cover materials, ranging from genuine leather (rarely used for yearbooks) through plastics and fabrics to paper.

Plastics that simulate leather come in textures that duplicate those of tanned animal skins as well as those in a pure, abstract design. Large and pronounced textures cannot be used when fine detail is required in printing.

Linen, vellum, buckram, and other *book cloths* are impregnated with Pyroxylin for a smooth, dirt-resisting surface. The natural texture of the fabric is pleasant but will not interfere with printing detail.

Cover papers come in a wide selection of surfaces. Paper is not as durable as the other two materials and is suitable only to smaller books.

All three of these cover substances come in many colors.

Printing Methods

Five methods are used for printing cover designs: letterpress, lithography, silk-screen, stamping, and embossing. Often a combination of two methods is used.

Letterpress is used almost exclusively for paper covers.

Embossing uses dies to press the design into the cover from below, raising it above the surface of the rest of the cover.

Modeled embossing uses two dies, concave and convex. Cover ma-

Silk Screen

Embossed

Modelled Embossed

Fig. 74. Three popular styles of yearbook covers. (Courtesy Wm. J. Keller, Inc.)

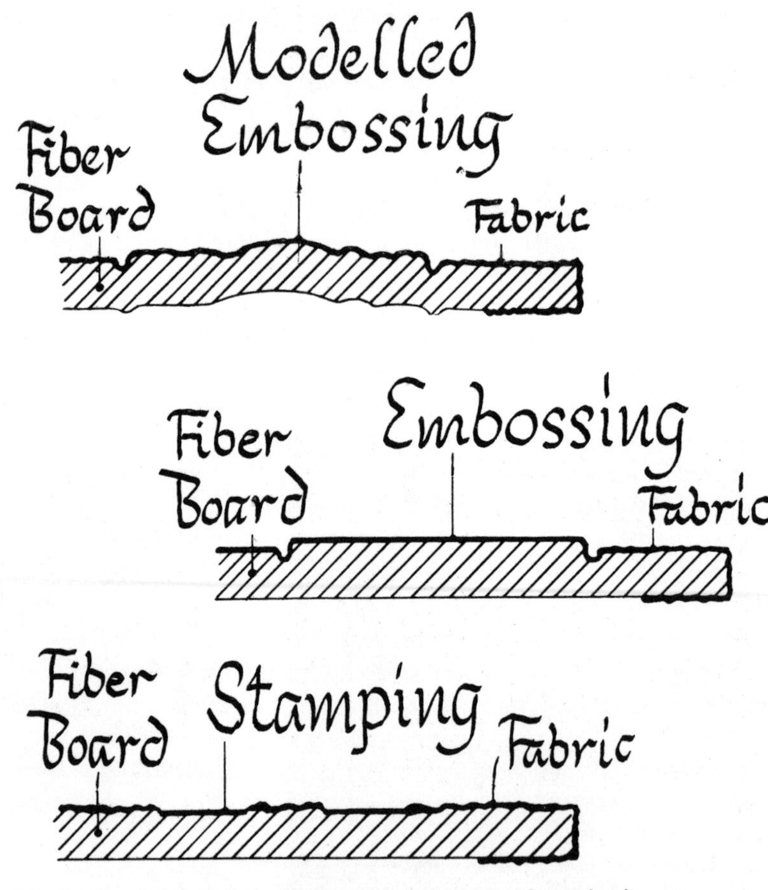

Fig. 75. Cross-sections of three-dimensional decoration of yearbook covers.

terial is pressed between them and the image is contoured like a bas-relief. This is the costliest method, as dies are expensive and two of them are required.

Flat embossing raises the design but in a flat plane. Silk-screen color can be combined with flat embossing, and both kinds of embossing are often used on the same cover.

Stamping depresses—*debosses*—the design into the cover.

Silk-screen printing uses stencils through which ink or paint is applied to the cover. The method can produce fine detail or large masses of color. Versatile, it can be applied to any surface, smooth or rough, and is often used with embossing.

Lithography is a comparatively new development for cover work. Using those principles we discussed in Chapter 16, the method can place black-and-white or color photography directly on the cover or on a separate sheet of paper that is then *laminated*—sealed and covered by a clear plastic—onto the cover.

Sometimes smaller pictures, reproduced by any method but most often by offset, are printed on separate paper which is then glued—*tipped on*—to the cover. This is expensive as it requires much hand work, and the result is often not as durable as might be desired.

There are two other practical ways to add color to the cover. An *overtone rub* is created by hand-rubbing a harmonizing color into the crevices of the grain and embossed surfaces to highlight the texture and embossed design. Or, with stencils and a hand sprayer, color can be added as a halo around the design or in some complementary shape.

Binding

The most durable and convenient binding is *sewn-round and back.* Each 16-page signature is *saddle sewn* by a sewing machine down the inside fold. Signatures are then glued to each other under extreme pressure and are rounded on the back, or *spine,* where they adhere to a piece of stout cloth. This fabric is then glued to the end papers and the cover itself. Sewn binding enables the book to be opened easily and to lie flat. It is durable and will withstand years of use. In normal usage, it is almost indestructible.

The same method of sewing individual signatures, then gluing them together and onto the cover, but eliminating the rounding of the spine, is called *section sewed-square* binding.

For smaller books, 80 pages or less, saddle sewing or *saddle stitching* is the most inexpensive. Saddle stitching is used for many magazines. Staples are driven through the folded spine from the outside of the cover and clinched in the center fold. Saddle sewing replaces staples with heavy thread sewn along the spine, cover, and all. These two saddle methods are not as attractive as the first two methods. But if that is all your budget allows, don't mope; the result is still acceptable.

Mechanical bindings are relatively inexpensive but usually do not have a connotation of quality. In *plastic binding,* each page is prepunched with square holes along the binding edge and then placed onto the teeth of a plastic comb, which curls tightly to hold pages in place. A similar method replaces the plastic with chrome-coated rings. A familiar trade name for this process is *Wire-O.*

Wire-O and saddle bound books do not have a spine that can be imprinted; all the other methods do.

There are three basic kinds of covers. *Hard covers* are made of sturdy board to which the cover material is glued. These covers afford maximum protection for inside pages and will never wear out under normal usage.

Padded covers have a layer of soft padding applied by hand between the cover material and the cardboard. The book is soft and rich in appearance—and also more expensive because of the added manual operation.

Paper covers are the least expensive and least durable. They should be used only on books of a hundred pages or less.

Cover Design

The design on the cover has the primary job of identifying the book. It is also useful in developing the theme.

The method of printing and of binding as well as the cover material will influence the design. Always, simplicity is desirable.

Many a handsome cover uses only the name of the book, and sometimes, the school. The seal of the school or community is always an attractive motif. Photographic art is practical only by lithography on a relatively smooth cover. Hand art can be adapted to almost any surface or printing method if it is kept free of minute detail.

Covers are almost always in colored materials. The designer must keep in mind that this background will give an effect much different from his black-on-white sketches. He may want to do his roughs on colored stock so he can more easily visualize the finished job.

Color of the printing on the cover must be selected to give enough contrast for legibility.

As the design is developed for the cover, the designer must keep in mind the adaptation needed for the spine. Usually the spine will carry only the name of the book and the date. Only by using small type—and/or if the copy is brief—can the title be run crosswise on the spine. Often excessive hyphenation is used to fit copy on the spine, resulting in low readability.

More commonly, spine copy reads lengthwise. Customarily—in this country—copy runs from top to bottom so the reader would have to tilt his head far to the right to read the title as the book stands on a shelf. As the book lies flat, top up, the copy on the spine reads normally.

If photographic copy is printed by offset, it is often *wrapped* from the front, around the spine, to include the whole back cover.

There are three major ways to produce a cover design. It may be done by the staff, by professional artists, or by a stock design.

The student artist prepares copy just as he would for any printing process. For flat embossing, stamping, silk screen, stencil, or printing, copy is prepared in India ink on white drawing board. If more than one color is used, mechanical separations must be furnished. These are discussed in Chapter 16.

Offset copy may be a black-and-white photograph, color photograph or transparency, or hand art in color or black-and-white.

For modeled embossing, skilled craftsmen must make the three-dimensional dies. A good pencil sketch will be adequate to show them the copy involved.

★ No matter what the cover is, don't use handlettering.

For maximum legibility, use one of the many type faces available from commercial sources.

Yearbook covers are often produced by a firm other than that which prints the books. The printer usually ships signatures flat to the binder who then folds and binds them into previously manufactured covers. Some printers have their own cover-manufacturing facilities. In either case, the maker of covers usually makes the services of skilled artists available at no cost to student staffs. Use this high-class talent if it's available to you.

Manufacturers have thousands of *stock designs*. These are least expensive because you will not have to pay for custom-made embossing dies. Of course, you'll know that other schools have used the same designs and will use them in the future. But with the many materials and colors available, chances are mighty slight that any school, especially one in your area, will duplicate the cover of your book.

Before you choose your cover, examine all the variables. Often a less expensive method will give you just as good a cover and often an even better one than that produced by a more expensive method.

Speaking generally—the only way possible when so many variables are involved—silk screen is the most economical printing method. Next is one-color offset, then stamping, flat embossing, and, finally, modeled embossing and full-color offset.

Letterpress is the most inexpensive for paper covers, which, by the way, can use all the other methods, too.

Paper covers cost least for stock; the varieties of other materials available are far too many to be graded by cost.

Saddle stitching or sewing is the least costly. Then come plastic and metal mechanical bindings, sewed-square, and, the highest, sewn-round and back.

Paper covers are least expensive; padded, the most.

★ Note well that if an insert is planned, this must be told to the cover manufacturer as early as possible. For he must make the cases so extra pages fit in neatly.

Planning the cover is one step where the printer or his representatives must sit in. The staff must use mature judgment to steer a neat course between extravagance and false economy. It's not wise to sell gravel in plush-lined gift boxes; it's stupid to choose a container for a book that will wear out before the content has been used.

24. *Yearbook Business Operations*

The student as publisher

A high school yearbook entails an investment somewhere between the price of a motorcycle and the cost of a house. This imposes a substantial responsibility upon the business staff.

Sound financing is as important as good editorial content. For a yearbook can never be just an artistic success; like any other publication, it must be financially sound.

The Budget

★ The secret of financial success is a good budget.

The best source for data to draw a budget is the past records of the business staff, especially for last year's book. Budgeting is usually educated guessing. But there is a recurring cycle in school life, and a careful study of past patterns enables us to anticipate the future.

These are the points to consider:

Receipts

Number of books sold
Price of the books
Advertising rates
Advertising revenues
Appropriations by student government or the school itself
Sale of space to organizations
Sale of pictures
Contributions

Expenditures

Printing cost
Cost of cover and binding
Photography costs
Office expenses
Mail and express charges and other distribution costs
Publicity costs
Miscellaneous costs
Contingencies

Let's examine the individual items.

The major portion, at least, of the cost of the whole book must come from its sales. This requires a salable book and an aggressive sales effort. The price is, of course, an important factor in sales. The book must be planned so it can be sold at a price that most—if not all—students can afford and that they'll be willing to pay.

The greater the number of books produced, the lower the cost per unit. This is the basis of all mass production. So a successful sales campaign will result in either a lower price to the student or a better book for his money.

Advertising is rarely as important a source of revenue for a yearbook as for a student newspaper. But it can be substantial. The business staff must establish a fair rate and do a conscientious selling job. These two go hand in hand; the more equitable the ad rate, the easier it is to sell space.

In most instances, yearbooks are "subsidized" by student government appropriations. Actually this is not a subsidy in the strictest sense; rather, it's a hidden sale. The student's dues to SG are split to include all or part of his purchase of a yearbook.

In many schools, organizations are charged for the pages in which their activities are reported in the yearbook. While this method is accepted by many staffs as a normal way of doing business, there are pitfalls. A large and/or wealthy organization may wish to buy more space than it would be entitled to by pure editorial judgment. On the other hand, there may be a group whose activities are far more important to the school but whose treasury is lean. To skimp on coverage of such an organization just because it can't buy large space is to distort the report of the school year that a yearbook must give.

Sale of pictures can be a lucrative activity. In most cases this doesn't have to be pushed; if students know they can buy pictures, they'll leap at the opportunity. Usually 8 x 10 glossies sell for a dollar apiece; if more copies of the same photo are ordered, the price can drop sharply.

This sideline should never be allowed to grow so large that it handicaps the photo staff from doing its basic job of making pictures for the book. But, as the photo staff completes its normal work late in winter, the spring months can be devoted to custom work.

Staff attitudes to contributions vary sharply. At those schools where gifts have been solicited over the years, both staff and donors take it for granted. Most donors are happy to make a contribution; they realize the value of a good yearbook and look upon their gift as a deferred payment for all the pleasure their own book has given them over the years.

Where gifts are not normally sought, there may be adverse reactions the first time this is attempted. In either case, contributions should be sought without any tinge of "blackmail." No one likes to be sandbagged into a contribution, and solicitors must do their work with a mature attitude, being just as courteous after a turn-down as if a generous gift had been made.

Some schools solicit gifts entirely by mail to avoid any semblance of pressure by personal contact.

There are varying systems for making charges against the book. Costs of printing and binding are, of course, paid on a schedule given in the contract. Those that involve student work can become sticky.

If Joe Brown uses his car to take a shipment down to the express office, should he be paid mileage for the trip? If Sandy Jones works all weekend to print pictures for sale, should she be paid an hourly rate?

★ No student should be paid for anything except actual out-of-pocket expenses.

When Sam Smith pays a $5.47 express charge on a shipment to the printer, no one expects him to use his own money. But when Joe runs his car down to the express office, it can reasonably be assumed that he would be using his car anyway and shouldn't be reimbursed. And those hours that Sandy spends in the darkroom have been matched by the nights that Editor Bob has toiled away up in his room—or a track man or Drama Club actor has spent practicing.

Each staff member should be happy for the chance to utilize his time and talents for the good of the team. It's this attitude that consistently makes high school yearbooks far better than those of colleges. At the college level, senior editors are paid for their work. All too often this monetary reward, rather than the satisfaction of producing a good book, becomes the prime motivation.

Don't forget those items that are small in themselves but accumulate to substantial sums. If your printer is out of town, postage will be a tidy item. Most materials, even if rather heavy, will be sent first class. There may be long-distance phone calls.

Photography supplies are costly, but as they are purchased in small quantities at one time it's easy to overlook their impressive total.

The staff will need many supplies, paper, clips, pencils, drawing board, rubber cement, and so forth.

Usually overlooked in budget planning—and too often in execution, too—is advertising. There should be a definite amount earmarked for promoting the sale of your book.

After close study of previous figures, a budget is drawn up. Any budget requires long looks into a crystal ball; no one can predict precisely the many figures involved. When guesses are necessary, they should be educated guesses and should be conservative.

The business manager must work closely with the faculty advisor and the editor-in-chief, as well as with the printer. Editors always want more pages, more color, better covers. The business manager must keep these dreams down to a practical level. While it's the manager's prerogative to state a flat "No!", he'll try to obtain the same result through diplomacy. After all, the editor is no dope; when he is given all the facts, he will understand that you can't buy a Rolls-Royce on a Falcon budget.

And it's lots easier to add a signature to the book in January, if increased revenues warrant that, than it is to cut down the size of the book for reverse reasons.

The business manager should constantly—and senior editors at frequent intervals—check the status of the budget.

If revenues do not meet expectations or if expenses start to run too high, added efforts must be exerted and retrenchment may be needed. If—glory be!—the budget shows some fat, it may be possible to buy some extras for your book.

Records

All this presupposes an adequate and accurate system of records.

The *ledger* is a permanent record, one that next year's staff will often consult. In it is written, neatly and legibly, each transaction. Consult with a teacher of business subjects on how to set up the ledger. It should be itemized in rather fine detail.

You must have duplicate receipt forms for the sale of books, advertising, and photographs as well as for contributions. You may use one basic form with boxes to be checked for the specific item involved. The customer gets the original copy; the carbon is filed for rechecking and transfer to the ledger.

There must be a detailed record of expenditures, too.

There is a whole battery of proverbs that attest to the value of paying attention to small sums of money. They're all still valid.

The wise business manager must be a penny-watcher. Too often a yearbook is bled white by almost invisible financial incisions.

Supplies will account for many a figure in the expenditures column.

And waste can become far too large a portion of this item.

In the darkroom, the photographer should cut large pieces of photopaper into small test strips. There's no point in using an 8 x 10 piece of paper when an 8 x 1 can perform the experiment just as well. Get maximum use out of developing chemicals, but don't attempt to use them when they're so weak they'll only spoil good paper.

Don't waste copy paper. Use spoiled sheets for scratchpaper. Save paper clips; it doesn't take many boxes of them to eat away what might pay for a good picture in the book.

Establish an inflexible policy on the purchase of supplies. Insist that authorization be given in writing, by the business manager and/or advisor. It's easy to spend money, especially when it's not your own. Students have been known to go on shopping sprees and buy materials which were not needed. Be sure to tell all suppliers with whom you do business that the yearbook will not allow any charges to its account without such authorization.

The business manager should control the petty cash fund and not reimburse any unauthorized expenditures.

You must be hardnosed about this; you can bleed to death from small cuts as well as from a severed artery.

Most purchases should be charged. The cash box should be kept nearly bare as a constant reminder to watch the pennies.

Subscriptions

A logical way to finance a yearbook is through appropriations by the student government. This assures widest distribution and a lower cost per book, and it is most convenient to the students. The yearbook is certainly a major student activity, and a persuasive case can be made for appropriations.

If it is not possible to use this method for the entire school, surely it ought to cover at least the senior class. A yearbook is as essential a part in the graduation "package" as the diploma.

Even if this "forced circulation" method is used, there are many opportunities for single sales. Faculty members, alumni, and adult friends of the school, perhaps the public libraries, all make an interested prospect list.

If there is no appropriation, or if it is only a supplement to sales revenues, the sales campaign must be well planned and conducted zealously.

★ Set a sales goal.

Usually 85 percent of the student body is considered good coverage.

★ Decide whether sales shall be cash or paid for in three or four instalments.

The instalment plan is a good one although it entails extra work and bookkeeping, of course.

The campaign should start as soon as school opens in the fall. The sales staff should have both briefing and pep meetings. Each salesman should know the reasons why a student should buy a yearbook:

1. As a permanent record of an important year in his life.
2. As a way of recalling old friends.
3. To have his own picture in a pleasant package.
4. As a handsome addition to his library at a low cost. (Compare a typical yearbook with a similar commercial book; the difference in price is striking—and all in favor of the yearbook.)
5. As a way of demonstrating loyalty to his school and class.

It should be stressed that, for all practical purposes, the fall sales campaign will be the only chance the student has to buy a book. The staff can't, normally, afford to order books on the speculation that they can be sold in spring. If there are such extras, they should be sold at a higher price than that charged in autumn.

The sales campaign will coincide with that for the student newspaper, if the paper is sold on this basis and if its campaign isn't conducted in the previous spring. The business managers of the two publications should meet frequently to coordinate plans and remove the element of competition.

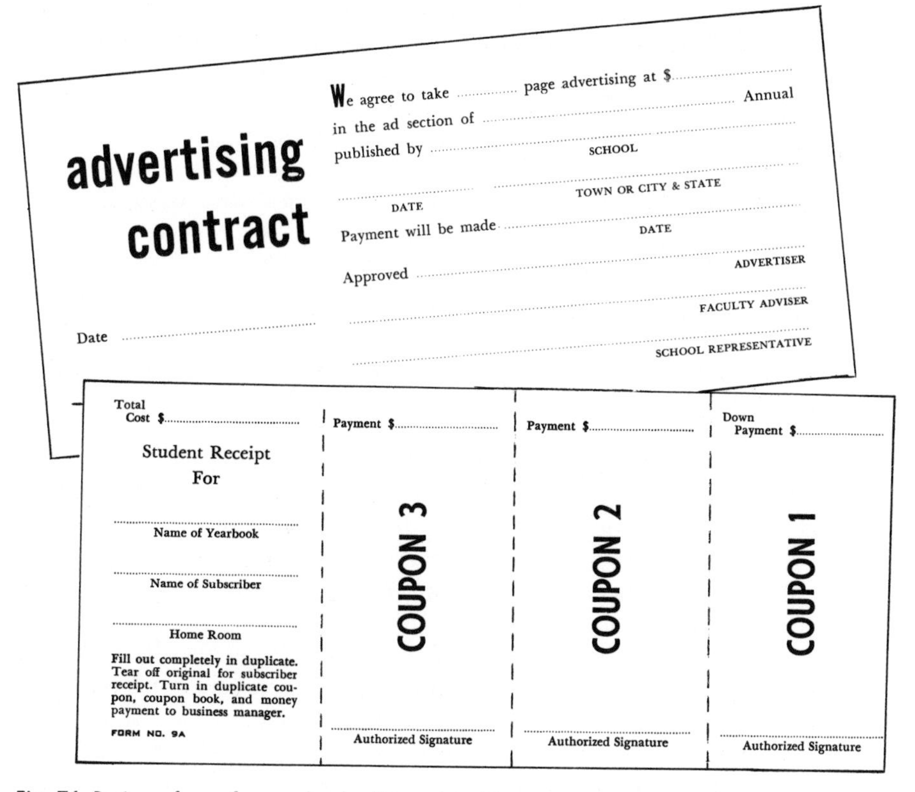

advertising contract

We agree to take .... page advertising at $..........
in the ad section of .... Annual
published by ....
SCHOOL
....
DATE TOWN OR CITY & STATE
Payment will be made ....
DATE
Approved ....
ADVERTISER
....
FACULTY ADVISER
....
SCHOOL REPRESENTATIVE

Date ....

Total Cost $..........

Student Receipt For

....
Name of Yearbook

....
Name of Subscriber

....
Home Room

Fill out completely in duplicate. Tear off original for subscriber receipt. Turn in duplicate coupon, coupon book, and money payment to business manager.

FORM NO. 9A

Payment $..........
COUPON 3
....
Authorized Signature

Payment $..........
COUPON 2
....
Authorized Signature

Down Payment $..........
COUPON 1
....
Authorized Signature

Fig. 76. Business forms for yearbooks. Top, advertising contract. Bottom, coupon for selling yearbooks in three payments.

The same techniques used by newspapers—and discussed in Chapter 14—can be used during the yearbook sales campaign.

A kickoff assembly should introduce the staff to the student body. This is a good sales device; the quality of the staff is a good assurance of the quality of the book. (It's also a good morale-builder to give the staff a moment in the spotlight.)

Use a musical group, band or vocal, to add excitement. (Perhaps one of your editorial staff can parody a popular song to become the theme song of the campaign.) Plan noon-hour rallies or record hops to keep the student body thinking about the book.

Use your student newspaper as an advertising medium. Maybe the paper will contribute space; if not, it's a legitimate expenditure to pay for it.

Signs, bulletin-board announcements, handbills, and commercials over the school P.A. system should be used, of course after the administration gives permission. Don't forget press releases to your local newspaper and radio and TV stations.

The bandwagon technique is a recognized way of making sales. If all his classmates have ordered a book, a student decides, "This must be a good deal; I'd better get in on it." So identify all purchasers by giving them a button or ribbon to wear. These may be imprinted with "Sure, I've ordered a yearbook!" Or it may be just a plain feather or a piece of bright woolen yarn. As long as it's conspicuous the student body will soon learn what it signifies.

★ Use direct mail to reach nonstudent prospects.

Always enclose an order form, preferably on a postal card so the prospect needn't write a letter or look for an envelope or stamp to accept your invitation.

★ Conduct a clean-up campaign.

This must be completed by December 1 because that's the time you'll have to give your printer the exact number of books you want.

The clean-up should be used to call again on those prospects who were hesitant during the first campaign or those who have allowed their instalment payments to lapse too far.

Some schools report success from a *two-edition* yearbook. Part of the total production is bound in hard covers; the rest—usually, but not necessarily, a smaller amount—are bound in soft-cover stock. Because the hard cover represents a substantial percentage of the total cost, replacing it with the relatively inexpensive paper cover enables the staff to reduce the price considerably.

Staffs that use this device find that seniors will usually order the hard-cover book; they are willing to pay for permanence. Underclassmen, whose interest may not be as high, often choose the economy model.

This is a good idea, especially in large schools or those where traditionally the yearbook is a senior record and sales to underclassmen

.we are educating.
..your children in..
..thrift through...
.our school savings.
BAY
RIDGE
SAVINGS
BANK
main office
54th st. at 5th ave. b'klyn.20
branch
48th st. at 13th ave. b'klyn.19
member. federal... deposit. insurance. company
70

Fig. 77. Yearbook advertisement was handlettered for use in offset book. (Courtesy *McKinleyan,* William McKinley Junior High, Brooklyn)

are usually small.

Two editions require extra record-keeping, of course, because the printer and binder must have accurate information on the numbers of both editions. But usually the benefits of longer press runs and wider distribution are well worth the extra effort.

Advertising

The points raised in Chapters 12 and 13 on advertising in the school newspaper apply to ads in the yearbook. (It will be worth your time to reread those chapters right now.)

Yearbook advertising has an added advantage. It is far more permanent than that in a periodical. For this reason, yearbook advertising must be written for long-term exposure. It will be "institutional" in tone; it will sell the store as a place to do business rather than sell individual items of merchandise.

Such advertising can use "posed candid" pictures of students to advantage. Such ads add to the editorial content of the book; here is another chance to use communicating pictures. If the book is done by offset, the extra cost will be slight, only that of photography. For letterpress books, an engraving will be required. Its cost can be included in the basic ad rate, it may be borne by the yearbook, or a surcharge may be made to the advertiser. In any case, the value of good illustrated ads to both the merchant and the yearbook will make the cost a good investment.

As in any publication, yearbook advertising is salable only for the business it produces for the advertiser. The salesmen should know the advantages of yearbook advertising and be prepared to submit them in a brief, persuasive, friendly, and courteous way:

1. Yearbook advertising is permanent. People will be seeing it and be influenced by it for many years.

2. Yearbook advertising is well read. Most readers give it the same attention they give to editorial matter.

3. Yearbook advertising approaches the reader under pleasant conditions. The reader who has been enjoying the editorial content of the book is most receptive to the sales message.

4. Yearbook advertising reaches a wide audience. Surely no book is read only by the purchaser; his family and friends read it just as avidly. A rule of thumb is that each book has a readership of at least six persons. This is a conservative minimum; the actual figure is undoubtedly closer to 10 or 12.

5. Yearbook advertising builds prestige. Just as a business that advertises in a slick magazine is more highly esteemed than one that uses coarse handbills, so the merchant included in a fine yearbook gives his store that "quality" image he seeks for it.

When the sale is completed, give the advertiser a duplicate of the advertising contract. Be sure that all details are given: size, total cost, date payment is due or amount of money collected, deadline for copy, and whether pictures will be furnished by the staff or advertiser and if additional charge—and how much—will be made for engravings.

The original contract goes to the advertising manager. He enters the data on his ad log, where he charts the progress of preparing the ad, on which page it has been dummied, and when it has been sent to the printer.

From the log the proper entry is made by the bookkeeper so payments can be recorded in the ledger or bills be sent out at the proper time.

★ A common formula for setting ad rate is: cost per page × 2.5.

This is the total cost for the page, not only that charged by the printer but the percentage of the cover and binding plus the percentage of photographic, mailing, and miscellaneous costs.

Books with circulation over 1,000 may add 5% to the basic rate; those over 2,000, 8%. In all cases your rates will be in line with commercial advertising.

To encourage larger space sales, graduate your rates. A full page carries the basic rate; a half-page is charged as 60% of a whole page; a quarter page is 35%, and an eighth, 20%.

These rates should never be presented in such a way that it seems the small space user is being penalized. Rather, it should be stressed that the larger purchaser is being given a bonus.

★ Never sell less than an eighth-page ad.

Ads smaller than that are useless to the merchant; furthermore, they fail to provide a profit for the book—and that's the only reason we're selling space.

Merchants who can't afford or don't want an eighth of a page can usually be grouped with other merchants into a single, large *cooperative ad.* Such an ad will then carry several, instead of only one, signatures. *Co-op ads* are useful for merchants in neighborhood shopping districts or in suburban plazas.

★ Don't accept charity ads.

Insist that ads do a selling job, that they be written as they would be for any commercial publication.

Best wishes to the Class of 1968

SAM'S DRIVE-IN

on River Road at Sunnyside Park

can (by stretching the definition a little) be classified as an institutional ad. At least it presents the name in a pleasing manner and the readers can be trusted to read, from between the lines, that Sam is soliciting their patronage.

But there is no justification whatever for:

Compliments of a Friend.

So-called "ads" like this are a disgrace to the yearbook. They can't possibly do the advertiser any good. It is far better to have the merchant make an outright and honest gift and list it with similar contributions.

Other Sources of Revenue

In recent years the custom of having yearbook *patrons* has grown

The Senior Graduating Class
of Clay High School
TAKES PLEASURE IN ACKNOWLEDGING
Dr. Michael Moore
AS A
Patron
OF THE YEARBOOK
THIS CERTIFICATE IS A TOKEN OF OUR APPRECIATION
Marjorie Kramer
YEARBOOK REPRESENTATIVE

PATRON CONTRACT

Please insert our name as patron in the ______ Date ______
of ______
for which we agree to pay $ ______ Paid cash ☐ Send bill ☐
Name ______
Address ______
per ______
Taken by ______ Homeroom No. ______
All checks payable to ______

CONTRACT PRICE DOES NOT INCLUDE COPY OF BOOK
FORM 121 7-61 WM. J. KELLER INC., BUFFALO, N. Y.

Fig. 78. Patrons who support yearbook with cash contributions are recognized by certificate of appreciation (top) and receipt which becomes a tax record. (Courtesy Wm. J. Keller, Inc.)

in popularity. Patrons are contributors who, by their cash gifts, support and publicly acknowledge a student activity which they think is worthy.

Doctors, dentists, architects, and similar professional men are often forbidden, by rules of their associations, to advertise in the conventional ways. They are often happy to be listed as a patron. School and city PTA's, church societies, service clubs, women's groups, and other organizations often are glad for the chance to support wholesome student activities. Parents, alumni, and other individuals are often equally glad for such an opportunity.

Patrons are usually awarded certificates. These may be printed especially for your book, or your printer, as many do, may have certificates to furnish you at very low cost. (Here student artists have a chance to show their lettering ability by inscribing the patron's name.)

Patrons are listed in nicely-designed pages in the yearbook. Running the names alphabetically removes the appearance of favoritism.

Solicitation of patronage should be made in a dignified manner. It should never have overtones of the tin-cup approach or of a squeeze play. Contributions should be acknowledged immediately by a personal letter signed by the business manager and editor-in-chief and, often, the advisor. In some schools, the principal himself writes a personal note or signs the students' letter.

In some schools, the staff—by tradition or necessity—conducts other fund-raising activities. Oddly enough, this custom is not restricted to small schools.

While such activities are certainly legitimate, there is always a danger that students will use time and energy that might better be devoted to doing a good book.

Some staffs form a Booster's Auxiliary, a group of students who don't actually work on the book but are happy for the chance to make a substantial contribution to its success. In some schools, the Honor Society or some service club takes as its main activity the support of the yearbook.

Candy sales are a favorite fund-raising activity. Students may be asked to contribute the merchandise. Or the staff buys materials and the home ec class makes the candy as a class assignment. Candy may be purchased wholesale; be sure to choose those items which produce the biggest profit. Vending machines at some schools are operated for the benefit of the yearbook either by the students themselves or by commercial operators who pay royalties into the book's treasury.

Baked goods sales, Christmas bazaars, book fairs, and similar sales are popular. These may be conducted in the school or in a downtown store which may be pleased to offer space in return for favorable publicity.

Some staffs sell pencils, book covers, imprinted pencils and notebooks, or school emblems. Paperback books are a favorite commodity in many schools.

Selling magazine subscriptions is an activity that can be divided among many people with a minimum of effort for any individual. Ask your local magazine distributor for details or write to the circulation manager of large magazines. Special package rates make such sales attractive to the purchaser.

A natural is auctioning off unused glossies. Because the cost of these pictures has already been absorbed in the budget, profits are 100 percent. The gala atmosphere of an auction is fun and often raises prices to a highly profitable level. And even if a student pays a few cents more for a picture, he has the pleasant assurance that he has contributed to a worthy school project. The auctioneer may be a student or several students, or a professional will often offer to serve in return for the good advertising he gets.

At least one school has an ingenious plan for swelling yearbook coffers. Five minutes after yearbooks have been distributed in homerooms at the end of the school day, a "dance" begins in the gym. By custom, this is the time when autographs are exchanged. There is no dancing, although phonograph music adds to the festive atmosphere; people are too busy signing their friends' books. But students find the quarter admission is a small price to pay for all the fun involved.

There are many other methods of raising money, of course. The staff should choose that one which renders a real service to the student body or the city, which will be fun to carry on, which will not make too pressing demands on the participants, and which will show a fair profit. Above all, it must be an activity which does not reflect unfavorably on either the yearbook or the school.

The business manager is largely responsible for the contracts between the yearbook and its suppliers. This is discussed in detail in Chapter 26.

The most pleasant task of the business staff is delivering the finished product. This, too, must be carried out in a businesslike way.

The printer is instructed—usually in the contract but sometimes in a supplementary letter—how and where to deliver the yearbooks. The circulation manager should make arrangements, well in advance, for a suitable "receiving room." This should be: (1) large enough to hold the cartons and the people who'll be working on them; (2) clean, so dust and dirt won't wreak damage; (3) convenient to the point of actual distribution; and (4) securely locked. (It's a sad fact that many a person who sneers at the book when asked to buy one will go to great lengths to purloin it.)

After books have arrived, they should be checked to determine that the number is correct. (The printer, of course, is not going to short-change you, but it's easy for a carton or two to be overlooked in his shipping room or delivered to some other customer.)

Have proper tools to open the cartons. It is too easy to damage books and knuckles if you try this job with makeshift instruments. Handle the books with care; they're valuable.

Use all the communications systems in your school to announce where and when books will be distributed. Some schools go so far as to give a half-holiday for this auspicious occasion; if that's the case in your school, you must, of course, arrange it with your principal.

If the receiving room is adequate, you can pass out books there or from tables set just outside the door. The staff room or part of the office may be convenient. If the main supply of books is distant from the distribution point, make sure there is a battalion of runners to keep the supply adequate at all times.

Rehearse your procedure before the actual delivery. The student must have some document to get a book, usually his receipt or the final stub, if he has been paying in installments. The circulation manager should be on hand at all times to supervise proceedings. The business manager himself should be there as a trouble-shooter.

If any dispute arises, the business manager should be prepared to settle it at once, not tomorrow. He should have ready access to all records so if there is any question about payments having been improperly recorded, he can resolve it immediately. If the student is entitled to a book, he's entitled to it—and wants it—right now.

If you sell books other than those prepaid, or if final payment is made at this time, be sure that there is adequate change on hand, and that there is a safe place to store your receipts.

If you have extra books to sell, this is exactly the right time to do so; your prospects are excited as they see their classmates enjoying their yearbooks.

The vast percentage of all books will go like hotcakes, but there will always be a few unfilled orders. Check on these right away.

If the student is home sick, have a staff member deliver his copy to him. This can be good medicine to speed his recovery.

For those students whose absence is casual, send word to their home rooms where they can pick up their copies. Ask those students who still have unpaid balances to take care of these at once, within a day or so. If there is extra demand for books, some staffs set a deadline. If the student doesn't claim his book by that time, his money is refunded and the book sold to someone else. Ten days is usually sufficient time, although this must be kept flexible for unusual circumstances.

Books should be delivered personally wherever feasible. If they must be mailed, do so with care; it would be a shame if improper packing were to mar an otherwise good book. Mailing boxes can be bought inexpensively. Or corrugated board can be used for protection, with stout kraft paper as the wrapper.

Be sure your return address is on the package with the notation that you guarantee return postage if delivery cannot be made. (Should that be the case, notify the customer by first-class mail, which will be forwarded, and ask where shipment should be made.) Note that books carry a special low postage rate. Don't send them as regular parcel post.

The circulation manager also distributes complimentary copies, if any, to the school library, principal, faculty, and others.

At least one week before school closes, the circulation manager should have his job completed. Completed, not almost!

As soon as the book arrives, the advertising manager checks to see that all ads have run. (Should the dire calamity occur—that an ad has been left out—he must immediately take a refund and profuse apologies to the advertiser. Neglect to do this can make it impossible for next year's ad staff to do business with the merchant. The same procedure applies if there is an error. Honest apologies, a sincere explanation if there is one—and never excuses—and above all, promptness, are the best oil to spread on these troubled waters.)

The bookkeeper also checks that all ads have been charged in the ledger. If there was no prepayment, the bookkeeper issues statements —which he has previously prepared—to the advertising salesman to take to his customer.

All receipts should be in by two weeks before the end of school. If there are any delinquents, write a concise but complete report and give it to your advisor and/or principal so that the person who has to do the follow-up will be adequately informed.

Pay all your bills as promptly as you collect accounts receivable. Major items—payment to printer, binder, and photographer—may be handled through the school office. In that case, fill out the proper forms or write a letter saying that shipment has been made, that the work is satisfactory, and that the disbursing agent is authorized to make payment.

Meanwhile the editorial staff has been examining the book with eagle eyes. If errors have crept in, *prompt* apology should be made to the offended party—in person, by the editor-in-chief.

At least one, and preferably two or three, books should have corrections noted in India ink. One goes to the principal's office, another to the school library (and perhaps public library, too) and the third stays in the staff's own reference collection. It is no more than decent to take every step to prevent an error from being perpetuated by those who take your yearbook as an authoritative source.

Finally, for the whole staff, comes the job of cleaning up. (Much of this should have been done earlier.)

Examine the files and throw out material which is no longer needed. Clean out desk drawers. If necessary, have the staff come down some Saturday and stage an old-fashioned cleaning bee.

Finally, have your last conferences with your successors. If this is a social affair, be sure some time is set aside for talking business.

And there you are. You have just completed a big job. You've learned many things that you otherwise wouldn't until well into adulthood. You've left a monument of your work that is as permanent as any that man can make.

A top newspaper executive once told one of your authors, "When you consider the magnitude of putting out a yearbook, the time and effort and skills required, the close coordination of so many different activities, it's just a miracle that the book ever comes off the press."

There will be times when you are convinced that only a miracle will help you meet your deadlines. But when you finally write —30— to your yearbook job, you'll know—as many great men have demonstrated—that a lot of "miracles" are really only the result of good planning and conscientious performance of duty.

BOOK FIVE

The People in Journalism

25. *Working with Teachers*

How to make friends and . . .

Smart school publication staff members can say, "Some of my best friends are teachers."

This is not just a philosophy recommended by teachers; if one polled a hundred editors of successful publications, the overwhelming majority would say it was true, too. There are good reasons for this.

Faculty advisors can show you short cuts in journalistic procedures that will save time and allow you to do a better job. They help fill in gaps in your limited training. Teachers usually know more about the school "world" since most of them have been around longer than any of the students. Thus they know its history, traditions, and other background that you could obtain nowhere else. They can help solve ticklish problems in deciding what is good taste and what is good for staff morale. They may aid in obtaining better office space, typewriters, and other conveniences that will permit a better publication.

Teachers other than faculty advisor are also important to a successful paper, magazine, or yearbook. Much news comes from teachers. Enrollment figures, class schedules, announcements of forthcoming assembly programs, lists of awards and honors all may be obtained at the principal's office. Plans for a school play may be released by the drama coach; details on next week's big football game may come from the athletic director or coach; the program for a Latin Club festival may be told by a Latin teacher instead of club officers.

The school librarian should rate an especially high position on any editor's list because all sorts of reference books and idea sources are in the library for staff members to peruse.

The Faculty Advisor

The faculty advisor should be considered an honorary member of the staff. He should not, in thought or deed, have to be policeman or censor. However, if student editors do not accept and assume their proper responsibility, then teachers may have to move in and do assignments that properly belong to students.

A faculty advisor's role on a successful school publication should be a combination of many assignments. He is an "older brother" who can steer staff members through difficult situations and around crises. He is official liaison agent with the school administration and superintendent's office, when such representation is needed. He is a source for useful news tips, background information, and general counseling. He is, in fact, a most useful and nearly indispensable person.

Among the faculty advisors assigned to high school publications today are many who have taken college courses in journalism, special workshops after their graduations, or summer training especially in publication supervision. To expand such training, the Newspaper Fund, Inc., supported by "The Wall Street Journal," had spent approximately a million dollars by 1963 for special courses, workshops, and institutes for high school teachers in scores of colleges and universities across the United States. Increasingly, state education departments are establishing regular specialities for teaching journalism in high schools or supervising student publications.

Other advisors have had experience working on newspapers, magazines, or at radio-television stations. Still others have undertaken extensive training by independent study. Many faculty advisors with years of experience have picked up valuable information from previous publication staffs that they happily and unselfishly pass on to the current year's editors. These tips will involve not only writing and preparation of editorial copy but also valuable suggestions on how to work with printers and businessmen in the community who want to purchase advertisements in the paper, magazine, or yearbook.

If the staff has a legitimate request to make of the school administration or from the student governing organization, a faculty advisor may be most helpful in planning and drafting the petition and the supporting arguments. You may desire more space for an enlarged staff, more filing cabinets in which to store records of advertisements and subscriptions, or permission for senior editors to meet during a free period during the next two weeks to plan an issue of the paper. The idea may be good, but unless the presentation is mobilized effectively the necessary approval may not be forthcoming.

Here, again, the faculty advisor should be considered as a helping friend—not as a conspirator who can get you and your staff colleagues something that you would like but which you really don't deserve.

★ Be sure you deserve support before you involve the advisor.

Advisors may help an enterprising staff to protect its "scoops" by explaining to the principal and other teachers who are news sources that, if possible, they should protect the school newspaper or news magazine. School administrators, especially the principal, should be told that when a school staff uncovers a feature article or other news by its own enterprise, faculty members are under special obligation to assist the students' efforts. They should not accidentally give the information to a regular reporter from the community paper unless he, too, stumbles onto the same idea. In that case, they should tell the students that the community paper is working on the news, too.

Faculty members also may assist the school paper or news magazine when releasing some stories. Obviously, spot news, such as an accident or the sudden resignation of the football coach, can't be delayed to favor students. However, many events can be controlled by administrative officers. For instance, release of the names of honors students may be held up so that both school and community papers print the news the same day.

In addition to useful ideas for procedures and operations on the publication, advisors may be a most valuable source for historical information and traditional procedures in a school. For instance, is this year the first time that a basketball team elected two cocaptains? Or, how many times in recent years have twins won identical scholastic honors because their grades were the same for four full years? Is there some way to get the principal to give out some information in confidence to the editor-in-chief? An advisor may know.

An editor who has established a good working relationship with a faculty advisor will wisely turn to him for help when the question comes up, "Should we print this material?" There are several reasons for this: (1) The advisor may have had previous comparable experiences and thus will know what is the best solution, (2) he has greater knowledge of the legal responsibilities in cases of possible libel, and greater sophistication in cases of possible poor or bad taste, and (3) he is able to bring an impersonal attitude to the discussion whereas students may be emotionally involved in the argument or situation.

★ The faculty advisor should act not as an authoritarian censor but as a friendly counselor.

Too many administrators, both in high schools and colleges, expect an advisor to scan every bit of editorial copy with a blue pencil poised. This is far from an ideal arrangement and does not build a sense of responsibility and democracy for the editorial staff. In this strained environment, frequently staff members play a game of getting suspect material into print. This is unfortunate, undesirable, and unfair to both students and faculty advisors.

A knowledgeable advisor will be able to provide guidance on matters which may affect staff relations. Every organization has its personnel problems, and high school publications, which pay off in glory and status rather than dollars and cents, have their full share. Since students have had little experience in managing people, even their contemporaries, a teacher who can give quiet but effective counsel is extraordinarily helpful to an editor.

Staff members, however, should not run to teacher every time something goes wrong. The initial responsibility on any school publication belongs to the students, not to teachers or the administration.

★ Student staff members should try to solve their own problems—at least the first time around.

★ A happy staff maintains its own chain of command; in other words, go through channels.

Some advisors have found it useful to have *press cards* printed. When students are recognized as regular staff members, they are presented with their individual cards by either the editor or advisor. Such a card might read:

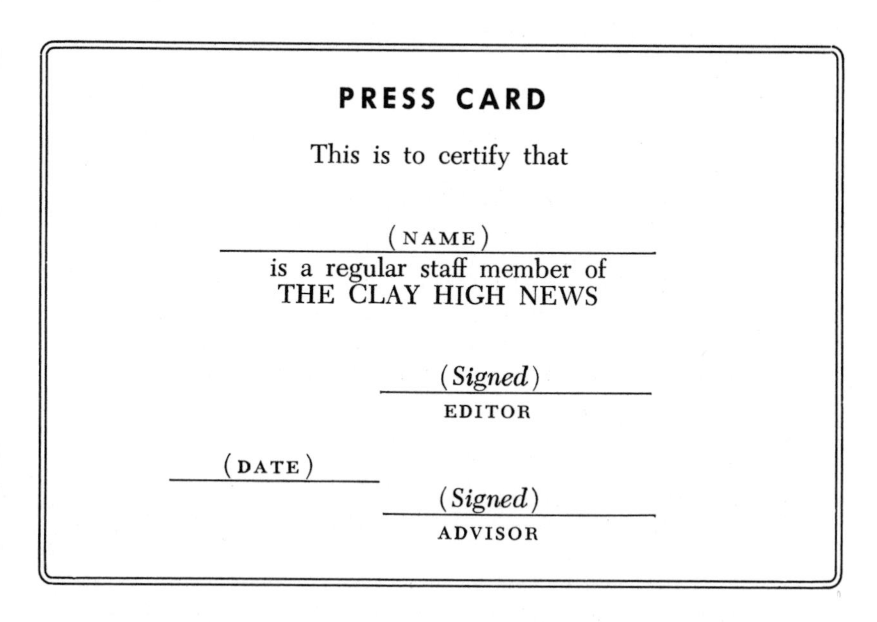
PRESS CARD

This is to certify that

(NAME)

is a regular staff member of
THE CLAY HIGH NEWS

(*Signed*)
EDITOR

(DATE)

(*Signed*)
ADVISOR

★ Holding a press card always should be a privilege that has to be earned by working for it.

Many successful newspaper advisors mark up a copy of the student paper, pointing out superior work and poor performance. This points out a student error so that not only he but all his fellow staff members may benefit—and, hopefully, none will make it again. Of course, a teacher's comments should not be caustic, unless the student has been stupid or stubborn.

A highly competent editor-in-chief can do this analysis extraordinarily well. If an editor has sufficient expertise, naturally the advisor defers to him.

The advisor may contribute immensely by directing efforts of students to evaluate their performances. For example, one school used the following form to have staff members rate themselves and then turn in copies to the editor-in-chief and advisor:

STAFF MEMBER'S SELF-EVALUATION SHEET

Name: Issue No.

(Collect your stale copy, evaluate it by filling out this form, and staple your copy together with this form on top. Place your folder in filing cabinet.)

Best thing I did in preparation of this issue:

Worst thing I did in preparation of this issue:

Grade I think I deserve for my work on this issue: ________

Circle "Yes" or "No" before each question:

Yes No 1. Did I meet the deadline on each story?
Yes No 2. Was the copy clean when I turned it in?
Yes No 3. Did I prepare my copy according to the style sheet?
Yes No 4. Did I find a feature and play it up in the lead?
Yes No 5. Did I avoid grammatical errors?
Yes No 6. Did I avoid wasting words in my lead(s)?
Yes No 7. Did I include only facts, stating sources for any opinions?
Yes No 8. Was my copy clear?
Yes No 9. Was my copy concise?
Yes No 10. Was my copy accurate?
Yes No 11. Did I follow the style sheet for names and identities?
Yes No 12. Did I avoid editorializing?
Yes No 13. Did I stick to the third person except in quotations?
Yes No 14. Did I avoid a "will be held" expression?
Yes No 15. Did I write with the publication date in mind?
Yes No 16. Did I avoid using passive voice?
Yes No 17. Did I use "tomorrow," "last Friday," in preference to dates of the month?
Yes No 18. Am I proud of the contribution I made to this issue?

My contributions to this issue included (be specific):

★ Expert evaluation should be helpful to all the staff.

Such careful study of performance is no childish action. Theodore M. Bernstein, assistant managing editor of "The New York Times," compiles a comparable analysis called, "Winners & Sinners: A bulletin of second guessing issued occasionally from the southeast corner of The New York Times News Room." Here are bouquets for good work, with staff members frequently mentioned by name, and adverse remarks on unidentified writers and copyreaders. In almost every issue of "Winners & Sinners," which comes out about once a month, are collections of such topics as "Inviting leads," "Bright passages," "Trophies of a head-hunter" (quotations of excellent headlines), and "Helpful hints for hatchet men" (pointers on grammar). So popular are Mr. Bernstein's sharp comments that many of them have been collected into a book that might interest school staffers, "Watch Your Language" (Channel Press: cloth, 1958; paper, 1962).

Advisors should introduce themselves to staff members at local newspapers and radio and television stations. Early in the fall term, a visit to a newspaper office will provide beginners with useful information on how a daily is published. Some of these facts will make them better staff workers; all will broaden their background about modern communications.

Professionals frequently are willing to talk to the school staff and pass on to them valuable hints. A well-known local reporter may be willing to tell some of his personal experiences while gathering news, the copydesk slot man to talk about editing and writing headlines, the chief editorial writer to discuss how the paper's policy is set, and the business manager to tell how to handle records of subscriptions and advertising.

Students on the business staff turn to the commercial, business practices, or accounting teacher for special help and guidance. He will assist them in setting up their account books and in establishing the proper procedures for selling and writing advertising and for keeping track of subscriptions. This teacher seldom is named advisor because that assignment traditionally is given to an English or journalism teacher. Nevertheless, for those on the business side, he may be of greater help than the regularly assigned advisor.

What business records should be maintained and how they should be set up were discussed in Chapters 12 and 24. Consult the teacher in charge of the business training courses in your school for help in inaugurating the system most useful for your publication.

Help from Other Teachers

Teachers are among the more important sources for both news tips and facts. They should be organized into a series of news beat assignments just as are other informational sources.

The No. 1 teacher news source is the principal's office. Some principals like to do all their own talking; others authorize an assistant or secretary to give out information on their behalf.

★ Find out the administration's ground rules, then follow them.

The principal's office keeps many records on school administration, and thus it may be used to check all kinds of information. If the principal permitted, you could obtain, for instance, home addresses of students you wish to contact outside of classes, statistics to be used for historical comparisons, and biographical information on faculty members.

This office probably could provide information about education beyond your own high school, too. Most state educational departments issue a statewide directory of teachers. This could be used to check the spellings of names of faculty in other towns, such as debating or basketball coaches at a school 50 miles away. Practically all school districts and county teachers' associations print and distribute rosters of the teachers in their areas.

An alert editor arranges with the principal for senior staff members to use these source materials; or, better still, he orders copies for his own publication if he finds them valuable enough.

Obviously, no student will be permitted unsupervised access in the school offices to the permanent, personal-data cards with confidential information from teachers.

Another key news source is the spokesman for athletic activities. This may be the sports director, a specific coach, or some other individual on the school staff.

★ Find out who is authorized to give out sports news and go to that person for it.

The same applies to all the variety of school activities. At the very start of the school year, compile a list of officers and faculty advisors for clubs and other outside activities. If students are not available, then news may be obtained from the teacher concerned.

Also make a list of home room teachers because they, too, may be news sources.

★ Always be polite and respectful to teachers, who are potential news sources.

★ But remember there is nothing wrong in trying to gather all necessary facts involved in a news item.

★ Don't be bashful, flustered, or intimidated because you are receiving news from a teacher instead of a student.

A good school librarian deserves special affection from almost any publication's staff. Among her volumes may be the only complete files of high school publications, including your own, that are available anywhere. Despite careful efforts, office copies of back issues of school papers, magazines, and yearbooks somehow seem to vanish. Possibly the library's don't because librarians make borrowers sign up when they take out periodicals as well as books and then require that the material be returned promptly.

To digress a bit, editors will be doing their successors a favor and making them less dependent on the library's files of their own periodical if they will have at least two sets of complete copies of the newspaper or magazine bound each year for the publication's own morgue. One should have errors corrected so next year's staff won't make the same mistakes again.

★ No scissors are EVER to be used on these bound files. Such careless action is ground for justifiable homicide—almost.

A school library also contains many of the standard reference books that a staff member needs to check his facts, although some references should be available in the office, as suggested in Chapter 7.

Here are a few references to be found in a school library, together with the kinds of information that might be obtained from them:

1. Local city directory—has names and addresses for all those living in the community when the directory was compiled. More complete than a telephone book (which should be on hand in the office) but generally more dated.

2. Almanacs and yearbooks—general compendiums of statistics, history, and biography for earlier years. Among the better-known almanacs are the "World Almanac," published by the "New York World-Telegram and Sun," and "Information Please Almanac." Both are available annually in paperbound editions and at least one copy might be added to a publication's morgue if there is a surplus of funds.

3. Encyclopedias—range from single-volume "Columbia Encyclopedia," issued by Columbia University Press, to the multivolume "Encyclopaedia Britannica," now printed under the sponsorship of the University of Chicago. Others that are widely used include "Encyclopedia Americana," "Collier's Encyclopedia," and "New International Encyclopedia." Several of these should be available in a school library. For the student who seeks extensive general background, any of them would be a rewarding storehouse of facts.

4. "Who's Who in America"—provides biographical material in near-statistical form on approximately 50,000 prominent Americans. Issued every other year, this volume would supply information on guest speakers, visitors, and so forth. This is not to be confused with "Who's Who," a comparable volume issued primarily for use in the United Kingdom. Regional and vocational biographical reference books, such as "Who's Who in the East" and "American Men of Science," are available.

5. "Current Biographies"—supplies more extensive biographical information on a far fewer number of prominent Americans. Issued monthly and cumulated annually, these are biographies in depth.

6. "Readers' Guide to Periodical Literature"—cumulative publication that lists contemporary magazine articles by topic, title, and au-

thor. If you want to learn what had been printed on, say, shifting college entrance requirements, you look under the appropriate topical listings and find listed recent articles in a representative cross section of mass circulation magazines and some specialized periodicals.

7. "The New York Times Index"—listing of every news story that appears in that paper. Since many libraries keep files of "The New York Times," a check of this cumulative and annual index could provide the dates, pages, and columns for stories on a desired subject.

8. For current facts, other publications, besides newspapers and news magazines, that give general factual background include "Facts on File," "Editorial Research Reports," "Deadline Data," and "Public Affairs Pamphlets."

Reference books, whether in the office or in the library, will make it possible not only to get a story but to get it right.

Working with teachers, whether they are advisors, news sources, or librarians, is a two-way street which makes it possible for publication staff members to perform professionally while still learning. Also they will be making friends that they will remember throughout the years.

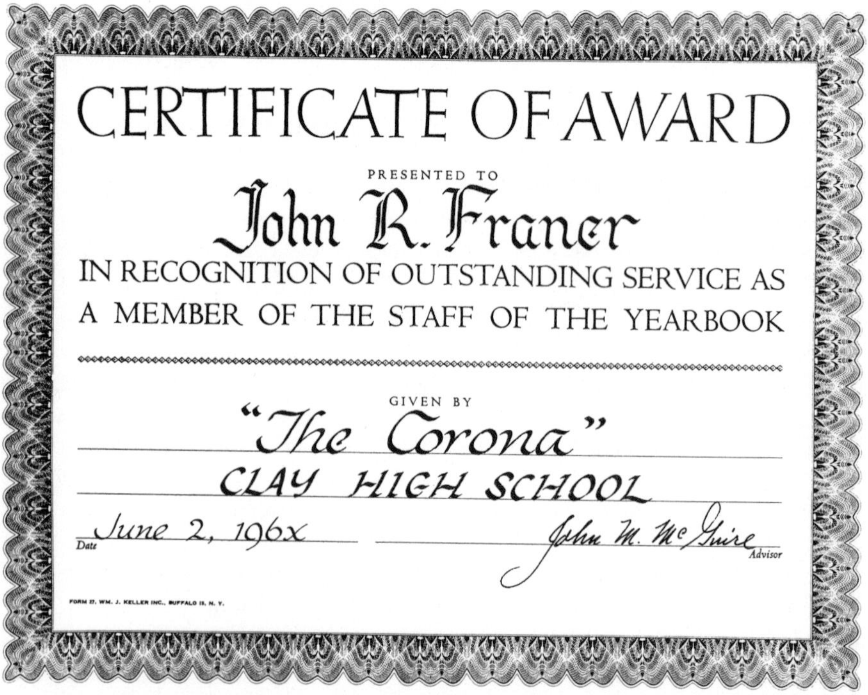

CERTIFICATE OF AWARD

PRESENTED TO

John R. Franer

IN RECOGNITION OF OUTSTANDING SERVICE AS A MEMBER OF THE STAFF OF THE YEARBOOK

GIVEN BY

"The Corona"

CLAY HIGH SCHOOL

June 2, 196x — Date

John M. McGuire — Advisor

FORM 27, WM. J. KELLER INC., BUFFALO 15, N. Y.

Fig. 79. Certificate of award testifies to loyal service by staff member. Certificates are inexpensive; many yearbook printers furnish them at only nominal cost. Keys, letters, and books are other customary awards to staff members. (Courtesy Wm. J. Keller, Inc.)

26. *Working with Printers*

Staunch allies of the staff

The phrase is "the printer's devil," not "the printer's a devil." Sometimes students get confused. For a printer is a strict disciplinarian; he insists that deadlines be met. Of course, he is under the same discipline. Every job he produces must be done on time; many would be worthless if they were late.

Printers work under the tension of deadlines and in those circumstances there isn't time for idle chit-chat. Conversation becomes terse and this may be interpreted as unfriendliness. It isn't, though.

The very fact that your printer IS your printer demonstrates that he is interested in your job.

The International Clubs of Printing House Craftsmen have as their motto: "Share your knowledge." This has been a characteristic of printers for generations. Printers are more than craftsmen; their work as preservers of all human knowledge makes printers well-informed people. Most are highly articulate and are willing to give the student staff the benefit of their own skill and experience.

The printer is anxious to do a good job for you. He has pride in his craft; he knows the work that he does for you may be examined by other prospects, so he wants the best example possible of the work his shop produces.

The first contact you will have with your printer may be at the start of the year. Newspaper staffs may meet with him early in the fall, although it's wise to do it in the spring. Yearbook staffs may do it as early as late winter of the previous year. At this time you will establish deadlines, standards, and prices.

Don't be afraid to speak freely during this conference. Many student staffers are afraid of being considered "hagglers." Many are just as afraid that a sharp operator is "taking" them. Neither is correct. Your purveyors are responsible businessmen; they're not selling gold bricks. At the same time, they're used to the give-and-take of commercial bargaining. There's nothing petty or disgraceful in seeking to get the most for your money; a good transaction is one that is mutually satisfactory. If discussions are carried on in good humor and good faith, it is possible to reach that point of mutual satisfaction in the most expeditious and pleasant manner.

Yearbook Contracts

Yearbooks are almost always produced under a contract. Newspapers and magazines more often do not have written contracts but depend on less formal letters or even verbal agreements.

Because the yearbook represents the major expenditure, and because for a one-time publication there isn't opportunity between issues to revise methods or conditions, its contract is most specific and we shall look at it first.

Most of the work of the yearbook staff comes to a focus in that legal document, the contract with the printer and/or binder and photographer.

The simple act of drawing up a contract helps the staff crystallize its thinking and evaluate its many ideas. The legal force of the contract is not only an incentive to fulfilling obligations; its clauses establish a practical timetable.

There are always preliminaries to signing the contract; each is vitally important.

First the *supplier* must be chosen, the printer, cover manufacturer, photographer. The basis is often price but that should never be the only criterion.

Laws that cover public contracts usually say that the business shall be given to "the lowest or best bid." Note that "best." Not always is the lowest bid the best one. A printer may shave his price to get a contract, then cut corners in production to make his profit; the result is an inferior book. Recently a school gave the contract to a photographer who was just establishing his trade. He was willing to shoot senior pictures at a little above cost just for the chance of showing his work to the community. This is perfectly legitimate, of course. Unfortunately, the photographer became seriously ill shortly after he had taken the pictures but before he had a chance to develop or print them. Because he had a one-man operation, there was no one who could step in and finish the job. The yearbook was three months late.

★ The purveyor should be chosen on the basis of past performance. A business becomes old and well established because it has given good service at a fair price over an extended period. It may not always have entered the lowest bid, but chances are good that its bid has consistently been the best one.

This doesn't mean, of course, that a new business should automatically be written off. After all, every printer had to start out some time. But assurances must be given, in writing, that the purveyor is able to meet the specifications of the contract.

Some schools, by habit or by school board, city, or state law, always ask for competitive bids. Two or more companies are invited to bid on identical specifications.

These specifications become the contract, with only minor, if any, amendments. They must be drawn with care.

Usually invitations are extended only to business firms that have already demonstrated their ability to do a good job. It costs money to prepare a bid—substantial sums. It is unethical to ask a bid from any company unless it has a fair chance of getting the contract. Many schools think they are doing a kindness to a firm, or at least avoiding hurt feelings, when they ask for a bid, even though it is well understood that this is but a formality and the real decision has already been made.

Just as the size and kind of yearbooks vary, so do the establishments that actually produce them.

Almost every town has at least one printing plant. And most printing plants can produce a yearbook. But often it is not feasible to use the local shop, which may not have the facilities to do the book efficiently. Or it may have regular customers whose work can't be postponed as the yearbook comes down to the final deadline. Or, as is often the case, yearbook work comes at the busy season for the printer and he just can't take on extra work.

But it is a deserved courtesy to ask the local printer whether he is interested. He is part of the business community that makes your school possible through its taxes and that supports school activities in many ways—through gifts, manpower, leadership, attendance at scholastic affairs, and warm interest. In smaller towns especially, the printer probably publishes the local paper, a stout ally for any school.

If it is not practical to have the book done locally, there are many specialists in yearbook production throughout the United States. While most business with them must be conducted by mail, these specialists have developed such efficient systems that there is little, if any, inconvenience involved.

All such suppliers have representatives who cover an area so small that they can come to the scene on short notice and give you the personal help you need.

These companies had to be good to grow to their present stature. So, no matter where your school is located, you have the finest talent in the world available to you. And they are geared to produce any kind of book that fits your budget. Few of them will decline a production job because it's too small; no company has been known to refuse because the book was too large.

These are the basic points that must be covered in the specifications, and later in the contract:

1. Dimensions of the book: page size, number of pages.

2. Number of books. Here should be included the date when the final number must be specified and change in cost if the basic number is changed, upward or downward.

3. Total area of pictures (for letterpress).

4. Total number of galleys of type. (Often the printer will not insist that these two elements—pix and type—be specified. He knows the average amount of type per page in a typical yearbook as well as how many pictures are used.)

5. Number of divider pages and other inserts. The kind of paper to be used for special pages and the use of color, if any, is specified.

6. Kind of paper. This is usually given by trade name: for instance, *Partridge Book, 40 lb. substance.* The phrase "or equivalent" is usually added. This allows the printer to use paper of the same quality and characteristics that may be cheaper for any number of reasons.

(This phrase "or equivalent" can create problems. "Equivalent" means different things to different people. Coca-Cola and Pepsi may be equivalent to you; to your buddy they may be totally different.

(The integrity of the purveyor is the best assurance against substitution of inferior quality. It may be added, in the contract, that "the purchaser shall specifically approve any substitutions.")

7. Number of pages of advertising. Composition of ads may vary considerably from that of editorial pages. The printer needs this information to make a good estimate; rarely need this be included in the contract unless the printer asks for it.

8. The use of color. Here shall be specified how many signatures will use color. How color is used must be given, too. (*Flat color* is least expensive; duotone costs a little more. Process color is most expensive; its use is usually covered in a separate item in the specifications.)

9. The cover. Method of binding, kind of cover style, cover material, embossing, stamping, or printed designs, or combinations thereof must be spelled out. If more than one color will be used on the cover, this must be noted.

10. Deadlines. On invitations to bids, the staff submits its tentative schedule for submitting copy. On the contract, a definite schedule, developed by the purveyor and the staff, is used.

11. Delivery date. This binds the purveyor to a final date for delivery. In some cases, if the staff will have to pay unusual postage cost to mail yearbooks delivered too late for distribution during the school year, the purveyor may be charged a penalty. This penalty is payable

only if the staff has met every one of its deadlines.

12. Method of delivery. Usually this is indicated only as the "best way"; the printer can then choose any method or carrier that is most convenient or economical. Sometimes schools specify the kind of containers that must be used. This is not necessary, though; if there is damage in transit, it is covered by insurance.

13. Pattern of payment. This is usually pegged to the deadline schedule. Payment is usually made in two or three instalments. The purveyor must pay for labor and material on a weekly basis; he can't wait for several months until the job is done before he collects.

If the staff plans on using commercial photolettering, the fact should be noted so the printer can delete the cost of the equivalent typesetting from his estimate.

If the staff plans to use the services of the printer's art staff, note should be made of this. It may be a factor in the bid, although, in many cases, the printer offers these services at no extra cost.

All these items except those noted will also appear in the contract. In many cases the printer will insert another clause; in essence it will say "No material will be accepted by the printer unless the advisor has initialed it." This is a protection to everyone concerned against practical jokes on the part of an irresponsible staffer.

It is wise to ask the printer of last year's book to discuss this invitation to bid before it is prepared and distributed. Often he will have ideas that will save money, time, or headaches.

The staff should rely heavily on the experience of the advisor at this stage. Some school systems require yearbook contracts to go through a central purchasing office. The officer in charge is another expert whose advice should be sought—and heeded.

When the lowest or best bid has been determined, the successful bidder is called in to draw up the contract. He will raise questions the staff must answer—and vice versa. He may show how to save money on some elements so you can afford extras in other places. He will have many ideas to make a better book, although most of them will not be written into the contract.

The final deadline schedule is drawn up.

Finally the contract is signed.

Perhaps the laws of your state won't allow a legal minor to sign a contract. In that case the advisor or purchasing agent of the school will do so. Often the student may sign but there must be an adult's countersignature. In any case, it's YOUR contract.

This may well be the first formal business transaction that the students have ever taken part in. A contract is a sacred document; in most cultures it is second in importance only to an oath taken in a court of law.

The staff shouldn't fear the contract; it protects them as much as it does the purveyor. At the same time it can't be taken lightly. Just as much as it places a legal responsibility on the staff, so it places a moral responsibility on them toward their school.

Once the contract has been signed, the staff has just received a valuable addition, the printer's representative. Here's a man whose experience is vast. He has been intimately involved in producing scores—maybe hundreds or even thousands—of yearbooks. He's anxious to help you produce a superlative book. After all, next year he will be competing for your school's business. He knows that the best prospect is a satisfied customer.

The art staff of the printer may also augment your own, depending on the contract.

The cover may be contracted for in the basic printing contract. Or it may be covered by a separate one. In most cases the printer will handle all details and usually accepts payment for the cover. There will be separate deadlines for the cover and binding; these must be spelled out in either the basic contract with the printer or the supplementary one with the binder. The printer should be asked about this while the contract is being discussed.

In selecting a professional photographer, the staff takes the same steps and signs the same kind of contract, with those obvious exceptions rising from a difference in the product being bought.

Let's consider senior portraits first. (Some schools run individual pictures of underclassmen as well. Their handling is identical with that of senior portraits.)

It must be specified when portraits will be taken, when proofs will be delivered, when they will be returned, and when finished glossies will be submitted.

(Portraits represent a large part of any yearbook and lots of time and effort on the part of the staff. Unless the deadlines are met by all concerned, some big roadblocks will soon loom in your path.)

How many shots will the photographer make of each subject?

If the subject isn't satisfied, how many shots will be made on the second sitting?

What are the prices at which the subject can buy pictures? Usually the student will want some small wallet-size pictures to exchange with classmates, several 5 x 7's for family and special friends, an enlargement or two and perhaps some of the photos in color. Because the student is, in effect, a captive prospect, this price schedule must be clearly specified and made known to the student.

How much must the staff pay for a portrait glossy? In most cases the photographer furnishes the portrait glossy for the book at no charge. The opportunity to take all portraits and the sales he can anticipate as a result are worth the cost of reproduction glossies to most studios. Some photographers even pay a commission to the yearbook on all business resulting from the book.

Will portraits be retouched? They should be. It should also be specified that all portraits be in sharp—not diffused—focus, that all poses be conventional, that all dress meet definite standards, and that all prints be of same area and head size.

If the photographer is to take group shots, the contract must specify where and when these pictures are to be taken. It must also be in writing how long the photographer will wait past the scheduled time—and how long the group must wait, should the cameraman be delayed. If reshooting is necessary, there must be definite written understanding on rescheduling.

Charges must be given in detail. Here again, the agreement is often that the photographer will take a certain number of group shots at no charge to the staff. His profit will come from copies he sells to members of the group. Again, the selling prices must all be clearly defined.

If the professional photographer is to take pictures of sports and other events, the basis of charges will vary greatly. The best way to determine a mutually equitable method of charging is to examine all previous contracts and to talk over the problem with all cameramen who will be invited to bid.

If the photographer is to do other kinds of pictures, the contract should specify when he is to be notified, when the first contact prints will be delivered, when the staff must return contacts to show which are to be printed as glossies and how they are to be cropped, and how long after this the finished prints will be delivered.

The contract should specify the size of individual portraits so they can be easily grouped into combinations.

Rarely will the photographer be able to furnish same-size prints for a layout without running the cost out of the question. He will furnish glossies in one of four standard sizes: 2¼ x 3¼, 4 x 5, 5 x 7 or 8 x 10. The platemaker can reduce a photo only as much as half the linear measurement. Thus, if a layout requires a 2 x 3 picture, the staff must furnish him a glossy no wider than 4 inches. So the photographer would be told to print the picture 4 x 5.

(The first number given in a photo dimension is its width. An 8 x 10 is a vertical rectangle, a 10 x 8 a horizontal one.)

If size specification is required in the contract—ask the photographer—it is covered simply by a phrase something like this: "Glossy prints shall be furnished only in standard sizes, cropped according to instructions of the customer."

If the photographer has an adequate studio and facilities and a reputation for reliable service, no penalty clause should be considered. But if there is any doubt about his ability to fulfill contract requirements, there may be a penalty clause which requires him to pay for any additional charges the staff may incur by having to bring in a new photographer on an emergency basis, or for overtime charges by other purveyors because deadlines haven't been met.

Each supplier will have modifications in the systems outlined here.

These have been developed over a long period in order to improve the quality of the product and the efficiency of the operation. So, when you are confronted by new forms to use or new procedures to follow, don't be alarmed. If you'll take a few minutes to study them, you'll find they are not as forbidding as they may appear at first glance.

Systems and forms are not important in themselves. They are useful only as tools in doing a job. There's no question that "your own way" may be efficient for you. But the "company way" works best into the operations of your suppliers. Besides, if the supplier has already devised these systems, you are saved from dreaming up your own and so will have more time to direct the yearbook itself.

Newspaper and Magazine Contracts

Printing of student newspapers and magazines is basically the same, so we can examine procedures for both at the same time.

Because a newspaper is more stylized than a yearbook, its specifications are easy to determine. Usually the staff gives the printer a copy of a previous issue and says: "This is what we want." All pages will have the same number of columns, of the same length and approximately the same area of advertising makeup. Paper quality rarely changes from year to year.

If no contract is drawn, a letter to which a sample issue is attached should be sent in duplicate to the printer. He and the staff will initial both copies as a *memorandum agreement*. This can cover the price, also.

There are two basic ways of setting the price. The printer may offer a *flat price* for each issue of a basic size, or for the entire year with a certain number of issues of a basic size. He will, then, also quote a price for extra pages.

Or the printer may offer a *cost-plus* pricing system. He will keep an accurate record of time and materials used to produce every issue, add his profit, and submit a bill for each issue as it is printed.

The cost-plus method is the most advantageous for the staff. Costs may vary considerably between given issues; but at the end of the year, the total may be well under that of a flat price.

A flat price must have a cushion for contingencies. Things may go wrong anywhere in the long and complex series of steps in producing a paper. The printer may have to pay overtime rates on occasion to make up lost time. Inadvertent and major errors may require considerable author's alteration. An engraving may be wrecked because someone dropped a quoin key on its face.

The printer cannot absorb such unexpected costs, so he must include a *contingency* item in his firm price.

In a cost-plus situation, the staff pays for such contingencies only if they actually happen and only if the staff is responsible.

Sometimes, by cost-plus pricing, the staff pays for material before it is used. If there are two galleys of overset, for instance, the printer's bill will include that composition. But if that material is used next time, the typesetting bill will be reduced by that amount. If ads are reused, the cost of making them up is charged only once.

This method is a good yardstick by which to measure the staff's efficiency. Excessive overset which must eventually be discarded, tricky ad layouts, too many author's alterations, late copy or proofs, all these will be pointed up by your bill. (You'd pay for those by any system of pricing, but the cost-plus method doesn't allow bad habits to be overlooked because their cost is hidden.)

One of your authors is copublisher of a company that prints several student publications. Both pricing methods have been used. But once a staff agrees to the cost-plus basis, it never wants to change back to a firm price.

Deadlines are always a critical factor in establishing a price. Late copy or proofs may entail night, or weekend, or holiday, work at high rates.

Discuss deadlines thoroughly with your printer.

★ Be sure deadlines are realistic.

There is no point in setting a Friday noon deadline when you know very well you'll want to get stories of Friday night basketball games in each issue. Don't set up a 12-hour deadline for return of proofs if it has been demonstrated that the staff just can't do the job in that period.

Days and dates of publication can also change costs.

Perhaps changing your publication day may enable the printer to give you better service or a better price. Suppose your paper goes to press Wednesday at 8 A.M. And at noon that day the printer must get a weekly price list for a wholesale hardware company on the same press. That leaves a narrow margin for your job. If it's only a little late and something goes wrong, your paper may still be printing at 12 o'clock. So, to make the deadline on the price list, pressmen may have to work overtime. Sure, it wasn't on your job, but if the delay is your fault you pay for it.

By moving up your press time by 24 hours, you may be able to avoid the time squeeze and the extra costs that might be occasioned by it.

Or the printer may say: "I have open time on my press Monday afternoon. If you can use it, I can make you a good price."

Printing equipment is expensive. Whether it's running full blast or standing idle, the printer must pay depreciation, rent, heat, lights, and, usually, wages.

The printer can't afford to let equipment stand idle. He may be far better off running his presses at only a slight profit than to leave them motionless at a loss.

Sometimes a change in page size will enable more efficient operation. If slicing a half-inch off two sides of a page will allow eight pages instead of four to be printed on one form, press costs are cut in two.

In some cases a newspaper can add four pages at only a little more cost than two.

In the case of magazines, changes in paper may produce a better publication or reduce costs.

If the magazine staff uses color, it can often save money by changing its mind about the hue.

The printer may say, "I'll be running a job in red next week. If you use red on your cover instead of orange, you can save yourself a *washup*."

Each time a different color is used on a press, the previous color must be taken out of the ink fountain and all the many rollers must be washed thoroughly. If your job can be run without this washup, by using a color already on the press, time is saved. And time is usually money.

Of course, this economy can't always be effected. If your cover design, for instance, requires a specific color, you wouldn't want to change it. A snow scene planned for blue would be less than sensational printed in orange. But jack-o'-lanterns are as effective in red as in orange and often a change in color has no bad effect whatsoever on your art.

★ The agreement with the printer should specify how engravings will be handled.

In some cases the staff buys cuts direct from the engraver. In others, all copy is delivered to the printer, who orders engravings, pays for them, and includes them in his bill. In some cases, of course, the printer may operate an engraving department.

★ Specify when and how delivery of the issue will be made.

The agreement will set up the time the job must be done, but this will depend on the staff's meeting its deadlines. If the staff has met all its obligations, the printer may be penalized for tardiness by a discount from the bill.

If the staff picks up the papers, some time may be saved. If the printer delivers the job, it may have to wait for the return of a delivery truck or your school may be the last stop on a regular run.

★ Another point to have clearly established is whether the staff may work at the print shop while pages are made up.

Many printers allow student editors to work at the stone just as a professional makeup editor does. He tells the printer what to do if any problems arise that haven't been anticipated in the dummy.

Working at the stone is great fun and valuable experience. The student editor shouldn't abuse the privilege by interfering with the printer's work or making unusual or capricious demands upon him.

Usually the number of students who will be in the shop must be limited. There is equipment which can be dangerous to careless people;

carelessness increases in direct ratio to the number of young people in a given area. Print shops are usually rather crowded; too many bodies in the aisles will cut down the efficiency of the printer's crew.

In union shops, a nonunion person may not so much as touch a piece of type. You can tell the makeup man that the story he's looking for is in this galley. But you can't hand it to him across the stone, even if he has to walk all the way around to get it himself.

Many union rules appear ridiculous; some of them are. Their enforcement is sometimes cavalier or picayunish. But they're there and the student must obey them. Composing rooms have been known to walk out on a wildcat strike because rules were violated, even though innocently or in ignorance. The poor owner takes the rap even though it was a customer who started it all.

One of your authors, on a visit to a printing plant that produces several student publications, asked: What are the main faults of student staffs?

"They don't make their deadlines.

"Their dummies aren't clear.

"They want things done that just can't be done, or at least without more time than we have.

"They know it all. They never take advice.

"They're discourteous.

"They change their minds too often.

"They make unnecessary changes.

"They horse around too much. It spoils our concentration on jobs that demand a lot of it. And we're always afraid some wise guy will stick his finger in the saw or Linotype gears."

The same complaints could be—and are—made of adults, too. But the wise editor will make very sure that his staff isn't guilty of these annoyances.

(It might be added that one of the complaining printers also said, "Don't get me wrong now. I like these kids and I enjoy working with them. The bad apples are few. I want to help the youngsters put out the best paper possible. I'm as proud of it as they are." With this he lit up a cigarette and proudly showed his lighter, which is engraved with a thank-you from last year's staff.)

The staff that considers its printer as a member of the team, that asks his advice, that treats him fairly and courteously, has a valuable ally and a good friend.

27. *Working in Professional Journalism*

The high school activity with a built-in future

Work on a high school publication, whether it is a newspaper, magazine, or yearbook, is one extracurricular activity that has a built-in future.

Few football or baseball players expect to join professional teams after they finish their education. Fewer actors in a school play find their way to success in Broadway plays, Hollywood motion pictures, or television and radio programs. But high school journalists quite often do go on into journalism after they are graduated. In fact, most surveys show that a job on a high school paper, magazine, or yearbook staff is one of the key factors in determining whether a student enters journalism when he goes on to college or into a vocation.

The professional newsman runs a wide range of human activity.

He may be with a successful presidential nominee when he wins election and receives congratulations and adoration from his supporters. Or he may sit mournfully with a defeated candidate who has worked to the limits of his endurance but still failed.

He may be the first to tell a Nobel prize winner the news of his world recognition. Or he may accompany a prison warden to death row to inform a murderer that he has been denied a reprieve.

He may give the world the first news of frontier violence that will lead to war between two nations. Or he may announce, as a public information officer at military headquarters, that peace at last has been agreed upon and fighting will stop.

He may provide the play-by-play description of an international tennis competition. He may unravel for his readers or listeners the complexities of an advance in nuclear physics. Or he may interpret and highlight events through feature stories, background sidebars, or documentaries.

When he becomes an editor or commentator and attains the right to express his own opinions in print or on the air, he may create editorials that move the public to vigorous action.

As an advertising executive, he may contrive a slogan that nets millions in sales—and in profits.

But regardless of what he does in professional journalism for newspapers, magazines, radio, television, advertising, or public relations, his actions differ only slightly from the basics he learned on a high school publication.

Why would one consider going into journalism?

★ It's an interesting, often exciting, and sometimes adventurous vocation.

One of the common sayings among professional newsmen and newswomen is that they enjoy their work "because you meet such interesting people." A wry addition often is heard, "Yeah, other newspapermen!" Both remarks are true.

You come in contact with all sorts of people when they are in the news—those in high and important positions and those in the gutter, those of superior intelligence and those who are stupid. Then, as a news reporter, you have entree to places that the ordinary citizens would never see.

For instance, foreign correspondents travel to faraway places in Africa, Asia, and Latin America where only a handful of other Americans have ever been. Other reporters are allowed to cross police lines at a huge dock fire or to enter a mine where a major disaster has taken place. Some sit in favored positions when world-awaited announcements are spoken. Several hundred Washington correspondents meet the President of the United States to question him at his press conferences; some he addresses by their first names in his replies. Important personages, who are protected from contacts with the public generally, will interrupt dinner or conference to speak to news representatives. By-line reporters and syndicated columnists obtain exclusive interviews from the world's mighty.

Even the "shop talk" of journalists swapping stories of their experiences is interesting and heady conversation.

★ News gathering, news writing, and news selling is a challenging and wit-stimulating assignment.

How to get the news when officials may not wish to talk to reporters, how to write up events so that readers and listeners may relive them, how to attract the largest possible audience, and how to snap a picture that tells the whole story yet is action-packed—these intrigue any intelligent and alert individual who wants to make his place in the field of communications.

After the newsman or newswoman has obtained facts for his report, he still has the exacting requirement of translating what he found into words. In some cases, he will have the help of pictures but always a primary and vital channel remains words, graphic words, precise words. He has to pick those that will make readers and listeners smile or cry as he desires.

The photographer tries to obtain one shot or a whole series of pictures that will be worth large masses of type. His challenge is to preserve in black-and-white or in color an event that may defy description by words alone. A cartoonist, another artist with black-and-white or with color, seeks to epitomize with a few bold strokes what would require many words for an editorial writer, columnist, or commentator to convey.

And for all this, a copyreader, headline writer, makeup man, or radio or television program manager strives to package it all so that readers and listeners will stop and stay to get the news that will truly make them informed citizens of a great democracy. Yet change of pace and humor are important and necessary, too.

It is an exacting, often tedious, sometimes impossible assignment to capture the reality of an event and preserve it—and still balance it with a light touch. But it is one that appeals to newsmen and one that always challenges them to do their best work.

For workers on the business staff, the job is to promote and sell this news "product" so that it will attract a large audience—the largest possible under the circumstances. A poor product seldom can be truly promoted successfully for any length of time. But when you have a good idea, there may be a number of ways to call attention to it; and that is where the sales and promotion staff faces its own challenge. If you provide news and comments that a sizable group of people want and need, then you will reach them if they know about what you are doing. The people concerned with subscriptions, circulation, and promotion have special responsibilities to let the public know. That group may be thousands in a small town that could be interested in a community weekly telling the local news, or it could be millions across the nation that might be persuaded to listen to a new television program. As a lubricant for such a smooth performance, a staff must keep efficient records in all the business subdivisions.

Equally important for those media that depend heavily on advertising revenues to help finance their continued existence are advertising staff members who plan campaigns to persuade individuals and concerns to use space or time to sell their products or ideas. Selection of the most widely circulated media may not be the best way to reach potential consumers, and the advertising staff members have to present convincing arguments to support their viewpoints.

New developments in mechanical production of print media and in electronics engineering challenge the ingenuity and intelligence of the "back shop" and the studio's technical staff. Original ideas here pay rich premiums, too.

★ Professional newsman or newswoman has a chance to stand up and be counted.

This opportunity isn't always available but it happens often enough to make the field attractive to a large number of young people who have made up their own minds about today's world and want to do something about it. News is not loaded with bias and prejudices, as was emphasized earlier, but editorial influence is used to shove the public conscience.

The National Conference of Editorial Writers says in its code of ethics:

> Journalism in general, editorial writing in particular, is more than another way of making money. It is a profession devoted to the public welfare and to public service. The chief duty of its practitioners is to provide the information and guidance toward sound judgments which are essential to the healthy functioning of a democracy.

Two famous journalistic credos are well in their second half-century but they still are exciting reading and they provide the cornerstones for two daily newspapers that are respected not only in their own communities but around the world. Since they present the highest ideals of two great newspapermen, they are worth quoting here.

The first is a statement by Adolph S. Ochs, which was published August 19, 1896, and outlined the late publisher's concept of what he hoped to do with "The New York Times." The key paragraph in his philosophy follows:

> It will be my earnest aim that THE NEW-YORK TIMES give the news, all the news, in concise and attractive form, in language that is parliamentary in good society, and give it as early, if not earlier, than it can be learned through any other reliable medium; to give the news impartially, without fear or favor, regardless of any party, sect or interests involved; to make the columns of THE NEW-YORK TIMES a forum for the consideration of all questions of public importance, and to that end to invite intelligent discussion from all shades of opinion.

The second is from a statement by Joseph Pulitzer to his staff when he stepped down from active control of the "New York World" on April 10, 1907. Now printed on the editorial page of the "St. Louis Post-Dispatch," managed by Pulitzer's grandson, the credo reads:

> I know that my retirement will make no difference in its cardinal principles, that it will always fight for progress and reform, never tolerate injustice or corruption, always fight demagogues of all parties, never belong to any party, always oppose privileged classes and public plunderers, never lack sypathy with the poor, always remain devoted to the public welfare, never be satisfied with merely printing news, always be drastically independent, never be afraid to attack wrong, whether by predatory plutocracy or predatory poverty.

Some critics of contemporary communications argue that increasing monopoly in newspapers, magazines, radio, and television has blunted the crusading spirit in American journalism. It is hard to measure the intensity of editorial impact by a well-written editorial or a striking documentary. But recognized awards for excellence to periodicals, radio, and television annually shout out a salute to outstanding crusades that have often supported unpopular contestants and have spotted attention on matters that required public interest. For documentation, look at the recent lists of Pulitzer Prizes and Peabody Awards. Year after year, you will find recognition for crusading that was not always popular and safe and which required courage and just plain "guts."

What are the major careers in professional journalism? This chart gives an over-view of opportunities in various fields:

			Commenting	Business		
	Writing	Copy Editing	Editorials Opinions Columns	Advertising Distribution Promotion	Mechanical/ Production	Research
Newspapers						
Daily	Yes	Yes	Yes	Yes	Yes	Yes
Weekly	Yes	Yes	Yes	Yes	Yes	Seldom
Press Associations/News Syndicates	Yes	Yes	Yes	Promotion/ Sales	Transmission only	Seldom
Consumer or Mass Magazines	Yes	Yes	Yes	Yes	Yes	Yes
Industrial Journalism						
Trade	Yes	Yes	Yes	Yes	Yes	Yes
House	Yes	Yes	Sometimes	Distribution	Yes	Seldom
Religious Journalism	Yes	Yes	Yes	Yes	Yes	Yes
Advertising						
Media Staff	Yes	Yes	Seldom	Yes	Sometimes	Yes
Agency	Yes	Yes	Seldom	Promotion/ Sales	Sometimes	Yes
Radio	Yes	Yes	Yes	Yes	Yes	Yes
Television						
Network	Yes	Yes	Yes	Yes	Yes	Yes
Station	Yes	Yes	Sometimes	Yes	Yes	Yes
News films	Yes	Yes	Sometimes	Promotion/ Sales	Yes	Seldom
Public Relations	Yes	Yes	Sometimes	Yes	Seldom	Yes
Free-Lance Writing	Yes	His own writing	Seldom	Sales	No	For his writing

Individuals who select journalism as a lifetime career may possess diverse talents that qualify them for a place among an exceedingly broad variety of possible assignments. Each must assess his own background and his own talents.

To make this assessment as realistic as possible, a student who is considering any field of communications will talk to his journalism teacher, advisor, or, when he gets a chance, the professionals in his community. These individuals are more likely to have details at hand than a vocational guidance counselor, who would have to look them up because he is responsible for hundreds of various vocations.

Some students may elect to go into gathering and writing news and features; others may handle the editing and preparation of copy and pictures.

Those with a commercial bent may join a business staff and be concerned with circulation, promotion, and advertising. Those who go into advertising and promotion may do such varied jobs as sell groceries in a supermarket to study consumer buying habits, manage an annual Golden Gloves boxing tournament, or supervise preparation of billboards and plant tours.

Still others may go into the service activities of advertising agencies and public relations counseling with industrial firms, nonprofit institutions, or specialized organizations.

Those with an artistic aptitude may join an art department. If they are exceptional they may become nationally known cartoonists for editorial or sports pages or even more widely recognized if they create popular comic strips. A highly successful comic strip may yield more financial return than a syndicated opinion column.

Some individuals may elect to work on specialized publications, including such a diversified range as employee magazines for industry, journals for labor unions, and religious and fraternal periodicals. Those employed by industry have a good chance to work their way into top management, as witness the many former employee magazine editors who now hold positions as vice-presidents and even corporation presidents. While salaries in the expanding field of religious journalism are not as high as those on commercial publications, status is particularly high, with some editors of religious periodicals getting the same preferential treatment as ministers, priests, and rabbis.

They may become public information men with the armed services, an opportunity that many journalism-trained college graduates seize, at least temporarily, when they join the military.

Still others may combine journalistic background with social science training to become research specialists and market analysts for media, advertising agencies, government, or independent groups.

A few may become highly successful as free-lance authors who sell their works to high-paying publications.

Others may go into teaching journalism in colleges or high schools.

What about a prejudice against women in journalism?

Doors are open to both sexes. Although it must be admitted that in some fields there is a slight bias in favor of men, women have advantages over their male competitors in others. For instance, some positions on women's interest magazines, accounts of women's products handled by advertising or public relations people, and editorships of women's departments in newspapers and networks would be the special province of females.

Exceptional women have served as publishers, city editors, and war correspondents. One won a Pulitzer Prize for her work during the Korean War when she covered front-line action on the scene.

What is the range of salaries?

Many college graduates with journalism training and experience on their school papers are now starting their first jobs at $100 a week. By the early 1960's, the median starting salary was approaching that figure and it was shifting upward a few dollars every school year. Increasingly, heads of schools and departments of journalism around the country were reporting two, three, or four employment opportunities for each qualified recent graduate.

The American Newspaper Guild, founded during the depression years of the 1930's, has campaigned steadily for higher wages and better working conditions for print media. Contracts covering thousands of newsmen and newswomen with print media across the nation set minimum salaries after five years ranging up to $9,000 a year. Most veteran staff members on the larger papers get well above this minimum.

While news executives admit that starting salaries are lower for newspapers and other periodicals than for some other professions and businesses, they point out that the tendency for pay to flatten off into a plateau is not so strong in journalism.

Comparable or higher salaries are paid for radio and television newscasters and those who write their scripts. Most salaries in advertising, public relations, and industrial journalism result from individual arrangements and thus are geared to the accounts or assignments handled by the person.

In the composing room, Linotype operators and makeup men now hold white-collar jobs with incomes near those of professional men.

Top salaries may run upwards to a quarter or half a million dollars a year for the exceptional newspaper owner-publisher, radio-television network executive, public relations counsel, advertising agency head, or widely syndicated columnist or comic strip artist. One syndicated columnist and television personality was reported to have earned more than a million dollars a year during his peak income period.

What training should one seek for a professional journalism career?

★ Learn to typewrite.

This is preparation that a high school student should make. Anyone who takes his work on a school periodical or yearbook seriously should do this as a first step toward professional performance. The staff member who doesn't type well is so handicapped that his chances for promotion to an important job are small. He will have to learn later, in any case.

More and more of the young men and women going into communications careers today are college and university graduates. Many of the more successful ones have specialized in some communications major or minor. The expanding vocational opportunities can't begin to be supplied by those with such a speciality.

Employers seek individuals who have a broad basic background, such as journalism majors now receive in all recognized schools and departments of journalism.

For newspaper, magazine, radio, and television editorial assignments, a free-ranging knowledge of liberal arts and sciences attracts favorable consideration.

For jobs on the business side of the mass media, public relations, advertising, and industrial journalism, more attention is given to background in economics, marketing, business management, and general commercial orientation. However, broad liberal arts and sciences should not be neglected by those planning to enter these specialties.

For those expecting to teach or perform communications research, training in education and social sciences is desirable along with the wide range of humanities and sciences.

After one has obtained his college degree, he should consider carefully whether he wants to join a large corporation and learn a small job with a wider future or to get a job with a smaller concern, be it publication, station, or agency, where he will do a wide variety of assignments but may not have such a rosy chance if and when he gets to the top of that organization. There are impressive arguments for both vocational approaches, and an individual should pick the one that he honestly thinks is better for him.

In considering his future, a student should keep in mind that many a weekly publisher or small-town station manager attains satisfactions and status that are unknown to the sometimes frustrated public relations counsel, advertising agency vice-president, metropolitan daily's promotion manager, or slot man on a big copy desk. Running a successful weekly is not the one-horse operation of half a century ago, and the rise of suburban weekly papers during the postwar era has upset journalistic traditions with hurricane force. Except for those in the very top positions, a metropolitan daily's staff members may be far less highly respected than those on a weekly's staff.

What should motivate a student to go into a journalism career?

Among factors found motivating ambitious young people to go into journalism, according to a recent survey, were an "urge to communicate," a desire to meet people and to get around, and the expectation to become involved in "the stream of events."

Down deeper but usually less exposed and talked about was a desire to perform public service and the chance to help create an informed public that is essential to any real solution of today's complexities in a democratic society.

But this is not quite the full story, as Dean Edward W. Barrett of the Graduate School of Journalism, Columbia University, told the 1962 meeting of the American Newspaper Publishers Association:

> Among high school students, particularly high school editors, there is today a wealth of young people who at least vaguely would like to go into the journalistic fields, who have an urge to communicate, who would like to have a feeling of serving society through journalism. Moreover, they have a fairly realistic picture of the salaries being paid and of the rewards that are attainable within five or ten years.
>
> What deters so many of them? Many at this stage are deterred by lack of confidence in their own abilities, some by lack of real respect for the dailies to which they happen to have been exposed in their own home towns, many by a broad feeling that the profession is not too widely respected or is not a so-called 'prestige' profession. . . .
>
> Down in the age ranges where the first impressions are crystallizing about our profession, we have two strong facts going for us. This rising generation looks upon journalism as "interesting work" and as being "useful to society." If we fail to justify these early impressions, we shall be injuring something very precious in the next generation of men and women who may be working with us.

This is a perfect peroration for this book. It might equally well be the preface to your own career in professional journalism.

APPENDICES

Style Book

This style book, adapted from that used by students of the Department of Journalism, Washington Square College of Arts and Science, New York University, may serve as a guide for high school student editors and advisors in working out their own publication's style rules. This style book was developed after study of standard newspaper and press association practices.

Format

All assignments must be typewritten.

Mark each page as follows in the upper left hand corner:

Slug line (story title, page number)
Last name, first name
Date Due (Date Submitted)

On the first page, begin almost half way down; on subsequent pages leave about an inch of space at the top.

Use 8½ x 11 typing paper (unlined white or yellow).

Never use both sides of the paper.

Double space all copy.

Indent each paragraph.

Leave wide margins on both sides of the paper and at bottom of sheet.

At the bottom of each page, with the exception of the last page, type the word "more." On the last page indicate "the end" with an appropriate symbol.

In general, follow the rules of good standard English.

Punctuation

The Comma

The comma is used to separate words or figures that might be misunderstood:

What the solution is, is a great question.
Aug. 1, 1965
1,307,653

The comma is used after a series of coordinate, qualifying words:

The woman was perfumed, dressy, short, slender, and old.
x, y, and z
Brown of Arkadelphis, S.D., said . . .

and between the title and organization (name and number):

Woodring, secretary, The Patheon Co.; American Legion Post, No. 110.

The comma is used to set off parenthetical words, phrases, or clauses, and also scores:

The work, he said, was exacting.
The basis will be found in Title XIX, chapter 2, page 15.
Milwaukee 7, Brooklyn 6.

The abbreviations Sr., Jr., and etc. are parenthetical and thus commas will set them off:

Joe Smith, Sr., said . . .
Letters, parcel post, etc., should be put there.

NOTE: The comma is not used for restrictive clauses:

The car which failed lost the race.

The comma is used to separate in apposition or contrast:

Smithwick, the favorite, won handily.

The comma is omitted before the ampersand, before the dash, and in street addresses, telephone numbers, years, and serial numbers:

Smith, Jones & Co.
ORegon 3-3617
1628 Oak St.
A16503421

In names of business firms, follow the individual firm's own usage.

The Semicolon

The semicolon separates phrases containing commas to avoid confusion; separates clauses where the conjunction is implied but omitted; separates statements of contrast or statements too closely related in meaning to be separate sentences; and separates phrases in lists:

No, sir; I did not see him.
The draperies, which were ornate, displeased me; the walls, of a light blue, were easy on the eyes.
George Lake, Waterloo; Henry James, Washington; Harry White, Kalamazoo; and William Smith, Seattle.
The party consisted of B. M. Jordan; R. J. Kelly, his secretary; Mrs. Jordan; Martha Brown, her nurse; and three servants. (Seven persons, but without semicolons the party would number nine.)

The Apostrophe

The apostrophe is used for possessives and in some abbreviations, and its use should be determined by the rules of grammar.

Usually the possessive of a singular noun not ending in "s" is formed by adding the apostrophe and "s." In the plural ending with "s" or "ce" the apostrophe only is added.

man's	men's	Prince's	Princes'	Essex's	Essexes'
Jones'	Joneses'	Hostess'	Hostesses'	Mars'	Jesus'
GI	GIs (pl)	GI's	GIs'	three R's	
class of '90		John Jones '01		(but 90s)	

His U's are like V's and his 2s like Z's.

Quotation Marks

Quotation marks enclose direct quotations and some words or phrases in ironical use, political controversy, or use other than true significance. Some accepted sobriquets or misnomers take quotation marks instead of parentheses but nicknames should be in parentheses: "Babe" Ruth; Nat (King) Cole.

When quotations are broken into several continuous paragraphs, each paragraph should be started with quotation marks, and the closing quotation marks be placed only at the end of the final paragraph.

The comma and final period are placed inside the quotation marks. Other punctuation marks should be placed inside quotation marks only when they are part of the quoted matter:

> The coach shouted, "Let's go!"
> Ruth said, "Whither thou goest, I will go."
> The question is, is she "for real"?

Where possible, quotation marks should be limited to three sets (double, single, double).

Capitalization

Capitalize the names of political parties, all governmental bodies, presiding officers and permanent committees, corporations and firms, military, naval, and similar bodies, races and their languages, religions, and geographical divisions. Do not capitalize "p.m." and "a.m." when referring to time of day. Capitalize and quote titles of books, plays, journals, pictures, poems, songs.

Spelling

The spelling, division, and hyphenation should be those of Webster's New International Dictionary, Second Edition.

Abbreviations

Abbreviate titles which precede personal names:

Dr. Robert Brown
The Rev. William Johnson ("Rev." never appears without the definite article.)

Abbreviate states, territories, and provincial names following names of countries, cities, and towns of the United States:

Philadelphia, Pa.
Manila, P.I.

Abbreviate names of scholastic degrees, decorations, and branches of military and naval service when they *follow* personal names:

James Spencer, M.A., Ph.D.
Lt. Robert Charles, D.S.C.

Abbreviate commonly recognized organizations and programs with long names (except when mentioned for the first time), such as:

YMCA, WCTU, PTA, UN, NLRB

Figures

In general, spell out numbers below 10. Use figures for street addresses, time of day, percentages, sports scores. Figures which begin a sentence are spelled out.

Glossary

NOTE: Phrases in SMALL CAPS appear in Glossary as separate entries.

accent face: type of markedly different design or weight used to contrast against basic letters used in ad or page.

add: new material to include at the end of a story already written or already set in type.

advance: story about an event which will take place in the future. Also copy of speech, resolution, etc., given to reporter before it is actually presented.

agate: 5½-point type. Also, as **agate line,** unit of measuring advertising, one column wide by 1/14 inch deep.

all-cap: caps, material set entirely in capital letters or upper case.

anchor the corners: LAYOUT technique that places strong DISPLAY elements in or near the corners of the front page.

AP: Associated Press, a major wire service.

armpit: the undesirable LAYOUT technique of placing a narrow HEADLINE immediately under a wider one.

art: illustrative material of all kinds except typographical in a publication: photography and HAND ART, prepared by an artist.

ascender: portion of letter that extends above MEANLINE. Also, those letters which have such extensions, such as b, d, h.

assignment: reporter's designated job.

assignment book or sheet: editor's record and announcement of jobs given to staff reporters.

assignment editor: staff member responsible for giving reporters assignments.

author's alterations: AA's, changes made in set type, not to correct typographical errors but to revise content.

backing up: printing second side of a sheet of paper.

bank: one line of a HEADLINE. Also that surface on which typographic material is stored before it is MADE UP.

banner: streamer, HEADLINE that extends across width of page. Also, largest head on front page.

baseline: imaginary line on which PRIMARY LETTERS align at bottom.

basement: lower half of front page of a newspaper.

beat: run, regularly assigned area covered by a reporter. Also an exclusive story.

beat reporter: one who covers the same territory regularly, in contrast to GENERAL ASSIGNMENT REPORTER who covers specific and changing events.

Ben Day: process of placing a shading pattern on LINE ENGRAVINGS or type; named for inventor.

billboard cover: that of a magazine which uses all-type to call attention to several inside stories.

Black Letter: TEXT, a race of type.

bleed: to extend a picture off one or more margins of a page. Also, the ENGRAVING so used.

block letters: GOTHIC letters.

body: metal rectangular bar which carries the printing surface of type. Also, the regular reading matter in a newspaper as contrasted to display lines.

body type: that style and size in which most non-advertising material is set.

boldface: form of an alphabet in which size remains constant but heavier strokes make the characters. Abbreviated bf.

bold graf: paragraph of a news story set in boldface to function as a SUBHEAD and change color of the mass.

boldline: line of boldface type opening a paragraph, used in place of a SUBHEAD.

bond: kind of paper usually used for letterheads.

book: name for magazine frequently

used in trade. Also applies to yearbooks. Also a prepared set of two sheets of copy paper and one of carbon paper used by reporters in writing story.

book method: proofreading technique which uses two marks for each error, one at the point of error, the correction in the margin. *See* GUIDELINE.

bowl: that area of a type character enclosed entirely or partially by curved lines such as the interior of o, a, b. Also, the lines that form such circular enclosures.

box: unit of type enclosed by a border. Sideless boxes use such border only at top and bottom.

bright: humorous or human interest news item, almost always short in length.

buddy system: ORIENTED LAYOUT.

budget: total amount of editorial copy and art available for one issue of a newspaper.

bullet: large period used for decoration or typographic COLOR.

bureau: out-of-town news-gathering office of a newspaper.

business department: staff of publication concerned with circulation, advertising, and accounting. Usually headed by **business manager**. Other departments include NEWS, EDITORIAL WRITING, and MECHANICAL.

by-line: writer's or photographer's name above story or under picture to indicate that it is his work.

calligraphy: beautiful writing, a letter form often used for NAMEPLATES or column HEADS.

canopy: headline which runs across related picture and story. Also, headline enclosed by three-sided box.

caption: heading above any illustration. Also, descriptive material accompanying pictures in a yearbook. Erroneously used instead of CUTLINES in newspaper usage.

catchline: line of large type between picture and CUTLINES.

chase: rectangular metal frame in which typographic elements are assembled for printing.

cheesecake: female figures photographed in saucy or suggestive costumes and poses.

circus makeup: razzle-dazzle, that which uses strong and sensational DISPLAY patterns.

city editor: executive in charge of publication's coverage of local news and director of local staff.

city room: area in newspaper office where local or city news is written and edited. On many newspapers called NEWS ROOM, where all copy is processed.

clamshell: PLATEN PRESS.

clapper: PLATEN PRESS.

classical: LAYOUT pattern in which elements are placed in patterns generally resembling certain letters of the alphabet.

clean copy: material relatively free of errors and corrections.

clip: clipping, cutting from periodical, especially one filed for future use.

clip book: collection of REPRODUCTION PROOFS of ART to be used for OFFSET work.

cold type: that produced photographically, by typewriting, or by preprinted characters; as opposed to HOT METAL.

collage: ART produced by pasting together various elements into a single composition.

color: typographic device used to change overall tone of masses of type. Apparent tone or density of a page as affected by varying type faces, borders, decorations, etc. ROP color is use of inks of different hues than black.

color, flat: use of additional hue or hues without attempting to create the spectrum of nature. In newspaper usage, commonly referred to as "spot" or "ROP" color. ROP (run of the press) designates that color, flat or PROCESS, produced on a regular, instead of specialized, press and on any page.

color, typographic: variations in tonal value of masses of type; created by using BOLDFACE, ITALIC, white space or ORNAMENTS.

column inch: unit for measuring advertising space, one column wide (this dimension varies among publications) by one inch deep.

communications theory: application of social science research findings to transmitting information.

compact: format of newspaper with pages approximately 11 x 15 inches. This is also called TABLOID format, but the compact format uses more conservative LAYOUT, and pages become smaller versions of conventional, FULL-FORMAT papers.

composed: set in type; typographic elements arranged in FORM for printing.

composing room: part of printing establishment or plant where type is set, then assembled into ads and pages.

composition: type set manually or by machine. Also, the act of typesetting.

comprehensive: detailed, same-size DUMMY which is almost a replica of finished printing job.

Condensed: form of an alphabet in which characters retain their height but are narrower than normal.

constants, newspaper: those elements which appear in every issue of a paper, such as NAMEPLATE, MASTHEAD, FOLIO LINES, etc.

contact print: UNCROPPED, same-size photographic print made from negative without use of enlarger.

continuous tone: picture in black, white and intermediate tones of gray, or their equivalent in color, without SCREEN dots.

contrast: introduction of markedly different typographic or art element into a layout for emphasis or interest.

copy: material written for possible publication. Also, materials from which printing PLATES are made.

copy desk: location, usually a U-shaped desk, where COPYREADERS edit COPY and write HEADLINES. Also, the collective group that mans that desk. Also, general term for news room management.

copyreader: staff member who edits COPY, writes HEADLINES, and frequently DUMMIES-UP pages.

correction fluid: material to cover over errors on Mimeograph stencils.

counter: areas within and around the printing surface of type that are depressed to prevent their contact with ink rollers and paper.

cover: to gather information.

criticism: broadly, a report on some performance in the arts, books, drama, etc.; frequently an evaluation and sometimes including subjective, opinionated comments. *See* REVIEWING.

crop: to eliminate unwanted areas of a picture. These are not actually cut away; the desired portion is indicated by marginal CROP MARKS.

crop marks: indicators that show areas of a photograph to be eliminated in making ENGRAVINGS.

cropper's L's: pair of L-shaped cardboard pieces that are manipulated to find the most effective area in a picture before CROPPING.

crossline: type of HEADLINE consisting of a single centered line.

CSPA: either Columbia Scholastic Press Association, with headquarters at Columbia University, or Catholic School Press Association, with headquarters at Marquette University. Both are organizations to serve high school journalists. *See* also NSPA and QUILL AND SCROLL.

Cursive: letterform resembling handwriting but with unconnected characters. *See* SCRIPT.

cut: ENGRAVING, PLATE, or ZINC. Also to compress a story in length.

cutlines: explanatory COPY that runs with pictures. In yearbooks, called CAPTIONS.

cutoff rule: thin line used for horizontal separation on newspaper pages.

cylinder press: printing machine on which paper is impressed upon a flat typographic surface by a cylinder. Also called flatbed press.

dateline: phrase showing origin and date of filing of out-of-town news story.

deadline: time when reporter has to submit copy, when copy must go to composing room, or when publication goes to press.

debossing: design depressed into paper or fabric. The opposite side of the sheet carries the image, which is raised or EMBOSSED.

deck: that section of a multiunit headline composed of one or more lines in the same face and size. When deck is subordinate to banner, it is called a "readout" or, more rarely, a "drop." Deck is often confused with BANK.

density: the quality of a negative or picture which gives well-defined gradation from black, through gray, into white.

departmentalize: to group news content of paper by subject matter.

descender: portion of letter that extends beneath BASELINE. Also those letters which have such extensions, as g, p, q.

desk: that place in news room where copyreading is done. Usually **city desk** or **news desk**. Also, that broad definition of duties which distinguishes editors from writers. Also, the administration of special departments such as sports, women's, etc. Also, general term to designate the executive levels of the news staff.

diagonal, common: system for determining size of ENGRAVING smaller or larger than original art.

dirty copy: written material with many mistakes and corrections.

display: that size of type larger than BODY TYPE which is used to attract attention. Use, rather than size, determines difference between body and display types.

divider page: page or pages in a yearbook that introduce a major division of contents.

documentary photography: that form of the art which concerns itself with recording facts rather than primarily or only with form and composition.

downstairs: lower half of the front page of a newspaper.

downstyle: COPY or HEADLINES set with minimum of capitals. So-called because of emphasis on lowercase letters. In body type, only key words of titles are capitalized, as in *Clay high school* or *Middletown Athletic association.* In headlines only first word and proper nouns are capped.

dropline: STEPPED HEAD.

dummy: drawing showing arrangement of elements of printed page or ad. **Thumbnails** are small, sketchy preliminaries. **Roughs** are larger but with little detail. COMPREHENSIVES are same size and in detail. Mechanicals or comprehensives are exact replicas of finished printed job.

dummy-up: to arrange news material in page form by preparing a rough DUMMY for printer to follow.

duotone: printing process in which a dark and light color are combined to produce a third color, the only one visible.

ear: small block of type that runs alongside a newspaper FLAG.

edit: to check copy for mistakes of any kind, including facts, style, spelling, grammar, and libel, and to improve it as a communication. Also abbreviation for editorial.

editor: staff member who edits news COPY, in contrast with gathering and writing news for publication. Also, executive in charge of specialized department of a publication, as, sports, women's, business, etc.

editorial page: edit page, that devoted to opinion and comment.

editorial writing: department of publication concerned with expressing opinions, usually through editorials. Also function of periodical sometimes known as OPINION FUNCTION. Usually directed by editor of editorial page or chief editorial writer. Other departments include NEWS, BUSINESS, and MECHANICAL.

Egyptian: SQUARE SERIF type.

embossing: process of pressing a design into the reverse side of paper or fabric, especially book covers, to create a raised image on the front side.

end mark: 30-mark, symbol that shows the end of a story in COPY or print.

engraving: photoengraving, process of converting photograph or art work into a printing plate by photochemistry. Also, plate so made.

evergreen pictures: photographs that are not subject to rapid obsolescence or "aging" after a specific date. Examples are seasonal pictures of beautiful young women, cats, dogs, exotic animals, and travel scenes.

exchange subscriptions: complimentary copies exchanged with other publications. Part or sometimes all of the FREE LIST.

Extended: form of an alphabet in which characters retain their height but are wider than normal.

family: a subdivision of a type RACE identified by a trade name and containing various sizes and forms of the basic design.

feature, news: material developed out of current happenings as background information or "with" story.

filler: short item used to fill space.

5 W's: who, what, when, where, why (or how), term to denote possible elements that may be included in SUMMARY LEAD PARAGRAPH. Also called 5 W's and H, to include "how."

fixative: clear material applied to face of art work, usually by blowing on tiny droplets, for protection against dirt.

flag: nameplate, the formal identification of a newspaper on its front page. Often but erroneously called the MASTHEAD. Sometimes called the LOGO.

flatbed press: CYLINDER PRESS.

flat embossing: design impressed into paper or fabric by only a single flat plate.

flong: STEREOTYPE matrix, mold of papier mache from which a printing PLATE is cast.

floret: typographic ORNAMENT, usually in the form of a stylized flower.

flush left: type of HEADLINE set so all lines are against left-hand column rule, and right-hand side is irregular. Also, any other type so set.

flush right: type of HEADLINE which is set so all lines are against right-hand column rule, and left-hand side is irregular. Also, any other type so set.

folio lines: those which give the newspaper name and page number. Erroneously, DATELINES.

follow copy: instructions to printer to set COPY as marked. Used to indicate unusual spelling, type arrangement, etc.

follow-up or **folo-up:** instructions to gather additional information on event. Or a story about an event that has been forecast in an ADVANCE story.

folo: short for follow, a second story that follows another item. Also instructions to reporter to get additional information.

font: collection of letters, numbers, and characters in one type FAMILY and of one size.

forced circulation: system in which subscription to publication is included in another fee such as membership dues.

form: type and ENGRAVINGS, assembled in a CHASE, from which a page is printed or STEREOTYPED.

formal balance: SYMMETRICAL LAYOUT.

format: shape, size, and general physical appearance of a publication. FULL FORMAT is usually a newspaper in eight columns of about 21 inches deep; TABLOID, or COMPACT, format is approximately half that size.

foundry type: reusable metal printing characters used in letterpress.

four-color process: printing method that combines four halftone PLATES to reproduce the full color spectrum of nature.

Fourth Estate: term applied to journalism, the press, newsmen. In feudal Europe the three estates were nobles, clergy, and commons; the fourth was not official but so named in deference to the influence of the press.

free list: complimentary and/or exchange subscriptions of publications. Many staffs exchange subscriptions so that they may study each other's publications.

fresh air: white space injected into LAYOUT.

full format: that of newspapers of seven to nine columns of approximately 21 inches in depth.

fullface: normal design of letters as opposed to CONDENSED and EXTENDED and normal weight as opposed to BOLDFACE or light. Lightface is often used as a synonym of fullface but confusion is possible when there is a weight lighter than normal.

furniture: wood or metal rectangles used to create white space in printing FORMS.

future book: editor's listing, under dates, of forthcoming events that should be COVERED.

gallery cover: that of a magazine which uses one picture, usually not related to any inside story.

galley: long, narrow, shallow tray in which type is stored after being set and before it is assembled. Also short for GALLEY PROOF.

galley proof: first printing of type to detect errors.

gathered: (printed sheets) assembled in proper order before binding.

general assignment reporter: one who covers a specific event or meeting, in contrast to BEAT REPORTER who has a specific territory to cover regularly.

geometrical layout: one in which typographic elements are arranged to form definite patterns of lines and areas.

gimcrack: typographic decoration, usually small, used to break up masses of type.

glossy: photograph made with the shiny finish usually preferred by ENGRAVER. Often, though erroneously, used as synonym for all photos.

Gothic: a form of SAN SERIF letter. In its earlier form it was ungainly and compressed, with heavy strokes and squared-off curves.

go up: to use one more column of space than type.

graf: paragraph.

gravure: intaglio printing. Method in which printing image is made of lines, incised into metal plate, which hold ink which is transferred onto paper. **Rotogravure** is the most common commercial application and is most frequently used for Sunday newspaper magazine sections. Gravure is too expensive in short runs for application to student publications.

Grotesk: European name for GOTHIC type race.

guideline: proofreading method in which error is circled and line drawn from it to margin where correction is noted. *See* BOOK METHOD.

gutter: the two margins of book and magazine pages that meet at the fold. A single margin there is called the inside or gutter margin.

hairline: the thin stroke in a type character. Also, the thinnest rule used by newspapers.

halftone: printing PLATE which reproduces continuous-tone art by use of a SCREEN.

hand art: all pictures and decorations produced by an artist, in contrast to photographs.

handout: PRESS RELEASE.

hanging indent: HEADLINE style in which first line is set flush left-and-right and each succeeding line is indented a specified, identical amount at the left.

hard copy: typewritten copy, usually produced at the same time tape for automatic typesetting is perforated.

harmony: arrangement of typographic elements to lead the reading eye pleasantly throughout the whole area.

head: short for HEADLINE.

headletter: type used for HEADLINES.

headline: heading, label, or CAPTION placed over news, columns, etc.

headline schedule: collection of all HEADLINE forms and sizes used by a newspaper.

hellbox: depository for discarded type, slugs, or other printer's metals.

H. I.: HUMAN INTEREST, feature or news material with high emotional or dramatic appeal, often of comparatively low news value.

hold copy: material which is to be kept and not used until notification, or at a specified later time or date.

horizontal makeup: typographic technique of disposing type in wide, flat areas to make it appear easier to read.

hot metal: or **hot type,** LINECASTER SLUGS and FOUNDRY TYPE as contrasted to COLD TYPE.

house publication: newspaper or magazine printed by business organization or institution, generally wholly subsidized and distributed free or for small fee to convey special message for its publisher.

HTC: head to come (or **HTK,** hed to kum), indication to printer that HEADLINE will follow but to set COPY ahead of receiving headline.

human interest: news with emotional impact about individuals or animals. May be fairly short items, such as BRIGHTS, or longer FEATURES about interesting but not necessarily well-known personalities.

impression: product of one cycle of printing press; also, clearness of printed sheet; also, force with which paper and type meet. "Kiss impression" brings paper and type together so ink is evenly deposited but no indention is made in paper.

informal balance: LAYOUT pattern in which elements are balanced by optical weight rather than by mathematical placement.

initial: first letter of a paragraph set in type larger than body type for decoration or emphasis. Its size is indicated by the number of lines of BODY TYPE it occupies, as a 3-line initial. Those aligned at bottom of body type and projecting upward are **rising** or **stickup initials;** those that occupy a corner cut out of type block are INSET.

inline letter: that form in which a white line runs down the center of each stroke of a character.

insert: new material that is to be inserted into COPY already written or type already set. Also, section of a yearbook printed after main book is complete and so designed that it may later be fastened into the cover with earlier material. Also, PORKCHOP, a half-column picture.

inset head: HEADLINE, used especially with typewritten COPY, which occupies a corner within the mass of body type.

internal silhouette: TINT BLOCK with an area removed so a SILHOUETTE HALFTONE will print on white background but be surrounded by color.

interpretation: explanation, background, REPORTING-IN-DEPTH, attempt to get below the surface in news reporting without becoming subjective.

interview: story obtained by talking with individual. Also the act of such talking.

inverted pyramid: style of newswriting

starting with most important facts first and following paragaphs containing information in descending order of interest. Also type of HEADLINE in which DECKS form upper portion of an inverted pyramid.

Italic: Itlx, variation of ROMAN type which slants to right and is often more decorative. Also, erroneously, used to designate slanting form of non-Roman faces, which are correctly designated as OBLIQUE.

jazz: LAYOUT pattern in which each side of a layout is suggested but not entirely defined.

jump: to continue story from one page to another. A story so continued, especially that portion on following page.

justify: to set type so it fills line completely. Also, to space type so a column is exactly filled vertically.

kicker: small HEADLINE that rides above main headline.

kill: to eliminate material, either in part, as within news report, or entirely. **Mandatory kill,** order from news service to its clients forbidding use of previously transmitted material.

label head: HEADLINE that indicates general story content or departmental classification. Also known as "**deadhead.**"

Latin alphabet: the 26 letters used for writing English. Also called Roman alphabet, although that can create confusion with ROMAN type race.

layout: application of principles of TYPOGRAPHY to specific problem. Also, a DUMMY.

lead: pronounced *leed,* opening of news story. Pronounced *ledd,* and spelled phonetically in this book, metal strip that produces two points of white space. Leading (pronounced *ledding*) is adding space between lines of type.

legibility: visibility, that quality in type that affects the quickness of perception of a single line or compact group of lines. Erroneously used instead of READABILITY.

leg man: staff member who gathers news, then transmits information to REWRITE MAN who does actual newswriting.

lettering guide: mechanical guide for producing characters on MIMEOGRAPH STENCILS or for COLD TYPE.

letterpress: method of printing from relief typographic elements.

libel: false and malicious defamation in print; includes type, pictures, cartoons, drawings.

lightface: FULLFACE.

light table: translucent working surface, through which light shines from below, used for preparing STENCILS and PASTEUPS.

line art: art work in only lines and masses of black and white, that makes line engraving printing PLATE, as opposed to HALFTONE.

linecaster: a machine that produces a line of type. The LINOTYPE, a trade name, was the first keyboard linecaster and the name is used almost generically. The LUDLOW has no keyboard.

line cut: PHOTOENGRAVING which prints only lines and masses of black.

lines of force: lines within a picture or created by type arrangement which act as directional guides to the reading eye.

Linotype: the first linecaster, a machine which casts type in lines instead of as individual characters. It is a keyboarded linecaster.

lithography: writing with stone. Printing method that uses repulsion between ink and water to transfer image from stone surface to paper. Modern development, **photolithography** or OFFSET, uses metal or paper plates prepared photographically instead of manually as in lithography, which today is used basically as fine-art form.

locked up: (printing FORM) wedged tightly into CHASE and ready for printing.

log, ad: record of advertising scheduled for future issues.

logotype: heading which identifies a section of a newspaper or magazine, such as sports or activities. Abbreviated **logo**. Sometimes used for NAMEPLATE or advertiser's SIGNATURE.

lowercase: minuscules, small letters; so named because in old print shops these characters were kept in the lower of two cases.

Ludlow: trade name of linecaster in which MATRICES are assembled by hand.

magazine: a periodical publication, usually bound and smaller in format than a newspaper. Also, container in which LINOTYPE MATRICES are stored.

makeup: to assemble type, ads, and CUTS in CHASE.

makeup editor: representative of NEWS DEPARTMENT who directs assembly of type and cuts in MECHANICAL DEPARTMENT. Not to be confused with MAKEUP MAN, a printer, who actually handles type and cuts.

makeup man: printer who assembles ads or pages in composing room, frequently under direction of MAKEUP EDITOR.

managing editor: executive in charge of all news functions of a publication. The title varies; sometimes it is EDITOR or NEWS EDITOR.

mass media: communication channels to the general public. Generally considered to include newspapers, magazines, radio, television, newsreels, and, in some cases, nonfiction or informational books. Sometimes, but rarely, direct-mail and billboard advertising is included. Used in contrast to personalized approaches, such as individual letters or lectures to comparatively small groups.

masthead: that collection of data, usually appearing on the editorial page, which lists publisher, editors, and staff of a publication. Often but erroneously used to refer to the FLAG.

matrix: mold from which type, decorative materials, advertisements, and illustrations are cast for letterpress use. LINECASTER MATRICES are brass; STEREOTYPE MATRICES, of papier mache (*see* FLONG). Abbreviated to **mat.**

matte: photographic surface of tiny pebbling, usually used for studio portraits.

meanline: imaginary line at the top of PRIMARY LETTERS.

measure: length of line of type.

mechanical: PASTE-UP, COLD-TYPE material arranged for PLATE making. Also, a DUMMY that is the exact replica of the finished printed job.

mechanical department: section of publication concerned with production of newspaper or magazine. Usually headed by MECHANICAL SUPERINTENDENT.

mechanical separation: art work, prepared by hand, for each plate to be used in multicolor printing.

mechanical shading: SHADING SCREEN or SHEET.

mechanical superintendent: M.S., executive in charge of MECHANICAL DEPARTMENT.

milline rate: cost of one AGATE LINE of advertising per million readers.

Mimeograph: STENCIL duplicating machine. This is a trademark and should be capitalized, although, because the machine was the first of its kind, there is a tendency to use the name as a generic term.

minuscule: LOWERCASE letter.

modelled embossing: design in bas relief produced by pressing paper or fabric between two dies.

Modern: form of ROMAN letter with sharp, straight SERIFS, maximum difference between thick and thin strokes, and BOWLS on perpendicular axes.

mold: MATRIX.

montage: picture produced by using portions of various negatives in a single photographic print.

morgue: publication's library of reference materials. Probably called "morgue" because it stores obituaries or "OBITS."

mortice: area removed from ENGRAVING to allow type or other engraving to occupy that space. Most common is the "NOTCH," where a rectangle is removed from one corner. Area removed within an engraving is **internal mortice.**

mousetrap cover: that of a magazine which lures the reader to a specific inside story by means of picture or type.

naked column: one without head or picture at top of page.

nameplate: FLAG.

news: reports of anything timely which has importance, use, or interest to a considerable number of persons in the publication's audience.

news angles: aspects of event which make it of special interest to communicators and their audiences. Among most common are: today angle, local angle, prominence angle, consequence or importance angle, human interest, paper's policy, and good taste.

news department: that organization of publication concerned with gathering, editing, and displaying of news items. Usually it is headed by either MANAGING EDITOR or NEWS EDITOR.

Other departments include EDITORIAL WRITING, BUSINESS, and MECHANICAL.

news editor: executive in charge of news department. *See* MANAGING EDITOR.

news hole: that area in newspaper devoted to editorial, as opposed to advertising, material.

newsprint: inexpensive paper usually used to print newspapers.

news room: areas of publication office where news COPY is written and EDITED. On smaller papers it combines with the CITY ROOM.

noise: interference in transmitting information. Applies to COMMUNICATION THEORY.

no-orphan system: ORIENTED LAYOUT.

no-run: advertisement which was not printed as scheduled.

notch: simplest form of MORTICE, a rectangle cut out of one corner of a printing PLATE.

Novelty: ORNAMENTED LETTER.

NSPA: National Scholastic Press Association, an organization for high school journalists with headquarters at University of Minnesota. *See* also CSPA.

obit: obituary, biographical material used on death of individual. Often this is prepared in advance from material entered on printed obit form.

Oblique letters: those letterforms, of races other than ROMAN, which slant to right. Slanting Roman forms are ITALICS.

offset: planographic method of printing using a plate on which the printing image is neither depressed nor raised. Technically this is offset LITHOGRAPHY, although the second word is commonly dropped.

Old English: a form of the TEXT type RACE.

Old Style: form of ROMAN letter with minimum difference between thick and thin strokes, bracketed SERIFS, and BOWLS that tilt to left.

one-up: LAYOUT technique which uses one more column of space than of type, the extra space being distributed between columns. When two more columns of space are used, technique is called **two-up.**

opaque: to remove, in a negative, unwanted shadows and other elements before PLATE-making.

opinion function: one of aims of periodical. Others include information, entertainment, and service. Opinion function applies to editorials and columns that express opinions. Includes EDITORIAL WRITING.

optical center: that point at the vertical center and 10 per cent above the horizontal center of a page or ad.

optimum line length: that width of a line of type which is most easy and pleasant to read. Determined by multiplying lowercase alphabet length by 1.5.

oriented: buddy or no-orphan system, LAYOUT pattern in which each typographic element is arranged to align horizontally and/or vertically with at least one other.

ornaments: those typographic elements other than characters making up a normal FONT. Most common are stars, FLORETS, borders and INITIALS.

Ornamented letter: NOVELTY, letter form with variations in shape or texture of strokes or additional elements around the letter itself.

overlay: transparent paper or plastic laid over a picture to create MECHANICAL SEPARATIONS; to indicate CROPPING, especially of intricate shapes; or to give instructions to platemaker.

overline: line of display type over a picture. Also, erroneously, called CAPTION.

overset: COMPOSED type in excess of current available space. Usually such matter must be discarded because of loss of timeliness.

overtone rub: method of decorating a book cover by rubbing a contrasting color over an EMBOSSED area.

padded covers: book covering that has soft material between the fabric and the heavy boards.

page proofs: sample impression of whole page or form.

pagination dummy: rough, small folder showing number of pages and arrangement of magazine or yearbook.

pasteup: assembling various COLD-TYPE elements into a form from which printing PLATES are made. Also, the material so prepared.

pattern shot: a photograph which repeats the same shape of objects many times to create a pleasant composition.

pebble: texture of paper with tiny hemispherical depressions.

personal: brief news item about individual or small group, frequently found on society page. Unlike

BRIGHTS, personals generally do not give humorous or amusing incidents.

photoengraving: RELIEF PRINTING PLATE that reproduces pictures. Also, the process of converting photographs and art work into printing plates.

pica: unit of printer's measurement, 12 points, 1/6 inch. Also the larger of the two standard typewriter faces.

pick up: instruction to COMPOSING ROOM to add material indicated, usually already set type or available CUT.

picture editor: executive in charge of all pictures, local, mail, MAT, and wirephoto. Generally assigns local photographers to cover local news events.

pix: pictures, plural of **pic.**

plastic bindings: method of binding using rings or spiral fastening of plastic or metal.

plate: a piece of metal that carries a printing image in relief, depression or planographically.

platen press: LETTERPRESS printing press, also called clamshell or clapper press, which impresses flat typographic surface upon paper in a hinged motion. Also, the surface upon which the paper rests during printing and typewriting.

play: emphasis given to news and pictures. Also applies to extensive display given to a story or picture.

point: unit of printer's measurement, 1/72 inch. Also, a punctuation mark.

porkchop: half-column picture.

poster layout: that used in typical TABLOID FORMAT for page one, consisting of one or two HEADLINES (with stories inside) and a large picture.

P.R.: public relations.

press associations: press services or wire services, organizations which supply regional, national and world news and pictures. AP and UPI are two leading ones in United States.

press release: information given to newsmen or sent to publication, usually by public relations man, on behalf of organization anxious, or obliged, to have such news widely disseminated.

primary letter: those lowercase letters without ASCENDERS or DESCENDERS, such as a, c, m, r.

primary optical area: that portion of written or printed page in the upper left corner where eye instinctively begins reading or inspection.

process color: that printing operation which combines halftones in two or more colors to create an optical illusion of colors which are obtained when such pigments are physically mixed, as in paint. Three-color (commonly used in newspapers) and four-color process can duplicate all colors in the spectrum.

progression: arrangement of total material in a magazine or yearbook.

proofreader: person who examines first impressions of printing to correct errors, primarily typographical, but also in fact and style.

proportional spacing: device giving different amounts of space to wide and narrow characters in typewriting.

put the paper to bed: complete work for publication; give final approval before publication is printed.

pyramid: ad pyramid, placement of advertising on newspaper page. Pyramid head, arrangement of DISPLAY type in which centered lines are progressively shorter.

Q and A: question and answer, used for transcript of court trials, hearings, etc.

quality magazine: superior publication. Journal which is concerned primarily with expressing opinions or subjective evaluations, usually on contemporary scene.

Quill and Scroll: honorary society for high school journalists with headquarters at State University of Iowa. Also the name of society's quarterly magazine.

quoin: metal wedge, used in pairs, to fix typographical materials firmly into CHASE.

quotes: quotations used in story. Also quotation marks.

race: basic subdivision of type, ROMAN, TEXT, SANS SERIF, SQUARE SERIF, SCRIPT, and ORNAMENTED.

razzle-dazzle makeup: CIRCUS MAKEUP.

readability: that quality of type which affords maximum ease and comfort in reading over a sustained period.

reading diagonal: basic, instinctive motion of reading eye through printed page, from top left to lower right.

readout: secondary HEAD under a BANNER.

rectangular layout: LAYOUT pattern in which the area is subdivided into rectangles that harmonize with the whole and each of its parts.

register: arranging position of impressions of different colors so they match properly on printed page.

reglet: spacing material, usually wood but often metal, 1 pica or more wide.

release: PRESS RELEASE, material prepared for newsmen, usually by public relations man. Also authorization to print material sent out to composing room to be set into type and marked to be held.

relief printing: LETTERPRESS, method of printing by applying ink to raised surfaces and impressing on paper.

reporting-in-depth: explanation, background, INTERPRETATION.

reproduction proof: repro, carefully produced impression from relief type, used to make printing PLATES.

Resisto: trade name for water-resistant photographic paper.

retraction: correction of error in previously printed news story. Generally important as means of showing willingness to rectify mistake. A retraction may help establish lack of malice if LIBEL action is taken.

reverse cut: printing PLATE which produces effect of white letters on black or gray background.

reverse kicker: large, short HEADLINE above a smaller main headline. So called because it reverses ratio of regular KICKER to main head.

review: broadly, a report on some performance in the arts—books, drama, etc.; frequently comments resemble a news item in objectivity. *See* CRITICISM.

revise: second proof of type in which errors discovered in first—or GALLEY—PROOF have been corrected.

rewrite man: staff member who either writes information received from LEG MAN or rewrites COPY, already submitted, which needs major revisions.

rim: group of copyreaders as opposed to SLOT MAN.

rim man: regular copyreader who may be under supervision of SLOT MAN.

rippletone: popular texture of paper with irregular valleys and hills.

Roman: RACE of type distinguished by swelling and thinning of curved strokes and by SERIFS.

ROP: run of the press, color work produced on regular newspaper press, not a special one, and on any page.

rotary press: LETTERPRESS printing press in which paper is impressed upon curved typographic surface by a cylinder.

rough: *see* DUMMY.

round-up: summary in one story of numerous news developments from different sources.

run: reporter's beat. Also the number of copies being printed.

running head: material in display type that reads from one page to another. Also, name and number of BOOK, and sometimes of chapter, that appears on every page.

saddle staple: method of binding in which staple is inserted into the fold from outside.

Sans Serif: monotonal letter without SERIFS.

scaling: determining and marking size of ENGRAVING when not the same size as original art work.

schedule: collection of headlines used by newspaper.

scoop: exclusive.

screen: device used by ENGRAVER to reproduce continuous tone art work in a PLATE. Also, indication of fineness of engraving when combined with number—as 65-line screen—which indicates lines of halftone dots per lineal inch. Also, erroneously, a TINT BLOCK.

Script: letter form resembling handwriting in which characters are connected. *See* CURSIVE.

self cover: magazine or booklet cover of same paper as that used for inside pages. Also, a periodical so bound.

series: a subdivision of type FAMILIES that contains various sizes of one form of an alphabet. Identified by size and family name.

serif: tiny finishing stroke at end of main strokes. Major distinguishing feature of ROMAN type.

sewn-round and back: the most common permanent method of binding books, in which pages are sewn to each other for easy opening.

shading sheet: regular pattern printed on transparent plastic sheets and pasted onto line drawings for the equivalent of a BEN DAY.

short: any brief news story, but frequently used for humorous incident told in few words. *See* BRIGHT.

sidebar: second story that goes with another. Also known as **"with story."**

side staple: binding method in which

fastener is inserted through side of sheets near the fold.

sig cut: signature, that typographic element which performs the functions of a trademark and identifies an advertisement. Also called a LOGO.

signature: SIG CUT. Also group of pages printed on single sheet of paper.

silhouette: HALFTONE ENGRAVING from which background has been removed.

silhouette, modified: printing plate with one to three straight sides with the subject outlined in the other(s).

silk-screen: a reproduction process using STENCILS, often used on yearbook covers.

single wrap: copies of a publication which are packaged and mailed individually.

slot man: staff member in charge of COPY DESK. So named because he sits on inside of U-shaped desk and directs activities of copyreaders on outside edge, or RIM.

slug: a line of composition produced on a linecaster. Also, a blank printing unit six or more points thick.

slug line: word or several words used to identify news COPY.

spec: specify, to instruct printer which types and sizes to use on page or ad.

spike: to kill or eliminate COPY. Also hook on which such copy is placed.

spine: backbone, that portion of a book where all folded edges are joined.

spot: small decorative drawing. May be hand or photographic.

spread: two facing pages of a book. Also, the LAYOUT that occupies such area.

square halftone: halftone printing plate with 90-degree corners.

Square Serif: letterform made with SERIFS of the same weight as the main stroke.

S/S: abbreviation for **same size,** instruction to engraver.

staff: group of people who produce a publication. Most commonly this refers to those performing EDITORIAL and writing functions, although BUSINESS DEPARTMENT personnel are also designated as the business staff. Mechanical and circulation personnel are usually called the "crew."

stamping: impressing type into paper or fabric.

standing head: or STEREOTYPE HEAD, heading on a recurring feature used repeatedly without change.

stencil: sheet of cellulose material through which ink is forced to reproduce written, typed, or art material. Used in Mimeographing and silk-screen process.

stepped head: dropline, HEADLINE form in which three lines of approximately same length are arranged so first is FLUSH LEFT, second is centered, and third is FLUSH RIGHT.

stereotype: process of making FLONGS from printing forms and casting printing PLATES from them. Also, the plates thus made. Also, STANDING HEADS. Shortened to **stereo.**

stone: smooth surface upon which printer works. In old days an actual marble-topped table.

streamer: BANNER.

stringer: area correspondent of a newspaper. So called because in old days payment was made on amount of material which was printed, and which was pasted in a long strip as proof of claim.

style book: handbook for publication's style in grammar, capitalization, etc. Less detailed instructions may be merely a **style sheet.**

stylus: pointed instrument to produce stencils, or illustrations thereon, for Mimeograph and similar machines.

subdivider: page in a yearbook that introduces a subdivision of the contents.

subhead: GRAFhead, a displayed line, usually BOLDFACE and centered body type, within a story.

summary lead paragraph: initial paragraph which tells highlights of news at beginning of story.

supplement: INSERT to a yearbook.

swipe file: collection of pictures and ideas used by artists and LAYOUT men for their own guidance and inspiration.

symmetrical: LAYOUT pattern in which each half is a mirror image of the other.

syndicate: service organization which provides comics, features, pictures, columns, etc., to newspapers.

tabloid: newspaper format with pages approximately 11 x 15 inches. Also a philosophy of presenting news of sensational content and in circus form. Shortened to **tab.** The same format but with conventional typography is called COMPACT.

tearsheet: single "torn" sheet of newspaper or magazine delivered to advertiser as proof that his ad has been properly run.

telegraph editor: WIRE EDITOR, executive in charge of copy originating outside locality of publication. Handles PRESS ASSOCIATION and SYNDICATE copy.

Teletype: machine for sending electrical impulses which will print a message simultaneously on typewriters at distant points.

Teletypesetter: development of TELETYPE permitting electrical impulses to punch a paper tape at distant points, which tape then automatically actuates a Linotype machine to set type.

Text: BLACK LETTER, RACE of type using only thick and thin straight strokes, no curves. Erroneously called OLD ENGLISH.

texture: surface quality of paper.

theme: unifying idea connecting various portions of a yearbook.

thirty: symbol meaning "The End"; sometimes written "30" at end of story copy. As **30-dash,** END MARK.

thumbnail: the first small, sketchy DUMMY drawn by a LAYOUT man.

time material: time copy; material that is not directly under pressure of deadlines for immediate publication. Sometimes called **"AOT copy"** (Any Old Time).

tint block: background of color over which is printed type or picture. Erroneously called a SCREEN.

tombstone: placing HEADLINES side by side, especially those of same or similar form.

tracing paper: sturdy but transparent paper used for making LAYOUTS.

Transitional: a form of ROMAN letter that combines characteristics of OLD STYLE and MODERN.

trim: to cut or compress COPY.

turn rule: instructions to COMPOSING ROOM to reverse SLUG so its blank, bottom edge will print and thus indicate some change is to be made in copy above or below.

two-digit code: system for marking HEADLINES. The first digit indicates column width, the second the weight of the head in that width. Thus, a 2–3 head is two columns wide and the third heaviest in that width.

typo: typographical error, mistake made in COMPOSING ROOM.

typography: basic plan for use of typographic elements. *See* LAYOUT.

unit count: method of determining the number of letters which can be set in a line of a head.

upper-and-lower (u & lc) head: HEADLINE in style which capitalizes every major word.

UPI: United Press International, a major PRESS ASSOCIATION.

upstyle: COPY or HEADLINES set with maximum of capitals. So called because of emphasis on capitals or upper case letters. In headlines all words are capped; in body copy all words in phrases that are proper titles, as: *Clay High School.* In contrast to DOWNSTYLE: *Clay high school.*

vignette: printing PLATE which gives effect of picture blending almost imperceptibly into white of paper.

void: COUNTER.

wire editor: TELEGRAPH EDITOR executive in charge of COPY originating outside locality of publication, from PRESS ASSOCIATION, SYNDICATES, BUREAUS, and STRINGERS.

working title: tentative headline given to story as aid in identification and before title has been selected. Usually applies to fiction material and is not entirely comparable to SLUG LINE given to news item by writer or copyreader.

wrap: to continue type from one column to the next. Also, type set in different MEASURES to fit around an ENGRAVING.

x-height: height of PRIMARY LETTERS, from BASELINE to MEANLINE.

zinc: ENGRAVING, especially a LINE CUT.

zinc etching: LINE CUT. Sometimes erroneously applied to all photoengraving.

Zip-A-Tone: trade name for shading screen.

Index